To

Preparing for Secession . . .
(or for Being Driven into Exile)

Gloria in excelsis Deo,

C. Roy Mc

Beverly McMillan

Preparing for Secession . . .
(or for Being Driven into Exile)

My Life and That of My
Wife, Beverly McMillan

C. ROY McMILLAN

VANTAGE PRESS
New York

FIRST EDITION

Published by Vantage Press, Inc.
516 West 34th Street, New York, New York 10001

Manufactured in the United States of America
ISBN: 0-533-12162-0

Library of Congress Catalog Card No.: 96-90752

We have gone beyond the point of no return.
Christianity has made an "unholy alliance" with Caesar.
We have lost our biblical basis for self-government, irrevocably.

Contents

Preface

Christianity and Its Unholy Alliance with Caesar

I'm not a theologian; I'm not a prophet. In fact, I'm not even particularly bright; but I do read the Bible, study biblical and postbiblical history, observe our culture, and believe we are in serious trouble, in desperate times, as a nation.

Basically, our national problems and moral deterioration are due to Christians and Christianity refusing to be the "salt and light" to the world that we are called to be. While our God does "call" us to be "salt and light," "their" god/s "call" them to be "sugar and darkness" to the world. And eating a candy bar in a dark corner is often more appealing, even to "us" and our children, than getting salt in one's eye (or wound) in the bright sun. Yes, salt is a seasoner and a preservative, but it is also an irritant. We have not only failed to be the major force for social services (the social gospel or charity); we have been all but totally unwilling to offend those who need offending (in love, of course).

Christianity has made an unholy alliance with Caesar.

Caesar has become "God" in this land! Caesar feeds, clothes, houses, heals, rehabilitates, and educates, for the most part, in our culture.

While I accept the premise that government, especially the federal government, has willingly taken over the social services, Christianity has not resisted the challenge of government to take over the God-mandated responsibility of Christians and Christianity to be the agents of charity and mercy as well as education. We have withdrawn from the public square and thereby left the square empty, and as you know, a void will be filled by something or someone. In this case the government has filled the vacuum and increasingly denied God as it ministers to the needs of the people whom it identifies as "needy."

Also, Christianity has failed to provide the moral impulse that defines right and wrong for the culture in order for individuals in public service, the media, the arts, entertainment, medicine, science, law, garbage collection, and every other vocation to do and say what is expected of them in their spheres of influence based on Christian principles and precepts.

The reasons Christians and Christianity have become almost irrelevant in our society are (1) we have great heresy within our camp, which has made the defining of "right" and "wrong" almost impossible to discern for Christians and non-Christians; and (2) we have abandoned our "call" to social charity and education, with a few exceptions, as well as abandoned our "call" to impose God's morality on the culture.

Morality, like art, begins with the drawing of a line! Those who would tell us that we ought not "legislate morality" on others don't have any problem with "legislating [their] morality" on us. They have no qualms with taking away from your earning and other incomes (and assets) in order to give a "portion" of it to others. This is the "legislating of morality" in its most basic elements. The collective society's identification of those who have too much and those who have too little and taking from the first group to give to the second group "is" imposition of a moral value and comes from a moral decision!

The "don't legislate morality"-ers would probably deny you and me the "fundamental right" to duel to the death on our property if we chose to do so. They would probably, at present, deny a heterosexual or homosexual couple, married or unmarried, the "fundamental right" to engage in sex stark naked in their own front yards in the middle of the day.

We have gone backward in so many areas of law, decency, and common sense over the last forty years, and our enemies would call that progress. While they would, most likely, unanimously deny the legal "rights" enumerated in the previous paragraph today, they are working to (1) take away arms from law-abiding citizens; (2) legalize all types of smut, including child pornography; (3) expand the right to kill (as in doctor-assisted suicide) and to kill one's self; (4) permit the use of illicit drugs; (5) endorse any and all types of sexual unions and elevate them to the level of heterosexual civil marriages; and (6) erase Christianity as an ethical/moral guide in public policy. And there are others, many others.

Our society/culture/government (which is a reflection of our collective morality) has blurred the lines between "right" and "wrong." In many cases we have endorsed wickedness and condemned righteousness. We have, indeed, called "evil, good, and good, evil."

And, following the theme of this book, I believe we have "gone beyond the point of no return."

I am a son of the South, born and raised in Louisiana and Mississippi. After a few years of being away from the South for military service, education, and employment while in my twenties, I returned to the South. The South has a rich heritage. We have, individually and collectively, been right as well as wrong, just like everyone else everywhere else has been.

Part of our legacy is the knowledge of a failed attempt in 1861 to succeed from the Union. The signs of that failed attempt are everywhere in the South and are often remembered: our flags, our battlefields, our reenactments.

If one can overlook the reason for our secession attempt, and that is hard even for us to do, the secession documents were brilliantly written from the Christian perspective, as were the documents of the "founding fathers" of the United States of America. We, Southerners, simply wanted (in 1861), as did the colonies (in 1776), the right to independence, to self-determination. We wanted, in particular, the right to personal, private, moral "choice" regarding the decision as to how to obtain laborers for our plantations. (While some wanted to hire someone to pick their cotton or to pick their cotton themselves, others, "the pro-choicers" wanted the option of buying people to pick their cotton.) Most Southerners endorsed this right to choose as a fundamental, constitutional right.

Then came the Union Army to "impose their morality" on the South. And the Union Army used force and violence to do so. Need we be reminded that the nation was conceived in the national sin of slavery as well as force and violence (the War of Independence)? What a horrible price we paid for that national sin, that national crime against humanity.

I've never understood how anyone could have defended the institution of slavery! But I can remember when I, in my youth in Mississippi in the 1950s supported segregation, which was obviously separate and unequal.

I believe there are legitimate reasons to study/consider/advocate and prepare for secession from the United States today. I'm not advocating violence or the violent overthrow of the government. I am simply planting the seed in your minds that we ought to at least think about secession, abandoning the nation, or being driven into exile. Perhaps we will have to rebuild a nation that is destroyed (from within) from the chaos of race war, financial collapse, anarchy, gender or age warfare, etc. or (from without) from a foreign foe, earthquakes, flood, drought, fire, etc. I am certain that we are under judgment and have "gone beyond the point of no return."

Perhaps we will find it necessary to abandon this land. Perhaps we will be allowed to choose a section of land and secede. It may be God's will that Christians understand one day that we can no longer pledge allegiance to and finance this government. Perhaps we will be driven into exile due to our persecution, as were Moses, Abraham, Lot, Joseph and Mary with baby Jesus, and our American, Christian forefathers.

I believe there is more justification to declare our independence from the United States of America today than there was for our forefathers to declare independence from King George in 1776. All they wanted was to be left alone and maintain the right to keep what they earned and exercise a little self-determination. They just wanted to vote on whether or not their tea was to be taxed.

Yes, we vote today; we have self-determination. But look at what is being done in the name of "government of, by, and for [we] people"! And many in the government want you to pay for child killing via abortion for those mothers who can't afford to pay the executioners. The government wants you to pay for health care, which may soon include doctor-assisted suicide or the killing of oneself.

Government wants you to pay for a painting of Christ on a cross in a vat of urine but denies your children the right to conduct a student-initiated prayer in the government schools that your taxes pay for. I have said this regarding government (public) schools: "David said in Psalms (chapter 19), *The Heavens declare the glory of God.*' When our government schools deny the existence of God, it is time to close down government schools."

Government wants you to pay for condom distribution in schools and government health centers (?) to singles, heterosexuals and homosexuals, as well as providing "clean" needles for people addicted to illegal drugs. The government wants to use your taxes to pay for medical benefits for homosexual partners of government employees.

And government wants to use your taxes to arrest, convict, and imprison an elderly couple who refused to rent a vacant apartment in their duplex to a homosexual couple and a heterosexual couple who were not married.

How far are you willing to go? I heard a Catholic bishop recently state at a statewide pro-life convention, "I'm not sure I can serve you communion if our taxes are required to pay for abortions and you pay your taxes." Interesting.

I am convinced that two things will hold back the serious discussion and consideration of the theme/thesis of this book. They are: (1) our "stuff"; and (2) the lack of persecution.

Our jobs, our homes, our cars, our recreational things, our savings (our assets) may prevent us from seeing the obvious. Our "stuff" can be an anchor, and our "stuff" can blind us. Our "stuff" may drag us down. Our "stuff" may keep us from being the "reckless" Christians that God would have us be at times. Our "stuff" may drag some of us to Hell, as the Rich Young Ruler was dragged.

Persecution and the "call" of God on our lives, along with the losing of our "stuff," may cause many of us to see what I believe to be true. Yes, I've been in jail sixty times for trying to obey Proverbs 24:11, which says: *"Rescue those unjustly sentenced to death."* It does not mean to rescue only "me and you (and our kids)''; it means to rescue the sojourner, the stranger, too.

On the point of "loving your neighbor as yourself," if you include the unborn child as your neighbor in America today, which he/she is, this means it is illegal to be a Christian. What that God requires of us will be illegal to do tomorrow? Remember, the "sin" of omission is as evil as the "sin" of commission.

I predict as the sun goes down on the United States of America (as some of us see the "dusk" and the stormclouds) and God's judgment settles on our land and its people, many will agree with me. I predict as we lose our "stuff" and are persecuted, many will agree with me that we have "gone beyond the point of no return." Souls may be saved by this conclusion and appropriate actions.

Please continue to read. Read what I predict may happen. Read of preparations that I suggest for the coming chaos that I believe will grip our land.

Introduction

In December of 1993, I read that a funeral home in Pensacola, Florida, had opened a "drive-through" window in order that family, friends, co-workers, and acquaintances could say good-bye to the deceased and register their "paying of last respects" to the next of kin of the deceased.

"Have we really 'come this far,' or 'gone this sour'?" I asked myself.

I believe we have. I believe we have "gone beyond the point of no return." I believe "we have lost our biblical basis for self-government, irrevocably." I believe "Christianity has made an 'unholy alliance' with Caesar."

This is the theme of this book, *Preparing for Secession . . . (or for Being Driven into Exile)*. I have concluded that we are not just "on the edge of a new dark age," as Chuck Colson suggested a few years ago in his powerful book, *Against the Night*, but, as a nation, as a culture, as a former Christian society, we have "gone beyond the point of no return."

What am I suggesting the future will hold? I'm not sure, but I will explore that in this book. Secession, abandonment of the nation, being driven into exile, and civil war are all real possibilities in my view. Do I expect to sell many books or to have many embrace or welcome this idea or accept my theme/thesis? No, I don't, but I'm convinced I am right.

I hope (no, I pray) that I am wrong. I may be; I've been wrong before and will be wrong again. But, what if I am right? Ought not you and others at least hear me out by reading this book?

Perhaps I have been unduly influenced by the events of my life over the past decade or so, during which time I have been jailed sixty times for my pro-life "rescue" efforts on behalf of the precious perishing unborn at abortion centers in my town, Jackson, Mississippi, and elsewhere around the country.

I will admit that being behind bars as often as I have been has made a profound, negative impression on me not only because of the pure injustice of my arrests, convictions, and imprisonments for trying to obey

God by "doing for others" what I would want others to do for me, but because this nation, which we support with our confessed allegiance and finances, sanctions and protects the killing of some (the unborn) by others.

The personal experience of getting to know many of those imprisoned, the so-called underclass, has educated me and frightened me of the discontent with this culture and Christianity by so many. And they are not all in jail!

As I have said, I hope and pray that I am wrong, but what if I am right? What if God has departed this land? What if God has closed His ears to our prayers? What if God is withdrawing or has withdrawn His protection/discernment from the few Christians left in the United States of America?

If you say, "He would not do that to us," I say, "You do not know Scriptures."

Again, what if I am right? This is the theme of this book.

Many believers, many of you, believe this: "Perhaps we are in the twilight of 'the home of the brave and the land of the free.' " But have you faced the possibility that we may have already "gone beyond the point of no return"? Perhaps you are not so rushed now that you would drive through a "drive-through" window at a funeral home, but have you slowed down enough to ponder what I have: "Have we 'gone beyond the point of no return'?"

Often in the Bible these five words are written: "And God departed their land." What might that mean to America if this has, indeed, already happened, as it happened to "His people" in bygone years?

In Isaiah, the first chapter, verses 10–15 and 20, these words are written:

Hear the word of the Lord, you rulers of Sodom; give ear to the instructions of our God, you people of Gomorrah, "What are your multiplied sacrifices to Me?" says the Lord.

"I have had enough of burnt offerings of rams, and the fat of fed cattle. And I take no pleasure in the blood of bulls, lambs, or goats.

"When you come to appear before Me, who requires of you this trampling of my court?

"Bring your worthless offerings no longer, incense is an abomination to Me. New moon and sabbath, the calling of assemblies—I cannot endure iniquity and the solemn assembly.

"I hate your new moon festivals and your appointed feasts, they have become a burden to Me. I am weary of hearing them.

"So when you spread out your hands in prayer, I will hide My eyes from you, yes, even though you multiply prayers, I will not listen. Your hands are covered with blood."

....

"If you refuse and rebel, you will be devoured by the sword." Truly, the mouth of the Lord has spoken. . . .

Much of the emphasis of this book will be on the slaughter of the innocent unborn. The slaughter of these children in this generation is applicable to the Scriptures identified above, I believe.

I believe the matter of abortion is settled in this nation, with the exception of a few minor adjustments such as parental notification/consent, clinic regulation, waiting periods, and informed consent, because of the inadequate response by Christians, individually, and Christianity, collectively, to the unholy sacrifice of much of our nation's posterity to our modern-day gods such as convenience, reputation, and finances.

While this book is not limited to the national sin of abortion, I do believe "as go the children will go the nation." God has willed it, I believe, in Scriptures and throughout history.

In late 1993, the U.S. surgeon general, Joycelyn Elders, encouraged parents not to give their little boys toy guns for Christmas '93 and the very next day, before the National Press Club in Washington, D.C., she advocated the exploration of legalizing illicit drugs. Are we so far gone that we are going to take away toy guns from our little boys and replace them with drugs and condoms, which former surgeon general Elders and her boss, Bill Clinton, both "so-called" Christians, advocate? I believe we are that far gone and beyond.

My perspective after several years of reflection, and some of this time with plenty of "time" on my hands, as I was being held as a POW as a result of my "trench warfare" with the abortion industry and our government, which protects the killing, is that three conclusions have to be affirmed before one can explore (A) secession; (B) abandonment of the nation; or (C) being driven into exile. They are:

1. One must be convinced that we have, indeed, "gone beyond the point of no return";
2. one must conclude that we need not, nor does God require that we, remain for the judgment coming to the land and its inhabitants from a vengeful God; and

3. one must believe that we are losing more of "our" people, especially "our" children, to "them" and "their" god/s, the god/s of darkness, than we are winning "them" and "their" children to our God, the God of light.

In addition to exploring this thesis, I have written an autobiographical chapter on myself, "I Always Knew That I Was Special" (one who was abandoned at birth in a shoe box, naked, in the middle of night in the middle of winter, on the steps of a Baptist church); a biographical chapter on my wife, Beverly McMillan, M.D., "Not 'Born on a Mountaintop in Tennessee' but Born at Kings Mountain Memorial Hospital" (the story an ob-gyn specialist who opened the first abortion center in Mississippi in 1975, before she became a Christian and denounced abortion as a sin against God and a crime against humanity); and a chapter about the years that Beverly and I have known one another, "Time Together."

The last chapter, chapter 4, "Their Destiny Is Their Destruction. . . . Their Glory Is Their Shame" (Phil. 3:19), details the theme/thesis of this book.

Acknowledgments

I divide this section into two sections, a dedication and acknowledgments. I dedicate this book to several people whom I know and love so very much, as well as to a larger number of people, many of whom I know only slightly and millions whom I was denied an opportunity to know and of whose continued presence we all were denied the blessings of.

Then I single out a few people to acknowledge who were either a special inspiration or assistance to me as I wrote the manuscript that has become this book.

I dedicate this book to my daughter, Amanda, and my grandson, Troy. Amanda, Troy, and I have something in common: we were all conceived out-of-wedlock. We three are living testimonies how God can use our mistakes for His purposes and glory, and we three are valuable creations, at least to ourselves and to one another, who love life and hold sacred human lives.

I dedicate this book to my wife, Dr. Beverly Ann McMillan, M.D., an ob-gyn specialist, who, in 1975, opened the first abortion center in Mississippi. Within a few years she realized the error of her ways, became a born-again Christian, and denounced abortion as a sin against God and a crime against humanity. She is a nationally known pro-life speaker and the first former abortionist to be jailed for resistance to government sanction of the killing of preborn humans and for protecting those whom she once was killing. Like Paul, the persecutor had become the persecuted.

I dedicate this book to the many (probably millions) children who have been spared death by abortion by the heroic efforts of Christian, pro-life direct activists. These people comprise a wing of "the remnant church" in America. These Christians understand that folks can't be "born again" until they are "born alive" first. Most of Christianity continues to respond wholly inadequately to the slaughter of the innocent while a large element of Christianity, sadly, condones the killing and thereby participates in the killing by supporting "pro–choice to kill" politicians.

I single out for dedication in this section the more than seven hundred babies, many of whom are now walking and talking and whom are now children of God, I have played a part in rescuing from death by abortion in my city. My praise to the few who have been a part of the "rescuing of the perishing" in Jackson and across this land.

I dedicate this book to the heroes of the faith who have been engaged in the battle as at least passive warriors, for almost none of us have made the effort, including myself, to be classified as warriors to the point of having been taken as "prisoners of war" in solidarity, in fidelity, with the preborn who have been exterminated. How God must grieve at our inappropriate response to mass murder as we carefully measure our willingness to sacrifice and take risks.

Last, I dedicate this book to the millions of human beings, our brothers and sisters, who have been destroyed in this land by abortionists and their accessories to murder while an impotent Christianity responds inadequately to these slaughtered beings. God have mercy on us, especially the spiritual leadership, who are, in my opinion, for the most part spineless, gutless cowards.

* * *

I thank my friends at Vantage Press for helping me produce this book; their willingness to offer suggestions and constructive criticism has been invaluable.

1

I Always Knew That I Was Special

I always knew that I was special. I can't remember when I was told that I had been adopted. I just always knew it. I even bragged about it as a youngster, though rarely, and only to a few people. When there was sibling rivalry/strife, I could brag that I was "especially" chosen as a member of the family and not just in the family by chance, as were my older sister (by two years), Joy, and my younger brother (by nine years), Stokes.

I even always knew the mystery of my origins, having been found, abandoned, naked, in a shoe box in the middle of the night in the middle of winter on the steps of Emmanuel Baptist Church in Alexandria, Louisiana.

My parents, Mr. and Mrs. Billy McMillan, read about my abandonment in the newspaper. They were in their midtwenties and were living and working in Baton Rouge with their two-year-old daughter.

The date that I was abandoned was February 25, 1943. The month that I was officially adopted that year was August.

As I have been very active in the pro-life movement as an abortion abolitionist and have been arrested sixty times for peaceful intervention to try to stop abortions, one of my "standard operating procedures" is to answer, "I don't know," when asked, "What is your date of birth?" during the "booking" process after arrest and before confinement. Then I tell the person "booking" me that I use as my date of birth February 25, 1943, which was the date that I was "rescued" after having been abandoned on those cold steps at Emmanuel Baptist Church in that central Louisiana city.

My Identification/Fidelity With the Unwanted Unborn

I have an identification with the precious perishing unborn of this generation, for I, too, was obviously unwanted, unplanned, and endangered.

Of course, I don't remember being abandoned or unwanted, I don't know the circumstances of my conception, and I don't remember being in my biological mother's womb. (Bet you don't either!) But I was me at each stage of my human development, just like everyone else.

I don't remember the Baptist orphanage I was placed in or being introduced to my adoptive parents, much less the months of routine background checking and paperwork that were required.

I have concluded, based on the fact that I was born a healthy, full-term delivered "found," baby on February 25, that I must have been conceived in the late spring of 1942. The "summer of '42" (remember the movie?)—what a troublesome time for our nation, for the world, and, most assuredly, for my biological mother!

The Japanese attack on Pearl Harbor had happened five months prior to my conception. We were not sure that the Japanese were not going to attack the West Coast. In Baton Rouge, where Dad was working for DuPont, which was manufacturing needed war chemicals and supplies, he told me that air-raid practice alerts were held routinely at night. Windows were covered to conceal homes, factories, and other buildings from potential aerial observation by Japanese bombers.

My parents were married in 1937, had attended Louisiana State University (LSU), and were living in Baton Rouge when World War II began. After the war ended, they returned to central Mississippi, to Kosciusko, their hometown, which was to become my hometown, too.

My Hometown, Kosciusko

Kosciusko, the "Beehive of the Hills," as it is called, is the country seat of Attala County. Attala County, named for an Indian chief, is located in the red-clay hill region of central Mississippi. The area is a rural, agricultural-based economic region situated in a pine-covered area of rolling hills. It is sixty-eight miles north-northeast of Jackson.

The historic Natchez Trace, an old pathway that connected Nashville and Natchez in the late eighteenth and early nineteenth centuries, runs from the northeast to the southwest corners of the county (and the state). The French Camp community and French Camp Academy are located about a dozen miles "up the Trace" (from Kosciusko) and add to the historical roots of which Kosciuskoans are so proud.

2

Kosciusko was a town of about seventy-five hundred people during my formative years (1947–61), the years from when I can first remember, from about age four until the time I graduated from Kosciusko High School.

My first memories must have been when I was about four years old. We, my mom and dad, my six-year-old sister, and I, were living in the basement of my maternal grandparents' old home. The basement apartment faced the backyard of Stokes and Della Sanders's very nice home, which was a split-level. It was the home that my mom had lived in most of her life.

I have, I'm sure like all of you, attempted to recall my first memories. I can remember playing with kittens beside a large oak tree near a sandbox. I remember a playground swing set. I remember a bunch of kids being in our yard playing on the playground equipment. Mom ran a day-care center for about ten kids. According to Mom, I was four or five at that time.

I remember the rooms of the basement apartment that my parents said we lived in between 1945 and 1948. I remember the room that Joy and I shared and slept in, the small living room, the small bathroom and the small kitchen/dining room combination, and the fact that there were windows only on two sides of the house. (The other two sides had been built into the bank.)

I do not remember a bedroom in which my mother and father slept. It may be that they converted the living room into a bedroom at night after Joy and I had gone to bed.

The Stage Is Set for My Formative Years

Now, I have outlined my humble and precarious early days in order to set the stage for the days and years that I remember better and when my world, through relationships, travel, and experiences, expanded. In these "formative years" my education and moral foundations that would follow me all the days of my life were established.

Those of you who are younger than I am will be better able to understand why I have the beliefs that I do as you complete this chapter. You will understand that the culture we live in today is far different than when I was having my "foundation poured." Today's culture is far more hostile to you and your children and the family unit. We live in critical and, I shall say it, desperate times.

I believe that by outlining my past forty-five years I will help you better understand why I believe we are living in near-chaos and permanently divisive times. I will expand (through this narrative) my territory and experiences from age five (1948), from home, yard, and family. I will relate my educational years, my military experiences, social relationships, growing into adulthood times, occupations, and becoming a Christian and living a Christian life amid national and international developments that impacted my life and the lives of everyone in Kosciusko and Attala County, in the United States, and in other nations.

In 1948, when I was five years old, we moved into the first home that we owned or did not share with other people. It was in a west Kosciusko subdivision called the Oaks. The house came to be known as "the Stone House" (due to the fact that it had a stone facade). It seemed large to me and had a huge backyard that was covered with trees and underbrush. We, my neighborhood male buddies and I, played in that backyard a lot. We played games of confrontation such as Cowboys and Indians, Army, Tarzan, "Hide and Go Seek," and other games.

These were preschool and first- and second-grade years. I remember having fun, playing outdoors most of the time, and the childhood bickering that is, has been, and shall always be commonplace. I remember "having to take baths" and eating a lot of peanut-and-butter sandwiches. I remember a lot of unsupervised time playing outside with my neighborhood male playmates.

Going to Sunday school and church at First Baptist Church was a "big deal" and part of the routine. I remember the teachers teaching us "the Golden Rule" and things that we ought not to do, such as fight with our brothers and sisters, as well as things that we ought to do, such as obey our parents.

Sunday school and vacation Bible school at First Baptist Church were relevant to our family lives and our relationships away from home, i.e., school and around the neighborhood. My horizons were expanding as I was able to be trusted with my safety and ability to find my way back home. In the first few grades of school, as well as in the neighborhood, my "chums" were exclusively boys. As I got to know other guys my age at school, my "world" expanded to their neighborhoods and theirs to mine.

What we were instructed at home by our parents and grandparents and aunts and uncles was reenforced by our schoolteachers, our Sunday school teachers, our pastors, our buddies' parents (and there were almost always two per buddy), our "big" sisters and brothers, our friends' "big" sisters and brothers, and society and all of its institutions.

There was no television and I spent little time listening to the radio. I recall evenings when the family would sit in one room, the living room, and listen to the radio while individual family members did their particular "quiet thing." Joy would play with her dolls and dollhouse, Mom would sew or knit, Dad would read the paper or clean his pipe or fishing reel, and I would play with toy soldiers or with my little cars and trucks.

I can remember listening to *The Lone Ranger, Fibber Magee and Molly, My Little Margie, The Shadow*, and other half-hour and one-hour programs. The "good guys" always won, the bad guys always lost, and we could easily tell them apart! The sound effects were dramatic, and I can remember often being very excited and occasionally very scared. There was no cursing and no sexual material broadcast at all.

The Good Guys Always Won, the Bad Guys Always Lost, and We Could Easily Tell Them Apart!

A major highlight was going to the movies on Saturday afternoon at either the Strand or the Pix theater. We called this weekly ritual "going to the movies."

For about four hours each Saturday afternoon, year-round, most of the kids who lived in town were at the movies. There would be previews of coming "shows," a cartoon or two, a "serial," and two cowboy-and-Indian, cavalry-and-Indian, cowboy-and-rustlers, or "war" movies. Roy Rogers and Gene Autrey were big stars and heroes in my life at that time.

No horrible violence was shown (I don't ever remember seeing blood), and there was no sexual content or cursing. Yes, Roy (Rogers) would get too affectionate with Dale Evans at times to suit me and even sing to her. That was my cue to head for the concession stand, where I would be met by about two-thirds of the boys in the first through the fourth grade.

You could tell the good guys from the bad guys, and, I repeat, the good guys, the ones in the white hats, always won, and the bad guys, the ones in the black hats, always lost.

Dad would give me a quarter for "the movies." Ten cents was for admission. The three nickels were for (1) a fountain soda, (2) a bag of popcorn, and (3) a candy bar.

5

Times were simple. When television came on the scene in the mid-fifties that was easy, too. There were but two stations and the reception was terrible during the day, therefore there was only nighttime television. There was no color. Selections were a breeze.

But back at the "Strand" (or the "Pix"). I was always "full" of the three purchases from the concession stand. We were always satisfied that "justice had been served"; we were having defined for us right and wrong and the fact that sin "hurts" and righteousness has "its rewards"; and we thought everyone in America, if not the whole world, was doing and believing the same thing.

I thought that we were pretty much rich and thought everyone else had about what we McMillans had, with one exception: the Negroes. (More about this later.)

Our family moved to a home in the country (about five miles from "the square" in downtown Kosciusko) in the summer of 1950. Mom, whose name is Mrs. Della McMillan, drew up the floor plans for the home as well as a paper model of the "home-to-be." I was impressed. Mother was not real thrilled about the move but agreed to it so that Dad could have his "dream home in the country."

I don't know why I was so impressed that Mom could make a paper model house. She was an artist and had majored in elementary education at LSU during the depression. Mom says that she was a substitute teacher when we were in school some days. I don't remember that. In fact, I hardly remember Mom anywhere but at home. In fact, I don't ever remember coming home from school and Mother not being there to greet me. What security!

In the summer of 1950 (the summer the home in the country was built), Dad was managing the county newspaper, the *Star-Herald*, along with his father-in-law, editor Stokes Sanders. Many days during that summer Dad would take me to the building site with him early in the morning when he would inspect the progress and consult with the builders. He would leave me there all day to play, explore the woods, and watch the house "go up" and pick me up late in the afternoon.

At the end of that summer, we moved into this brand-new, modern home in the country. It was so modern that it was an "all-electric" home, which was something new. Everyone was happy and proud to be in our new home. But happiness soon turned to grief.

While Dad was out of town (out of state, in fact, on a business trip) we had an ice storm (in early 1951). We lost all electricity for about a month. I know Mom was none to happy, and I'm sure Dad knew it when he finally got back to town and to us. I thought it was very exciting. We lived in the living room, where the fireplace was. We used the fireplace for heat, for light, and for cooking. I loved it; Mom hated it!

Soon as the ice thawed, we moved back to town. Mom won that argument even though I never saw or heard my parents have a real argument about this or anything else. Dad was in charge; at least, we thought so. Dad probably thought so, too. Mom and Dad were not "too cross" during the "ice storm of '51," for baby brother Stokes was born nine months later, on November 28, 1951.

By that time we were living on South Natchez (named after the Natchez Trace) Street in south Kosciusko. I found out many years later that my dad "traded even" the house in "the country" for the older one on Natchez. Have you ever heard of someone doing that? I haven't.

It was in that home on South Natchez Street that I lived for the next ten years. We lived there from the time I was in the second half of the third grade until the time I graduated from Kosy High, in May of 1961.

My Beginning of Spiritual Wisdom Was a Healthy Fear of God

Concentrating now on the years from when I was nine through high school, I recall these general categories, if life can be compartmentalized: (1) education; (2) recreation (including organized and unorganized sports activities); (3) friendships with guys; (4) interactions with girls; (5) family time and activities; (6) jobs and responsibilities; (7) travel; and (8) spiritual and moral teaching and training, including the development of a personal relationship with Jesus Christ.

My parents cared for us and were good parents. Particularly comforting was the fact that my mother was "always" home! Dad worked very hard and very long hours, but he did not neglect his children and his time with us was quality time. He was committed to leaving his "imprint" on his children. He especially desired that we learn to think for ourselves and to challenge conventional wisdom.

Dad and Mom were born in October of 1914, and Dad and his family had a hard time, financially, through the depression. Many "people" products of that generation developed a strong "work ethic." I believe Dad worked too hard, worried too much, and attempted to shield his family too much from material wants. Dad's mother died when he was four years old due to complications while delivering Dad's brother, Clarence, into the world.

This tragedy brought displacement and economic hardship to Dad and his family (a father and two young sons). Dad's dad remarried and moved to Kosciusko when Dad was seven years old. Two younger sisters, Eleanor and Mary, came from Dad's dad's second marriage. Soon came the stock market crash and the Great Depression. (Interesting to me is the fact that the four kids in Dad's family were spaced out in four-year increments.) The McMillans struggled, as most Americans did, during the depression years of the 1930s.

The work ethic was ingrained into my dad, probably by his father as well as those hard times, and he instilled it into his three kids. He wanted to succeed in his work and he did. He not only wanted to provide for his family, but he wanted to be a part of the American Dream, which included self-reliance, self-confidence, financial independence, comfort, and materialism. He made us proud of him and proud to be McMillans.

I thought we McMillans were pretty well off financially. When compared to other families in Kosciusko and Attala County (the only world I knew) we seemed extremely well off financially and materially. I was later to realize that beyond my small world was enormous wealth. But that was to be several years later.

Being the son of the newspaper owner and editor helped me to be secure, proud, and, I confess, a bit arrogant. Dad was a "big fish" in a small pond. Everyone knew him and almost everyone knew who I was, the son of Billy McMillan. I didn't realize how small the pond was at the time, not that it mattered then or matters now.

Mom's family roots in Kosciusko's soil went deep. Her great-grandfather had come to Attala County to live in the middle of the nineteenth century. He had established a newspaper in Kosciusko by the end of the Civil War. And succeeding generations of male heirs continued the legacy of owning and operating the newspaper and accompanying printing shop. The Sanderses were active in the political, moral, military, economic, and social affairs of their community and state (and nation).

My mother's father, Col. Stokes Sanders, had a profoundly positive effect on me. He had been mayor of Kosciusko and a representative (and senator) to the Mississippi legislature for almost three decades, as well as editor of the *Star-Herald*. He had risen to the rank of colonel in the U.S. Army, having served in the First and the Second World Wars. He was, for a number of years, the commanding officer of the national guard unit located in Kosciusko and a high-ranking officer in the Mississippi National Guard. He was a quiet man, but he had enormous influence. I was very proud to be his grandson.

When I was twelve, I went to Jackson, our state capital, for two weeks to live and to serve as a Mississippi State Senate page. I lived with my grandfather in the then-famous King Edwards Hotel on Capitol Street in downtown Jackson. This was an honor, an exciting experience, and I got paid for it (and did not have to go to school for two whole weeks).

Early in my life, I understood that what I did and said not only would reflect on what people thought of me but would reflect on what people thought of my family and extended family. I was sensitive to this and concerned that our family reputation be guarded. That was good. I did not want to bring dishonor or shame to my family. On the positive side on the ledger, I wanted to do what I could to make my family proud of me and to bring added honor and glory to our family.

How could I do that? I could do that by making good grades in school, by being respectful of my elders, by being successful in sports, and by being "morally straight," as we were taught to be in Cub Scouts and Boy Scouts. I was a good kid. I did well in about everything to which I applied myself. And I was a part of about everything young men were offered. I had not only a healthy respect for my father but also a healthy fear of him. I knew he was boss.

I remember joining the First Baptist Church when I was twelve years old. I remember Mr. Lamar Nesbit, my Sunday school teacher and father of my good friend (to this day) Lamar Jr. Mr. Nesbit was my barber, too. He was a good man, a good dad, and a good Sunday school teacher. I guess he was a good barber, too, but when I was twelve getting a haircut was just something you did when told to and you didn't particularly care how your haircut looked.

Between Mr. Nesbit and our pastor, Rev. Lloyd Sparkman, I developed a healthy fear of God, too. I realized that He saw me at every moment and knew my every thought. I was convinced that "the beginning of wisdom is the fear of God." We don't hear that much in the 1990s, but Brother Sparkman reminded us of this eternal truth routinely.

Brother Sparkman was short and fat and convincing. I remember being scared not only of God but of Reverend Sparkman also.

When I walked to the altar of the First Baptist Church in the spring of 1955, soon after my twelfth birthday to acknowledge God as my God,

9

I don't believe I gave much thought to Jesus. Yes, I believed He was the Son of God and that He did and said what the Bible said He did and said when He was one of us here on Earth in every way but sin, but I don't remember walking and talking with Jesus as a part of my personal journey in those early years.

I wanted to be a "Christian" because I was scared not to be. I was scared that I would go to Hell if I was not when I died. I, to this day, remind people that "the fear of God is the beginning of wisdom." It was true when I was twelve years old in 1955, is true today, and will be true until the end of time.

Schoolwork, School Activities, and Friends Dominate My Life

It seems that being at school and studying our "homework" at home as well as school activities and being with school friends dominated my life as a young man between the ages of twelve and eighteen. I had many close friends. And I hated the thought of staying at home on Friday and Saturday nights. I don't guess I ever stayed at home on a Friday or Saturday night after the age of fourteen until I was married.

My close friends were (1) classmates; (2) guys with whom I had similar interests; (3) neighborhood buddies; and (4) guys with whom I shared social/economic similarities.

As I reflect on the past, practically all of my close friends were within a year or so of my age and were sports and outdoor enthusiasts and white. The schools were segregated, and I did not know one black person other than my family's maids and the maids of some of my friends. (We changed from calling African-Americans Negroes to "coloreds" to "blacks" over the past forty years as they preferred. That was fine with me.) I regret that I did not have black friends when I was young. I missed much by not knowing black folks.

Racism/Segregation, My First Moral/Social/Justice Challenge

I guess my first major challenge on what we would call a social/ moral/justice issue was the plight of the black race, especially in my hometown, local area, and state. As it ought to be for youngsters, parental

10

influence was to be important and critical in all areas for me, especially my view of truth and moral/social justice issues.

My father, more than anyone else in Kosciusko, was a critic of segregation and racism. He believed that government ought not to discriminate. He believed that blacks should be allowed to vote and have equal educational opportunity. He believed that racism was wrong, sin, but that changing the hearts of people, both black and white, would be difficult. He said that "law is a great teacher" and believed that if government policy was colorblind then the hearts and eyes of white and black people would eventually be colorblind. He realized that this was going to take a long, long time.

I'm not exactly sure how far Dad, who died in 1983, would have mandated, by law, desegregation of public accommodations, privately owned country clubs, civic clubs, racial quotas, etc. But he would ask the Ford and Chevrolet dealers this question: "How would you like to sell twice as many cars next year?" His inference was that the auto dealer and his employees would be better off economically if the blacks were better off financially and that would come via better education and equal job opportunities. This is obvious today, but it did not seem at all obvious or logical in the 1950s and 1960s.

I do recall Dad railing against the religious leaders, particularly the pastors, for not denouncing racism as sin more strongly or at all. He believed that the moral/religious leaders should address segregation and racism as well as denounce violence against blacks in the public square and from the pulpits.

As Dad understood then and I see so clearly today, the fact that most ministers, especially the Baptist, were elected (read: "hired") by their congregations is the reason most ministers did not denounce racism and segregation as the evil that it was (and is). I believe the fact that most ministers are elected by their congregations is a major reason that pastors do not speak out forcefully today on moral/social justice issues.

I believe that the election of "shepherds" by the "sheep" is a major leadership obstacle in Christianity today, and I guess it has been in times immemorial. When the pastor can be "fired" for any reason, such as taking a correct moral position on matters of social justice, by the congregation, the pastor is less likely to do so. After all, most pastors have groceries to buy, rent to pay, car payments to make, and children to clothe.

Back to racism and segregation in the 1950s and 1960s. I know that you agree with me that racism and segregation are sin and unjust, but most whites in Mississippi did not believe this forty years ago. I now believe that during that era most white Americans, North and South, East and West, believed in "separate and unequal" everything for the blacks.

My father did not march in civil rights marches, although he was sympathetic to them and said he would have been at the front of the marches if he were black. He did not call segregationists hate-filled racists (even though many were). He tried to keep the "lines of communications" open and tried to be very reasonable. He was most successful. White southerners were simply scared and apprehensive of change. Aren't we all, and about most changes?

Editorially, Dad would write about fairness in education and job opportunity and equal treatment before criminal justice courts. He would say that a black person who tries to register to vote or whistles at a white woman ought not to be hanged.

I must confess that as a teen I was not as "fair" and open-minded in my thinking as Dad was. I feared going to school with blacks (the unknown) and thought that it was easy for Dad to advocate desegregation of the schools, for he was no longer a student. (By the way, there were no private schools around in those days in Kosciusko.)

What changed my opinion on the injustice of segregation and the plight of the blacks was the violence against blacks by law enforcement officers when civil rights demonstrators were protesting and some of them, including Martin Luther King, committed acts of civil disobedience. I thought that what they were doing was wrong and counterproductive and done for publicity in order to make the South look bad. We did (look bad), but I was repulsed by the violence against the blacks. While I thought they ought to "cool it" because things were getting better, in the back of my mind gnawing at me was the belief that I would be with them if I were black as my dad said he would be.

I was hostile to black agitators because I thought they would cause change too rapidly and the change would affect me negatively. I was afraid of change. My personal journey toward advocating "justice," now, for blacks and to joining the civil rights movement as a demonstrator when I was a student at Ole Miss in 1965 came about as I wrestled through what my dad had said: "What would you do if you were black?" and "What would you want me to do for you if you were black and I were white?" Case closed!

12

I Guard Against Using the L and C Words

You may have noticed that I have not used the *L* or *C* words, *liberal* and *conservative*, though I am, for the most part, comfortable with the "conservative" label as it applies today in our political debates.

I have described my evolution from being a "lukewarm" segregationist to a "moderate" intergrationist. I would have cringed at being called a liberal when I marched with Dr. King. While I did "liberalize" my views on racial discrimination, I guard against using labels for myself or for others. I always have.

We ought to be liberal where Christ was liberal, i.e., in charity, forgiveness, humility, open-mindedness, and solidarity with the oppressed and tormented, while remaining conservative where Christ was conservative, i.e., in defining the family by biblical definition, affirming the traditions of Christianity, conserving natural resources, conserving and protecting the animal population, conserving judgment on others, conserving innocent blood, and conserving Christian, moral values.

While the individual search for personal evaluation of one's moral position on racial justice for the society and culture as well as one's inner conflict about racism was the number-one debated issue in Mississippi in the 1950s and 1960s, the growing strength and threat of world communism presented the number-one challenge and was the most debated issue on the national/international front.

I spent a lot of time as a teenager talking with my father and grandfather and listening to their opinions on these weighty matters. In fact, I believe I was too serious during those years. I was very concerned about the possibility of a nuclear war and a nuclear winter or being conquered by the Soviet Union.

It is appropriate for young men and women to be concerned with public dilemmas—they always have and always will be—but we ought not to rob our children of the "summers of their youth."

Like Gaul, My Life Was Divided into Three Parts

Prior to my teen years, my life, like Gaul, was divided into three parts: (1) family and its close environments (neighborhood events and activities); (2) school and extracurricular activities; and (3) community, including church, organized activities.

13

As for home/family and neighborhood events and activities in the preteen years, my parents had a good idea of where I was, what I was thinking, whom I was with, and what I was up to. They knew all the neighborhood kids and their parents. They knew our activities and games. Most of our activities involved sports, "cowboy and Indian" and the like games, and simply "palling" around with best buddies.

School was school and, I suppose, about the same for everyone educated in the 1950s and early 1960s. We knew little of kids who were not in our grade unless they were classmates of our brothers and sisters, and we knew the ones in the our grades and classrooms very well. We were together day after day, month after month, and year after year. We stayed in one classroom with the same teacher, no matter the subject, until the seventh grade.

I began the first grade in 1949 with a class of about sixty-five, and twelve years later I graduated in a class of about seventy-five, two-thirds of whom I had begun the first grade with. We were from the same small town and went to the same few churches, and our parents knew one another.

Each morning in class there were Bible readings and prayer, first by teachers and later by volunteers from the class. Prayer was offered over the public address system in the junior and senior high school years. No one objected and everyone was educated, encouraged, inspired, challenged, and blessed through the Scripture readings and prayers. I do not believe anyone was "warped" or injured by them.

As we grew older, our world expanded into Little League Baseball, the city park, where we played tennis and on the playground equipment and went swimming, and institutional-sponsored events such as Cub and Boy Scouts (sponsored by the major denominations' churches), and other community-accepted activities (sponsored by civil clubs and similar-minded groups).

This is important: either the public schools, churches, or civic organizations were the sponsors of our activities, clubs, sports teams and leagues, or other events. With the one exception of the public schools, government was not involved. And we didn't think of the schools as the government. Sure, they were operated and financed through public funds, but the "hands" that controlled the schools were local people whom we knew well and who had total control of the schools. Many local unpaid volunteers, including our moms, did much of the work and supervision of extracurricular activities.

It was not uncommon for Baptist boys to be in Boy Scout Troop 44, which was sponsored by and met in the Methodist church. I was. And there were Methodist boys in Troop 45, which was sponsored by and met in the buildings of First Baptist Church. We joined the troops our best friends were in.

As we evolved from preteens to the teen years, the common thread to our lives and to our society as young people was the fact that the values and principles we were being taught and that we were learning came "as one voice" from the public schools, the civic and cultural clubs and institutions, the entertainment industry, the media, the churches, and the families. The message was unmistakable and unanimous. There were boundaries to our conduct. There was shame, and there was a line that separated good from bad, right from wrong, and righteousness from evil. Thank God for that!

Another couple of points before turning my thoughts from the pre-teen years to the teen years.

I'm not sure what the girls were doing during my preteen years. Sure, we went to school with "them"; some of "them" were even our sisters. But we did not seem to have much to do with (or use for) them or they with us. They were not on our Little League teams; Cub Scouts and Brownie Scouts as well as Boy Scouts and Girl Scouts were separated by sex (imagine and fancy that), and it seemed that girls did not want to play the games or to do the things that we guys wanted to do and we were thankful for this.

The girls couldn't run as fast or as long as we could, they couldn't kick a football or bat a baseball as far as we could, and they could not throw at all. I mostly had pity for the girls for their lack of athletic prowess but had "no use" for girls, period.

I did begrudgingly acknowledge that their spelling and other school-related skills were better than "ours" but chalked that up to "if you can't do anything else" you can excel in those areas. Girls could write better, spell better, add and subtract better, and read better. We guys pretended those things didn't really matter much. I figured that we could excel at schoolwork if we wanted to and figured we would want to one day. But for then we didn't; there were more important things to do.

I really didn't understand for sure why Dad liked and enjoyed being with Mom so much, but that was his business and I didn't see any potential relevance in my life for girls at that time and didn't give the future much thought.

15

Sure, at times girls were useful. We guys ate what they couldn't or wouldn't in the cafeteria; we found girls fun, at rare times, to be with and funny most of the time. We wanted them on our terms and were not "futuristic" at all concerning girls or much else, for that matter.

The other point that I wanted to make and reemphasize is that we had almost no contact with black people. Yes, we knew there were a lot of black people in our town, but we kept our distance from them and they did the same. We were never told to "keep our distance." It was just understood.

The only blacks I knew were the few who served and worked for us or my close friends' parents. (A few blacks worked for my dad at the *Star-Herald*, in menial jobs, and I knew them and called them by their first names. They called me Mr. Roy.) As near as I could tell, every white family I knew had a black family working for them, i.e., doing housecleaning, cooking, washing clothes, ironing, doing yard work, and "minding us kids." I knew the kids of the blacks who worked around our house. We played together some when we were together.

I can remember vividly going to Pearl's home at times and being with her kids. I can remember Pearl cooking her clothes in a big black kettle in the front yard of their home. I regretted that we did not wash our clothes the same way. I remember their poverty! I remember our "used and worn out clothes" going to them. I remember their "outhouse." I remember their children always having runny noses and their being sick with coughs and colds all the time. I pitied them and as I grew older the pity I had for them (and the knowledge of their living conditions) played a part in my changing views regarding segregation and our discrimination against blacks as individuals and through the white-controlled government.

I guess I had the feeling of "better them than us," but I was never comfortable with that reasoning.

The Teen Years (1956–63)

The junior and senior high school years were great years for me and my friends. We thought we were really important, and we were, to ourselves and to our families. We thought everyone was impressed with us (we had an eleven-win, no-losses football team my senior year while scoring 254 points and yielding but 34), and we thought that we had to be "God's gift" to the masses! Of course, we were "gifts" from God and "the heritage of the Lord," according to Psalms 127. Our self-worth was probably a bit inflated, which is typical of teenagers, I presume.

We had confidence, good looks, skills, and brains, and, other than a few negatives, e.g., the success of the Soviets in rocketry and space exploration and the buildup of military hardware, we believed that the youth of America were the "knights in shining armor riding the white horses" who would save the nation and the world from itself.

Almost everyone did pretty well in school, grade-wise and conduct-wise. There was good, wholesome competition in schoolwork and on the athletic fields, the boys and girls began to talk to one another, and our little-boy hearts began to go "pitter-patter" for the girls even though we were not sure why. We did realize they smelled good and their laughter made us "tingle" right down to our toes. We were not sure why we were beginning to appreciate them. We didn't have "a clue" about sexual matters, but we were beginning to spend more time with them. We observed another phenomenon, which was that the older guys from the grades "above" us were spending a lot of time in our hallways with the girls in our classes. We did not appreciate that but were helpless to combat it.

We had no condoms and had not received any "sex education" at school or at home, but we began to care what girls thought of us and we did things in attempts to impress them, some which, in retrospect, must have made us look like fools to them at the time. I repeat, in case you passed over it, we had no condoms and had received little sex education, not even the so-called plumbing education, i.e., anatomy lessons. To this day, fifty-four years into my life, I have not touched a condom! People can live without condoms.

In health classes in the seventh grade and in biology class in the tenth grade, we skirted around human reproduction and sex education with nothing more than a few drawings on the human body on a page or two in the textbooks.

We were not using illicit drugs (haven't touched any of "that" either in my life). We saw and committed hardly any violence. No guns or knives in schools or anywhere else, unless we went "can" shooting with our fathers and, later, bird hunting with one another in our teens. The only violence other than good, clean, hard contact on the athletic field was a rare fight between a couple of guys when tempers flared in unorganized sports games on the sandlots.

About the worst thing anyone did was smoke in the rest rooms at school and elsewhere (usually to "prove" that they were nonconformists) or run in the hallways at school (only to get into the cafeteria line ahead of a few others. I can't remember anything else we were in a hurry to do, unless it was to get out of the school building at 3:15 in the afternoon when the bell rang sounding the end of the school day), use a few mild curse words, and, as we turned seventeen or eighteen, drink a few cans of beer with a few other guys on a Friday or Saturday night in roadside parks. Alcoholic beverages, including beer, were illegal to buy, sell, use, or possess in Attala County when I was a kid. Adults had a hard time finding alcoholic drinks. It was doubly difficult for us teenagers.

I remember that on Saturday nights, Mom and Dad would buy items that they were short on, including gasoline, due to the fact that all the stores, shops, and service stations would be closed on Sunday. Today in Mississippi you can buy or do about anything on Sundays. There is an abortion clinic in Mississippi, situated beside a Baptist church, that is open on Sundays, performing abortions! Imagine standing up during the church service singing "Rescue the Perishing" while observing moms and dads as well as grandmoms and granddads offering their children and grandchildren "up" as human sacrifices next door. And there are casinos all over our state today.

Also today in Mississippi, our shopping centers as well as our bars, gambling casinos, and topless (and one topless and "bottomless") dives are open (and going like gang busters) on Sundays! I ought to be able to close this manuscript here as proof that "we have gone beyond the point of no return." However, there's more. I'll continue.

My teen years' social life revolved around school activities and events, mostly athletic, church activities and programs, and Friday- and Saturday-night parties at alternate homes sponsored and supervised by parents. We were always closely supervised and well behaved by to-day's standards.

About the only thing that we did independent of organized social events was date at the movies and "hang out" at the Gate-Way Drive-In (mostly in the parking lot, sitting and talking in parked cars). We went to the one outdoor drive-in theater with dates, usually double-dates because most parents (of the girls) required it.

Sure, we guys tried to kiss our girlfriends and dates and to "persuade" them into "more," but for their sake and ours they said, "No!"

18

I'm not sure we guys would have known what to do if they had allowed us to continue. I remember being relieved with the "stop" signs.

About the only "sex education" we had, in addition to what has been mentioned, was an implied, unspoken promise from our dates' fathers that went something like this: *You touch her and I'll break your arms off!* Regarding sex and human sexual organs, we knew little. We guys were not sure "what went where" and did not talk among ourselves about this. Naked women and those experiences would have to wait. I can remember a few of us decided to try to find a "men's magazine" and we couldn't find one. The stores, convenience stores included, didn't sell *Playboy* or any other "men only" magazines in the late fifties in Kosciusko. My, have times changed!

I can only remember one girl getting pregnant while I was in high school. The young lady, and she was a fine girl from a fine family (who made the best of the bad situation), was a couple of years younger than me. One of her older sisters was a classmate of mine (a major Christian influence on our class), and I believe we were seniors at the time. This girl who became pregnant as a sophomore and her boyfriend (who was a sophomore, too) got married. They were both from very respected families, and I remember what a scandal her pregnancy was. The families and the community (including their two churches) were loving and accepting of the young couple and their child when he arrived, but we were all shocked at the pregnancy and were warned by our parents to "stay pure."

No one that I know of was shipped off to a drug rehabilitation treatment program. Only the one girl got pregnant. The word *abortion* was never heard! There was no talk of sexually transmitted diseases.

Were we naive by today's standards! God knows how innocent and lucky we were. We were protected; we thank our lucky stars and Heaven above for the times in which we were nurtured.

Some of my memories and experiences did not change as I went from my preteens to teen years. In fact, many overlapped, e.g., love for and participation in sports, organized and unorganized, striving for achievement by making good grades, and a desire to be appreciated and accepted.

Also a carryover from preteens to teens was my feeling that my family was an affluent one. I thought that we McMillans were "wealthy, healthy, and wise." I'm sure that I believed this due to my lack of knowledge of what true wealth, health, and wisdom were. Very few homes that

I visited in my youth had more than we did. My friends' big brothers and sisters were not going to Harvard, Yale, or Princeton but to Holmes Junior College, Mississippi State University, Mississippi College for Women, or Ole Miss. There were no "Charles Atlases" or "Bridget Bardots" in Kosciusko. We all had about the same thing, visited the same doctors and dentists, and had been educated in the same public schools by the same teachers (some had taught our parents) and were to attend the same colleges or universities, those who were fortunate to go to college (about 50 percent).

Television had come into Kosciusko and into a few of our homes by the midfifties. What we viewed on TV was "tame" by today's standards, which are pretty much "no standards." *The Rich and The Famous* had not been produced yet; therefore, we watched (and identified with) *Ozzie and Harriet* and *The Life of Riley* both in values and materialism. Monitoring our "viewing" was simply for our parents. There were only two stations, WLBT-TV (the NBC affiliate) and WJTV-TV (the CBS affiliate).

As I look back from age fifty-four to my preteen and teenage years, I realize that I was guilty of a few things, pride and arrogance chief among them. Not only was I wrong about us McMillans being "healthy, wealthy, and wise," but I was proud, sinfully so, in thinking that we were among the elite of this world.

What We Did Not Have

Let me tell you what we did not have. We had, as I have just related, no television until the midfifties; we had no home-delivered daily newspaper, but we did have twice-a-week delivery of bottled milk; we had few Coca-Colas (Coke was a rare treat; mostly we kids drank milk and inexpensive Kool-Aid); we did not have air conditioning (I remember when we added room air-conditioners to the living room and to Mom and Dad's bedroom); and I don't remember eating steak but remember a lot of ground beef (I think I lived on peanut butter sandwiches until maybe age fourteen).

Even though we did not have so many things we take for granted today (much of which we feel we could not live without, i.e., leaf blowers and automatic ice-makers), we did not think we were poor or deprived. I did not feel as if I would become a misfit or socially irresponsible if I

20

had to walk to school (which I did every day until I got a car at age fifteen) or live without a Coke or Dr. Pepper every four hours.

No, we were not affluent, but we were spared "the four horsemen of the apocalypse"—no, not the four from the fourth chapter of Revelations, written by John the Apostle ("Conquest, War, Famine, and Death"), but the four that our culture is submerged in ("Power, Pride, Privilege, and Materialism").

Through my teen years my interests, along with sports, friendships, girls, and moral living, turned to more serious and potentially long-ranging and far-reaching things, especially media, the newspapers in particular, politics and government, and the military.

My family's involvement in these three areas obviously influenced me. My father and his father-in-law, Colonel Sanders, owned and managed Attala County's only newspaper, a weekly, and the corporation that Dad oversaw purchased or began several other newspapers in several other counties. By small town standards, their newspaper printing plant, consolidated in Kosciusko with state-of-the-art equipment, along with a parallel commercial printing plant, was a considerable operation. It was a major benefit to the community as well as a business that was rewarding, profitable, fun, influential, and worthy of pride of ownership.

Almost everyone in town knew who my father and grandfather were and that I was their son/grandson. I was proud of them and wanted to emulate them. What interested them interested me. Dad was a photographer, so I was a photographer, developing black-and-white film and prints in the newspaper's darkroom by age thirteen. I worked for the newspaper from the time I was a little boy and grew up reading the editorials and stories that my father and grandfather had written.

Colonel Sanders had been mayor of Kosciusko for many years in the early days of the century. He had, also, served as a member of the Mississippi state legislature (both as a member of the House of Representatives and the Senate) for approximately twenty years. I was, understandably, proud of him and interested in politics and government myself. Editor Sanders had served with considerable distinction in the U.S. Army and the Mississippi National Guard through the 1910s, 1920s, and 1930s and into the early 1940s. He had served as an infantry officer in the First World War and at the beginning of the Second World War (as a colonel). Due to his age, Colonel Sanders retired just as World War II began. He had commanded the National Guard unit in Kosciusko and was well known in that capacity.

I would question him about the military and his war experiences. While he was reluctant to talk much about the actual combat, he did tell me about his "travels" while in the military, and this was fascinating to me. Like my grandfather, I was interested in the military, politics, commerce, and government. I wanted to be just like my grandfather when I was a teenager.

My father was following Colonel Sanders's path in community involvement and improvement, particularly in the areas of economic development and social justice. During the 1950s and 1960s, Kosciusko and Mississippi were making giant strides in convincing industry and manufacturing executives from the North to move south or establish industrial or manufacturing expansion branches in the South. State and local government assistances and incentives such as BAWI (Balance Agriculture With Industry) programs, along with aggressive local leadership, combined to convince many business executives to locate plants in the South. Inexpensive labor was abundant (as were raw materials, water, and energy), and labor unions hardly existed. The "climate," literally and figuratively, was favorable for business development in the South.

My dad, even though his age was appropriate to having served in World War II, was not able to because he was an employee of Du Pont in Baton Rouge and Du Pont was involved in war chemical production.

The effect of working for my father and grandfather at the *Star-Herald*, listening to them while they talked between themselves and with me, reading their columns, editorials, and stories, and witnessing their "hands-on" involvement in the social/commercial/governmental life of our community had an enormous influence on my future. I came to the decision in high school that I would study journalism and business in college at the University of Mississippi (Ole Miss), and I joined the National Guard unit in Kosciusko, the unit that my grandfather had a long history of involvement in, as soon as I was eligible, the day after I reached my seventeenth birthday. For the last one and one-half years of high school I attended National Guard drills (meetings) every Monday night, monthly weekend drills, and a two-week summer camp (in Anniston, Alabama, at Fort McClellan). I was off to Fort Jackson, South Carolina, within a few days of graduating from high school to attend U.S. Army basic training.

Other than the fact that I had made a long-term commitment to the U.S. Army through the Mississippi National Guard while in high school and had decided on a college to attend and a profession to major in and to pursue after college, I don't believe my activities, interests, and experiences were much different from those of others my age, at least no different from those of my good friends.

We attended public schools through the 1950s and into the 1960s, we dated and many went steady with a number of girls our age or a few years younger, sharpened our social and interrelational skills with those of our sex and of the opposite sex, and did not participate in serious sexual relationships.

We appreciated and coveted our close friends, many of whom are still close friends (four decades later). Homosexuality was not even discussed, and if it existed (and I'm sure it did), we were unaware of it. We were largely ignorant as to what petting and lovemaking consisted of, and we had never heard of homosexual, anal intercourse. Even the most "worldly" of us would have probably gotten sick to our stomachs at a description of a homosexual act when I was a teenager, or a college student, for that matter. The only reason we are not all totally repulsed today by descriptions of explicit homosexual acts is that we have been inundated with the perverse conduct and acts of homosexuals.

My teen years were during an "age of innocence" (as far as I am concerned) and of little tension or heartbreak, even though we would have been hard-pressed to believe the latter when our "puppy love" romances disintegrated. In retrospect, I believe our parents gave us (and we give our children) too much latitude in single dating. These "single dating" experiences led to "going steady" and that to "breaking up." We were, I believe, being "trained" to expect and endure divorces, which became commonplace for our generation in years to come.

I would identify the racial tension and the growing communist menace as the two major regional and national/international (the communist threat) dilemmas facing my generation.

Due to the publicity engendered via the civil rights (of the blacks) movement in the 1950s and 1960s as well as usually unsubstantiated reports of vigilante activities of the Klu Klux Klan elements in our area, we "privileged" white kids were having to come to terms with racial discrimination. I remember going to the Attala County Courthouse to register to vote after I turned twenty-one. I paid my two-dollar poll tax and took a short written and verbal literacy test about fifteen or so minutes long. I remember an old, poorly dressed black man trying to register to vote when I was registering. While I did not think that a two-dollar fee was a major obstacle to voter registration (after all, we paid for other "rights and privileges," i.e., to enter a state or national park or to rent a paddleboat in a park) nor did I believe it to be unfair for a potential voter to have to pass a simple literacy test to "earn" the right to vote, I was troubled that I might be wrong. I was troubled that day by the verbal "test" to which the elderly black man was subjected. All that I had been required to do was read something simple. The black man was required to read something far more complicated and then required to interpret something (which I was not required to do). I passed; he failed.

Immediately I became convinced in my heart, if not in my mind, that we whites, who were in charge of the power structure (we gave the literacy test in the case above), were capable of being unfair, and did "rig" who could vote and who could not. I'm sure the two dollars the elderly black man paid (and was not refunded) for his voting registration attempt was more precious to him than the two dollars I had paid as a poll tax was to me.

I had long been aware of the major economic disadvantages that blacks suffered. For example, I had never seen a street in the black business area, such as Beale Street, or in the black residential area, such as Tipton Street (the street that Oprah Winfrey lived on, I believe), that was paved. There were no paved streets in the black areas at all. However, almost every street in the white business and residential areas were paved.

I remember the separate rest rooms! At my Uncle Channing's Gulf service station on East Jefferson Street there were three rest rooms, one for "White Men," one for "White Women," and one for "Coloreds." I can, to this day, remember how filthy the "colored" rest rooms were. (A few times I looked into them out of curiosity.)

I can remember with a bit of envy the fact that the "coloreds" sat in the balcony at the Strand Theater. (I can't remember whether or not the Pix Theater had a balcony.) I thought, as a little kid, that I would rather sit in the balcony than downstairs. We had so few two-story (or more) buildings in Kosciusko that being in the balcony would have been a rare thrill. (I can remember the thrill of riding in elevators and on escalators when we went to Jackson or Memphis!)

I can't remember much racial tension, conflict, or violence between the races in Kosciusko when I was a child or teenager. I believe it mostly simmered under the surface. I never witnessed any tension, conflict, or violence. I guess the closest thing to racial conflict I ever witnessed was an occasional cup of soda being thrown from the balcony (by the "coloreds") down onto us "innocent whites" below.

24

There were occasional rumors of violence such as church burnings as a result of voter registration drives in other Mississippi towns and counties or other southern states. I'm not saying church burnings and the like did not happen. Such occurrences were not prominently reported by the white-controlled news media in our area, such as the *Clarion-Ledger* and the *Daily News* (which has ceased to publish). Of course there were the famous acts of violence, including lynchings and, a little later, organized acts of violence by law-enforcement agencies in the South (including Jackson and Philadelphia, Mississippi) which received local, national, and international media coverage (rightfully so). Of course, we (southerners) realized there was racism and discrimination in the North, East, and West, but it was not institutionalized there as it was in the South.

Most white southerners and many "colored" southerners were resistant to integration at first. We were mostly resistant to change of any sort and feared change more than anything. We did not "hate" the "coloreds," and I would guess the "coloreds" did not "hate" us whites. One has to know someone or something to "hate" them or it. Ashamedly, we "mainstream, churchgoing Christians" had little to do with our "colored" brethren. "Knowing them" would not have meant interracial dating and marriages or forced socializing together. (Not that this is sin. It is not and ought to be a part of the fabric of our culture.) "We" did not know "them" and their needs and pains in any real sense of the word, as the Word required of us.

As far as the communists and their rise to world political, economic, and military prominence and power, I have a few reflections to make. When the Soviets launched *Sputnik I* on October 4, 1957, Americans were shocked and scared. If they could put a spaceship into outer space, they could deliver a nuclear weapon to our doorsteps, we feared—rightfully so.

Americans realized that we had a formidable enemy who was committed to "burying" us (as Nikita Khrushchev, one of Russia's premiers, once predicted) and who would be identified, rightfully so, as "the evil empire" (by Pres. Ronald Reagan) at a later date. We were soon to be scared of "nuclear blackmail," and I was scared. Dad's actions didn't help any either.

In the late 1950s, Dad built a fallout shelter at our home in our basement. I remember the canned foods, the water bottles, the pillows and blankets, and the flash lights. I remember the designated fallout shelters around Kosciusko and the fallout-shelter public service announcements on radio and television. Really (I now ask myself), how many nuclear bombs were pointed at Kosciusko? What and who in Attala County could have threatened or devastated "the evil empire"? In retrospect, not much or many.

But there were real scares based on real knowledge and real events. I remember the Berlin Crisis in late 1958, when Soviet Union premier Nikita Khrushchev closed off West Berlin from Western Europe, and in June of 1961, the month I entered the U.S. Army, there was another showdown between East and West.

In 1961 and 1962, when I was in the army, we again risked nuclear war with the USSR over the confrontations in Cuba with the ill-fated Bay of Pigs invasion and the Cuban Missile Crisis. These were frightening times that "tried men's souls," especially those men in the military or of draft age.

There was a reverence for the military when I was a youngster in the post–World War II era and prior to the Vietnam War. There was a respect for practically all institutions, private and public, and vocations then. We understood the need to be militarily prepared. We understood that the best defense is a good offense and a good defense. We knew the bully never picked on a stronger, faster, and wiser foe.

As I close this section, about the formative years of my life, of this chapter, my intent is that you can better understand where I came from, which will help you grasp why I have reached the conclusions I have regarding the future of this nation, which are "laid out" in chapter 4: " 'Their Destiny Is Their Destruction. . . . Their Glory Is Their Shame' (Phil. 3:19)."

The significant realization that I come to when I reflect on my past is that my generation (and those immediately before mine) had common fears, struggles, and values. Our commonly held values and principles were, for the most part, being taught and reinforced by all of the institutions that existed. Yes, racial injustice and prejudice was the major exception. With this exception, we were fairly innocent (and nice to one another), hardworking, self-reliant, optimistic, happy, and of one mind, but people vulnerable to the coming upheaval of the 1960s and beyond, which was to radically transform our culture and lives forever and mostly for the worse, I fear.

Off We Went into the "Wild Blue Yonder"!

Friday night, May 26, 1961, seventy-two seniors graduated from Kosciusko High School in the school auditorium. We would never play on the Whippets sports teams or in the KHS band together again, and we would not have to be present to hear the first school bell ring weekdays, nine months of the year, in the morning at 8:05 or to be in our homerooms for roll call when the second bell rang at 8:10. Most of us would not go fishing, hunting, or water skiing together again. We were "flying the coop" and heading into seventy-two different directions.

I left within a few days for Columbia, South Carolina, for Fort Jackson for basic training in the U.S. Army. After basic training came advanced infantry training and then an assignment to a combat unit for the duration of my first tour of duty, which lasted about a year.

In August of 1962 I attended Fraternity Rush Week at Ole Miss, located in Oxford. Then came college registration.

A man named James Meredith, also from Kosciusko, was attempting to register along with about seven thousand others for the fall semester at Ole Miss that year, too. He wanted to enter Ole Miss's Graduate School. There was one problem, a major one at that: Mr. Meredith was black. If admitted, he would be the first black to ever attend Ole Miss or, for that matter, any other state college or university in Mississippi other than the ones created for "blacks only." There were no black faculty members at Ole Miss at that time either.

What a time in my life! National attention to my university as a result of the looming desegregation of a major university in a major segregation state! National attention was being given Ole Miss that fall, too, because its football team, the Rebels, was a preseason Top Ten team in all the polls. What an interesting time was this beginning of my college career and the beginning of many new relationships in my college dorm, Lester and my fraternity, Phi Kappa Psi, to which I had just "pledged."

As a result of Mississippi Governor Ross Barnett's unwillingness to surrender his state's right (as he saw it, as did most Mississippians, the white ones, that is) to control who entered what schools in Mississippi to the federal government through a mandate of the federal courts, there was much tension and attention to those first days of the 1962–63 school year at Ole Miss.

During the half-time ceremonies of a football game in Jackson (Ole Miss versus Kentucky [we won!]) the Saturday night before the Monday registration at Ole Miss, Gov. Barnett issued a "call" for loyal Mississippians to join him and the Mississippi Highway Patrol and the Mississippi National Guard on Monday as Mississippi refused to "bow" to federal authority over the matter of Mr. Meredith's attempt to become the first

27

black to enter Ole Miss. By midnight of that Saturday night I had drunk more than my limit of adult beverages; I knew that I had been called into active duty as a member of the Mississippi National Guard in order to prevent Ole Miss from being desegregated. I was to report, according to the news being broadcast over the radio, along with thousands of others to our local National Guard armories at daybreak the next morning. I was there; I was not in too good of a shape (the morning after my first major frat party), but I was there.

As we prepared to journey the 190 miles from central Mississippi (Kosciusko) to north central Mississippi (Oxford and Ole Miss), we were activated into federal service in order to desegregate Ole Miss, if military units were needed to help the U.S. marshal corps that was to be at Ole Miss that fateful Monday in September of 1962. We had gone from being under control of our segregationist governor, Ross Barnett, to the federal control of Pres. John F. Kennedy, who was obligated, according to the federal courts, to see that Mr. Meredith was registered at Ole Miss and was able to attend classes.

What ensued that Sunday night and Monday morning was called a riot. I was there! I was in army fatigues as a newly commissioned second lieutenant. I saw what happened. And what happened was a major legal confrontation between a state government and its superior federal government in an area that the federal government rightfully had jurisdiction, in my opinion.

A few cars were turned over; a few of them burned. Three or four people (I can't remember which, but it was either three or four) were shot to death. There was some physical damage to a few buildings and a lot of angry shouting. Most of the students wanted the federal government to "butt out." But most students enjoyed being "where the attention was," and a few made "butts" of themselves as they helped the national news media malign what little reputation Ole Miss and Mississippi had that was positive.

Where was I? I spent the first month of my first semester of my first year of college living in a pup tent, eating in the woods in our unit's bivouac area, and taking my turn standing guard at various intersections, buildings, dorms, and the like in order that a "show of force" would prevent any added violence against people or damage to property.

My "uno one" remembrance of those days was the great amount of media "hype" orchestrated by the national news media representatives who were on campus covering the story and not just covering news as bystanders but "manufacturing" it. They would convince a group of students to shout slogans that the newspeople would create. The students would follow the media representatives' "script" in order to be on national, network news that evening.

Also, I remember the hundreds of federal marshals who descended on Ole Miss. They were rude, crude, arrogant, and, in my opinion, very unprofessional and unskilled law enforcement personnel.

The presentation of the "riots" at Ole Miss in the fall of 1962 and the confrontation between the state government of Mississippi and the federal government forever jaundiced my view of "news." I was already skeptical of media bias from watching the media coverage of the civil rights movement from my southern perspective. The one-sided and slanted national media coverage of the events at Ole Miss that fall totally reinforced my lack of trust of the "fourth estate," and that mistrust continues to this day.

As I studied journalism at Ole Miss and became a part of the media as an employee after graduation, I understood the disastrous effect the media has had on our culture due to its written and broadcast perspective of the news, which is, in general, in my opinion, anticapitalist, pro-death via abortion, infanticide, and euthanasia, pro–sexual emancipation, pro–the homosexual agenda, anti–U.S. military preparedness, pro-government "takeover" of the social/charity service (including health care) from Christianity and its individuals and institutions, pro–"tax and spend" government, and anti-Christian position.

Things settled down at Ole Miss and I eventually was able to attend classes by day and study by candlelight and flashlight by night in my tent as I remained on "active duty" for a couple of months.

While federal marshals remained on campus for the remainder of the school year, the National Guard was deactivated and I became a full-time student. Well, I was a full-time student on weekdays, for at Ole Miss weekends were dedicated to social life, "partying" and supporting the Ole Miss football, basketball, and baseball teams.

Ole Miss was considered a "party" school, and they had me convinced that it was so. Of course, I had nothing by which to judge whether it was true or not. It sure seemed to be true to me, and I was determined to "join in," not to be a spoilsport or anything like that. There was little else to do at Ole Miss or in Oxford. Memphis was the only large city nearby, and it was more than two hours' drive away. Oxford was a small town and "rolled up" its sidewalks, a familiar term, at dusk; therefore,

29

our weekend nights were occupied with fraternity parties, football games, and attending entertainment concerts given by such notables as Peter, Paul, and Mary, the Mama and the Papas, and other leftist, social-liberating, free-sex, "anything goes" advocates.

What was occurring across the country in the colleges and universities was coming into the "heart of the Bible Belt," the South, i.e., free love, pot smoking, and antiestablishment, antiwar, and "anti everything" of traditional, moral, biblical values. Ole Miss was not Berkeley, and we were given only a small "dose" of what was to come to the next generation.

There was much to hold me and my peers to our past at Ole Miss. We attended a great university with a historic tradition; we came from mostly small, conservative southern cities and towns; we were in a small city in a relatively small university in a rural state; and our parents were more socially and economically conservative than parents in the North, the East, and the West.

We were "tied" more to the past than those students in other regions, I believe. Oxford and Ole Miss were the home and school of William Faulkner, for example. It was not unusual to visit with Mr. Faulkner in "the Grove" as he meandered around the campus. He would tell of his life and times as well as about the "soul of the South" for hours at a time as we sat under elm and oak trees mesmerized by the famous novelist's stories and remembrances.

I was occupied with my studies and going to classes during weekdays and weeknights, with Monday night National Guard drills, and with campus social and sporting events on weekends as well as concerts and lectures as well as one-a-month weekend National Guard drills and maneuvers. Occasionally, on weekends, I would visit home, Kosciusko, to see the folks, put in a bid for more money, and see a special young woman whom I cared very much for.

Continuing Military Training

This interesting, growing, and educational experience (attending college) lasted for three and one-half years. I spent my summers in U.S. Army schools at Fort Benning, Georgia, and elsewhere. I attended Officers Candidate School for two summers and rose in rank from a sergeant to a second lieutenant in the infantry.

I graduated from Ole Miss in January of 1966 with a B.S. degree with a major in journalism (from the School of Business). I was healthy, educated, and still quite optimistic about my future and the future of my culture/society/nation. I was idealistic, single, debt-free ("fancy free," some would say). I looked at the world as my "oyster"!

I was proud of what I had accomplished in my twenty-two years and thought that my values and lifelong principles and precepts had been unalterably settled.

I loved life, my nation, my future, and myself. Perhaps I, like many of you, did not understand how fragile life was and how quickly a person and a nation could lose his and its moral foundation and soul. The completion of the first twenty-two years of one's life is either "the end of the beginning" or "the beginning of the end" of the journey. I would call it the former, as this period lasts but a score and two years and is but a quarter of the actuarially predicted four score and "change" of the average life today. Anyhow, I believe when one reaches his or her twenty-second birthday, he or she has completed the "autumn of one's youth."

I was independent when I finished college. I was a confirmed "conservative" where I thought one ought to be conservative and a "liberal" where I thought one ought to be liberal.

As a Christian, I believe one ought to be conservative where Christ was conservative, i.e., in holding onto the best of individual and cultural traditions that are good for the individual and for the group. I believe that one ought to be liberal where Christ was liberal, i.e., in forgiveness, patience, tolerance (to a point [more later]), and charitable. While I did not always do what I knew to do (sins of omission) nor did I refuse to do what I knew not to do (sins of commission), I had a little voice (conscience or "Holy Spirit" for us Christians) convicting me of my sins of omission and my sins of commission. I, like everyone else, was a product of my faith, my family, my heritage, my education, my culture, my nation, and my generation.

For better or worse, I was ready to "fly" on my own, to see distant shores, to complete my military obligation (which I enjoyed), to be gainfully employed full-time, to be a part of this "great experiment in freedom," to make new friends, and to find one to love and to be committed to in marriage.

Heaven help the world and Heaven help us, was my prayer on my college graduation day.

31

Thus far in this chapter, I have written an autobiographical sketch, chronologically, of the first twenty-two years of my life, which spanned the years from 1943 to 1966. I have done so in depth so that you can compare my "formative years" with yours, especially for those of you born since 1960, who didn't experience the post–World War II era through the mid-1960s. Those born after 1960 were influenced much differently by the education system, the entertainment industry, the media, and, sadly, Christianity and, in general, for the worse, in my opinion. You who were born after 1960 have been tremendously influenced by a culture/society/nation that has not the sense of "right" and "wrong" and by many Christian denominations that have fallen into various degrees of apostasy (some into total apostasy) due to the fact, in my opinion, that they have rejected the Bible as the inerrant, infallible, inspired word of God Almighty.

From Age Twenty-two to Meeting and Marrying a Former Abortionist

I am going to spare you most of the events of the next eighteen years of my life. The reason I went into great detail of the first twenty-two years of my life was because I believe it will be important for you to understand how I arrived at the very difficult, and unhappy, conclusion that is the theme/thesis of this book, my belief that we have (as a nation/culture/society) gone beyond the point of no return. I believe it is essential for you to understand what I had learned and experienced in my formative years to arrive at such a startling prediction. I carefully did not say that I "predicted" a future that would be "detrimental" to the individual Christian or for Christianity. Yes, I believe we are in for hard, even disastrous times, physically, emotionally, and spiritually, but I believe this can be good for Christians and Christianity if we prepare for it and do what we ought to do before and during it.

All of us understand what Adolf Hitler meant when he said, "Give me the minds of the children and I will transform the culture in one generation." We believe that.

We understand the truth to this statement: "What is taught in the schools in one generation will be public policy in the next." We are a nation that is simply "reaping what we have sown."

What began in the 1960s and continues practically unabated to this day influenced my life and yours, but it did not dominate our values as it has those who have been born after 1960. Their minds and hearts have been developed and influenced much more than those of my generation by humanist teachings and examples, mostly for the worse and in a way, I believe, that will lead to the destruction, the moral "meltdown," of our culture/society/nation.

Yes, my generation and the generations still living who came before me have been influenced greatly by the humanist propaganda, but it did not lead to total self-destruction and the chaos that is upon us. Our generation has participated in the humanist lifestyle of this generation, but we have not totally capitulated/surrendered to the teachings and actions of these times.

For example, I never used illegal drugs, with the one exception of alcholic beverages (as a high school and college student when alcholic beverages were either banned and/or illegal for minors and, in some places, for adults). As high school students, a few of us bought beer from local bootleggers or drove the eighteen miles to Holmes County (Durant), where beer was legal. Beer sales to minors were illegal, of course, but we always found some adult who would buy beer for those of us underage.

We drank beer while in high school, ages fifteen to eighteen, because it was the "forbidden fruit," to impress others, and to see what it made us feel like. Does that sound familiar, i.e., like all illicit drugs? We did not, I repeat, we did not drink beer because it tasted good. We hated the taste! We hated getting sick as a result of drinking too much! We hated the vomiting and headaches that it caused!

In college, where we drank stronger alcholic beverages, we, again, did not drink because it tasted good. We drank in college, speaking for myself, to become uninhibited, primarily at social events. In high school, back in Kosciusko, dancing was hardly allowed. Therefore, we went to college not knowing how to dance and too inhibited to dance with our dates in a crowd without a little "lubricating." I now believe that many of us who came to colleges from small towns where dancing was forbidden got into the bad habit of overindulging in drinking due to our shyness in social situations, particularly at college dances. I think that the Baptist ban on dancing was wrong.

There was one "silver lining" that resulted from our drinking to excess at times during my high school and college days. We alienated and embarrassed so many of our dates that we never got to know them well enough to develop close relationships that might have resulted in sexual sin.

Understand, when I was in college the coeds easily could be alienated and embarrassed by the conduct of young men. Today it is far more difficult to cause a young woman to walk away from a socially disgusting and repulsive young man who has done or said something that ought to cause a young woman to leave his presence.

Coming to Grips with the Eastern Mind Set

I was sexually pure, a virgin, until age twenty-six, just months before I married my first wife. I had never seen or held a condom (still haven't ever touched one). I hardly ever cursed, a habit I picked up primarily in the army. I never, never cursed around women or young people. I even opened and held open doors for women and children as well as waited for women and children to enter and exit elevators before me (and still do).

I was never a violent person! Never had a reason to be.

I was pretty much "morally straight," which was and I pray still is contained in the Scout oath.

After college and the completion of my military service, I moved to New York City and was employed in the Advertising Department of the *New York Daily News*. I was about the only social, political, economic, and religious conservative in my circle, even though the *Daily News* was conservative, compared to the *New York Times*, the *Post*, and the *Herald* (which was operating at that time). Even my social contacts and the congregation of the Baptist church that I attended in Manhattan were much more liberal in all areas of life than I was.

At times I felt as if I were the only, or the most, conservative soul in the Northeast. I witnessed and heard the rantings and ravings of those who thought (1) we ought not to have intervened in Vietnam (in order to allow those helpless people determine their own destinies); (2) illicit drugs ought to be legal; (3) all sexual activities was good, healthy recreation; (4) homosexual relationships were as acceptable morally as heterosexual relationships; and (5) God was dead.

Most of the people I got to know in New York as well as up and down the eastern seaboard were not just anti–Vietnam War (again involvement to protect the helpless and to stop communist aggression); they were clearly antiestablishment and challenged about everything I had been taught in conservative, rural, "buckle of the Bible Belt" Mississippi. (Boy, were they wrong, but, boy, were they winning the hearts and minds of the people!)

I did not give in, I tried to hold my own, but I did not aggressively challenge and confront their liberal positions as I could and should have. I assumed they would go away and no one would be injured by what they were advocating and doing. I wanted to be "tolerant" and wanted to be accepted and liked. That was a mistake. I believe, looking back twenty-five years, that I was being more influenced by them than I thought I was at the time.

We who know better ought to stand "toe to toe" with the liberals who have been and are destroying our culture in the pubic debate, in the public squares, at the abortion mills, at the steps of the "topless bars," and in the liberal churches. (Indeed, we are required to. To whom much is given, much is expected.)

Bit by bit, I realize now, the liberals and their failed policies were transforming our culture "in their images" for the worse. While we conservatives were sitting quietly by the side of the road, humming hymns, studying our navels, and feeling bad about what was happening, they were taking over our land!

Many women, thanks to the radical feminists and exploitative men, were becoming sex objects, and illicit drugs were coming into our schools along with knives, guns, vile language, and condoms, while prayer, Bible reading, Judeo-Christian morals and values, and Christ-centered Christmas plays were being removed.

Abortion was being legitimatized and legalized, and abortion death centers were being situated beside our churches while the subject of abortion was being debated ("Abortion: Right or Wrong?") within Christian churches. Homosexual conduct was being blessed in many of our churches while active homosexual pastors were being ordained. It all was "being tolerated" because many in our churches believed "what *they* believed" and "did" would not affect "us" or our families or our culture.

Free speech became pornography and was even "stretched" to non-verbal speech or print, i.e. burning draft cards, bras, and the Stars and Stripes as well as dancing naked on tables and in the aisles of bars and, in some areas, parading on beaches.

But "free speech" prohibitions included the use of the biological facts of human life in the womb before juries in defenses in criminal cases for those few who took risks and made selfless sacrifices in efforts to protect the unborn from death in our courts of law. Of course, the reading of Scriptures to juries in our courts of law regarding the existence of human beings, including Jesus, in their mothers' wombs has been routinely prohibited, as have been references to Scriptures that require Christians to protect the innocent.

Juries are no longer "our peers," for Christians are systematically expunged from our juries. Most Christians who believe abortion is murder and that murder ought not or cannot be legalized by a legitimate government readily excuse themselves as jurors when challenged by prosecutors or judges as to whether or not they can be "fair" jurors. These Christians somehow believe that their religious, moral values prohibit them from not condemning/convicting someone who has been "obeying God rather than man." When these so-called Christians leave the jury pool, the only people left to judge "good" and "evil" are the amoral and the immoral who don't believe anything anyway and can be conjured into any verdict or sentence by prosecutors and judges.

A Failed First Marriage

When I was in my late twenties, I decided it was time to get married. I envied married men and women and revered the institution of marriage and the family and thought I would be happier and more fulfilled married than single. While this is true, this is not the reason to get married. I married my first wife within a few months of meeting her and after she had become pregnant. I am aware that everyone says, "It happened [pregnancy] the first time." It was true in our case. Perhaps we would have married had she not have become pregnant, perhaps not, but getting married because one's girlfriend is pregnant is not the way God desires.

Perhaps I loved her; perhaps I would have loved her more had we not had to get married. Those considerations didn't really matter, because we believed getting married was the right thing to do for our child, Amanda, who was born on February 3, 1970. I cared (and still do) a great deal for my first wife, and I think she did and does care a great deal for me today, in that we do not wish each other ill. I loved being married, I loved my daughter, I love my wife's son, Andrew, by her first marriage, and I loved having and owning a home in the suburbs.

We had, by most people's expectations and standards I suppose, a good life together for about ten years. After twelve years, my wife wanted "out" of the marriage. I realized (too late) that I was not giving her, our daughter, and my adopted son the attention and devotion they deserved. I was trying to succeed in the manner that "the world" measures success. My wife and I had slowly become not "one" but "separate" people living in the same house. Our difficulties, which were not manifested on the surface to one another, much less to others, included selfishness and the lack of communications. She failed to tell me of her loneliness and about the times I hurt her through neglect, and I assumed that "no news is good news."

There was never any abuse, or neglect, harm to one another or to the kids; no dishes were broken; no pillows (or worse) were thrown at one another. There was just an emptiness that God did not intend to exist between a husband and a wife. I believe this hollowness exists in far too many marriages today.

My married life for those twelve years, from 1969 to 1981, was that of a married white male, between the ages of twenty-six and thirty-eight, who was a father and stepfather. (My first wife's first husband had died of cancer only two years before we married.) I was committed to work, my reputation, "good works," and involvement in my church, but with little spiritual intensity and growth.

My career, business-wise, was in advertising, journalism, publishing, printing, public relations, and communications with several newspapers, from the newspaper with the largest circulation newspaper in the country at that time (the *New York Daily News*) to about the smallest weekly newspaper, a freely distributed newspaper in southwest Jackson, Mississippi, which I owned and operated as a minority partner with my uncle, and with a ten-state life insurance company, Southern Farm Bureau Life Insurance Company, which was headquarted in Jackson. I was the public relations director with responsibilities in public relations, employee relations (there were 600 employees in the home office building), publications, advertising, media relations, and sales promotion. The company was represented by more than twenty-five hundred insurance sales and services representatives affiliated with the Farm Bureau organizations in ten southern states. I really enjoyed my work at Southern Farm, particularly the people I had the privilege to work with and for. (More about this in chapter 3.)

When my marriage ended, I faced my "Damascus road" experience. My life shattered. I was embarrassed; I was pained. I could not sleep or eat regularly for months. My daughter, Amanda, was eleven at the time. She lived with me and I had legal custody of her. I'm not sure I could have survived without her. Even though it was not easy for a father to raise his daughter alone as she reached her adolescent years, it certainly kept me occupied and was a sacred trust to be her father and sole guardian. I grieve for fathers who lose the company and companionship of not only their wives but often their children also when families are split apart in divorce.

It was during this "divorce recovery" phase of my life that I, for the first time, truly turned my life over to the Lord and had long, passionate prayer time with Jesus.

We know that the same heat that melts butter will harden an egg. Adversity can either destroy us or make us! Heat will melt steel so that it can be molded into a cast iron for the purpose for which it is needed. "Spiritual" heat, I believe, can be used by God in our lives during times of trials and tribulations so that the Holy Spirit can "make" us into the tools that God desires if we will allow it to be done.

I believe and thank God that the character that I had been molded in during my formative years as well as the spiritual guidance that I had been given in my youth gave me the foundation to repair my life, giving me my confidence back, providing me a reason for living, and bringing me into a deeper, closer, more personal relationship with the Lord Jesus Christ. I spent much time in prayer and Bible reading and study during that "recovery" and "healing" period of my life. For several years early in the morning I prayed earnestly and read the Bible. (For three years consecutively I read the Bible through annually.)

I grew steadily in the Christian faith. There was much fruit in my life. I discovered that the fruit of prayer is faith, the fruit of faith is love, the fruit of love is service, and the fruit of service is peace. I had a peace in my life that I had never had before as I recovered from the aftermath of a failed marriage. I had hope in the future. I clearly understand now that there can be no peace in the present until there is hope in the future. All Christians ought to take great comfort in this knowledge that Christ is our hope, our only hope, and through him alone is there "peace that passeth all understanding."

I became very active in my church (First Baptist Church in Jackson, the largest church in Mississippi). I volunteered for many projects. I was active in the adult singles group to which I belonged. I taught Sunday School for six-year-old boys. My partner in the six-year-old-boys department was Ross Barnett, Jr., the son of the former governor of Mississippi who had resisted the federal courts when Ole Miss was desegregated. Ross was and is a smart, compassionate, successful attorney who is a delightful person to be around. I became active in a number of Christian charities and outreaches. My responsibilities at work and in pubic relations gave me the perfect opportunity to "do" for charities and to "gather laborers" for charities in the Jackson area.

Then There Came Along Beverly Smith, M.D.

In the spring of 1982 I met an extraordinary person who has altered my life in ways I could never have dreamed that my life could be altered. I sometimes am asked by friends, "Would you have run from Beverly when you first met her if you had known what the future was going to hold for you?" (Sixty arrests, "public enemy 'number uno' " in Mississippi!) Of course not, but it is an interesting question and a "yes" answer would be understandable.

That person was Beverly Ann Smith, M.D., an obstetrician-gynecologist who lived in Jackson with her three young sons and practiced medicine in her medical clinic office and at several hospitals in the Jackson area.

She was a divorced mom. Her three sons, Emory, Tony, and Chardo, at the time we met (April of 1982), were six, eight, and ten years old. She was a fairly new Christian and had had the experience of opening the first abortion center in Mississippi in Jackson in 1975.

I heard her testimonial as to why she had gotten out of the abortion business and had become a Christian when she was debating the owner of a Jackson abortion facility at the one where Beverly had previously performed abortions.

She explained that day that she quit performing abortions due to three reasons: (1) she could no longer look at the bodies of the little human beings she had killed; (2) some of the mothers whose unborn children she had destroyed were coming back to her for other medical needs grieving for what they had done to their children and themselves during a past time of personal crisis in their lives; and (3) the Lord Jesus Christ, the "Hound of Heaven," as she had described her experience with Him, had broken out of the "underbrush" and become real to her and her "savior." That meant that her entire life, including her medical practice, had to conform with His will, and His will would not be for her to kill His little ones.

While she gave her most moving presentation that day, I recalled the fact that I had been abandoned at birth, naked, in a shoe box, in the middle of the winter in the middle of the night on the doorsteps of a Baptist church in Alexandria, Louisiana, thirty-eight years ago. It occurred to me that if abortion had been legal and accepted with no more than a little moral debate as to whether or not it was right in the summer of 1942, a few months after my conception, I most likely would have been "history" in the summer of '42.

I talked with Beverly after that meeting. I got to know Dr. Beverly well, very well, and the rest is history.

The next chapter of this book is a biographical sketch of Beverly's life. After that chapter, I will relate our "time together," the name of chapter 3.

2

Not "Born on a Mountaintop in Tennessee" but Born at Kings Mountain Memorial Hospital

Beverly Ann (Bushore) McMillan was born August 22, 1942, in the beautiful, mountainous region of northeastern Tennessee. Unlike "Davy" Crockett (1786–1836), who was, reportedly, "born on a mountaintop in Tennessee" near Rogersville in northeastern Tennessee on August 17, 1786, Beverly was born at Kings Mountain Memorial Hospital in downtown Bristol, Tennessee/Virginia. (Bristol lies partly in Tennessee and partly in Virginia. The main street in downtown Bristol divides the two states.)

Obviously Beverly was born much later than fellow Tennessean Davy Crockett.

While Beverly is not nearly as famous as Crockett and other eastern Tennessee "favorite sons" such as Daniel Boone (1734–1820), Andrew Jackson (1767–1845), and "Tennessee" Ernie Ford (1919–1990), she is a native of the same region and "her days" (and legend) have not been completed (or written).

Not unlike Crockett, Boone, Jackson, and Ford, Beverly has not spent her entire lifetime in eastern Tennessee.

Crockett, Boone, and Jackson lived during eras when transportation/ travel was a bit more difficult, time-consuming, and dangerous than during Beverly's time; however, they, not unlike Beverly, "got around" to various places, too. Crockett, for example, meandered throughout the frontier, fought in Indian wars all over the place, lived in Murphreesboro, which was the capital of Tennessee when Crockett served in the Tennessee state legislature (1821–24; Tennessee was admitted into the Union in 1796 as the sixteenth state), resided in Washington, D.C., while serving the people of Tennessee as a member of the U.S. House of Representatives (1828–31), and died in 1836 at the Alamo as a martyr in the fight against Mexico for an independent Texas.

41

Boone, though better known for his life and achievements in Kentucky, played a vital part in "taming" the Wilderness Road, which passed through Virginia, Tennessee (northeastern Tennessee via the Cumberland Gap), and Kentucky.

Jackson, the seventh president of the United States (1829–37), was a military hero and is revered in Tennessee. Though born on March 15,1767, in either North Carolina or South Carolina—no one really knows which—he made his "mark," to a large degree, in Tennessee. He spent a lot of time in and traveled often through the area where Beverly grew up, northeastern Tennessee. Jackson, a hero of the Battle of New Orleans against the British in late 1814 and early 1815 during the War of 1812, died in and was buried at the Hermitage (his home), near Nashville, in 1845.

"Tennessee" Ernie Ford was born on February 13, 1919, in Bristol, Tennessee. He claimed Bristol as his hometown and spoke often of Bristol while onstage and on television. While well known for his beautiful deep singing voice, especially his singing of Christian hymns as an entertainer and comedian on his weekday network television program, *The Tennessee Ernie Ford Show*, Ernest J. Ford was best known for encouraging others from the Grand Ole Opry stage in Nashville as he said, "Bless your pea-picking heart!" And who could ever forget his singing of "Sixteen Tons"!

Much of what was said about Crockett, Boone, Jackson, and Ford, the first three in particular, was fables and exaggeration. It is the folklore of this marvelous region of America, which is steeped with beautiful people and wonderful and exciting stories of "times and people past."

Most of us have heard the rumor that Crockett killed "a b'ar when he was only three"—far from me to dispute it—but fewer of us have heard the tale of the raccoon who, reportedly, said this to Crockett when he (the raccoon) saw that Crockett had taken "dead aim" at him with his long-rifle as he (the raccoon) sat in a tree in eastern Tennessee: "Don't shoot, Colonel! I'll come down! I know when I'm a gone 'coon!'"

Born in August of 1942, Likely Conceived in November of 1941

Born at 3:15 A.M. on Saturday, August 22, 1942, the second of six children of John and Dot Bushore, Beverly was likely conceived in late November of 1941. During those months that Beverly was conceived, born, and taken home from Kings Mountain Memorial Hospital, much of the world was at war and uncertainty for the short and long run was evident for Beverly's parents and all Americans.

Nine months before Beverly was born would have been late November of 1941. A few weeks later Pearl Harbor was attacked by the Japanese, and we now know well the outcome. However, Mr. and Mrs. John Bushore, young, married, in love, working and beginning their family and life together, did not know what the future would hold for them, their young family, or the nation.

Beverly was born into a devoutly religious home. John Henry Bushore's Irish-Catholic mother was a Donahue. Dorothy May Bushore's maiden name was Meub. Her family was deeply religious, too. The Bushores were to have six children, as large (number of kids) families were the rule rather than the exception in those days, especially for Catholics.

Major recollections of Beverly's early childhood involved her parents and siblings. She remembers, fondly, her father "wrestling" with the kids on the floor in their spacious two-story home on Georgia Avenue. Older brother Arthur was born twenty-three months before Beverly in September of 1940. Beverly's only sister, Judy, a public school teacher living in Kingsport, Tennessee (only a twenty-minute drive from Bristol), was born in November of 1943.

Beverly's first younger brother, John, a physician in Knoxville, came along in October of 1946 and evened "the score" at two boys and two girls. Beverly's two youngest brothers, Alan and Mike, both career military officers (the navy and air force, respectively), were born in October of 1947 (Alan) and July of 1951 (Mike).

The six children were raised in Bristol, where they lived with their parents. These parents lived as one husband and one wife for forty-nine years before John died on Palm Sunday in 1990. Dot Bushore lived in their family home on Georgia Avenue until recently. She is very active, bright, and a joy to be with.

The six Bushore "kids" have fourteen children, who are all living and doing well, ranging in age (in 1995) from one in preschool (the youngest, living near a navy base in Charleston, South Carolina) to a third-year medical student (at Washington University in Saint Louis).

Just like all American families, the Bushore family has experienced "the good and the bad." (In fact, the "good and the bad" and the "sad and the happy" are common to all families in all nations in all generations around the world whether rich or poor, educated or uneducated, living in democracies or dictatorships, residing in Hindu, atheist, Muslim, Jewish, or Christian nations or north or south or east or west.)

The Bushores have experienced good health among all members of their families, military and governmental service, the death of the patriarch of the family (of natural causes after a blessed eighty years of life), excellent public and private school education (all six Bushore kids graduated from universities and include two medical doctors, an educator, two military officers, and a recipient of a graduate school degree in computer science), church involvement (only Beverly remains a Roman Catholic), athletic participation, a suicide, excellent incomes (resulting in excellent taxpayers), and several divorces. Sound familiar these days?

Beverly and her parents and her brothers and sister as well as their children have been affected by and are affecting our culture (the latter mostly positively). The changing culture, however, has affected the Bushores, just as it has all American families, as the standards, customs, lifestyles, and morals have undergone major transitions.

"Baptismal Remembrance"

In Beverly's personal archives scrapbook/box is a lovely Catholic document, "Baptismal Remembrance." This paper records the fact that on September 20, 1942, Beverly was "baptised" at St. Anne's Catholic Church in Bristol, Virginia (the parish was just across the state line), by Fr. James J. Hickie.

Father Hickie was the priest at St. Anne's Catholic Church, which Beverly attended until she left for college at the University of Tennessee (in Knoxville) in the fall of 1960, and St. Anne's Catholic School, which Beverly attended from the second grade through the eighth grade. (The school did not have a high school; therefore, Beverly attended the public high school.)

Although Beverly would "turn her back" on the Catholic Church and Christianity as a sophomore in college, Father Hickie, a tremendous Irish-Catholic priest, Beverly says, was to influence her life from when she has her first memories of him to the present. Wherever Beverly was and whatever her spiritual belief or lack of belief was at various times in her life, Father Hickie, like the "Hound of Heaven," had been buried "alive" in her heart and soul.

For fourteen years, beginning as a sophomore in college, Beverly did not attend mass and rejected the Christian way of life in much of her life. She was to return to Christianity and, later, to return "home" to the Roman Catholic Church (in 1990). (More about this later.)

Another certificate, "This Honor Certificate," testifies that Beverly was recognized 'for the effort shown to improve her work in Religion for the term ending June 30, 1946." It was signed by Sr. M. Constance. At age three, Beverly was doing something right spiritually, or at least her parents were, according to Nun Constance of St. Anne's Catholic Parish/School.

Beverly was a good daughter, a good sister, and a good student. She made excellent grades, to put it mildly. One does not become eligible for universities and obtain college loans at the University of Tennessee (undergraduate school at Knoxville), the University of Tennessee Medical School (at Memphis), and residency training at the Mayo Clinic (at Rochester, Minnesota) unless grades were unusually good, as Beverly's were. This was especially true in the 1960s if you were a female.

For example, for the official record, Beverly's first grade report card, signed by Margaret Baumgardner of the Bristol Public School for the year 1948–49, showed straight A's! This is not at all uncommon for first-grade students, but for Beverly it was A's and B's for some twenty years.

700 Georgia Avenue

Beverly and her family lived at a home on Lawrence Avenue in Bristol, Virginia, until she was five. (That was in 1947.) For the next forty-seven years 700 Georgia Avenue, Bristol, Tennessee, was the home of the Bushores. The house is within walking distance of downtown Bristol.

Georgia Avenue is a picturesque street running north and south in the rolling hills of Bristol. At one time, large Dutch elm trees lined the street on both sides. Beverly says that she remembers when the elm trees were small and growing to maturity and she thought they were reaching for the sky. Unfortunately, the elms contracted Dutch elm disease a few years ago. Today all the elms are gone, just as are almost all Beverly's friends and acquaintances from her childhood in the neighborhood.

Other than the elms and her friends and acquaintances, not much has changed up and down Georgia Avenue. The homes are about the same as they were forty-five years ago. A few of the homes are occupied by members of the families who lived there when Beverly played in the neighborhood with her brothers and sister as well as childhood friends.

Streets in the neighborhood are named after states of the Union: Virginia, Kentucky, Maryland, Alabama, Pennsylvania, and Carolina. The "cross streets," which run east and west, are named after trees. There's Spruce, Pine, Maple, and Cedar.

Fairmont Elementary is the public school where Beverly attended first grade. Beverly and the other kids on Georgia Avenue walked a couple of blocks uphill (southward) on Georgia and turned right, and there was Fairmont. A little to the east of Fairmont is King College, a well known Christian college founded in 1867. Anyone traveling through Bristol ought to detour to King College for a short visit. It is a most attractive school situated in a beautiful setting. It is located on "a mountaintop in Tennessee" and is a lovely, tranquil campus to behold.

Beverly transferred to St. Anne's Catholic School in 1949, the year it opened, for the second grade and was there through the eighth grade. Her grades at St. Anne's were near perfect. A review of her report cards through high school revealed nothing but A's. As stated earlier, Beverly returned to the public schools in the ninth grade through her senior year, as St. Anne's did not offer a high school education.

Anyone would be impressed with her scholarship whenever and wherever Beverly attended school. Grades for Beverly's freshman year at Bristol HS were English I: 96; Algebra I: 97; Latin I: 96; and General Science: 90.

Beverly and her four brothers and sister were outstanding students, due in large part to parents who emphasized their children's studies and their responsibilities. Beverly's father supported his daughters' quests for high scholarship achievement and Beverly's ambition to be a medical doctor from an early age. He gave Beverly the confidence she needed and told her that she could be whatever she wanted to be, if she would discipline herself and pay the price that achievement requires.

The Bushore house at 700 Georgia Avenue deserves more attention. It was located on a corner lot, Georgia and Spruce (the southeast corner). The yard was sufficiently large even for a large family (if any lawn/yard in a small city can be large enough for six kids to play in).

The white, wood-frame, two-story house appears to be large enough for a family of eight, but upon closer inspection there is some doubt (by today's standards). The house had but one full bathroom! Yes, they had but one tub! The answer to surviving with only one bath is explained by Mrs. Bushore: "There was a 'system' for nightly baths and an 'order' for morning use of the bathroom."

While there was a half-bathroom downstairs, there was but one tub in the house. It is a porcelain "claw-foot" relic of bygone years.

Mrs. Dot Bushore, a "Stay-at-Home" Mom

Things were always lively at the Bushore home. With six kids spanning ten years in ages, there were people (lots of little people) around the house much of the time, especially on weekends, after school, nights, and in the summertime.

One person was home most of the time, and that person was Mrs. Dot Bushore. Most Americans born after 1960 will find this, a "stay-at-home" mom, to be a novelty, an anomaly, of bygone days, something archaic/out-of-date/even useless, as well as oppressive of femininity; however, it "worked" for the Bushores, according to the record.

Beverly and her brothers and sister will tell you that there was something marvelous, comforting, and stable about walking home from school, regardless of their ages, and finding "Mother doing what mothers do" in the midafternoon.

And what exactly did mothers do after school at home? They greeted the kids, one by one, provided or supervised afternoon snacks, gave kids permission to do something and go somewhere as well as denied permission to do some things and to go some places, supervised schoolwork, broke up fights, arbitrated and/or "judged" disputes between siblings, and were "mommie figures" for the few kids in the neighborhood whose moms were at work, gone, or nonexistent.

John Henry and Dorothy May were married in August of 1939 in Indianapolis, Indiana. The first two years of their marriage were unsettling for the Bushores, employment-wise, as John worked for the federal government, first in Washington, D.C., then in Columbus, Ohio. Remember how unsettling these times (the late 1930s and early 1940s) must have been for everyone.

Soon John and Dot Bushore and not-yet-one-year-old son Arthur moved to Bristol, where they would remain. John and Dot were married for forty-nine years, until John died in 1990. After they relocated to

47

Bristol, they would move but one more time, from a house on Lawrence to their home on Georgia.

John was employed by Eastman Kodak for thirty-two years, beginning in 1943. Eastman had (and still has) a large chemical plant in Kingsport, which was approximately twenty miles from the Bushore home. Mr. Bushore carpooled to work with other Eastman employees those thirty-two years that he worked in the accounting/payroll departments.

The Bushores did not have an automobile the first eleven years of their marriage. (John had a cousin, who was his good friend, who lost an arm in an automobile accident, and John did not want to nor did he do much driving during his entire life.) Dot Bushore had pretty much "sole custody" of the Bushore cars until the kids were old enough and qualified to drive.

What stability it must have been to have Father work at the same company for thirty-two years, to have Mother at home practically all the time, and to live in the same house throughout your childhood!

Arthur, Beverly, Judy, John, Alan, and Mike, born over an eleven-year period, lived in the same house until they left home to go to college or into the military, shared the same two parents, saw their father leave home at the same time of morning for thirty-two years to go to the same job with the same company (a prestigious one at that), and, to this day, enjoy and look forward to getting together during holidays, vacations, and other special occasions!

This nation is "poorer" without these types of family histories and legacies even though the "modern, progressive, more mobile, busier American family" may think they are "richer" because we count blessings today mostly in materials, i.e., dollars and cents, rather than rich memories and stable families.

Families too often today have these characteristics: (1) kids don't know who their fathers are; (2) fathers are at work or on business trips much of the time; (3) kids are neglected and abused; (4) kids open their homes with their latchkeys when they come home from school or from neighborhood gang meetings; (5) kids live in "blended families"; (6) kids are traumatized by divorce and separation; (7) kids are confused as to where home is when they spend weekdays with mommies and weekends with daddies; and (8) kids aren't sure who their "father figure"/role model is (if they even have one) or who is in charge when Mommie changes "live-ins" like she changes the sheets. And we wonder why

48

these "kids" grow up to be misfit adults who are looking for peace, security, and happiness in all the wrong places.

Beverly, a Ballet Student and Baby-Sitter

Beverly was a student at the Constance Harding School of Ballet while in high school and was a "nymph" (defined as "a lovely young maiden" in Webster's dictionary) in the three-act performance of *Garden of the Gods, Hansel and Gretel*, and *Moods in Jazz* given on April 19 and 20, 1956, when Beverly was thirteen and a freshman at Bristol High School.

Beverly earned spending money as a neighborhood baby-sitter. While a college student at the University of Tennessee she worked occasionally at Smith Floral on weekends and special occasions when she was home in Bristol.

High school life for Beverly and her brothers and sister in the 1950s and early 1960s in many ways was like it is today. They were active in clubs, ballet/dance, sports, as well as studying for their classes. Beverly was admitted to the Beta Club in November of 1957, and she served on the staff of the school newspaper, the *Maroon and White*, while in high school (as editor of the feature section her junior year and as editor-in-chief her senior year).

Kids are active in many of these same things and more today, but there is something missing in too many cases. There was a moral underpinning in the schools in the 1950s that is missing today. There was a teaching and an understanding of Christian values, virtues, and morality. Today for the most part, we are financing and sending our kids to our ideological and spiritual enemies, the government schools and, in some cases, sadly so, Christian schools, many of which are marginally better than public schools.

U.T., Change, and Trouble

Beverly graduated from Bristol High School in May of 1960, and after a summer with family and friends she packed and was off to Knoxville, some 110 miles to the southwest (in September) for her freshman year of college.

Beverly had made up her mind in junior high school that she wanted to be a physician. She liked the idea of helping people with their medical and health care needs and realized that physicians were respected and admired in our society. Also, she was aware that medical doctors were well paid and medicine was opening up for women as a profession.

Beverly had done well in her scholastics all her life, particularly in the sciences, and she enjoyed studying and experimenting in science courses, i.e., biology, chemistry, botany, etc.

Knoxville and the University of Tennessee are a beautiful city and campus. Knoxville is situated on the Tennessee River in the heart of the continuingly, rapidly developing economically (industrially, "informationally," chemically, and in about every other way) area of eastern Tennessee. Knoxville, with a metropolitan area of about five hundred thousand, is the third most populous city in Tennessee and is the gateway to the Great Smokey Mountains.

Knoxville was settled in the last quarter of the eighteenth century. The area was a most suitable site for a settlement due to its good soil, water resources (the Tennessee River, good for travel and transportation as well as finding the location of a settlement for travelers), highlands, and location on the popular east–west route to the frontier of the new nation. Knoxville was named in honor of the nation's first secretary of war, Henry Knox, a Tennessean.

U.T., as the University is commonly called (along with "the Big Orange" of sports fame), is positioned a little west of downtown Knoxville on beautiful rolling hills. U.T. was found in 1794, is a public university, and has about thirty thousand students on its Knoxville campus today. There are U.T. campuses in Chattanooga, Martin, and Memphis.

Immediately upon entering college Beverly immersed herself in her studies, and she continued to be at the top in her classes in scholarship. She realized that good grades would be more difficult to earn and competition would be keener than before.

Back home the Bushores had four kids. Beverly's older brother, Arthur, was attending Holy Cross (Catholic) University in Worchester, Massachusetts. Beverly's parents helped her with her college expenses as best they could, but Beverly had to work and to borrow funds, through federal government student loans, in order to finance her way through college and medical school.

While Beverly spent much of her time immersed in her studies and attending classes, she did "emerge" from time to time and "scout out," like a good Tennessee frontiersman (scratch that word *frontiersman*, make it *fronteirsperson* as the "feminization of America" and political correctness movement may be offended), and see what was going on in the world around her.

What Beverly found was that everything that she had been taught back home, in her home, in her schools, and in her parish was being challenged on every front by the college culture and her professors. Dating relationships and activities were becoming redefined as per limitations of conduct and morality. In class, she was being taught evolution as the only "theory" and she came to believe that *Homo sapiens* had simply "ousted" from the primeval swamp. These new relationships and theories were challenging what she had been taught and what she had believed all her life.

Within a couple of years, Beverly was confronted with a major choice: *Am I going to continue to live and believe the way I have been taught and to hold to the values that I have inherited, or am I going to join the "NOW" generation and accept and adopt their principles and values (or the lack thereof)?*

Beverly will tell you, as I have heard her give testimony many times during her pro-life presentations (from her perspective as a former abortionist), that she made a "bad choice" as a sophomore in college. Beverly knew at the time what she was rejecting (Christianity), but she did not know at the time what she was embracing. She could not put a name to it then, but she knows now and calls it what it is: secular humanism.

By dictionary definition, she was accepting "secularism," or "living in the outside world"/"not bound by religion," and "humanism," "following human nature." While modern-day secular humanists would say they live "at peace" with the Christian faith and do not advocate a "morality" or a "religion" as a guideline for individual behavior, Beverly understands now the secular humanists do have a moral and theological position on everything. And the majority of those positions run counter to Christianity. And the secular humanists are trying to persuade others to accept their "doctrine" and to impact everyone else's beliefs and conduct.

Essentially "Existential Liberty"

While Beverly was not aware of it, what she was "buying into" was what I choose to call existential liberty. Many of us, beginning in the 1960s, accepted this notion. Essentially, "existential liberty" means that each of us is "free" to choose as we please on everything. We want something to validate our desires to "choose to believe whatever we want."

According to Jean-Paul Sarte, the French existentialist philosopher, it was not the rightness or the wrongness of a choice that mattered, but that one is free to make one's own choice. If one wishes to believe in God, for example, one can do so; if one wishes not to, one can do that, too. And many believe in our culture the choices one makes ought not to matter to anyone else because, we reason, the consequences of our choices involve only the ones making the choices (on faith and morals). Most of us like that. We have forgotten what John Donne said so powerfully: "No man is an island," and "Ask not for whom the bell tolls; it tolls for me."

Beverly at first made only mental choices as part of an intellectual game, like so many of us. Then, she began to make real-life (and death) choices, rejecting certain biblical/traditional values from her past, not because there was anything wrong with them, she analyzed, but as a way of "authenticating" herself and her new alternative values.

Dr. Francis A. Shaeffer in his book, *The God Who Is There*, tells us modern man's rejection of absolute truth in every area of life began with the existential philosophy that Beverly and many of us embraced in colleges and universities beginning in the 1960s.

Beverly considered herself a "good person," and she was in many ways. She was a "good student," a "good part-time employee," a "good eater and exerciser," a "good friend," a "good daughter," a "good sister," a "good girlfriend," and a "good citizen," but she was lost from God and her beliefs would eventually be manifested through the killing of unborn human beings via abortion, which she considered "good for women" and would have "cast" her into Hell if she had not changed her ways and accepted the "faith of her fathers."

Beverly, not one for excitable, emotional, and dramatic stories and experiences, tells of "going one last time to mass as a sophomore in college and telling God good-bye." She had dropped to her knees at the altar of the Catholic chapel in Knoxville and prayed this prayer: *Lord, if You are real, come and get me one day. Today You don't seem relevant or real to me. My friends and professors do. I'm joining them. I refuse to be a hypocrite and believe one thing and do another.* Beverly ended her prayer in 1962 with the sign of the cross, never dreaming the journey she would take or the circumstances in which the Lord would claim her "again" as His own in 1976. It would be fourteen years before she would set foot again in a church, but "the hound of Heaven" would "fetch" her out of the world's underbrush one day in the doctors' parking lot at the Mississippi Baptist Medical Center in Jackson, Mississippi.

Three M's: Memphis, Medical School, and Marriage

After three years of undergraduate school in Knoxville at U.T., Beverly moved to Memphis, where she was to attend medical school at the U.T. Medical School and be an intern at Baptist Memorial Hospital.

She set up housekeeping for the next three years (1963–65) in a rented house with two of the other nine women in her medical class. Her medical class consisted of 115 students (ten women and 105 men). Eighty-five graduated three years later, including nine of the ten women.

The occasional drive home to Bristol in her Volkswagen Beetle took most of a day, as Memphis is situated in the extreme southwest corner of Tennessee while Bristol is located in the opposite corner of the state (the northeast corner). The distance is about five hundred miles.

As Beverly moved farther from home and matured as a young woman, she was experiencing a "distancing" of moral absolutes. Times were "progressive," she was told (and she believed). Much of what she was being exposed to, as was the case with many of us educated in colleges and universities the 1960s, was called progress but was "progressing backward" morally. Others might say we were progressing as a person would "progress" who has jumped off a cliff.

Beverly enjoyed her close relationship with her two roommates, her classmates, and her fiancée, who was in the same medical school class and whom she had meet in premed school in Knoxville.

She enjoyed her "home" life with her roommates, which was much cozier than residing in the women's dorms she had lived in at U.T., including her last year at the more quiet and prestigious Honors Dorm. Medical school and the year of internship in Memphis were consumed with study, labs, and hospital work under physicians' supervision.

Upon completion of her intern year at Baptist Memorial Hospital in January of 1968, Beverly had completed three years of premed undergraduate school and three years of medical school. She earned her medical doctor diploma in December of 1966.

Beverly married in December of 1965, and the two were off to the Mayo Clinic in Rochester, Minnesota, for thirty months of residency and specialty training after they had completed their residencies.

Family Grows, School/Training Continues and Ends

Beverly and her husband had their first of three sons, Chardo, in July of 1970.

Six months of Beverly's thirty months of training with the Mayo Clinic were spent at the well-known charity (and research) hospital in Chicago, Cook County. Six weeks of that six months at Cook County Hospital was spent in the Infected Obstetrics Ward. *Infected ob ward, wonder what that means*? Beverly asked herself.

Practically all of the patients coming into this ward were coming from the back-alley abortion mills of Chicago. The years was 1969, four years before the U.S. Supreme Court would render its infamous *Roe v. Wade* abortion decision. Approximately two dozen women suffering from botched illegal abortions were admitted to the ward each night that Beverly was on call.

Pro-Choice by Conviction, an Abortionist by Action

The experiences of treating women at Cook County who had undergone illegal, unsafe abortions in Chicago convinced Beverly that abortion ought to be "safe and legal." Beverly reasoned, through her secular humanist thinking, that if women were so desperate as a result of unwanted pregnancies that they would endanger their health and lives by submitting to illegal, unsafe abortions, then abortion ought to be legalized and the medical profession ought to take some social responsibility and perform abortions. While Beverly was not active, politically, in overturning the state laws that banned abortions, she supported the abolition of the laws banning abortions and became a dues-paying member of the National Abortion Rights Action League and the National Organization for Women.

Other things were taking "center stage" in her life at that time. Number-two son, Tony, was born on April 29, 1972, and Emory, her third son, was born on December 9, 1973. By that time Beverly and her family were living in Lexington, Kentucky. Beverly was teaching in the ob-gyn department part-time at the University of Kentucky Medical School in Lexington and later went into private practice with another female ob-gyn physician in Richmond, Kentucky.

When the U.S. Supreme Court legalized abortion during the entire nine months of pregnancy on January 22, 1973, in all fifty states, Beverly was surprised, relieved, and somewhat happy. After some time passed and Beverly and her partner discovered that abortions really were being performed legally (and in Lexington), they offered first-trimester abortions as a service in their "progressive," full-service ob-gyn medical practice.

Everything was going well for Beverly. She was happily married, she had three healthy sons, her medical practice was becoming well established, she was not too far removed from her family down in eastern Tennessee, and she and her family were enjoying all the comforts that a two-physician household could afford.

Then in the fall of 1974 a tragic thing happened in her life! Her husband announced to her that the family was moving to Jackson, Mississippi! Beverly, to put it mildly, was not too pleased with this news. She knew of the less than favorable national media reputation that Mississippi had. She was not sure that her preconceptions of Mississippi were not true.

In fact, Beverly was not sure folks in Mississippi wore shoes. She was not a "happy camper" as she prepared to move. She realized that she had no "choice" in the matter; her husband had told her they were moving. This did not set well with a budding feminist who had a profitable and satisfying medical practice in central Kentucky. But what was she to do? She did not think she could manage three sons under the age of five alone. She became a less than thrilled new resident of Mississippi.

1975 Was One of the Worst Years of Beverly's Life

When the Smiths arrived in Jackson, Mississippi, in September of 1974, Beverly would begin one of the worst years of her life. She knew no one except her husband, and she was angry and not speaking to him. Her solo practice of medicine, an ob-gyn's nightmare, was opened and in the red, as she knew no one and had no patients. The struggle of moving the family was a giant chore in itself with many adjustments such as selling and closing on one house and buying and "opening" another house.

One bright spot did occur in the spring of 1975 that was to change her life dramatically. A group of "concerned citizens and clergy" had banded together for the express purpose of opening the first abortion facility in Mississippi. More than two years after abortion had been legalized in the country by the U.S. Supreme Court, there was not one place in the entire state of Mississippi a woman could go to "terminate a pregnancy." Spokesmen for this group approached Beverly and asked her to become the physician who would "stick her or his neck out" and carry the distinction of becoming the first and only abortionist in Mississippi.

Beverly at first declined the offer, even though it would only be a part-time, after-hours, "moonlighting" position. Though Beverly had been in Mississippi only a short time, she was very aware that Jackson was in the "buckle of the Bible Belt" region of the country, and she would have been putting her reputation on the line by becoming the state's first and only abortionist.

"Here in Mississippi we were," Beverly has said to tens of thousands of people at pro-life meetings and rallies, "more than two years after *Roe* was 'handed down' and there was not one place in the state of Mississippi that a pregnant woman could go to terminate her pregnancy. I knew that things moved slowly in Mississippi as well as sometimes backward, but this was ridiculous! That's what I thought at that time."

Beverly was, however, troubled that she had made the decision to turn down the offer to "serve women" at the abortion clinic, which was named the Family Health Services Clinic ("what a contradiction in terms the name of the clinic was," Beverly now says) due to likely recrimination rather than genuine conviction. She did not like that and was ashamed of herself! She realized that she had flinched in the face of adversity and this was a cowardly thing to do.

The group organizing the abortion facility was having no luck in obtaining a physician willing to be labeled "the town abortionist"; therefore, they continued to "keep the door open" for Beverly to reconsider, and she did. She accepted the position as medical director and became Mississippi's first abortion provider in December of 1975.

Soon after she had become the physician who was performing abortions at the Family Health Services Clinic Beverly met a lady, Barbara Wellborn, at a child-birth education tea who was so horrified that Beverly was the abortionist at the first abortion clinic in the state that she went straight home from the tea, contacted one of her "prayer warrior" friends, and made a compact with her friend that they would pray daily for Beverly's conversion to Christianity and out of the abortion industry. Within a couple of years Beverly was a Christian and out of the abortion business.

Beverly realized that Barbara was a Christian and Barbara realized that Beverly was a heathen. But they liked one another in spite of their differences and became friends even through they had major different points of views on many things. For the next few years, Beverly performed abortions and trained a few residents from the University of Mississippi Medical School to perform abortions. She firmly believed that she was helping, indeed emancipating, women who were burdened with unwanted and unplanned pregnancies.

As You May Recall, 1975 Did Come to an End

In January of 1976, Beverly, who is a very organized and methodical individual, was reviewing 1975 and making plans for 1976 via New Year's resolutions.

Yes, 1975, a very difficult and harried year for Beverly, had come to a close. She realized this and was glad that she had survived. She realized that things were improving in so many ways as 1976 dawned. Her medical practice was growing; it was already in the black financially. She was living in a nice home. She had a new car. She had all the clothes she could put on her back. Her boys were healthy and growing and were enjoyable company. She was now speaking to her husband (you can't stay mad forever!), who was pleased and doing well with his new position at the Mississippi Baptist Medical Center. Beverly's private practice of ob-gyn (separate from her "moonlighting" abortion center), located in the Baptist Hospital Medical Arts Building, adjacent to the Baptist Hospital, was well equipped and had an excellent, likable staff.

Beverly had every "worldly" reason to be happy, but she was not. In fact, she was in great despair and had even comtemplated suicide. Even though she was not a psychiatrist, she knew enough about psychiatry to know that "thoughts" of suicide did not indicate a "healthy" state of mind.

Considering that she had so many positive things going for her, she reasoned that all she needed to do was to "think positively." Therefore, she went to a secular bookstore to find something to read that would reinforce her "positives" so that she could become "mentally well." She did not realize that she was spiritually, not mentally, ill. She saw a book, *The Power of Positive Thinking* written by Dr. Norman Vincent Peale. She bought it because, as she read the dust-cover, the book "nailed her." The book was written for people, just like her, who did not want to get up in the morning and who did not know the meaning or purpose of life.

When she got home and read further, she realized that Dr. Peale was not a *philosophiae doctor* (Latin for "doctor of philosophy") but a *divinitatis doctor* (Latin for "doctor of divinity"). Her first reaction to this knowledge was: *I have picked up a religious book, religious trash.* She originally had not realized that Dr. Peale was a religious writer. She thought he was a medical doctor. "I was a snob at this point in my life," Beverly confesses, "and I thought through education and reasoning, best taught by educators, all 'truth' would be revealed and all 'problems' could be solved. I had rejected the spiritual dimension of life altogether."

Beverly wanted to discard the book, but she realized that Dr. Peale had identified, "pegged," her as one who needed to read it and could be helped by it.

Confession Time: "I Eat My Meal One Thing at a Time"

Beverly, as stated earlier, is a very organized and methodical as well as emotionally controlled person. That's the kind of person you would want cutting you open. Surgeons, for example, count each sponge they insert into a body cavity during surgery and recount each sponge they remove when the operation is over. Why? So the patient won't leave the hospital a few days later with "hospital property."

Beverly's personal life is no different than her professional life in many respects. She is big on making lists, for example, and "checking them twice," crossing off items as they have been completed.

Beverly is so neat and systematic, as her stomach (and husband and children) will testify, that she eats one item on her plate at a time.

In the first chapter of *The Power of Positive Thinking*, the writer challenged the readers with a list of "things to do." One of the "things" was to affirm ten times a day Phillippians 4:13: *"I can do all things through Christ who strengthens me."* This made Beverly choke as well as furious! She would not, could not, say this verse once, much less ten times.

Beverly stopped reading the book. Even though she had been "pigeonholed" as if this book had been written just for her, she would not continue to read on. (She could not read chapter 2 if she had not done what chapter 1 required! If you don't eat your peas, you can't eat your corn!)

She carried *The Power of Positive Thinking* with her on the front seat of her car for days, then weeks.

The "Hound of Heaven" Breaks through the Underbrush!

"One morning in February, probably a Monday," Beverly says, "it seemed like a Monday [and the beginning-of-the-week blues]," as she was pulling into the doctors' parking lot at Baptist Hospital, "I could not stand it any longer," she says.

She was depressed; it was cloudly, raining, and cold. (Surely it was February, the monsoon season in Mississippi!) Beverly broke down and said it. *"I can do all things through Christ, Who strengthens me."*

Beverly, we have already said, is not one prone to emotional experiences or to relate them when and if they exist, but she was, and tells with passion, moved by what happened that morning in her car. She realized, even though she had not recited Phillippians 4:13 out loud with any conviction, that she was not alone in the car. "It was as if the 'hound of Heaven' had broken through the underbrush and had grabbed me," she tells.

"As I think back," she explains, "to that prayer I had prayed many years ago when I asked God to 'come get me one day if He really did exist' (when I was a college sophomore), I now know that He is and He had [come get me] that day as I sat, confused and bewildered, in my car that morning in early 1976.

"I didn't know exactly what was happening to me or what to do," Beverly relates. "I did what seemed natural; I cried. Then I put my makeup back on. I went into the hospital and made rounds. I felt much better. I must have said that verse that day not ten times, but a hundred times.

"And, importantly, I continued to read Dr. Peale's book and I finished it. Dr. Peale recommended to new Christians three things to do:

(1) read the Bible daily; (2) spend time among Christians; and (3) join a church. All of those would be hard for me to do.''

Beverly went back to that same secular bookstore to buy a Bible, as she did not own one. "I found that there were lots of choices of Bibles to read," she says. "There was the New American Standard Bible, the Good News Bible, the Family Heritage Bible, the King James Bible, the Catholic Family Bible, and many other Bibles.

"I chose the King James Bible, reasoning that I would at least get a little culture by reading Elizabethan English, if nothing else."

Beverly was not sure what the future held for her regarding her renewed belief and faith in God, for she had believed in Him before; at least she thought that she had.

As far as Christian friends, Beverly could only recall one Christian friend, Barbara Wellborn. She arranged to spend more time with Barbara.

As she read through the Word of God, starting with the New Testament, naturally, from Matthew to Revelations (you can't eat your dessert until you have finished your entree), Beverly's life began to change, sometimes little by little and at other times in huge leaps. Her belief in God and her understanding of what He desired and expected of her became clearer.

In addition to Barbara, Beverly met and became friends with Randy and Nancy Shuman. Randy was a seminary student at Wesley Biblical Seminary, which had opened recently in a large home two doors north of the Smiths' home. Nancy worked at the seminary as well as attended classes. She and Beverly became close friends. Randy was the youth minister at Riverside Independent Methodist Church, located in the neighborhood.

Nancy and Randy invited Beverly and her family to come to church with them. Beverly and the boys went. Beverly realized that attending church and its youth activities would be good for her boys. (A sidebar: Several years later, Beverly had the opportunity [the privilege] of helping a young pregnant mother give her son up for adoption. That young man, Jeremiah, is the son of the Shumans.)

As Beverly grew in the knowledge of God through Christian fellowship, Bible reading, and study, under the preaching of the Scriptures and prayer, she was becoming uncomfortable with performing abortions.

Nothing she was reading in Scripture was telling her: "Thou shall not perform abortions." She realizes now that the Sixth Commandment, *"Thou shall not do murder,"* means precisely: "Beverly, you shall not perform abortions.'' The godly admonition does not make an exception when the civil government permits legal murder. She understands this today.

She was becoming repulsed by her abortion trade. Many of the women she had performed abortions for were coming back for repeat abortions. This went against Beverly's grain, for she had little tolerance or patience with irresponsibility. (''The first blunder, shame on you; the second blunder, shame on me.'' [''At least,'' Beverly would say, ''if I am asked to destroy the consequences of your blunders.''])

She realized that many women were using abortion simply as a ''backup'' to birth control and totally irresponsible sex. She reasoned, correctly, that she was being used, and that angered her!

No one was giving her a ''hard time'' about her abortion business. Most Christians she knew, including the pastor of the church she was attending, didn't know that she was performing abortions or had not, sadly, come to a strong, challenging, and confronting stance against it at that time. Mississippians were slow to oppose abortion and weak in responding to it once they opposed it. This was, in part, due to the lack of a significant Catholic population in the state.

''I Was Trying To Run the World's Best Abortion Center''

God was moving in Beverly's life as other things were happening in Beverly's mind and heart. Many of the women she had performed abortions for were coming back to her private practice, which, it has been stated previously, was separate from the abortion business, for other, legitimate, medical services, including checkups and care for ''wanted'' pregnancies. Several of these ''postaborted'' women had gotten married and were ''happily'' pregnant.

While some of these women were in states of ''denial'' regarding their abortions, many of them were grieving for what they (and Dr. Beverly) had done to their children during their previous times of crises.

Beverly was beginning to see the sadness, the hopelessness, and the despair (apart from God) in these women's lives as well as in the abortion trade. She was beginning to realize that when people turn to death to solve problems, the problems are only exacerbated. Proverbs 14:12 clearly addresses this: *''There is a way that seemeth right unto a man, but the way thereof is the way of death.''*

Beverly was now seeing the fetuses in a different "light" and from a different perspective, from God's perspective.

Fortunately (for her patients) and unfortunately (for her own comfort), Beverly was trying to run the world's best abortion center. She prided herself on being a competent surgeon. She had even gone to Colorado to an abortion procedure teaching seminar conducted by the nationally known abortionist Warren Hearn, who performs many and late-term abortions and who had "perfected" the abortion techniques. Beverly was willing to perform only first-trimester abortions, not because second- and third-trimester abortions were (are) illegal, but because she did not want to deal with the greater medical and emotional complications that arise for the pregnant mother from late abortions.

After performing an abortion, Beverly would take the cloth socklike container off the vacuum cleaner–like machine, the suction aspiration machine, and go to the sink. There she would go through the aborted fetus's body parts in order to be sure that she had removed all of the fetal matter. If she could not account for four extremities (two arms and two legs), a spine, a rib cage, a skull, and the placenta, she would have to return to her patient and suction and scrape some more. Otherwise, the patient would be going to an emergency room at a hospital within a couple of days suffering from the effects of an incomplete, unsafe, legal abortion, just like those women whom Beverly had taken care of in Chicago at Cook County Hospital in 1969.

For the first time, under the anointing of the Holy Spirit, Beverly was starting to see what she was doing to unborn human beings when she destroyed them through abortions. Even though, I repeat for emphasis' sake, Beverly was only performing first-trimester abortions (during which time the little ones are much less recognizable as human beings than human beings in later gestational life), she could recognize the body parts of the little boys and girls whom she had killed.

For the first time Beverly was beginning to see what she was doing to the unborn babies who were destroyed during abortions. She was beginning to realize the sheer lunacy of trying to help some women become pregnant and other women remain pregnant as well as to ensure that mother and child stayed healthy while destroying the children of pregnant mothers who did not want to be pregnant on the other hand. All the little ones were human, alive, observable, nonrepeatable, and growing beings with little heartbeats and bodies of their very own.

The last straw was one day when a clinic worker from the administrative end of the abortion center asked Dr. Beverly, "What is it you do when you go to the sink when you are performing an abortion?"

Beverly invited her to come and see for herself what she was doing. Beverly remembers to this day showing the coworker the remains of a dismembered fetus, particularly a beautifully formed bicep of a little boy she had just aborted. She recalled, to herself, silently, that her youngest son, Emory, who must have been around three at the time, had been "showing off" to her and others his muscles, his biceps, recently. That abortion was the last abortion that Dr. Beverly would perform.

Fresh from the "Hands of God"

That clinic employee did not remain an employee at the abortion center for long. Nor did Beverly. Beverly asked herself, *What am I doing? I went into medicine to heal people and to relieve human suffering. What am I doing killing these little ones, who are 'fresh from the hands of God'*?

When Beverly reflects on those days when she could not "see" the babies, she is reminded of an incident in the Gospel of Mark, the ninth chapter, when Jesus gave sight to a man who was totally blind.

Beverly presents the story this way: "What was happening to me as I stood 'spiritually blind' at that sink reminds me of the story from chapter 9 in the Gospel of Mark. Jesus, upon preparing to give this man vision, took spittle and put it on the blind man's eyes.

"Jesus then asked the blind man, 'What do you see?' The man answered, 'I see men walking around as if they were trees.' The formerly completely blind man was seeing something, but he did not see perfectly clear. Jesus touched his eyes again, and the man was able to see clearly. This was to be the story in my life. I was now seeing something that made me very uncomfortable, but I was not seeing perfectly clear."

As Beverly was the clinic medical director and had trained other physicians to perform abortions, she was able to stop performing abortions herself and delegate the "procedures" to other physicians, who were happy to perform more abortions, as they were paid according to the number of procedures they performed.

Called to Identify Publicly with What God Had Done in Her Life Privately

Soon Beverly reached the point in her Christian walk when she realized that she must join a church and acknowledge publicly what Christ had done in her life, in her heart, privately. She understood that she could not "stain" with the innocent blood of unborn children the holy sanctuary, the house of God, Christianity, by bringing in with her the "abortion trade." Therefore, Beverly resigned from her position as medical director of the Family Health Services Clinic and joined Riverside Methodist Church.

She became very close to her newfound friends at church; Barbara became a faith friend and adviser, a member of Beverly's incorporated medical practice's board of directors, and her marriage soon ended. This was the "best of times" and this was the "worst of times" for Beverly, but God saw her through it.

Brothers in the Lord and Brothers in Medicine

Beverly was invited to attend a "brown bag" luncheon one day at noon in 1980 at First Presbyterian Church in Jackson, which was almost directly across the street from her home, by Paul Fowler, D.D., a professor of the New Testament at Reformed Theological Seminary in Jackson. This was within a couple of years after Beverly's leaving the abortion trade.

Dr. Fowler was trying to help the newly formed Right to Life organization in Jackson by organizing ancillary support groups. Dr. Fowler envisioned support groups for RTL such as Lawyers for Life, Accountants for Life, Pastors for Life, Athletes for Life, Educators for Life, Media Persons for Life, Physicians for Life, etc. It was his belief that professional and reputable secondary organizations could add their specialized expertise and aid the fledgling new main body in areas that it would need help, i.e., fund-raising, church coordination, accounting, education, media relations, political and legislative relations, public speaking, and others.

It was during this "brown bag" luncheon, a full two years after Beverly had resigned from the abortion center, that Beverly had her medical/embryonic/scientific biological reproduction knowledge of the humanity of the preborn person "strained" through the Bible.

Up to that point, Beverly was like a lot of people uncomfortable with abortion who know that abortion is evil because it destroys human beings at the beginning of their lives but who could not give you one, much less ten, good reason why abortion ought to be illegal, condemned, and restrained. She had many of her questions answered that day and and came to understand that abortion (1) was a "gateway" to the denial of the intrinsic sacredness of human life; (2) would lead to the rapid decline of a nation's morality; and (3) invites the judgment of God on a civilization. This was to be her "second touch" from the Lord, and she began to see clearly.

During that landmark meeting and subsequent meetings with Dr. Fowler and fellow medical doctors who were brothers in medicine and brothers in Christ, Beverly saw much more incontrovertibly why abortion was evil and an abomination before the Creator. Revealed to her were fetal development characteristics that she, as an obstetrician, ought to have expert knowledge of. Will Thompson, M.D., a family medicine physician from Yazoo City, shamed Beverly with his knowledge of the anatomy and physiology of the human zygote, embryo, and fetus as well as the abortifacient effects of IUDs.

Will identified many scriptural passages in which God's inerrant, infallible, and inspired Word spoke of His involvement in, creation of, and purpose for human beings prior to their births while they were still in their mothers' wombs. God *"knitted"* David (Psalms 139) and every one of us together in our mothers' wombs into His human family and told us in many places in the Scriptures to honor, respect, protect, care for, defend, rescue, and love one another as He loves each of us.

Familiar passages to ardent pro-lifers include but are not limited to these biblical passages: *"For thou has possessed my reins; Thou has covered me in my mother's womb. . . ."* (Ps. 139:16, scripture where David refers to his preborn life; Beverly calls this passage "the pregnant mother's passage"); *"Thou [Mary] has found favour with God. Behold thous shall conceive in thy womb, and bring forth a son, and shalt call His name Jesus. . ."* (Luke 1:26, the announcement by Angel Gabriel of the Annunciation, that Mary would conceive a child as a virgin and birth the son of God, God/man); *"Before I formed thee in the belly I knew thee; and before thou camest forth out of the womb, I sanctified thee, and I ordained thee a prophet unto the nations"* (Jer. 1:5, a reference to Jeremiah's humanity before birth); *"The Lord hath called me from the* womb. . . ." (Isa. 1:49, the story of Isaiah's call to be a prophet before he was born).

"Conceived by the Holy Spirit. What Could That Mean?"

Beverly sums up her understanding of why abortion is wrong this way: "The reason that abortion is wrong is that it destroys people, who are made in the image and likeness of God. In Genesis 1:27, the Bible says: '*God created man in His own image.*' In the next verse the Bible states that we are to '*be blessed*' and '*to go forth and multiply and replenish the earth and to have dominion over it.*'

"What finally sealed my understanding of God's perspective of the humanity of 'in utero' people was what occurred to me one day in church when we were, as a part of our order of worship, reciting the Apostle's Creed.

"As I spoke the familiar, memorized words of the Creed, 'I believe in God, the Father, Maker of Heaven and Earth; and in Jesus Christ, His only Son, our Lord, who was conceived by the Holy Spirit,' I was stunned and stopped. I asked myself, *Conceived by the Holy Spirit. What could that mean?*

"I answered my own question, *Well, gynecologist, you know how everyone else was conceived. Here's this female egg and here's this male sperm. They come together and make a new, unique, unrepeatable, observable human being at the exact moment of conception. That's how everyone was created. How else did it happen? No other way.*

"It suddenly occured to me that the Holy Spirit must have taken the form of a male sperm and fertilized Mary's egg. How else could it have happened? The creed that I had just recited said 'conceived by the Holy Spirit,' didn't it? I had never had any problem visualizing Mary, pregnant out to here [arms extended and fingers connected], with Jesus in her womb, riding on a donkey trying to get to Bethlehem to deliver Jesus in the stable where he was to be born and lain in a manger, but I had never carried it back to when and where His earthly life began, at the moment of His conception.

"If Christ Himself would identify with us as true God and true man from the moment of His conception, what ought to be our regard for everyone else from the moments of their conception? If God, through His only Son, Jesus Christ, would become one of us in every way but

66

sin from the moment of His conception, it is clear that we should regard everyone else as 'one of us,' a human being, our 'little brothers and sisters,' from their moments of conception.

"This position," Beverly contends, "does not contradict the 'natural law' of human reproduction science. It affirms it! Good science never contradicts Scriptures or sound Christian doctrine. Anyone who tells you that we do not know when human life begins either lies or does not know basic human reproduction biology."

Dr. Paul Fowler discovered when he met Beverly during the first meetings that he had a former abortionist on his side. He nurtured his friendship with Beverly and groomed her to be a public speaker against abortion and an advocate for our "little and vulnerable brothers and sisters" via assistance, and charity, if necessary, for the mothers.

Dr. Fowler realized, rightfully so, that he had a potentially terrific pro-life speaker in Beverly, a woman who knew what it was like to be pregnant as she has three sons; who was a board-certified ob-gyn physician who monitored daily the growth and development of her "second patients," the preborn children, in her busy medical practice that she now shared with three other lady ob-gyn physicians (all wives and mothers); and who is a former abortionist.

On the Speaking Tour

For the next couple of years Beverly was busy with her medical practice, had help from several seminary couples (as 'live-ins'') in caring for and instructing her three sons, and was helpful to the Right to Life of Jackson organization, principally as a public speaker. She was available as much as possible for her three sons, who were attending a Christian school at First Presbyterian Church and active in the Youth Department at their church, Riverside Methodist Church. Beverly had been asked and accepted a position as a member of the board of trustees at Wesley Biblical Seminary in Jackson, a multi-denomination graduate school of theology within the Christian evangelical, Wesleyan-Armenian tradition.

Beverly was becoming well known as a pro-life speaker across the country and was being invited to speak at Christian, pro-life meetings as well as on Christian and secular media programs. She was cooperating with Christian alternatives to abortion agencies such as Bethany Christian Services, Birthright, and Catholic Charities and would one day be of vital support, along with other physicians in her medical practice, to the Crisis Pregnancy Center, which opened in the late 1980s.

Carmack's "Pledge to the South"

On the steps of the Tennessee state capitol in Nashville is a pledge chiseled in granite written by a Tennessee native son, Edward Ward Carmack. (Carmack was a member of the Tennessee legislature, elected to the U.S. House of Representative and to the U.S. Senate, representing Tennessee, and a candidate for governor of Tennessee. For many years, Carmack [1859–1908], who was editor of the *Nashville Tennesseean*, was a well known and colorful personality in Tennessee.) While Mr. Carmack's impact on Tennessee was enormously greater than Beverly's, I choose to close this chapter about Beverly with the commemoration written by Carmack below.

Carmack's experiences seem to have been as varied (even more so) as Beverly's. One day, when many more risings and settings of the sun over Tennessee (and Mississippi) have occurred, perhaps Carmack's pledge to the South will not be that different from Beverly's.

The South is a land that has known sorrows; it is a land that has broken the ashen crust and moistened it with tears; a land scarred and riven by the plowshare of war and billowed with the graves of her dead; but a land of legend, a land of song, a land of hallowed and heroic memories.

To that land every drop of my blood, every fiber of my being, every pulsation of my heart, is consecrated forever.

I was born of her womb, I was nurtured at her breast; And when my last hour shall come, I pray God that I may be pillowed upon her bosom and rocked to sleep within her tender encircling arms.

3

Time Together

It was a beautiful spring morning in 1982. I had just returned to Jackson from a business trip to Little Rock with a group of Farm Bureau Insurance Companies coworkers. Saturday and time to relax.

I set my luggage down in the middle of the living room, turned on the television, and prepared to waste a few minutes watching television and reading the morning newspaper.

Featured on one of the local television stations was a debate about abortion, two for and two against. One side advocated abortion, its moral justification, and the need for its remaining "safe and legal." Making that point was the manager of a Jackson abortion clinic. Speaking against abortion were two women, a physician who had once performed abortions in Jackson and Kay Sheldon, the wife of a coworker at Southern Farm Bureau Life Insurance Company, Curt Sheldon, a company actuarial officer whom I liked and respected.

I had meet Kay at a company function and had been with Curt and Kay a few times at company social functions and was impressed with her. She was making convincing points for her side. The former abortionist was making powerful arguments against abortion (why it was wrong, ought to be discouraged, and should be legally banned).

I Supervised Monthly Forums for Company Employees

One of my responsibilities at Southern Farm Bureau Life was to supervise monthly forums for the company's 600 home office employees on matters of public interest. The program, Responsible Citizens Program, as the name implied, was established by management to further the community interest by promoting responsible citizenship among our employees.

The company, headquartered in Jackson, was (and still is) a great place to work, and its executives were (and still are) sensitive to the needs of its employees and agents. The company was (and still is) a good corporate citizen of the community. SFB Life is owned by the Farm Bureau Federations in ten southern states, roughly the states that comprised the Confederate states. Through some twenty-five hundred insurance agents working out of Farm Bureau offices in every county and parish (in Louisiana) in the South, scattered from El Paso to the Chesapeake Bay, the company offers life and health insurance to Farm Bureau members.

My title was Public Relations Director. I was involved in corporate public relations and advertising, publications for the home office staff and the agency force, and some aspects of employee relations. Communications was "my game" and I enjoyed it immensely.

I enjoyed every phase of my job, loved my coworkers, and appreciated the service the company provided the agricultural community across the South. I was allowed to travel a good bit, covering company news and announcements for a monthly publications that I edited for the sales/agency force, and was most impressed with their capable management staffs in both the home office and offices in the various state and county Farm Bureau offices.

The following Monday morning I went to Curt and told him that I had seen Kay on the television program the previous Saturday. I told him that I thought a debate on the subject of abortion would be an excellent program at a future Responsible Citizens Program Meeting. He agreed and said he would help me recruit speakers.

I Thought, My God, I Might Have Been Killed in the Summer of '42!

Within a month a formal debate with me acting as moderator was held at Southern Farm Bureau Life between Dr. Beverly Smith, the former abortionist whom I had seen on television, and the daughter of an abortion clinic owner in Jackson. The name of the abortion center owner was Martha Fuqua; I don't remember her daughter's name, but she did work with her mother at the abortion center in north Jackson.

The arguments of the abortion rights proponent, who claimed that all abortions were morally justifiable if the pregnant mother believed it to be the case, paled in comparison to the arguments against legal abortion and against the moral efficacy of abortion with the one exception of saving the life of the pregnant mother.

I introduced the program and the guests, asked the guests questions from the audience after the two speakers had given their presentations, and closed the program. I was a "neutral" participant during the one-hour program, which was held before a packed auditorium. I believe more employees attended this program than any other program we had ever held. Attendance by the employees was voluntary.

The presentations had hardly begun before I knew that I was not neutral on the debate that was unfolding before my eyes, for I immediately realized that if abortion had been legal and as accepted as our society accepts it today when I was in my mother's womb, I most likely would have been aborted in the summer of '42, a few months after my conception. As Dr. Smith explained a number of abortion techniques, it was as if I felt the "curette," the knife-like instrument the abortionists use to perform abortions (in addition to other killing instruments and chemicals), pierce my body.

As Dr. Smith explained through the reading of selected Scriptures God's inestimable value placed upon preborn human life as well as Scriptures that require Christians to "rescue the perishing" and to "do justice," I wondered why I had never heard a word of condemnation of abortion from the pulpit of my church, First Baptist Church in Jackson, the largest church (far and away) in Mississippi.

I remember several impressions that I came away from that meeting with about "Dr. Beverly," as she is affectionately known by so many people. I remember that she made a most convincing argument of the humanity of the unborn from both human reproduction science and Scriptures. I remember how believable and graphic were her descriptions of what she had seen after she had performed abortions, i.e., "little arms and little legs." I remember that her religious conviction was apparent when she explained that God had "*possessed my reins*" when she identified what David had said in Psalms 139 concerning the period when he was "*fearfully and wonderfully made*" in his mother's womb.

I recall her reminding the predominantly conservative Baptist audience of the Golden Rule: "Do unto others as you would have them do unto you."

I remember contemplating to myself that this woman possessed "quiet strength," a term I have used many times to introduce Beverly to audiences she has addressed when it was my honor to participate in the programs. And I recollect that at this first meeting she was most articulate, small, well dressed, soft spoken, and very attractive physically. I believed her to be about my age.

At the time I had no idea that she was single. I found out later from Curt that Beverly was a divorced mother raising three sons. I wanted to get to know Beverly and desired to become involved in the pro-life movement. I saw Beverly again, and did I ever find out how to become active in the right to life movement and did it ever change my life!

To Know Her Is to Love Her

Within a few weeks of the abortion debate at Southern Farm I had contacted Beverly and asked her out to dinner. Within a year we were married. To know her was to love her.

The first few times we were together we went out alone to dinner or to the movies. Then we "mixed" her three sons and my daughter in a few outings: swimming, movies, water slides, etc.

Beverly and I had many long conversations in her living room and my living room. We talked about our backgrounds, our kids, our extended families, God, our hopes, dreams, aspirations, and, eventually, the possibility of time together as a married couple with four kids, two dogs, a cat, two homes, and two excellent jobs.

By fall of 1982 I had asked Beverly to marry me and she had accepted. In October we drove to Bristol so that I could meet her parents and asks her father for permission to marry his forty-year-old daughter. He had opposed her first marriage.

On February 12, 1983, we were married.

After a week's honeymoon my daughter, Amanda, thirteen, our two dogs, Captain Jack (a mongrel) and Bartholomew of Nordvic (a young registered Siberian Huskie), and I (with all of our belongings) moved into Beverly's "mansion" (by most Mississippians' standards) with Beverly; her three sons, Chardo, twelve, Tony, ten, and Emory, eight; and their cat (Adam). Beverly and I were forty and thirty-nine, respectively. We were well-educated and we had good jobs and good incomes. (Mine was "good," hers was "excellent.")

I believe we did a pretty good job of "blending" our families. That's not to say we did it "perfectly" nor to say it was an easy job. It is not, no matter the new couple's ages, education levels, incomes, or strong religious, moral convictions and practices. These "blending families" times are the times that "try men's souls," and it is imperative, in our opinions, that parents be mature, together, and Christian.

Raising children in all situations is not easy, especially today. There are so many outside influences, and most of them are negative. Rearing children reminds me of the three books a child psychologist wrote (so goes the story). The first book, written when he was single, was titled *How to Raise Children.* The second book was written after he was married and when his children were adolescents. That book was titled *Suggestions on Raising Children.* The last book he wrote, when his children were teenagers, was named *Helpful Hints on Raising Children.*

My daughter and I had a nice home in south Jackson. It had four bedrooms, three baths, a large living room with a fireplace, and a fenced-in backyard. Our dogs lived in the backyard, and Amanda and I spent a good deal of time with them in the backyard whiling away the time together.

In our premarital planning (and we did use professional counselling), Beverly insisted that my family "move in" with her family. No objections from us. Beverly's boys' school, their church, and Beverly's office as well as the hospital where she admitted her patients were within a few blocks of her home. She was ideally situated, home location–wise, to "her world," and her home was very, very nice.

Her home, set high on a hill on the major thoroughfare of Jackson, was a two-story pink, ninety-year-old, wood-frame home. It contained five bedrooms, three full baths and a half-bath, many spacious rooms, high ceilings, and beautiful views throughout the home of the neighborhood we lived in, Belhaven, a residential area of fashionable downtown historic Jackson. There was a multileveled lawn and a cottage behind the two-car garage.

Three more things about the house.

I can remember the first time that I went out with Beverly. As I located the house and drove up the very narrow driveway (constructed when autos were very small and very narrow) to the backyard where cars were parked, I was a bit awed by the home and, therefore, intimidated by the person I was dating that night.

Many nationally known pro-life Christians, who will surely be in God's "Pro-Life Hall of Fame," have favored us as guests to our home. Among those persons are Randy Terry, Keith Tucci, Joe Scheidler, Jack and Barbara Willke, Bernard and Adelle Nathanson, Joe and Anne Foreman (and family), Penny Lea, Andrew Burnett, and Carol Everett. Even "George [Grant] slept here."

The third point I make is this: I love that home. The many times that I have been imprisoned for trying to peacefully stop the killing of precious preborn children, I have longed for the beauty and the comfort of that old southern mansion and the company of those who resided and visited there.

Beverly's three boys had a lot going for them when they were young. They were handsome, healthy, bright, curious, and humorous kids. They were (and are) close to one another. Their father, a physician who had remarried and given them stepbrothers and stepsisters, lived in Jackson just a few blocks away, spent time with them, and was very supportive of them, particularly in their quest for high scholastic achievements.

At this writing, the oldest, Chardo, who graduated from Mississippi State University in 1992, is a third-year medical student at Washington University in Saint Louis. The middle son, Tony, who graduated from Baylor University in Waco, Texas, in December of 1993, is a CPA (he passed all four exams the first time!), is married to Jessica (the daughter of a Southern Baptist minister and his wife), and works for an accounting firm in Waco. Emory, the youngest, is a fifth-year architectural student at Mississippi State University who, like his older brothers, makes exceptionally good grades.

These kids were (and are) excellent students, stayed out of trouble, and have been a delight for Beverly and me as well as for everyone else their lives have touched. Amanda did well and continues to. She was an independent sort and adapted well to the many changes she was forced to make. The adjustments to the blended family were far more of a challenge for her than for Beverly's boys. Amanda was "thrown" into a new home with an adult woman, her stepmother, and her three sons and had to make major changes in her life at an age, thirteen, that is difficult enough without major changes.

She was to attend much more difficult schools that she had been accustomed to attending. She had attended good public schools, but they were no match, scholastically, for the private schools she was to attend in junior and senior high school. We are proud of her. She adapted well and was savvy and "streetwise," having been a "latchkey" kid for a couple of years. She is married to Charlie Vyles. Their son, Troy, and their daughter, Elaine, have brought much joy to everyone, especially their grandparents.

Beverly and I had a lot going for us when we married, mainly great kids. As a new blended family (I'll brag just a bit), we did a pretty good job. It was hard work and it was expensive!

Beverly continued to be a much-sought-after pro-life speaker and lecturer, and I "tagged along" to many of her in-state and out-of-state speaking engagements and became more deeply involved in the pro-life movement in Jackson and in Mississippi, which was just getting started when we got married.

Beverly and I had, at the time of our marriage, (1) excellent jobs that we enjoyed; (2) kids who needed and demanded our time, attention, and energy; (3) extended families we cared for, cooperated with, and liked to be with; (4) a church to attend, support, and "draw" from spiritually; and (5) the tremendous "cause" of the unborn, which was a major "calling"/"ministry"/"hobby" in our lives.

Within the first few months preceding and following our marriage, there were two deaths in our families. Just prior to our marriage, Beverly's oldest brother, Arthur, committed suicide in Saudi Arabia; and a few months after our marriage, my father died of a heart attack.

I regret that Beverly did not get to know my father better. She had been with him only a few times. I regret that I did not know Arthur. I never met him. He had been a major influence on Beverly.

A Decade of Ups and Downs and Trials and Tribulations for the Pro-Life Movement

While Beverly was a major spokesperson for the pro-life movement in Jackson and Mississippi, I was active as a member of the governing boards, the boards of directors, of Right to Life of Jackson and, a little bit later, Mississippi Right To Life (when RTL of Jackson organized the statewide organization).

Many people whom Beverly and I have gotten to know well and love deeply were involved in the organizing, incorporating, recruiting of volunteers, and working for the Right To Life organizations in our city and state. The Right To Life organizations were primarily educational and political/legislative movements from which alternatives to abortion and direct action organizations "spun off."

75

The areas I initially concentrated in were the areas that I was educated and trained in, not to mention comfortable with and enjoyed, i.e., public relations, publications, communications, media, and advertising. This was a labor of love, and I was able to solicit help from others I knew who worked in these areas of expertise.

Committee members, committee chairmen, and other project volunteers for Right To Life worked in such areas as: education, legislation/politics, speakers' bureau, church coordination, school coordination, media, communications, fund-raising, special events (such as Mothers' Day Eve March for Life, Pastors' Protest against Abortion, and Life Chain), national Right To Life liaison, and other pro-life organizations' liaison (contacts with and support of other pro-life groups such as crisis pregnancy centers and adoption agencies).

Many persons came forward to take leadership positions and to be "worker bees" in RTL and other pro-life organizations. The pro-life movement did not begin in Mississippi until the early 1980s, but when it did, it became a steady, growing influence for righteousness and to, in my opinion, "sound the alarm" as to what happens to nations that "shed innocent blood."

I know it is not wise to mention people by name who were "mighty instruments of God" in Jackson and Mississippi for this "cause" of "causes," in the early stages, but I will anyway. Mason Swinney and Bill Conlee came forward at the very beginning to spearhead the movement. Bill was the first president of Right To Life of Jackson. He was a Jackson police officer. When Mississippi Right To Life was organized, Bill became president of it and Mason Swinney, who was vice president of RTL of Jackson, became president of RTL of Jackson.

Harriet Ashley was a member of the board of directors of Right To Life from its inception and has been the organization's full-time paid office manager for more than a decade. Bill, her husband, became a member or the board of directors and has been a valuable contributor for many years.

Ned Walsh has been a faithful member as a leader and worker of RTL from its origination. Ned, a naval academy graduate and retired navy officer and a businessman, has been a critical policy-making leader for many years. Rev. Jack Keene was an early cleric leader who was a key player in the direct activist movement that evolved from the RTL organization. Rev. Doug Lane has been a longtime major player in the movement, both when he was a seminary student (at Wesley Biblical

Seminary) and afterward as a pastor at Trinity Wesleyan Church. And there are many others who have contributed. Some have made their impacts and have had to drop away or have moved to other areas of the country where, I am sure, many are still active in the battle to save lives and to restore legal protection to the unborn.

As years passed and the pro-life movement progressed and occasionally regressed one constant, initially, was the fact that the media did not give our "issue" the attention or coverage that we felt it deserved. We believed that dead and dying babies and the activities of those who were trying to save them (as well as the activities of those who killed them and who validated their killings) ought to be of major news concern.

I put in quotations marks the word *issue* in the last paragraph because I cannot bring myself to call dead babies by the millions, an "issue" and will not again. Abortion is more than "an issue" such as "advocating that a stop sign ought to be replaced with a stop light" or a school bond referendum! Abortion is a matter of life or death, blessings and cursings, not only for the babies, but for Christianity and the nation. Abortion is a holocaust, not an "issue"! It is a paramount struggle between good and evil!

Deuteronomy 30:15–20 reads:

> I have set before you today life and prosperity, and death and adversity; in that I command you today to love the Lord your God, to walk in His ways and to keep His commandments and His statutes and His judgments, that you may live and multiply, and that the Lord your God may bless you in the land where you are entering to possess it.
>
> But if your heart turns away and you will not obey, but are drawn away and worship other gods and serve them, I declare to you today that you shall surely perish. You shall not prolong your days in the land where you are crossing the Jordan to enter and possess it.
>
> I call heaven and earth to witness against you today, that I have set before you life and death, the blessings and the curse. So choose life in order that you may live, you and your descendents, by loving the Lord your God, by obeying His voice, and by holding fast to Him;
>
> For this is your life and the length of your days, that you may live in the land which the Lord swore to your fathers, to Abraham, Isaac, and Jacob, to give them.

The workers of Right To Life in Mississippi, were, are, and, I believe, will continue to be a mixture of Christians, representing Protestant denominations as well as independent churches and the Roman Catholic Church. I have never attended a pro-life meeting or event where Christ and the truth of the Bible have not been center stage or have been compromised. Yes, we present the humanness of the preborn from medical science and "call" upon the civil government/s to protect the unborn, but we do not deny or fail to acknowledge the humanity of the preborn and our Christian duty before God to "do justice" to them as related in the Scriptures.

Interwoven with the humanness of the preborn has always been a "call" of not only "peace through justice" between mother and unborn child, but the Christians' "call" by God to *do justly, and to love mercy, and to walk humbly with thy God*" (Mic. 6:8).

Through the years, Right To Life in Jackson has not only recruited workers and disseminated the message of the sacredness of all life, including the preborn (which is obviously the one of greatest concern today because they are the ones under the greatest attack) to many groups and churches, but has been constructing a statewide organization of affiliates.

Monthly meetings were held by the Jackson chapter and some of the other affiliates across and up and down the state. These meetings have been used to promote the intrinsic value of every person, as well as our obligation, as Christians, through the law of civil government, to protect everyone from aggression. Also, these meetings afforded a perfect opportunity to promote the "social services/gospel," especially through Christian charity, to poor and needy pregnant mothers.

Perennial side issues such as (1) chastity education; (2) adoption options; and (3) anticontraception services to singles, especially minors and especially minors without their parents' knowledge or consent through government agencies (including the public schools), have been addressed at the meetings and have received broad consensus and have never been sidestepped. However, the use and availability of contraception among married couples has been avoided by the Right To Life movement, locally, statewide, and nationally. (More regarding my thoughts on this "abortion connection" later in this chapter and in the next chapter.) Support for alternatives to abortion organizations, particularly Christian charities, has been addressed and emphasized.

Annual conferences and conventions as well as special-occasion events have featured luminaries and nationally known speakers whom the organizations' leaders believed would "draw a crowd" as well as be valuable contributors to the meetings and conferences. Former abortionists such as Dr. Bernard Nathanson, Dr. David Brewer, and Mississippi's own Dr. Beverly would explain why they entered the abortion business and why they exited the abortion business. These former abortionists have contributed to ways of combating abortion.

Former abortion clinics nurses, such as Ollie Harper and Angie Ford (locally), have spoken at our meetings and detailed poor medical practices within the abortion centers they once worked in as well as outright lies and deceitful practices by their doctors (bosses), in addition to giving reasons why they quit the abortion industry and felt obligated to speak against abortion. Always they acknowledged that abortion does, in fact, kill little human beings. They have, to a person, told of their personal witness of viewing the remains of identifiable dead human beings' body parts.

Carol Everett, a Texan who came to own several abortion centers after having worked in an abortion center, told of the circumstances of the death by abortion of her third child, whom she calls Hedi, and that abortion is a skillfully marketed service. She said, "Abortion is not about 'choice'; it is not about rape or incest. Abortion is about money! We skillfully marketed abortion just as any salesman markets his or her product or service. And we preyed on the fears, apprehensions, and desperations of our patients, who really are victims, the pregnant mothers."

Joy Davis of Birmingham, who had no medical training and who was the "right-hand person" of abortionist Thomas Tucker, a notorious circuit-riding abortionist who owned a chain of six abortion centers in Mississippi and Alabama, explained how he taught her to perform abortions and how malpractice and negligence led to the deaths of two pregnant mothers. Ms. Davis was the featured speaker at the 1995 Annual Banquet of Right To Life in Jackson. Additionally, she testified of a "complication" abortionist Tucker described to her that had upset the workers in one of the abortion centers (in Southaven, Mississippi). That complication was the birth of a "live" child. She said she asked abortionist Tucker, "What did you do?" He told her, "I killed it!"

Tucker, after many years of killing babies, many past viability (he advertised second-trimester abortions up to twenty-four weeks; Davis said he performed abortions on babies in their third trimester of life), lost his medical license in Mississippi and was put on probation in Alabama, which denied him the right to practice medicine until his probation is lifted. After years of killing unborn babies, as well as maiming many women and killing a few women, Tucker finally lost his "right" to practice "choice" in Mississippi and Alabama.

Dr. Jack Willke, president (at the time he came to Jackson) of the National Right To Life Committee for many years, and Mrs. Wilke; Joe Scheidler, head of the Chicago-based Pro-Life Action League; and many other knowledgeable and well known pro-lifers graced our podiums and shared their expertise and experiences with our faithful.

Heads of organizations that provided support for pregnant mothers in crisis pregnancies would speak at our general membership meetings and appeal for volunteers and financial assistance in order that they could continue to offer alternatives to abortions to those they hoped to serve. These organizations and their volunteers provide physical, medical, emotional, and spiritual help for pregnant mothers and their friends and family members during pregnancies and after the babies are born.

Many pro-lifers who first became active in Right To Life have joined the Christian alternatives to abortion movement as a result of learning of these ministries and meeting their representatives at RTL meetings and functions. Many have chosen to be involved in the battle to save the lives of the unborn and the souls of their parents (and the nation) via the Christian alternatives to abortion organizations.

Pro-life political candidates have been given opportunities to come before pro-lifers to share their pro-life convictions and platforms and to appeal for support from our ranks. Many of our number have worked for and with pro-life candidates at the state and national level in an effort to elect lawmakers who would enact legislation and/or appoint or elect judges who are committed to protecting the innocent unborn, who can't vote for "self-protection," and to help mothers in their times of need.

Through education and legislation, Mississippi Christians have tried to (1) prevent unwanted and unplanned pregnancies; (2) offer alternatives to abortion to pregnant mothers; (3) explain the risks of abortion to pregnant mothers; and (4) provide the scientific facts regarding human procreation/reproduction, as well as biblical evidence of the humanity of preborn people, which often will prevent a pregnant mother from offering her unborn child as a human sacrifice at abortion mills.

Through the 1980s and into the 1990s (as of this writing), Mississippi has the most "preborn-friendly" and "pregnant mother–friendly" laws in force among the nation's fifty states.

The Mississippi legislature passed (in this order) legislation that would encourage the protection of and honor the sacredness of unborn human life: (1) a two-parent-parental-consent-prior-to-an-abortion-on-an-unemancipated-minor law; (2) an abortion-control act law (which identifies and regulates the abortion industry); and (3) an informed-consent-with-a-twenty-four-hour-waiting-period-before-an-abortion law.

While all three of these legislative initiatives were passed by substantial majorities in our state's House of Representatives and Senate and were signed into law (or approved by a two-thirds majority of both houses when a governor, Ray Mabus [a pro-abortion governor], vetoed two of the three laws), all three of these laws were held up by abortion advocates' challenges in federal courts for years. Each law finally "cleared" the U.S. Supreme Court's review. They were approved by the federal court in this order: first, the abortion-control act; second, the informed-consent-with-a-twenty-four-hour-waiting-period law; and last, the parental-consent law.

The ACLU, popularly known in the Deep South as the "Anti-Christian League for Un-American activities," bragged in one of their publications that the "temporary restraining order/injunction" issued by a Reagan-appointed federal judge, Henry Wingate, against Mississippi's parent-consent-law was the longest temporary restraining order ever approved by a federal court in U.S. history.

I have recommended to my ACLU acquaintances that they ought to have an affiliate, the ACLULUP affiliate, the American Civil Liberties Union for Little Unborn People. Come to think of it, the "NOW gang" ought to have an affiliate, the NOLUW, the National Organization for Little Unborn Women.

Mississippians acknowledge with great admiration, respect, and appreciation, and a bit of envy, that other states, namely Louisiana and Utah, as well as Guam, have passed legislation that has gone much further than Mississippi has to protect unborn babies. Those two states and this U.S. territory have gone as far as to actually ban the extermination of some unborn babies, but the U.S. Supreme Court ruled their laws unconstitutional.

The fact remains that no state has had as much pro-life/pro–pregnant woman legislation to pass its legislatures and pass "federal muster" as Mississippi has. For this we are proud and give thanks to God and to two ladies, Mrs. Teri Herring and Mrs. Julie Soutullo, who organized Capitol Connection, a pro-life, pro-woman, and pro-family lobbying organization and spearheaded a grass-roots effort to pass the legislation to which we have referred. These two ladies and the many volunteers who worked with them, mostly ladies, did so as nonpaid volunteers.

Many of our state's legislators are pro-life, pro–biblical/traditional values, and pro–local control of solutions to moral and economic dilemmas, and I am sure these lawmakers are often frustrated by a federal government that is hostile, and growing more so, to these three concepts. We thank God there are some legislators and government bureaucrats who fear God more than Caesar and understand that God's laws are immutable and will rule supreme when all is said and done; and we ought to align ourselves with His laws.

In the Early Days There Was Only a Three-Legged Stool; a Fourth Was Needed

In the early days of the pro-life movement in Mississippi as well as across the nation, the development of and life and growth of the pro-life movement was centered on three components, i.e., (1) education; (2) politics and legislation; and (3) alternatives to abortion ministries and charities. There was little attention given to the abortion debate by the media. The pro-abortion forces preferred this because they had the public policy, via the federal courts, they desired and they did not want any attention called to the abortion debate. This lack of public debate and coverage that only the mass media can provide stymied our growth.

This caused many of us, especially those of us who worked in the area of communications to the general public, frustration and was a continuing annoyance. I now know why we were not taken seriously by the media nor was abortion given the attention it deserved. We were not being aggressive enough in trying to protect the unborn under attack, and we were not confronting the evil at the place of evil that such an evil warranted.

In other words, our actions were so far removed from a proper response to "mass murder" that there is no wonder the media was not paying us any attention when we called them and asked them to attend and "cover" our banquets and conferences.

We were to learn that the babies were not being killed in the Supreme Court chambers, in the halls of Congress, or in the committee meeting rooms of our state legislatures (nor in our church sanctuaries). We were trying very hard, too hard, in my opinion, to "be liked" and to "not offend anyone." We were so careful not to have any enemies or to "turn over apple carts." I now believe that when the ship is sinking and tilting to one side our first action should not be to straighten the picture frames on the walls but to stop the flooding! America's ship is sinking! The first place we should have gone, the killing mills, was the last place we actually went! Shame on us! We ought to have gone there first, and we should have put up quite a ruckus. We ought to have offended people, disturbed the peace, and "rescued the perishing"!

When our organizations would invite the secular and, sadly, the Christian media to our banquets, conventions, vigils (at the government buildings), and other events, there was little interest shown by the media, which resulted in little or no media coverage, before or after the fact.

Yes, it was frustrating. Our cause was just, our points of view were logical, widely accepted, and shared (especially in Mississippi and the Deep South), and our political/legislative agenda was reasonable, just, and needed. Even our passion was evident. Why, then, we asked ourselves, were they, the media not giving us the attention that "opposing the murdering of babies" deserved?

We were to finally learn that the problem was not the media but us.

We Were Not at the "Foot of the Cross"!

Needing an "action" photo in the early 1980s for a publication for Right To Life I was preparing, some on the "radical fringe" of our organization, who routinely went to the abortion centers (we had three in Jackson at the time), said to me, "You ought to come to where the 'action' is, where the babies are 'actively' dying." Paul Hill was one of these radicals. (Paul was to later be recognized as the first recipient of the Mississippi Right To Life Volunteer of the Year Award.) I had not been "called" to the "sidewalk counselling" ministry, I had been telling myself.

However, I did need the photo, and the argument of the "radical few" was compelling. It made sense. *If you know where and when babies are being "torn limb from limb" and where and when pregnant mothers can be reached who need information about alternatives to abortion, facts about the risks to pregnant mothers' bodies, minds, and emotions (and spirits) from abortion, and the truth concerning human reproductive biology (including when human life begins), which could lead to some babies being spared death, doesn't it make sense to go to that place?* I asked myself. I thought the abortion center's site might provide the needed "action" photo.

I loaded my camera one Saturday morning and went to the abortion center nearest my home (approximately one mile away), the one on Lakeland Drive. I had driven by it often but had never stopped. It was situated across the street from the Catholic hospital, St. Dominic's and adjacent to the Hinds/Madison Counties Baptist Ministers Complex. (It is interesting, at least to me, that such a blight in the community [a "thorn"] would be situated between two worthwhile institutions [two "roses"]. Also, it is interesting that it operated there with little contention from representatives of the two honorable institutions.) The abortion center, the New Women's Medical Clinic, was the continuation of the center that Beverly had served some half a dozen years before.

After I had taken some photographs of emotional scenes of hostility from abortion-bound pregnant mothers and their likewise young (some obviously minors), hostile, vulgar boyfriends and gut-wrenching conversations between our sidewalk counselors and "willing to listen" pregnant mothers and their friends, I decided to stick around and "picket/demonstrate" (I will only call it "witness" now) with the faithful few.

I remember asking for a sign to hold. I wanted to have something to hide behind (I must confess) in case someone drove by that I knew. God, forgive me! What an impact that one morning had on my life! The after-effects of that single morning were to change my life dramatically, not just my Saturday mornings, but almost every awake moment of my life. As Rev. Keith Tucci, a former head of Operation Rescue, said, "I went from being 'principally' pro-life to 'personally' pro-life." My involvement in direct activism at the abortion clinic that morning was to change the direction of the pro-life movement, in large part, in Jackson and Mississippi, as I was to use my influence (and that of Beverly), which turned out to be considerable, to get more people to the centers and to emphasize the necessity of a presence there, at the site of the "massacre of the innocent."

I realized there was a fourth leg to the pro-life stool that was missing. That leg was a concentrated, ongoing, sustained, direct action campaign at the "gates of Hell," at the "foot of the cross" of the babies, at the abortion mills.

By not having a strong, vocal, and continuous presence at the abortion mills, we were not giving the "abortion debate" the urgency it deserved! We were not "on" the battlefield! We were conceding victory to the enemies of life by forfeiting our right, our duty before God, to enter the contest! We were not on the playing field!

Even if we could not stop the killing of all (or any) of the children earmarked and scheduled to be massacred on a given day, we ought to have a Christian witness at the mills decrying the act of abortion to be "a crime against humanity" and a "sin against God." I recall that all but one of the apostles of Christ, as well as many of His followers, were not at His crucifixion, and they were not there for good reason. Many were afraid; some were indifferent; some had jobs to attend to; and others had personal matters to take care of. Also, they did not want to be controversial, saw no need to be confrontational, and didn't think their presence would matter, much less change the course of human history. And they wanted to be sure that they did not "join" Jesus at Calvary on their crosses!

No, Mary, the mother of Christ, Mary Magdalene, the former prostitute, and John, "the Beloved Apostle," were not able to stop what was ordained to happen before the beginning of time to the "true man, true God," but they, and a few others, were faithful to Him to the end. They were "with" Him at Calvary. They proclaimed Him to be "Lord."

There were many others at Calvary. Some of them carried out the murder of Christ or made sure "potential rescuers" were unable to stop the "legal execution," crucifixion. Many others angrily shouted, "Crucify Him! Crucify Him!" And there was a large contingency there just watching. They, most likely, had "no opinion," and could be characterized similarly to those modern-day folks who have no opinion on abortion or who are "personally opposed to abortion, but . . ."

Unlike Mary, Mary Magdalene, and John, I discovered that first day at an abortion center, standing on a public sidewalk, that Christians who cared for the pregnant mothers and their children (and friends) could make a difference. We could change, and were changing, hearts, opinions, and planned abortions. We were saving babies!

As a result of this "touch of God" on my life during that first day of being at an abortion chamber to witness that abortion was, indeed, murder, and could prove it, and participating in the offers of charity, armed only with the truth, I became a faithful, regular sidewalk counselor at the three abortion mills in Jackson.

I shall never forget the first pregnant mother I persuaded not to kill her unborn. It was a lovely spring morning, just a few weeks after my first "witness" at a mill. The young black unmarried couple gave me some time to talk to them. They listened attentively. I compared that spring morning with the "springtime of life," seeds germinating, flowers blooming, the smell of freshness in the air. I explained that their little unborn child was growing this day, during his (or her) "springtime of life."

The couple acknowledged that they were Christians. In a prayer together, I thanked God for "the birds and the bees, and for the trees and all seeds." I thanked God for "the springtime, for new life, for new beginnings, for His washing away our sins and our 'born again' lives through His shed blood during a springtime almost two thousand spring-times ago, and for the forgiveness of our sins by God, the Father." I thanked God for "His mercy and grace in our lives." I thanked God "for bringing this young couple into my life and for their unborn child, fresh from your hands, O Lord." I thanked God for the blooms of the azaleas that blossom each spring and for the knowledge that spring has arrived and that our children, including the unborn, are a sign from Heaven that God desires that human civilization continues so that we can praise His holy name and establish His kingdom on Earth.

While praying for and with this young couple, I thought that if I prayed long enough and they stayed with me, they would not be able to abort their child that day because the clinic would eventually close for the day. The couple did not abort their child, and six months later I visited the young married couple in their little apartment and celebrated the arrival from the hospital of their newborn son, Luke.

Since that day, a faithful few and I have persuaded hundreds, perhaps thousands, not to kill their precious unborn. Many times we were not articulate, other times we were not pretty (as we stood in the rain, in the heat, or in the bitter cold), but people knew we were determined and we cared. Sometimes that has been enough; other times it has not. Sometimes we have been told only our presence was required to convince pregnant mothers and their "significant others" that abortion was wrong and, therefore, they could not go through with planned abortions.

Many times, confronting and challenging Christians who had ap-pointments to abort their offsprings with the knowledge that "the killing" would be sin and that the Bible says "the wages of sin is death" con-vinced these Christians not to abort their young. Many times this warning made little difference. Many have told us that they feared eternal separa-tion from God "in the lake of fire"/"separation from God forever," and this understanding caused them to change their minds regarding planned abortions.

Many times, "self-identified" Christian abortion-bound couples and/or parents who had brought their preborn grandchildren in their children's wombs to the abortion centers with the intent of killing them have been convinced not to go through with "it" when told by Christians that Christ said, in John 14:15, "*If you love me, you will keep my commandments.*"

It has been my experience that so many "self-identified" Christians, or "so-called" Christians, truly believe all one has to do to be a Christian is believe in God. They honestly believe it matters not what they do and that God will usher them into Heaven regardless of what they do (that is prohibited) or fail to do (which is required) while on Earth.

We must tell these "self-identified" Christians that there is more to salvation than believing Who He is. After all, the Devil acknowledges Who God is; however, the Devil is not "saved" and will not be in Paradise with the Redeemed.

While we have persuaded many not to abort their children, we have been at the "Calvaries" for many of the little ones, tens of thousands, who were not spared. Oh, how this grieves my soul! I estimate that I have spent more than ten thousand hours at the abortion mills in my town over the past ten years. I estimate that I have been alone about two-thirds of those hours and there have been less than four people there about 99 percent of the time. God, help us! God, have mercy on us all!

"We Are All God's Imperfect Children; God Has Every Right to Destroy Each One of Us"

One of the great privileges of my life has been hearing my wife speak at dozens of pro-life meetings and at a few "neutral" events where she debated pro-abortion opponents. I have heard her testimonial, in which she explains why she got into the abortion business and why she got out, so many time that I can give it for her. I have listened to her explain human development in the womb, from the moment of conception until birth, countless times as well as present slides and explain each slide (of preborn children) all over this country as well as in Canada.

I have watched her handle medical instruments that can be used to perform abortions and illustrate how abortions are performed with them.

I have seen her present slides of aborted babies from various abortion techniques very delicately, to the point that I have seen the corpses frequently in my sleep.

In my very prejudiced opinion, no one speaks more eloquently and compassionately against abortion than my wife, Beverly McMillan.

Beverly believes, and I concur, that a major obstacle to pro-life conviction and, thereby, legislation has been the advocacy of abortion when a life has been conceived as a result of what are typically called "the hard cases," i.e., assault rape, statutory rape, date rape, incest, and fetal deformities and/or abnormalities.

Beverly and I know that while all of these "hard cases" combined comprise but only a very small percentage, perhaps 3 percent, of all abortions performed, these "exceptions" undermine the entire reasoning as to why abortion is intrinsically wrong: the simply fact that all human lives are of inestimable value.

Whenever people question my "purist" position (abortion is wrong and ought not to be legal even when the "products of conception" are conceived in one of these "hard cases"), I reflect upon and tell of two cases that I am familiar with in which the conceptions occurred during one of the "hard cases," assault rape. (Incidentally, everyone reading this book, in fact everyone on the planet, is a "product of a conception." No exceptions. No one reading this book is a "product of osmosis" or grew on a tree or once was inside a nut, even though I have had my doubts about some persons. [Perhaps a few came from "nuts"? Not so, and the abortion advocates, you, and I know it.])

Ethel Waters, the great and godly, gifted singer who sang with evangelist Billy Graham for many years, was conceived as a result of assault rape. Waters (1896–1977) was born in Chester, Pennsylvania, and overcame many hardships to become the person who made the song "His Eye Is on the Sparrow" (the name of one of her two autobiographies) more famous than any other singer.

The world would be much poorer today if Ethel Waters had not been allowed to have been born alive.

Second, Beverly helped a Christian family face the consequences of their teenage daughter's victimization as a result of assault rape in the 1980s. The teenager's parents, especially the father, were "leaning" toward abortion to eliminate their precious daughter's crisis when Beverly met the teenager and her parents. Beverly, whom they were urged to confer with as a second opinion regarding this second-trimester pregnancy (the daughter had not told anyone, including her parents, what had happened to her until she was approximately halfway through the pregnancy), told her parents, "My heart goes out to you and to your daughter. I wish I could 'un-rape' your daughter, but I can't; you can't; no one can.

"What has happened to your daughter was a horrible crime against her, against her body, and a sin against God. An abortion would be a crime against the little innocent person in her womb and a sin against God and ought to be a crime against humanity. I know that the latter is not the case in this nation today," Beverly continued.

"What I can do for you is 'walk' with you and your daughter through this pregnancy. I will help you and your daughter as your friend and as her physician," Beverly promised. "Please let me do this." They did and she was (their friend and the teenager's physician).

The little boy was born at the Mississippi Baptist Medical Center.

After the successful delivery of a healthy baby boy and after Beverly had done the necessary paperwork, she visited the baby in the nursery. She walked to a place near the girl's father, who was crying over the child. It was an uncomfortable moment for Beverly when the father began to talk to her.

He said, "Doctor, I have hated this beautiful boy since I knew of his existence for what he had done to my daughter. I now know how wrong I was to hate him. This is my own grandson, he is so innocent, he is so helpless, and he is so beautiful. I could take him home and raise him as my son or as my grandson, but I don't think that would be the best thing for him or for my daughter."

The boy was given up for adoption. Beverly and I know the young man and his parents and see him regularly. He is a fine young man, a fine young Christian. His parents love him so.

And Beverly has continued to be the physician to the boy's birth mother. She is now a college graduate and is married. Her life was not ruined. Recently Beverly delivered another child for this young mother. We know that she must feel good about what she did when circumstances, God, put her to an enormous test.

Three Scriptures come to my mind regrading this true story. First, there is Proverbs 14:12: "*There is a way which seems right to a man, but it is the way of death*." Second, regarding the justifiable sorrow of their daughter's victimization by a rapist and the ensuing pregnancy, I am reminded of 2 Corinthians 7:10, *"For the sorrow that is according to the will of God produces a repentance without regret, leading to salvation; but the sorrow of the world produces death."* The third reference that comes to mind involves the time needed for understanding and the happiness that comes as a blessing from God from doing what is right in the face of adversity. Psalms 30:5 reads: *"His favor is for a lifetime; weeping may last for the night, but a shout of joy comes in the morning."*

Frequently in the time allotted for questions and answers Beverly is asked, "What about fetuses who are handicapped? What about 'imperfect babies'?"

If there is a time when I search for tears in the eyes of Beverly's Christian audiences, it is when she answers this question. "We are all God's 'imperfect children,' " Beverly laments. "None of us are the children God desires us to be. We are all marred by sin. We, all, in our own way, disappoint our Father with our disobedience and rebellion.

"Our Father, the Perfect Parent, has every right to destroy us for what we do and for who we are. But what did God do for His 'imperfect children'? He sent His perfect son as payment for our 'imperfections' to die a painful, necessary death for you and for me and for all the 'imperfect people' in the world.

"I believe a lesson can be derived from His example as to how we ought to think of and treat the 'imperfect children' entrusted to us and living among us," Beverly continues. "God is patient with us, He forgives us, and He adopts us into His home, His kingdom, not based on the degree of our perfection or our ability to think or do things for Him, but based solely on our willingness to be 'as a child' and to be dependent upon Him and to love Him.

"With that principle in mind, we ought to regard and treat our children, even our own physically and mentally 'imperfect children,' as God's children and as He treats us. Our children, all of them, are our *'heritage from the Lord . . . gifts from God'* (Ps. 127), and are *'made in His image'* (Gen. 9). Also, let us remember God said, *'Who made man dumb or deaf or seeing or blind? Was it not I, the Lord?'* (Exod. 4:11)."

I have scanned the audiences right after Beverly has made these biblically logical comments and not seen a dry eye in the crowd.

I estimate that Beverly has spoken in more than three dozen states at pro-life meetings over the past fifteen years. She has been to Portland, Oregon (on the west), and to Providence, Rhode Island (on the east). She has addressed thousands in Saint Louis and less than a dozen in D'Lo

(Mississippi). She has spoken before probably one hundred audiences in Mississippi and from Gulfport (on the Mississippi Gulf Coast [on the south]) to Southaven (a suburb of Memphis [in north Mississippi]). She has spoken in Meridian (in east Mississippi [on the Alabama line]) and in Vicksburg in west Mississippi (on the banks of the Mississippi River, which separates Mississippi from Louisiana). She has done so without compensation and many times without even reimbursement for her expenses. It has been my privilege to accompany her on many of these trips, and I have had the honor of participating in many programs.

She has appeared twice on both *The 700 Club* and *The Oprah Winfrey Show*. She has been featured on *Focus on the Family*, CBS's *Street Stories*, and NBC's *Evening News*. She has had her testimonial printed in a number of secular and Christian publications. Focus on the Family and Easton Publication Company have produced tracts on Beverly's conversion from being an abortionist to an opponent of abortion. *How One Doctor Changed Her Mind about Abortion* and *Know the Facts Before You Choose* are the tracts available from Focus on the Family and Easton Publication Company, respectively.

She has been interviewed by foreign newspapers, magazines, radio networks, and television stations and networks, and on most occasions when she speaks at a prominent pro-life conference or convention she is featured at a news conference.

Then there are the pro-life talks she gives behind closed doors at her medical clinic in her private office or in our living room or den to women who are considering abortion. I have been present at a few of these many conferences. Beverly presents a compelling argument against abortion as well as making an offer of assistance (and charity, if needed). The "fruits" of those conferences are evident; many of them are walking among us.

East Lakeland Ob-Gyn Associates

Beverly practices medicine with three other women ob-gyn specialists and a medical staff and office staff who are most competent and genuinely concerned for their patients. One of her partners, Dr. Freda Bush, is black and a member of the board of directors of the Crisis Pregnancy Center of Jackson. Dr. Donna Breeland and Dr. Rhonda Powell were on maternity leave at the same time (late 1993 and early 1994).

All four of these ladies have husbands and children and work with and are supportive of the pro-life movement as Christians, particularly the alternatives to abortion and adoption agency ministries of the Crisis Pregnancy Center, Bethany Christian Services, Birthright of Jackson, and Catholic Charities.

The staff and nurses at their "truly" women's clinic, East Lakeland Ob-Gyn Associates, cooperate with the physicians to "preserve life" and to heal the sick and relieve suffering as they answer God's call on their lives to minister to women. (I say "truly" a women's clinic because every physician, employee, and patient [with the exceptions of the unborn, male children] is a woman.)

Last, I want to say a few things in this section of this chapter regarding Beverly's "public" ministry. A major reason why those involved in the "sidewalk counseling" ministry so faithfully for so many years in the Jackson area, myself included, have been as successful as they have been has been because we know that Beverly will help us. Among those loyal to the babies and their mothers "on the streets" have been the following: Ester Mann, Rev. Doug Lane, his older brother, Rev. David Lane, and his wife, Janice, Stacy Wills, Barbara Beavers, Monica Baldwin, Harriet Ashley, Debi Ethredge, Becky Yawn, Ida Yerger, Robert Ainsworth, Martha Barton, Pat Cartrette and her husband, Rev. Phil Cartrette, Tanya Britton, Kathy Paulk, B. J. May, T. J. Mullens, Jim Whitehead, Bruce Stuckey, Ronnie Crawford, and Jonathan Loggins. The Christian alternatives to abortion organizations have been enormously helpful to us on the "front lines," too. We feel as if we are an "extension" of their ministries, and I'm sure they feel the same way toward us.

Many times pregnant mothers and their husbands and boyfriends have followed me in their cars from the abortion mills as I led them to my house or to Beverly's office for immediate counseling by a physician, Beverly, or her nurse, Pat Beasley. I shall never forget the time a black married couple from Canton (located fifteen miles north of Jackson), followed me home to talk with Beverly one Saturday morning. I remember praying all the way home that Beverly would be at home. She was and was I relieved!

The pregnant mother of four (three daughters who were home in Canton and the child in her womb) and wife of a truck driver was at the abortion center for an abortion because she had been told by her general practice physician, a racist doctor in Canton, that she needed an abortion due to her medical condition. I asked her what her medical condition was that warranted an abortion, and she told me that her doctor had told her that she had fibroid tumors on her uterus and an abortion was necessary for her health. When the lady told me this and when I saw where she was from, by looking at her license plate on their car, I said to her, "I bet Dr. —— is your doctor."

She said that he was and asked me, "How did you know that?"

I told her, "I suspect that Dr. —— is a racist. Many pregnant black women have come here for abortions as a result of recommendations by him for a variety of 'so-called' medical and other reasons, such as financial, educational, or being unmarried. I believe none of these reasons, including the medical ones I've been told about, warranted abortions."

She told me, "He did say, 'You have three children. Isn't that enough?' "

I told her that I believe he was trying to eliminate blacks from his area and she paused and contemplated that I might just be right. It was logical. I told her that I was not a physician but that I did not believe that fibroid tumors on her uterus were legitimate medical reasons for having an abortion. (By the way, no tumors were to be found!)

This lady's husband, a gentle-spirited and soft-spoken large man, and I sat quietly on a couch nearby as Beverly and the lady talked. Beverly convinced the lady to come to her office Monday and they would explore her medical condition. Beverly told her that fibroid tumors on her uterus were no reason for an abortion and were no danger to her health or life nor to the health or life of her unborn child.

When the lady said that she would not go through with the abortion unless Beverly recommended it, the lady's husband broke our silence (his and mine), saying, "We have three daughters. I've always wanted a son. I'm glad there is not going to be an abortion. I might have the son I always wanted."

I remember praying at that moment, *Lord, I know that the sex of this child was determined at conception, but I pray for a little boy anyway.* I was confident their fourth child was the son that the father had always wanted. It was.

I Was Dragged "Kicking and Screaming" into Full-Time Pro-Life Work

An abortionist, Mylan Chepko, who, at last knowledge was in a federal penitentiary as a result of his plea of guilty to charges of trafficking in illegal child pornography, came to Jackson in the early 1980s, first to perform abortions as a "circuit-riding" abortionist, then as a full-time, Mississippi-only, resident abortionist. He split his time between two of Jackson's three abortion centers and a clinic on the Mississippi Gulf Coast, in Bay Saint Louis.

One of these two centers in Jackson in which Chepko was performing abortions was affiliated with a chain of abortion centers headquarted in Charlotte, North Carolina, that operated in the southeastern U.S. The chain was owned/operated by one Ernest Harris and his children. Harris is dead. The chain of abortion centers was named after Mr. Harris's children.

After Chepko spent a few months performing abortions at the Harris-owned abortion center (on Terry Road in south Jackson), we discovered he was the abortionist at another abortion center in town (the center on Lakeland Drive in north Jackson), owned and operated by abortionist Larry Lipscomb and a few others (out-of-staters). Lipscomb was performing abortions along with his legitimate ob-gyn business at his private office in south Jackson on Robinson Road. We also discovered that Chepko was the abortionist at a Mississippi Gulf Coast abortion center (in Bay Saint Louis), which is about a three-hour drive from Jackson.

Reasoning that Chepko was completely occupied performing the abortions at three abortion centers in Mississippi, we believed that Chepko had moved to the Jackson area, but we did not know where he was living. After a few months, we found out that Chepko and his wife had purchased a home in an affluent Rankin County subdivision, Castlewood, for himself, Mrs. Chepko, and their son to live in.

A Gulf Coast Baptist minister, Rev./Dr. Nathan Barber, pastor of the First Baptist Church in Bay Saint Louis, where Chepko was performing some of his weekly abortions, found out where Chepko was living and went to the abortionist's neighborhood, alone, one day and picketed his house from the public right-of-way in front of Chepko's home. Dr. Barber carried a single sign that identified Chepko (by name) as a new neighbor in the neighborhood and as an abortionist. Reverend Barber had a "pass-out" that explained why he was there.

Dr. Barber explained that Chepko came to his neighborhood, his town of Bay Saint Louis, where he was the pastor of the First Baptist Church, to perform abortions and he, Dr. Barber, thought it was fitting that he go to abortionist Chepko's neighborhood in Rankin County to alert the residents that they had a known killer of little defenseless unborn children in their neighborhood. He, Dr. Barber, explained that abortionist Chepko could afford to live in his garish home on Arundel Drive because he made a lot of money killing little unborn children.

Within an hour or so, Dr. Barber had been arrested and taken to the Rankin County Jail in Brandon and told not to picket the abortionist's home again. Dr. Barber, whom the sheriff did not know was a Baptist minister, asked why he was being denied the constitutional right of free speech in Rankin County as a single individual on the public right-of-way while not interfering with traffic or disturbing the peace. The sheriff, a Southern Baptist himself, told Barber in plain language, "We do things my way in Rankin County, and if you do it again, I'll put that sign of yours in a place in your body where the sun doesn't shine." The sheriff is much like I have found most policemen, prosecutors, jailers, judges, and jurors to be. They are "pro–law and order" and "pro–peace and tranquility" more than they are "pro–truth and justice." They certainly don't like a favorite slogan of mine: "Without agitation, stagnation," according to my experiences.

We Jackson area direct activists found out from Reverend Barber, whom I did not know prior to his experience with the authorities in Rankin County (located adjacent to Hinds County [Jackson] on the east), abortionist Chepko's address and planned a Sunday-afternoon "witness" in his neighborhood with as many people as we could muster up. We, too, wanted his neighbors to know where he lived, to know what he did for a living in our area, to pray for him to stop killing the little ones and for his soul, and to speak to him about his grisly trade as they had opportunities to meet him as neighbors.

We contacted the legal authorities in Rankin County, the prosecutor's office (as it was), and asked what we had to do in order to demonstrate in front of a business or a resident in Rankin County, if anything. We were told that there were no prohibitions, no legal restrictions, to what we were planning to do. (We had told the prosecutor's spokesperson that we were going to have a quiet, non–traffic problem, small demonstration in a residential neighborhood that was in an unincorporated area. We told him that our cars would be parked in a church parking lot. [These facts were all true. We did not offer to tell him where we were going to demonstrate nor whose residence we would be singling out for our demonstration. They did not ask, either.] We were told by the county prosecutor's office that no permit nor notice was necessary as long as we did not disrupt traffic, did not disturb the peace, and remained on public property. We understood these points and adhered to them carefully.)

We met at a church parking lot at two o'clock on a Sunday afternoon, explained to the two dozen or so men, women, and children gathered there what we were going to do and how we were going to accomplish our mission, and appointed spokespeople (ladies only) to speak to neighbors who wanted to know who we were and what we were doing and why and spokespeople (a pastor and a lady) to speak on behalf of the group to the media that we expected and wanted to attend and report this event.

We had called the media in advance and told them of the event and its time and place. We had with us references to U.S. Supreme Court cases that permitted this type of activity as protected free speech. We explained to the media when we first contacted them about this project that we would welcome their presence during the event as well as coverage of the event after the fact. We understood that it was their "call" as to whether or not this event was newsworthy. It was the first of anything like this, residential picketing/protest, in Jackson, ever as far as we knew.

We did hope the media would come, because we believed we would be more safe from abuse and less likely to be arrested by the "Lone Ranger" sheriff of Rankin County and his deputies if the media were present. We believed that if the media covered the demonstration from beginning to end as unbiased entities and recorded it with their cameras and notes, we would not be treated rudely, abused, disbanded, or arrested. Boy, were we wrong!

We believe that Ephesians (5:11) requires that we expose evil and evildoers: "*Do not participate in the unfruitful deeds of darkness, but instead expose them.*" We believe that the Bible requires this type of confrontation as long as it is done for the good of the person exposed as well as for the community. That was part of our intention.

As we were concluding the approximately forty-five-minute demonstration, during which time we completed our purpose and were, generally, not treated with hostility by the abortionist's neighbors, Rankin County sheriff's deputies drove up and told us, in both a rude and threatening way, that we had to leave and what we were doing was illegal. This contradicted what their own prosecutor's office had told us only a few days prior to the demonstration, and we attempted to tell them this fact in a short, polite conversation. They did not want to hear this and brushed it off as meaningless. We were leaving as they arrived, and we tried to tell them this. They rushed us, telling a pastor that he would be arrested if he didn't leave faster and escorting us out of the neighborhood with their squad cars at the front and at the end of our procession of about half a dozen cars.

Rev. David Lane and I had gone to abortionist Chepko's front door, having walked on the sidewalk that began at the street and led to his front porch, rung the doorbell, and knocked at the front door. We had hopes of being invited into his home and, as representatives of the larger group, to be able to share with the abortionist our knowledge of unborn human life from the moment of conception from both the scientific perspective as well as the biblical point of view. We wanted to politely challenge part of his medical practice, the performing of abortions, as immoral and not in the best interests of the babies, naturally, their mothers, his coworkers, and himself. I had with me an outline of the points that we wanted to make with him, as well as my Bible with bookmarks identifying passages that we wanted to read to and discuss with him.

No one came to the door and there was no No Trespass sign in the yard. Understand, too, that no one had told us not to go onto his property, which is legal to do and done often by door-to-door salesmen, persons passing out flyers, and political candidates and/or their representatives.

The television cameramen and newspaper photographer followed us onto the property, and they were not later to be arrested and charged with criminal trespass as I was to be (the next day). They recorded with their video and still cameras this reasonable, nonthreatening, quiet, and nondestructive activity on David's and my part and telecast our venture onto Chepko's property as well as the demonstration on the 10:00 P.M. newscasts on all three local stations. It was the first item on all three stations. There was a major and fairly written story on the front page of the Jackson daily newspaper, the *Clarion-Ledger*, the next morning.

I got ''wind'' from news reporters the next day, a Monday, that the Rankin County sheriff had issued a warrant for my arrest. In fact, a major item on the news, radio, and television stations that Monday was the fact that I was wanted by the Rankin County sheriff for the previous day's alleged criminal trespass onto the abortionist's property.

That evening while I was eating supper with Beverly and our four kids, two Rankin County deputies and two Jackson police officers came to our front door, with media in ''tow,'' told me that I was under arrest, placed handcuffs on my wrists behind my back, put me in the back of a

Rankin County sheriff's department squad car, and drove me to the Rankin County jail. I was charged with malicious trespass with the intent of threatening or embarrassing another, though there was no such law in Mississippi or in Rankin County. (These were the early days of the "thought patrol" that would lead to "hate crimes.")

The media followed the deputy's car to Brandon, and the television cameramen and the newspaper photographer filmed me being taken out of the squad car and ushered into the jailhouse. Beverly bail-bonded me out that evening. There was an enormous amount of media coverage on this misdemeanor arrest. I don't know that a misdemeanor arrest had ever received as much attention as this one had in Mississippi. And the media attention given to the trial was extensive, too.

The pro-life community, of course, was "split" as to whether or not this was a "Christian" thing to do, i.e., challenge the abortionist for what he does to babies and their mothers and confront him "at his castle" and expose him via the news media. "After all," many said, " 'a man's home is his castle.' And everyone needs and deserves 'peace and tranquillity' while at home." Of course, those of us who advocated this action and participated in it explained that we could not control what the media reported or did not report. Also, no one said they would not confront him (or anyone else) on a Sunday afternoon at his house if it were their child/ children who was/were scheduled to be slain the next day.

Due to the large amount of mostly negative pretrial publicity, my attorney, Walt Wood, requested and was granted a change of venue for the trial. This was the first, ever, change of venue for a misdemeanor trial in Mississippi history, "court watchers" said! The maximum punishment, if convicted, would have been a $500 fine and a six-month jail sentence, which would have been "unheard of" in this day of overcrowded jails and violent criminals receiving "slaps on their wrists" for their punishments. It is conservatively estimated that the two mistrials that resulted through attempts to convict me before juries in Forrest County (in Hattiesburg, Mississippi [ninety miles away]) cost the citizens of Rankin County at least $5,000.

Two trials were held in Hattiesburg. Both trials ended in mistrials before the charges were dropped (or "remanded to the files," which, I understand, is about the same thing). The trial judge for both trials, Jim Smith, who had granted the change of venue, is a pro-life Christian who now sits on the Mississippi Supreme Court (an elected post). I believe he was most sympathetic to my plight.

My employer, Southern Farm Bureau Life Insurance Company, fired me as a result of the arrest and ensuing publicity. That was a sad, black day for me. I never dreamed I would be arrested for trying to talk to someone; who would believe there would be such a media "frenzy" over what David and I did? I still find it incredible that a person would be put on trial, twice, for going to someone's front door and ringing a doorbell with a pastor by his side, armed only with his Bible in his hands. (Incidentally, David was not arrested even though he did the exact same thing that I did. I call that "selective prosecution/persecution." I was the "leader," hence my arrest, in my opinion. It is called "decapitate the leadership" (in military terms.)

The month and year that I lost my job was November of 1985. I was disappointed that my employer would not "stand" with me. I loved my job! I was discouraged by the condemnation by many in the pro-life movement. *How and why could such a major incident come from such a minor, trivial thing?* I asked myself.

I have concluded that God wanted me to be "free" to serve Him more in the pro-life, direct-activist movement. I believe He wanted me to be able to be "more reckless" in my efforts and methods (as well as an example) to save as many babies as I could from abortion as well as to do what I could to force abortion into the public and Christian debate.

The loss of my job did give Beverly and me the opportunity to make the decision that I ought to organize a new pro-life organization and work full-time for a pro-life, direct-activist, more confrontational, more challenging (to the abortion industry and civil government [and Christianity]) organization.

I named the new organization the Christian Action Group/Mississippi Abortion Abolition Society (CAG/MAAS). The first newsletter of this organization included this explanation of its purpose under the heading: "What's In a Name?"

> An organization usually chooses a name that identifies it with its cause. The Christian Action Group/Mississippi Abortion Abolition Society chose its name for three reasons.
>
> *First*, of all, the name was chosen to convey an aggressive, activist image. An abortion abolitionist is one who sees no middle ground on the subject of abortion; it is morally unacceptable and ought to be illegal. He believes the practice should be abolished, ceased, terminated, obliterated, totally wiped out. As such, he wants it to be that he is one who is aggressive in his stance against abortion.

It has been suggested that if C.A.G./M.A.A.S. chose a name that was more positive and less aggressive, it might attract more participants. It is our belief that there are plenty of pro-life groups already in existence that are broad enough based to include wide support and we support each of them.

C.A.G./M.A.A.S. sees itself taking the truth of abortion, the holocaust of abortion, to the streets, neighborhoods, schools, and businesses that are purveyors of abortion. It recognizes that the vocal denunciation of abortion and its profiteers in the community might be viewed as undignified or uncivilized by many, even by many who consider themselves to be pro-life and believe abortion to be murder.

Nevertheless, C.A.G./M.A.A.S. believes that aggressive activism among the people is appropriate, indeed, necessary, and called for strategy in bringing the needed change in the minds of the people of this land and in the law to the senseless killing of preborn babies. At this point [this was written in December of 1985] 20,000,000 dead babies after Roe v. Wade, we ask, "How many babies must be sacrificed before people rise up against this legal atrocity?"

Men and women banded together to bring an end to abortion, not merely through speeches, lobbying, and negotiations, but in an aggressive, persistent denunciation and a call to sacrificial and risk-taking actions and repentance in the midst of the people, is what C.A.G./M.A.A.S. is purposely all about. Abolitionists are aggressive activists by name.

Second, the name, The Christian Action Group/Mississippi Abortion Abolition Society, is reminiscent of a movement of great historic significance in American history. An abolitionist in the 1800's fought against legal slavery. Those abolitionists, at that time, did much to bring about an end to the national shame, and sin, of slavery. It is hoped that the work of C.A.G./M.A.A.S. may, likewise, help bring an end to a practice far worse than slavery. Slavery is the owning of another person. The two are hardly on the same plane. While restricting one's freedom is terrible, the extermination of a person is horrendous!

It is the belief of the C.A.G./M.A.A.S. that the greatest abolitionist movement ever to occur in America is now emerging. C.A.G./M.A.A.S. is affiliated with other abortion abolition societies across this great land. There are men and women willing to sacrifice their reputations, pride, jobs, time, and freedom all over this country to put an end to this slaughter of infants. If our forefathers were willing to even fight with arms to death over a lesser issue, slavery (and lesser numbers, as there were but 3,000,000 slaves held captive in 1861), then where are the men and women in this great land with the courage and determination to join this holy fight against abortion? We must rise up before we and ours are next! We must rise up before the Lord brings final judgment on America!

100

Third, the name, the Christian Action Group/Mississippi Abortion Abolition Society, may suggest unlawful acts, but it need not. One friend of C.A.G./M.A.A.S. said the name sounds like a lynch mob. Certainly, the abolitionists of yesterday performed some daring and destructive acts, as did others who advocated needed and righteous change (George Washington, Jeremiah, the Underground Railroad [in the United States to free slaves and in Nazi Germany to save Jews and others], and Jesus). Some of their acts were illegal (John the Baptist, Susan B. Anthony, Corrie ten Boon, all the apostles of Christ, and Christ, Himself). Interestingly, all of those persons and their acts have since been called heroes and heroic.

When protests and outspoken denunciation become the norm rather than the exception, our country will then change their toleration of abortion and the law will protect the children. Until then, it will take men and women of conviction and principle, who are undaunted by criticism, as well as willing to take risks and make sacrifices, to stand up and be heard and to be persecuted. Some, many, must be able and willing, I fear, to identify with and be in solidarity with the precious, perishing preborn.

If this happens, and I predict it will, criticism of them one day will give way to respect and even honor. Let us not allow this opportunity to speak out for the preborn and rescue them from death to be missed and let us join them in suffering or else we will face utter shame and the possibility that our posterity will curse our graves.

I wrote the preceding introduction to the Christian Action Group/ Mississippi Abortion Abolition Society in December of 1985 and believed it when it was written. It was an attempt to inspire others to join me to a greater degree of risk taking and shared suffering with our unborn brothers and sisters in acting as if abortion was, indeed, murder.

I believed Christians, in large enough numbers to touch God's heart, would become a part of the "confessing, confrontational, challenging, and charitable church"! I was wrong! The movement has failed and, I believe, the abortion debate is over, for all intents and purposes. I believe we, as a nation, as Christians, are ripe for the judgment of God!

Thanksgiving Weekend of 1987, Cherry Hill, New Jersey

As I traveled with Beverly on her speaking engagements to regional and national pro-life conventions and conferences, I met and got to know many people in the pro-life movement. I "gravitated" toward those who were active in the "sidewalk counseling" and "public witnessing" efforts of pro-life work. They, too, were seeking out "birds of a feather." Many of us were advocating stronger and more challenging/confrontational efforts to save babies in immediate "harm's way" and to cripple the abortion industry, particularly the abortionists, who were and still are the weak link in the abortion advocacy/industry movement.

There were Joan Andrews, Joe Scheidler, Penny Lea, John Cavanaugh-O'Keefe, Joe Wall, Mike McMonagle, John Ryan, Christi-Anne Collins, Tim Dreste, Tom Herlihy, Andrew Burnett, Joe Foreman, Paul deParrie, and others. Many of them I have since been arrested with and have gotten to know well and respect and admire greatly.

Some of these (and others) wrote essays and position papers that were circulated as such or as articles in pro-life publications condoning and advocating the breaking of laws, peacefully, as an acceptable method of saving babies, injuring the abortion industry, and bringing needed publicity to the pro-life cause. Many organizations and publications became "splinter" groups that chose a different path to combat abortion. Some publications began as "underground/splinter"–type newsletters and magazines, concentrating on direct-activism news and methods, as opposed to the mainstream publications that dealt with the usual educational, political/legislative, and alternatives-to-abortion areas of involvement, which were good in and of themselves but were not the only ways to save babies under immediate threat and to bring about legal protection for the unborn.

I was fortunate to hear many of these people speak in person, to get to know some of them, and to read their writings and to hear their points of view via audio cassettes and videotapes as a result of attending conventions and conferences of the "mainstream organizations."

I heard a beautiful and articulate woman, Penny Lea, speak. She told of experiences she had in which babies were saved by counseling at or "in" abortion centers. That was a new "angle" to me: "in" the clinics. She explained how she had persuaded one pregnant mother out of an abortion when she, Penny, followed the young woman into the abortion center, sat down with her in the reception room, and continued the counseling effort of persuasion that had begun a few minutes before on the public sidewalk outside the abortion center. Boy, was I impressed!

Penny said, "I believed the young woman would not go through with her planned abortion if I could just talk to her a little longer. And I thought the tension created by my going into the abortion center with her would help convince her not to abort her unborn child and that I really cared for her and her child.''

Penny said that the young woman told her, after the abortion center employees threatened to call the police and have Penny arrested if she did not leave immediately, this: "Ma'am, if you do not leave, they will have you arrested.''

To which Penny responded, "I'll be OK if I am arrested. They will not harm me; they will not kill me like these people here at the abortion clinic will do to your child if you have an abortion. I love you and your child so much that I am willing to go to jail to protect you two from these people.''

The pregnant young woman left the abortion center (in Pensacola, Florida, where Penny lived with her family for many years and where Penny ran a crisis pregnancy center near an abortion clinic) with Penny, and the child was saved. I loved this true story! I admired Penny's boldness!

As I heard this story, I recalled, with grief and guilt, the many times I believe I could have stopped abortions if I could have continued to talk to women who were pregnant, who stopped to listen to me for a few moments and went into the abortion centers before I could complete my offer of help to them and plea for mercy for their unborn children. I have heard so many times: "I'm late for my appointments''; "My parents told me not to come home still pregnant''; "My boyfriend is tugging at my arm and wants me to stop listening to you''; or similar statements.

Not long after I had sat in the audience and heard of Penny Lea's tactics that saved babies from death by abortion, I was confronted with a similar situation on the sidewalk in front of an abortion center in my town. The circumstances that had developed were uncannily identical to the one that Penny had described. The pregnant mother was a minor, and her most likely "of-age" boyfriend was strongly persuading her not to stop and listen to me. She had a tear in her eye, and I knew that she did not want to have the abortion. I knew she was in a major crisis in her life.

I waited a minute or so after they had entered the abortion center, and then I went into the center, found the teenage girl, knelt in front of her, and continued my conversation with her regarding (1) alternatives to abortion; (2) the risks to her; and (3) the fact that an abortion would kill her own child. She had told me outside that her parents loved her, did not know that she was pregnant, and would be disappointed in her.

I told her, while kneeling in front of her, "If your parents love you, they will stand beside you through this ordeal, they will do what's best for you, and they will love and provide for their grandson or granddaughter just like they love and provide for you."

Needless to say, the abortion center personnel and the abortionist "flipped"! Nothing like this had ever happened!

To make what could be a long story short, the beautiful young woman left with me, leaving her stunned boyfriend sitting there in the lurch. I drove her home and we told her parents the crisis that she was in. They cried for and with her and with me. Seven months later a beautiful little boy was born to this young woman. All "four" thanked me for what I had done in their own words and way. (The newborn smiled at me.) God gave me such a peace about what I had done (trespassed), not to mention the joy and reward for the "deed."

I was not arrested for this trespass. This was not to be the case the next six times I entered abortion centers in Jackson with pregnant mothers I thought were not enthusiastic about their contemplated abortions and would not go through with abortions if I entered the clinics with them and their friends, husbands, and/or parents.

All six of these women backed out of planned abortions. All six times I was arrested either at the clinic while in the reception rooms or later at home or when I came back to the abortion center. However, I was never convicted for criminal trespass, the charge in all six cases. All the arrests and the "not guilty" verdicts received much media attention.

Why was I not convicted? The first few times, the abortion center personnel who signed the affidavits against me did not show up for the trials in Jackson Municipal Court for the alleged misdemeanor offenses to testify against me. No witness, no conviction! One time the prosecutor for the city did not show up for the trial. "Case dismissed," said the judge. Another time the prosecutor lost my "arrest papers." "Case dismissed," again. Another time, the judge, Bill Barnett, who I thought was sympathetic to my "cause," found technical grounds for dismissing the charges.

Even though I don't profess to be supersmart, I was beginning to understand several things. First, the abortion clinic personnel did not like being in court. They despise media attention. One of the abortion center employees, Angie Ford, who had signed several affidavits against me for trespassing told me, after she had resigned from working for abortionist Larry Lipscomb and had publically joined "our side," that she was ashamed of working there and that she "dare not let Mother know that I worked in an abortion clinic" (which might have happened via publicity if Angie had gone to court and testified against me).

Second, I discovered the "legal people," including the police officers, the prosecutors, the bailiffs, and the judges, don't like to handle abortion-related cases. They do not like the public attention either.

I believe in Mississippi most of the "legal people" are against abortion and would prefer that it be illegal. While they might not be "abortion abolitionists," they were, in my opinion, based on my experiences, uncomfortable prosecuting those of us who were arrested for trespass while trying to stop abortions.

Also, I became convinced that even the "legal people" who support "abortion rights" didn't want to get involved in a high-profile abortion-related case. They have friends who oppose abortion and they know it. They, prosecutors and judges, often have political ambitions, and they know that becoming involved in abortion-related cases presents a "no-win" situation for them. Jurors don't like to sit on criminal cases in which defendants who committed criminal trespass were on trial and testified, "Yes, we did commit criminal trespass but were obligated to in order to save lives." We argued that the breaking of "lesser laws" for a "greater good" was justification for our trespasses. And we outright challenged the laws that permitted abortion through the appeal of "jury nullification." Prosecutors, judges, and jurors do not like these moral high-profile cases. They wished they would go away; we said, "Sorry, we can't oblige."

I drove to other cities and states (Saint Louis, Missouri; Atlanta, Georgia; and New Orleans, Louisiana) in the early days of the "civil disobedience" movement to attend direct-action conferences. At those meetings there was an "urgency" to stop the killing and a greater grief for "the shedding of innocent blood" than I had ever observed at the other pro-life meetings that I had attended. I believed there was a deeper commitment to protect the unborn and a willingness to take risks and to make sacrifices for the preborn by the participants in these "direct activists" conferences than among the participants at the other conferences that I had attended. I sensed a "holiness" among the people connected with the "direct activists" that I had not sensed before among the people attending the general, "mainstream" pro-life conferences.

A major event during those early "direct activists" conferences was a "sit-in" at the abortion centers. I participated in them. I realized that this "is" the response that God had called me to and believed it would be the vehicle through which abortion would be "crushed" in the United States. I believed that this was the path to fidelity and solidarity with the unborn. I reasoned, *If they (the abortionists and their accessories to murder) are going to kill babies and if government leaders and employees are going to sanction/endorse/protect the killing, the abortion industry and the civil government people ought to be compelled to arrest, prosecute, convict, fine, jail, imprison, abort, and crucify us, too.* I reasoned that this was so obviously the way that millions of Christians should and would respond to abortion if this response was promoted and carried out by some of us as an example and that this would be the vehicle through which abortion would be "crushed" within a couple of years in our nation.

Two readings touched my heart so profoundly. John Cavanaugh-O'-Keefe's "No Cheap Solutions" and Joan Andrews's "If You Reject Them, Reject Me" ought to be read, not only by all Christians burdened especially by God about abortion, but by all Christians.

When Joan Andrews was serving a five-year sentence in Florida for trespass at a Pensacola abortion center and attempting to "neutralize" an abortion machine, a number of us from Jackson attended a rally there in an effort to call attention to and protest the sentence against and incarceration of Joan. She had already served about two years of the sentence at that time. It was in the fall of 1987.

A young man by the name of Randy Terry, a Yankee from New York, probably in his late twenties, was at that rally. I heard Randy speak and sing ("Where Were You When They Were Killing Babies?"). Randy Terry was to be the leader, I believed, who would lead Christians to "crush" abortion in our land. Randy Terry is a charismatic evangelist, not to mention a delightful entertainer. I was so impressed with his leadership that I drove from Jackson to Philadelphia, Pennsylvania, to attend a rally on the night after Thanksgiving in November of 1987. Randy had spoken of the rally when he addressed the crowd in Pensacola. Randy, at my request, had mailed me some information about the rally and an "event" that was planned for the next day, the last Saturday in November.

He called the Saturday activity, the "event," Operation Rescue. *What could that be?* I wondered.

After a two-day drive I arrived in Philadelphia that Friday night. I found the church where the rally was going to be held. I was eager to hear more about Operation Rescue. Randy Terry, Joe Foreman, Tom

106

Herlihy, Joe Wall, Mike McMonagle, and others presented the rationale for peaceful intervention "on" the abortion center grounds all over the nation as a reasonable, measured, rational response by Christians to "mass murder." They explained that this was "legal" before God just as surely as it was "legal" before God to rescue Jews from extermination, blacks from slavery, and the Hebrew newborns from death when the civil governments of Nazi Germany, the United States of America, and ancient Egypt had authorized those killings and enslavements. And it is legal in the United States of America to "break" or "bend" laws for a "greater good." However, for this to happen, judges, prosecutors, and/or jurors would have to accept our unborn brethren as "among us."

After the rally, I was the overnight guest (what little night was left) of a young couple in Valley Forge, Pennsylvania. At five o'clock the next morning we were to meet at a shopping center parking lot and go to an abortion center and stage an Operation Rescue sit-in. I remember thinking that this town that I was spending the night in, Valley Forge, was the town that George Washington and his ragged Continental Army had been quartered in during the winter of 1777–78 in preparation for "doing battle" with King George's far superior armed occupying force. As it must have seemed that Washington's army would be destroyed, it seemed natural that Randy Terry's "army" would be annihilated the next morning.

Another "rescuer" at the home that I was "camped" in overnight at Valley Forge was John Potts, a law professor at Valparaiso University in Indiana. He was confident and encouraging. I have had the great opportunity of meeting and getting to know so many "heroes of the faith," like John Potts, of this generation in the pro-life movement.

By six o'clock that Saturday morning in November of 1987 at an abortion center in Cherry Hill, New Jersey (just across the border from Pennsylvania [the Delaware River]), there were hundreds and hundreds of pro-lifers surrounding the center "on" the abortion center's property. It was very cold; some snow fell that morning. We "occupied," as God tells us to, the abortion center's grounds and blocked the doors all day.

I was arrested and carried to an awaiting bus in the middle of the afternoon. By night fall I had been released without a cent being put up as a fine, a bond, or a bail. I did not return for trial, which has been my policy during my many out-of-state arrests. I reason if Hitler's SS troops had arrested me for blocking the doors of one of his extermination camps, released me on my own recognizance, and sent me a letter at a later day to appear for my trial (and execution), would I be morally obligated to attend the trial? I believe not. I don't think it would have mattered if I had been a member of the German resistance or an American soldier with the Allied army captured as a POW, released, and then requested to come back to trial at a future date.

Likewise, I do not feel it to be immoral to tell a judge that you will pay a fine as a condition of being released and not pay the fine. The judge is "endorsing" and "protecting" murder. I owe him no moral allegiance and owe him no money (for a fine), I believe, and it is justifiable, in my opinion, to deceive him in order to get out of jail to rescue more children. In the U.S. Army Infantry School at Fort Benning, Georgia, we were, in counterintelligence classes, instructed to not to tell the truth (yes, to lie) in order to "deceive" the enemy if it would promote our cause and protect us or others.

I know many in the "rescue movement" disagree with me, seeing as the government is "ours" and we "pledge our allegiance" to the United States of America. I respect their opinion and believe they ought to follow their consciences on this matter. However, I believe it is justifiable to disobey this government when arrested unjustly and to "deceive" the government in order to gain freedom in order to return to the "battlefields" to save babies from death by abortion.

Back to Cherry Hill, New Jersey. The abortion center did not open that day at all. They had intended to; they were scheduled to kill babies that day. But they did not because Christians were willing to disobey the civil government and do what Peter said to do in Acts 5:29: *"We must obey God rather than man."*

Operation Rescue planned a "sit-in" campaign in New York City in May of 1988. The "Cherry Hill Rescue" was a prototype, a "dry run," in preparation for the New York City campaign.

I returned to Jackson, armed with the theme (the "message") of Operation Rescue. I believed that the "call" of Operation Rescue was not only the wave of the future, but biblically mandated of the collective Christian community. I believed it would save babies and, importantly, would create public attention for the "abortion holocaust" that would be the catalyst that would force government at all levels to ban abortion in the nation.

I wanted to be a part of the Operation Rescue movement (of God), which was to become a generic movement much like "right to life" is a generic movement. "Sit-ins"/"operation rescue missions" were to spring up all over the nation as small groups heard about its tactics and biblical mandate and acted unilaterally in their towns and cities. Many more were to answer God's call to *"rescue those unjustly sentenced to death"* (Prov. 24:11).

Jackson Police Officer Joe Daniels Resigns from His Job

To correspond with the May 1988 Operation Rescue campaign in New York City, I began to plan an Operation Rescue campaign in Jackson during the same period. I held Sunday-afternoon meetings at our home for twelve weeks in early 1988. I contacted pastors, pro-life leaders, and "regulars," urged them to attend the Sunday-afternoon meetings, and begged them to plan to participate in the mid-May "rescue" scheduled for Jackson, Mississippi. I told them of the Operation Rescue campaign to be held in New York City in May.

We made plans to have a Rescue Rally the night before the rescue at a Jackson area church. Rev. Jack Keene, pastor of New Testament Church, was a "regular" at the abortion centers. He agreed to host the Rescue Rally at his church. Jack became the second in command of Operation Rescue in Mississippi. We became dear and close friends over the next few years and are today.

I, to put it mildly, "desired" that Beverly participate in the coming "rescue" as one who would go onto the property, sit at the door, and subject herself, if necessary, to arrest. We call these persons rescuers. These "rescuers" were the one indispensable element of the "rescues."

Beverly had said that she believed that she was "called" to educate people of the humanity of the preborn and explain why she got into and out of the abortion business. She later confessed, "I didn't want to be arrested. I did not want the publicity that would come with being arrested, not to mention the criminal action that would be brought against me.

"But, at the same time, I read what Roy was writing and I listened to what he was saying. I was becoming uncomfortable with trying to come up with reasons why I ought not to subject myself to arrest, trial, conviction, and sentencing, if we were found guilty, which we believed we probably would be. After all, the babies were being punished and they were not guilty of anything. I told God one morning in prayer, *Lord, if you want me to do this, please make it clear.*

"I knew that was a dangerous prayer. A few days later, in my Bible reading and study I read Micah 6:7–8. It reads: *'Does the Lord delight in thousands of rams, in ten thousand rivers of oil? Shall I present my first-born for my rebellious acts, the fruit of my body for the sin of my soul?*

" *'He has told you, O man, what is good; and what does the Lord require of you but to do justice, to love kindness, and to walk humbly with your God?'*

"Those two words, *'do justice,'* jumped off the page at me!" Beverly exclaimed. "It didn't say to only 'advocate' justice, or to 'pray' for justice, or to 'petition' for justice, or to 'educate' about justice. It told me to *'do justice.'* " Beverly has told this story at more than a dozen rescue rallies.

Beverly told me a few weeks prior to Easter that she was going to join us on the May 14, 1988, rescue as a "rescuer." I was pleased. The person, a woman, who brought abortion to Mississippi was going to be arrested for trying to stop what she had started! I thought that would be a powerful witness. I made plans to give her time on the Rescue Rally program to explain to the audience the night before the rescue why she was going to "rescue" with us the next morning. I thought the previous story would help bring a few "maybes" into the "rescuer" fold. Things were looking good for the upcoming first rescue in Mississippi. I was working diligently for its success.

Getting herself "psyched" up for the coming "sit-in," Beverly became a more regular sidewalk counselor at the Terry Road abortion clinic, which was going to be the target for the rescue. One Saturday in April, just a few weeks prior to the rescue, she went to the abortion center to do sidewalk counseling and noticed that one thing had changed since the last time she was there. There was a yellow line painted on the pavement along the abortion center property on the driveway leading into the clinic's parking lot. She assumed that the line was to identify the separation between the clinic's property and the public right-of-way.

Within a few minutes a car drove from the street into the abortion center's entrance. There was a teenage black girl in the backseat, with two adults, probably her parents, sitting in the front seat. It appeared that this was a typical case of parents bringing their teenage daughter in for an abortion.

The car pulled up and stopped and they rolled down their window to see what Beverly had to say or to give them. Beverly, ignoring the yellow line, stepped across the line (by only a few feet) and gave them some alternatives-to-abortion literature and conversed with them a few seconds. One other thing happened. The security guard, the clinic's "rent-a-cop," took a picture of Beverly while she was standing on "their" side of the property line.

Five days later, on a Thursday night, when I was out of town (in Tupelo) "gathering" participants for the upcoming Operation Rescue mission, two Jackson police officers came to our house while Beverly and our children were eating supper. Beverly was presented with an arrest warrant and escorted to the police car. She was placed under arrest and was taken to the police station, where she was "booked" for criminal trespass (as a result of having stepped a few feet onto the abortion clinic property the previous Saturday).

Beverly has this to say about that incident: "I was embarrassed and humiliated. While I was waiting in the holding tank to have my photograph taken as well as my finger prints recorded, I looked up at the ceiling of the jail cell. I thought that through the years surely many prayers had been "lifted" to Heaven from this place. I prayed for my 'deliverance.' I was feeling sorry for myself and I began to cry softly.

"At that moment a silent voice from God came to me and asked, *Beverly, do you know what night this is*? I sobbed, 'No, I don't.' Jesus answered, *It's Holy Thursday. The anniversary of the night that I was arrested for you.* I thought, *Jesus was arrested, detained, tried, convicted, and crucified for me. They are not going to do anything remotely similar to that to me.* I got back my courage and composure. Soon I was released on bond, which I put on my MasterCard, and my oldest son picked me up. Within two hours I was back home."

A few weeks later, fifty-six of us blocked the doors of the Terry Road abortion center just before the clinic was due to open and where abortionist Thomas Tucker was scheduled to perform abortions. Several pastors and pastors' wives, a number of seminary students, professors, and their spouses, women who had, regretfully, experienced abortions, a former abortionist, and others of us were in that number. The last two persons removed from the entranceway to the front door of the abortion center, amid much media coverage, were a woman who had experienced an abortion many years before that she regrets, Bonnie Evans (who was at the time eight and one-half months pregnant), and the person who had brought abortion to Mississippi, which she now regrets, Dr. Beverly

McMillan. Their testimonies were "big news" in all the major Mississippi media that night and the next day.

We knew that many of the police officers were uncomfortable with arresting this group of kneeling, praying, and gospel-singing Christians. (It is a shame and a disappointment to me that practically all the Christian policemen [most of whom know that abortion is murder] across this nation have facilitated murder by arresting pro-life rescuers. One Boston Catholic policeman in 1995 said, "I am 'pro-law,' rather than 'pro-life.' " Nazi Germany had many of those types of law enforcement officers, too, regretfully.)

Nothing like this had happened in Mississippi since the 1950s and early 1960s when "other" civil rights "protestors" had been arrested and jailed for struggling for their civil rights. This "modern" act of civil rebellion was given enormous media attention in Mississippi.

We did not know how much what we had done affected one police officer, Detective Joe Daniels, a Christian who was assigned to the Child Protection Division of the Jackson Police Department, until we saw and heard him on the 10:00 P.M. newscast that night. Joe Daniels had resigned from his job, and this news was featured on all the local newscasts and in the Jackson's newspaper the next morning.

Daniels, a Methodist, had resigned from his job, which he had held for ten years (and enjoyed) and which provided the sole source of income for his young family, as a result of the guilt and shame he felt for his part in arresting "the wrong people today." He stated before the media, "They were doing what police officers are paid to do and what I am specifically assigned to do: protect children who are endangered.

"We," Daniels said before the media standing before the police academy, "myself included, arrested the wrong people today. I have always prided myself with protecting the innocent and arresting and holding back the criminals. Today, I arrested some 'good guys,' and I'm sorry. I apologize to them and ask God to forgive me. I feel I must, as an act of penance for what I have done, offer something to God that is dear to me as an act of repentance. I offer my job, which was 'my false idol' today and the reason for this wrongdoing on my part today, as that penance."

Joe, his wife, Annette, and their two preschool children, Luke and Rachael, were brought under the "wing" of the pro-life Christian community, both emotionally and financially, while Joe sorted out his situation and selected God's new direction for him. Joe became a vital part of the pro-life movement. He was invited to speak around the country at rescue rallies for a time. Joe reentered college, studied for the ministry at Mississippi College, Mississippi's largest Baptist college, and is now a Baptist minister.

Joe joined the crusade to try to protect the unborn children from abortion, which Joe says is the greatest "criminal activity" in Jackson and the nation. He was arrested in Jackson's second Operation Rescue mission and was featured on a segment of Dr. D. James Kennedy's Coral Ridge Hour television ministry called *Profiles in Courage*.

This act of "civil disobedience" shocked Mississippi! It received a huge amount of media attention. People, particularly the Christian community, were forced to evaluate what response, if any, was appropriate or required of Christianity, of themselves, in the face of "mass murder," when the government sanctions, endorses, pays for (in some cases), and protects "mass murder." Unfortunately, most decided, based on their "inactions," that they had no responsibility to do anything for the babies.

The success of Jackson's first "rescue," as well as the splendid, fast growth and success of Operation Rescue nationally, was an encouragement and gave us hope for the future. I thought (1) pastors and priests would lead their congregations into these acts of "godly obedience," sometimes referred to as "civil disobedience," which they are in large numbers; and (2) the attention to the abortion holocaust would be so profound that the political/legislative/judicial impetus would be created locally and nationally and the "gates of Hell would not prevail" much longer regarding human/child sacrifice in the United States of America.

In my opinion, Operation Rescue's call of repentance at the gates of Hell was not only warranted but necessary in aiding and augmenting the efforts to bring legal protection for the preborn and to help mothers in crisis pregnancies.

Education, political action, legislative efforts, alternatives-to-abortion ministries, and sidewalk counseling, all good and necessary in and of themselves, are not the total or appropriate response by Christians when we know where and when little babies are being slaughtered.

And, of course, the sit-ins and their ensuing punishments brought about a "fidelity and solidarity" with the unborn that all other efforts failed to do. I was so convinced of the need and potential success of the "rescue" movement that I began to plan Jackson's second rescue as soon as the "smoke" had cleared from the first rescue.

So Much Could Be Said and Written about Our Time Together These Past Years

Since Beverly and I first met in the spring (April) of 1982 there is so much that could be said (and written), about these years, "time together." I could fill volumes. Beverly, I'm sure, could write a book, if she could find the time, about her medical practice, her view of our modern-day culture and its values from her perspective as an ob-gyn physician, and her opportunities to witness to women and their friends, husbands, and parents that would be incredibly interesting. Maybe one day she will.

I have said before and it bears repeating that I have not taken any of the financial contributions to the Christian Action Group, the charity arm, and the Mississippi Abortion Abolition Society, the challenging and confronting wing, for personal use. In fact, Beverly and I have contributed thousands of dollars of our income (from Beverly's medical practice income) for the funding of the CAG/MAAS. Not only have we not taken any of the income for personal use (nor have we needed to); we have financed a great deal of charity for pregnant mothers and mothers' and their children's care after birth as well as paid for much of our travel and other expenses in our pro-life work. Additionally, we have contributed tens of thousands of dollars to charities and Christian causes through the years. I've never know anyone as charitable as Beverly.

I have, annually, documented the revenues and expenses of CAG/MAAS for our accounting firm as well as anyone else who desired to audit the finances of this organization. The CAG/MAAS is not a tax-deductible or tax-exempt corporation. I did not want to implicate board members in possible civil or criminal litigation, as the organization was intended to intentionally break laws, peacefully and nonviolently, and would be a target for criminal and civil action and suits, we assumed from the start. I have not been disappointed.

As for the accounting to the Internal Revenue Service, I annually merged the income and expenses into my personal tax report. The donations of the CAG/MAAS have averaged only about four hundred dollars per month. Much of those funds have come from the few rallies and other meeting that have been held and the few faithful who donate on a regular basis. Some additional funds have come via the selling of pro-life information and materials as a result of mailings, usually about quarterly, requesting financial help for specific projects and events.

The first couple of years, Beverly helped me get the organization going by contributing $250 per month from her income. I have not stressed fund-raising; that's probably been one of my major faults. I don't like to ask for financial help (donations), even though there is so much that could have been accomplished over the years to save babies if I had raised more financial support for the organization.

I believe people have hesitated in contributing to what they perceived as "my" (I use the word *my* because I have been the "most visible" leader identified with Operation Rescue in Mississippi) ministry due to the fact that (1) my wife is a physician with an excellent income; and (2) I operate the CAG/MAAS and Operation Rescue from an office in our home and do not "answer" to a governing board or body (when we planned direct action, we assembled a "project command staff" and governed by consensus); and (3) some people do not want to have a "paper trail" that would associate them with an "in your face," confrontational organization that is being sued, prosecuted, and persecuted with criminal conduct and conspiracy constantly.

In fact, some people have told me they refuse to donate to the CAG/MAAS or Operation Rescue for fear they might one day be sued in the civil or criminal courts under RICO, the Racketeering Influence and Corruption Organization act, other federal statutes or other legal actions by the government/s (including local and state) or abortion providers or advocates because of the organization's participation in and endorsement of illegal activities.

My "hat is off" to and my sympathy is with those few direct activists who have ventured into full-time antiabortion work who do not have a financial resource independent of donations.

Music Ministries versus Pro-Life, Direct-Action Ministries

I have researched the number of full-time or part-time salaried music ministers in Mississippi and estimate the number to be about two thousand. I'm not against music, especially Christian music, particularly when it is a part of the worship services in churches, but to have two thousand paid full-time and part-time music ministers and church employees in Mississippi and not one paid full-time or part-time minister attempting to save babies from being butchered by abortion in a direct fashion shows, sadly, where our values are. Where is the balance? Can you imagine what

115

could be done if there were 1,000 paid full-time and part-time Christians working in Mississippi trying to save babies from being killed by abortion through direct intervention and offering assistance to their mothers at the places of death to the children? I wonder how many of Mississippi's approximately ten thousand annual baby killings could be prevented? God have mercy on us Christians in Mississippi!

Yes, there is some support. A few churches and individuals support Right To Life and a few of the other educational and political/legislative organizations as well as the few Christian alternatives-to-abortion ministries, but those contributions (and ministries) don't ''hold a candle'' to the amount of funds donated to churches for internally used projects, many of them for entertainment, such as softball fields, gymnasiums, women's parlors, skiing trips during the holiday seasons, new choir robes when the present choir robes are in perfect condition, Christmas entertainment productions, etc. I wonder how much impact there would be in the areas of evangelism and social reform if we were being the ''salt and light'' that we are ''called'' to be in our culture if there were some balance.

I'm not against these things; there is a place for them. But I question the lack of balance in funding and working (volunteering) in areas that would affect the culture and change the hearts and minds of our neighbors through the fulfillment of needed social programs (Matt. 25), i.e., feeding, clothing, housing, healing, educating, jail ministries, and others, as well as through our ''calling'' to resist evil through public policy in the political process.

I submit there would be less ''friction'' within Christianity (such as the debates as to what color the new choir robes ought to be) if we turn our attention to ''others'' rather than constantly spending more funds and energy ''within'' the church ''on'' ourselves.

The ministry of the CAG/MAAS has focused on life-saving activities at the abortion centers, even though we have been involved in the other three legs of the pro-life stool that I have previously talked about: (1) education; (2) political/legislative/judicial activities; and (3) alternatives to abortion.

Members of the Christian Action Group/Mississippi Abortion Abolition Society have worked tirelessly for candidates who are pro-life. Beverly has testified before state legislative committees considering pro-life/antiabortion legislation. I remember her going to Baton Rouge, Montgomery, and Harrisburg (the state capitals of Louisiana, Alabama, and

116

Pennsylvania) in efforts to encourage legislators in those states to enact legislation that would protect unborn children and their mothers from the abortion industry. We have been a part of challenging abortion in the criminal justice court systems by use of the "necessity defense" as defendants and, in the case of Beverly, as a defendant and as an expert witness.

Juries have found defendants not guilty as a result of Beverly's unique testimonies in criminal trials along with the testimonies of others. At this time Beverly is being represented by the legal staff of Don Wildmon's American Family Association (headquartered in Tupelo, Mississippi, we Mississippians are proud to brag) as a defendant for a criminal trespass charge against her (and others) when she was arrested in July of 1993. This case is in litigation within the criminal justice system in Mississippi.

In that particular case, *Jackson (Mississippi) versus McMillan*, Beverly was arrested for blocking the entrance of the Mississippi Women's Medical Clinic, owned and operated by abortionist Thomas Tucker. (The clinic is now "out of business," and Tucker has lost his medical licenses in Mississippi and Alabama. [He owned and operated six abortion centers in these two states.])

Tucker performed some abortions on "postviable" babies. The case in question, which is still in litigation in Mississippi, challenges the Mississippi state government to determine if criminal trespass was justifiable to protect "viable" unborn babies from abortion. Beverly's (and others') position is that it was necessary to "break" a "lesser law" for a "higher good." This defense, the "necessity defense," ought to be accepted by the Mississippi courts. Beverly's attorneys maintain that if the human beings in question had been on the "other side" of the abdomen it would be accepted. The attorneys for the American Family Association believe this case could challenge abortions on demand on viable babies. And they believe a favorable ruling could lead to other reconsiderations concerning the federal judicial case law concerning all abortions.

It is ironic and a bit sad to me that the judge on this case initially was a black Roman Catholic who denied the necessity defense in his Hinds County Court. He said, "Abortion is not relative in this case. We are here only to decide if Dr. McMillan trespassed or not." Where is his religious faith? Where is his bishop? Can you imagine that statement in Syracuse, New York, a strong antislavery area, in 1858 if a member of the underground railroad was being tried for having extricated one of this

117

judge's ancestors and the "then-judge" (back in 1858) made this statement: "We are not here today to put slavery on trial. We are here only to discover whether or not the defendant stole this Negro slave, which is property of this plantation owner"?

And we know this type of scenario happened. How sad but how true the comparison.

"God Is Not Relevant in This Courtroom," the Methodist Prosecutor Said

I am reminded of a time when I was being tried for criminal trespass before a judge and jury in Hinds County Court. I was defending myself. (This is called *pro se*, which means you are not represented by an attorney but are representing yourself.)

The prosecutor, whom I like and who is a friend of mine, is a member of Christ United Methodist Church, the largest United Methodist church in Mississippi. I believe that he believes abortion is murder and ought not to be legal, but he was "doing his duty" and doing the best he could to convict me and to deflect "abortion" being on trial.

During my closing statement, when I was appealing to the Christians on the jury (they all claimed to be "devout" Christians) "to disregard the objections of the prosecutor and the instructions of the judge and to understand that you, as jurors, do have the right to 'not only judge the facts' but the 'law' itself" (I quoted U.S. Supreme Court cases that validated this), I made a reference to God and His law and the prosecutor shouted, "Objection, Your Honor! God is not relevant in this court."

I countered with, "Your Honor and ladies and gentlemen of the jury, if the prosecutor is right, if you agree with him, I suggest that before you render your decision on my fate we ought to climb to the roof of this five-story courthouse and remove the statue of Moses holding the Ten Commandments, the sixth of which is: 'Thou shall not do murder.' It is my understanding that God was referring to nations as well as individuals when He told us not to kill the innocent."

The judge, a friend of mine, a member of First Presbyterian Church, P.C.A. (the largest Presbyterian church in Mississippi), and a contributor to Right To Life, instructed the jury, as per the prosecutor's request, that they could not "base their decision as to my guilt or innocence" on whether they thought abortion was wrong or not. And the fine Christians

118

found me "guilty" (one of many times). (Jurors have called me at home and apologized for casting "guilty" votes against me.) I know that someone, probably an attorney, once said, "He who defends himself has a fool as a client." But I recall Jesus standing alone before Pontius Pilate.

Many Trappings of Christianity

In this nation, in my opinion, we have many of the "trappings of Christianity." They are everywhere, but I believe them to be meaningless to most people and certainly to most of those in government. These trappings are everywhere, and that includes on and in many of our government buildings; local, state, and national. They give us a "false sense of security," I contend. We mock God through our collective, church and state, hypocrisy by claiming today this is a Christian nation when it is clearly not, not in the "eyes" of our government/s.

I contend that this (to pretend to be a Christian but not be) is not just individually dangerous for us on our "great day of personal judgment" but is dangerous for our nation. I am reminded of what Thomas Jefferson said when he spoke of "the great national sin" that our nation was conceived in, slavery: "I tremble for my country when I reflect that God is just, that His judgment cannot sleep forever."

God has made no provision for punishing or holding nations accountable in the hereafter. Nations will suffer and be judged on Earth for bad judgments, unjust laws, and national sin, as individuals will suffer and be judged on Earth as well as in eternity for personal bad judgments and sin resulting from "personal choices," which includes, but is not limited to, denying Who He is.

I believe that many of our "religious trappings," such as wearing gold crosses on gold chains around our necks while undergoing abortions, lull us into a false security and become a "snare unto us." We say that we are a nation "under God" when we repeat the Pledge of Allegiance. This is a lie! We are not a nation "under God" but a nation that has "rejected God," denied "His hand in the affairs of nations." We sing that America is "the home of the brave" when we sing the national anthem, "The Star-Spangled Banner." I question if we are a nation of "brave people" when we are scared to defend little ones being murdered by the millions!

119

Beverly and I have been active in the establishment and support of Christian alternatives-to-abortion ministries. We believe it is the responsibility of Christians and our institutions to help these pregnant mothers in crisis pregnancies, not the government's responsibility. When Mary Michael, the driving force and the first director of the Crisis Pregnancy Center of Jackson (organized in the mid-1980s), spoke at its dedication banquet she said, "This center would not be a reality without Roy's help."

I mention this not to heap praise on myself but to explain that Beverly and I work with, support, contribute to, pray for, and encourage others to be involved in any or all of the pro-life areas of expertise as the Lord leads them and provides the energy and ability, as He has us. I'm convinced that, except for soul winning itself, the prevention of the murder of the innocent is the most important contribution a Christian can make (and the two are not mutually exclusive).

Beverly's medical practice is one of the very few, if not the only, private practices of ob-gyn medicine in our area that helps and works actively with the Christian alternatives-to-abortion ministries. There are several reasons why, in my opinion, other physicians, almost all white males, don't get involved.

First, they don't want to be seen as being partial to the pro-life side as opposed to the pro-abortion side of this "political debate"; second, they don't want poor black women in their reception rooms, as many of the CPC's clients are poor and black Medicaid recipients, with their white female clients; and, third, they won't accept the smaller amount of payment that Medicaid pays for medical care for pregnant mothers.

And these physicians and their families fill our churches! How this must grieve God, how this must enrage God, and how pathetic it is that our churches are full of people in all areas of business and commerce who do not understand that they are obligated, as Christians, to "merge" their business affairs with their Christian faith.

We, the Christian alternatives-to-abortion spokespeople, often say to pregnant mothers, "We can help with your needs, all of them, even medical care and places to live." While some assistance is given by Christians and Christian agencies, the real truth is that most of the "social services/charity/gospel" is provided by government/s through the Medicaid and other social system programs.

Yes, "we" (Christians) and others (non-Christians) pay the taxes that provide the public assistance programs; however, we Christians who direct the "needy" to government welfare programs do "hand over" the "needy," the vulnerable, to the government, which, in most areas, is our "ideological enemy."

The social welfare programs have been a failure, and an expensive failure. After forty years of experience, we ought to realize this. Some say we need to just "tinker" with the system and be sure that government practices a little "tough love." Some say, "Give the money taken in through tax revenues by the federal government to the state governments so the states can manage the welfare systems at the state level." I say this is foolhardy. I say we ought to end, abolish, government welfare and allow Christians and Christian agencies to do what "we have been called by God to do."

The fact that most Christians believe that civil government ought to have a prominent role in "the social gospel" grieves me. This "social gospel" is "our" responsibility as well as our legacy! Many Christians tell me that "we" can't possible take care of the needs of all those people on government welfare. No, not in ourselves do we have the intelligence, the manpower, or the resources to do this, but our God is a mighty God and He will provide for us what is required (and the intelligence) to do what is needed for His purpose, will, and honor. After all, does He not own "the sheep on a thousand hills"?

Our basic problems, in my opinion, are (1) we do "not believe this truth" (He will provide), and (2) we are unwilling to associate with or provide for "these" folks (we would rather do what we want to do with what God has given us). And this is because of our sins of selfishness. God, help us to see this truth; God, have mercy on us for our sins of omission.

Participation and Leadership in National and Local Levels of Pro-Life Direct Action

Beverly and I, through the late 1980s and 1990s, have been guest speakers at a number of national pro-life Christian events and conferences, including Operation Rescue campaigns.

We have (1) journeyed at our own expense and have paid for our expenses while in attendance at most of the events, as have many others; (2) been in "the streets"; and (3) ended up in jails (particularly myself) in a number of cities (Saint Louis, Saint Petersburg, Houston, Atlanta,

New Orleans, New York, Tallahassee, Baton Rouge, Birmingham, Washington, D.C., Dallas, Philadelphia, Montgomery, Memphis, Chicago, Kalamazoo, and Wichita).

I nurtured a great hope that the "rescue"/"intervention"/"shared persecution with the babies" movement would "take hold" and enough Christians, led by pastors, would join the movement, which would have ended legal abortion in my nation, in my humble opinion. This has not happened and I believe will not happen. I believe the Operation Rescue/ "sit-in" movement has ended because (1) Christians want, continually, something "new" to be involved in (we do not do well in long drawn-out campaigns); (2) the faithful who have been arrested so many times have grown weary and have run out of the ability or willingness to be "hammered" by jail time and fines (I have); (3) state and federal laws and injunctions have intimidated us and "hammered" us, while "singling out" our "civil rights," civil disobedience cause for special treatment (punishment); and (4) we realize that the political change, which was one goal of the rescue movement, will not come.

Locally, in Jackson, Mississippi, we have tried to stimulate others into all areas of pro-life labor as well as tried to lead by example. Beverly has done this principally as a public speaker and as an ob-gyn physician helping pregnant mothers who are in crisis. I have done this principally through my presence as a sidewalk counselor at the abortion mills and as a witness for truth and justice in civil and criminal courts as a defendant and in jails for refusing to pay fines for peaceful, non-destructive criminal trespass.

Beverly's Travel "Back to Rome"

Beverly, as stated earlier, grew up in a Catholic home and was Catholic until she rejected the teaching of her church, in particular, and of Christianity, in general, as a sophomore in college. She did not go to any church for fourteen years after her rejection of her Catholic faith. When she became a Christian, she became a Protestant. She, at first, attended and later joined an independent Methodist church, Riverside Methodist Church, and, still later, a Wesleyan church, Cobblestone Wesleyan Church.

I have been a generic Protestant all my life. I was raised in the First Baptist Church in my hometown of Kosciusko, Mississippi. But I have

122

been a member of a Lutheran church (Missouri Synod), a United Methodist church, an independent Methodist church, and a Wesleyan church. I have spent a lot of time in Presbyterian (PCA) churches and charismatic and evangelical independent churches, too.

In the late 1980s, Beverly began to talk about rejoining the Catholic Church and attending Catholic masses. I went with her to mass frequently and began to do something that I had never really done or wanted to do: comparative Christian religion studies. I had a better-than-average knowledge of the differences among the Christian, particularly Protestant, faiths and denominations.

In Mississippi only about 7 percent of the population is Roman Catholic; however, a larger percentage of the pro-life community is Roman Catholic. I have gotten to know, appreciate, and love many Catholics as well as much of the rich history, doctrine, and heritage of the Roman Church. I have been imprisoned for months with Catholics, and it has been there, in jails, that I have learned much about the Catholic faith.

I have gained a much better understanding from Catholics and other Christians that sacrifice, persecution, the withholding from one's self (fasting) pleasures and desires, and the willingness to absorb persecution and pain can "draw" a Christian nearer to God just as health, wealth, and happiness can, likewise, "draw" a Christian nearer to God.

As Beverly was "moving back" to the Roman Catholic Church, I was asking her questions about Catholicism, her past remembrances of it, and her thoughts on the Protestant churches/denominations. She talked a great deal about "the sacraments." I have learned about the seven sacraments that the Catholic Church believes in as well as a host of other biblical perspectives of the Catholic Church. I began to read more about the Roman Catholic Church's past and present doctrine.

To help me better learn of the Roman Catholic Church, I attended the Catholic education program RCIA (Rite of Christian Initiation for Adults). In fact, I attended RCIA classes four times. over four years I was "open" to becoming a member of the Catholic Church. I did not have a lot of negative preconceptions that I felt I would have to overcome concerning the Catholic doctrine before I could accept the Roman Catholic faith if I felt it was the move that God would have me make. Much of what I learned regarding the Roman Catholic Church doctrine and dogma I have accepted and believe does not contradict what I learned as a Protestant or from the Bible. However, I was not able to accept some of the teachings of the Catholic Church; therefore, I remain a Protestant.

123

I am not saying the Roman Catholic positions that I disagree with (according to my understanding of Holy Scripture) are wrong, but I was not (and have not been) able to accept the fact that the Catholic Church is correct on some points of Christianity that I believe.

I had interruptions in my weekly attendance of the RCIA classes, namely travel and jail sentences. But I do know a great deal about the doctrine of the Roman Catholic Church today. I am glad for this and have a great respect for the Catholic faith.

For now, I am "Catholic in my heart, Presbyterian in my theology, baptized Baptist, and evangelical and charismatic in my experiences," which is similar to what my friend Randy Terry says when asked, "What are you?"

I am convinced of a few points regarding the chaos in today's Christian faiths and denominations. They are (briefly):

1. I have a problem with the "sheep" electing the "shepherd," which is the case in Protestant churches and denominations.
2. There is a lack of specific prohibitions within the Protestant churches. For example: What is allowed to be done on Sundays and what is not? (I recall something called the Fourth Commandment. Seldom is guidance given anymore on this matter or any others.)
3. A major problem is the lack of discipline within the Roman Catholic Church with those who speak and act against the teaching of the Bible and the Church's infallible doctrines (including voting for candidates who have campaign platforms that will legislate against known Catholic doctrine as well as the politicians, after elected, who vote against their Roman Catholic Church's positions [such as voting for abortion rights]).

As I see it, most Protestant denominations have eliminated "anything as sin" or don't want to be "intolerant or judgmental" to the point that everyone is to decide for himself/herself what, if anything, is sin and will not be accepted by members of their denominations. There is little challenging of one another within Christianity anymore. (I welcome it, believe it is biblical, and believe it is sorely needed today.) Where there is a lack of discipline or disfellowship/disassociation/excommunication for speaking/teaching/acting/voting against church law/biblical truth on matters of faith and morals (where the denominations has taken a position), the integrity of the church/denomination is compromised and the person/s committing and advocating the sin/s corrupts the Body of Christ.

124

One last point about church faith/doctrine is this: When a denomination believes what they teach is "possibly with error," as do Protestants, there is less likelihood of enforcement of church law (church discipline, i.e., Matt. 18 and I Cor. 5) for fear that the position of the church/denomination may be wrong and may be changed in the next century, next decade, next year, next month, or next week or tomorrow. And this situation, along with "no absolute" "rights" or "wrongs," permeates the Protestant denominations and causes them to be just about impotent in calling their sheep to biblical holiness.

I believe that individual "interpretation" is destroying our witness as we decide, individually, what, if anything, is wrong, and what, if anything, is right (or required). The last verse of the book of Judges (21:25) speaks to this: *"In those days, there was no king in Israel; everyone did what was right in his own eyes."*

Perfect Example (Consistent Teaching): Catholic Teaching on Contraception and Artificial Birth Control

I have become totally and irrevocably convinced over the past five years that the constant, consistent teaching of the Roman Catholic Church on the immorality of contraception and artificial birth control is correct. I now understand clearly, for one thing, that contraception and artificial birth control are the "gateway" to abortion. There is, to me, no doubt of this truth! Where contraception and artificial birth control are approved and accepted by the culture, including the religious (including Christians) community, even within marriage, abortion will surely follow.

First, the "blurring" of the careful distinction between preventing conception and creating an environment (the female body) within which the new, very small, microscopic human being cannot live exists. Most so-called contraception at least occasionally causes the female body to be "hostile" to continuing human life "after" the conception of a new human being has occurred. Many "contra"-ceptions absolutely do not "contra" (prevent) conception at all! On this there is no doubt, no debate.

In fact, all "contra"-ceptions (even the ever-popular oral contraception) at times fail to prevent conception but prevent the continued life of the "conceptus" from continuing. Can it be that while we pro-lifers protest, rightfully so, the 1.6 million annual surgical abortions, there are more than 10 million (maybe as many as 30 million) "mini"/"micro"

125

chemical abortions performed annually? We ought to be equally protesting the destruction of these "mini"/"micro" people's deaths. After all, is it not we who say that a "little person's" life is as important and as intrinsically valuable as a "big person's" life?

The challenge, in my opinion, to the Protestant churches, all of which opposed all forms of contraception and artificial birth control prior to 1930, is this: "Did God change His opinion somewhere between 1929 and 1931 regarding the morality of the use of contraception and artificial birth control?" Another question that I can't dismiss as easily as most of my Protestant friends can, many of whom I have debated the finer points of contraception and artificial birth control with, is this: "Can we simply just throw up our hands and say, 'We were wrong then (1929 and before) and we are right now'?" I don't believe it is that simple. Magisterium anyone?

Of my Catholic friends I ask, "How can a member of the Roman Catholic Church who considers himself (or herself) be in good standing with the Roman Catholic Church (as a communicant) believe this to be true when he (or she) believes and/or practices differently than what the Roman Catholic Church teaches. Isn't this (the Roman Catholic Church's position on contraception and artificial birth control, for example) a matter of 'faith and morals'?"

If a Roman Catholic priest knows that a person disagrees (dissents) with the Roman Catholic Church's dogma and propagates this dissent, it seems to me the priest is required to speak to the person and challenge the incorrect position, and if the sinner does not repent (and change his position), the priest is required to withhold the sacrament of the Eucharist from the sinner who is in rebellion against the Roman Catholic Church.

To my knowledge, Beverly is the only physician or pharmacist (in this area), Catholic, Protestant, or otherwise, who does not prescribe or fill orders for prescriptions of contraceptions or sell devices or chemicals that are intended to prevent conception (most of the time). Through Beverly and her close friend, her fellow Catholic sister, Mrs. Geri Gray-Lewis, R.N., who has headed Natural Family Planning in Jackson for many years, I have developed a clear and, I believe, biblical perspective on contraception/artificial birth control as well as the heresy within Christianity that does not see children as a "blessing" from heaven but as a "curse" from Hell.

Back to "church discipline" on dissenters. Do we not understand the necessity for Christian discipline according to Scriptures? Do we not understand that the use of church discipline is for the good of the dissenters and necessary for the integrity of Christianity? Church discipline is clearly set forth in the Bible in many places, Matthew 18 and I Corinthians 5, for examples.

Do we not recall that Christ himself said in John 14:15, *"If you love me, obey my commandments"*? Is to not disobey God to love God, and isn't a person Hell-bound and a non-Christian who disobeys God and does not love God by virtue of his (or her) disobedience to His church and the Word of God?

I believe the route to (1) acknowledging the existence of, (2) regarding as sacred, and (3) protecting, through the civil law, preborn human beings is "rethinking" the artificial contraception/artificial birth control mentality as well as the understanding that children are "gifts" from God in our culture. Christianity must make this change before non-Christians will. I believe Christians and Christianity will not go "into the public square" with a clear, firm, and caring message of the personhood of the preborn as long as Christians (and Christianity) are confused and unsure of God's view of contraception and artificial birth control. Our nation needs a *"quiver of arrows,"* as Psalm 127 calls children.

"Rescues" Planned and Executed Locally and Nationally

As mentioned previously, I believed that Operation Rescue's "sit-in"/"solidarity-fidelity with the victims of abortion" movement was a "move of God" through His people that could have been the platform, through repentance and action, to give God a reason to look down from Heaven and have mercy on His people and everyone else in the nation rather than pour down His wrath and judgment upon the land.

I thought the movement, in the larger and grander scale, could have set the stage for revival in America. The elements of the rescue movement: (1) physical, peaceful, intervention and solidarity with the babies (action); (2) confrontation with Caesar when confrontation is appropriate and, in this case, necessary in order to show Caesar (and everyone else), Who is Judge, Lord, King, and the Mighty Prince, as well as Who Christians and non-Christians one day must bow their knees to; (3) Christians regaining their God-given role to be the agent of charity for those in physical, emotional, and spiritual need; (4) challenging "wickedness in high places" and in the public square not only in order to save precious lives but for the good of the evildoers; and (5) being the visible "salt and light" that not only flavors and preserves but also irritates were all present in the "rescue" movement for the reformation of Christianity and salvation for our nation/culture/society.

A number of pro-life direct-activist Christian leaders here in Jackson joined me in planning Jackson's second rescue as soon as the dust had cleared from our first rescue, Operation Rescue, Mississippi I. We set the date for the second rescue in Jackson, Operation Rescue, Mississippi II, for a Saturday in November of 1988, a weekend for which Operation Rescue National was planning a "National Day of Rescue" and encouraging direct activists all over the nation to have "rescues" in their localities.

My plans and thoughts went like this: to have the second rescue in six months (and November of 1988 was six months after the May rescue) and to have as a goal twice as many rescuers (those who would actually risk arrest by committing criminal trespass onto the abortion center property sitting at the entrance of the centers' doors, refusing to move when ordered to by the police, and remaining limp when arrested) as we had in the first rescue. Our goal, therefore, was for 120 (slightly more than twice the 56 rescuers who participated in the first rescue) rescuers for the second rescue.

Further into the future, we planned the third rescue to be held in one-half the time span between the first and second rescues, which was six months, with twice as many rescuers.

That would mean the third rescue would be held three months after the second rescue with 240 rescuers. The fourth rescue would be held in one-half the time span between the two previous rescues (the second and the third rescues), which was three months, or one and one-months after the third rescue, with a goal of twice as many rescuers participating in the third rescue (which would have 240 rescuers), which would be 480 rescuers. And on and on . . . until there would be so many Christians blocking Jackson's three abortion mills every day that the combined local, state, and federal law enforcement agencies would not have the power, resources, or will to prevent the "closing" of the abortion industry in Jackson, then Mississippi, then the nation.

That "plan" would have worked and would not have involved much time, effort, or sacrifice by the Christians in our city, state, and nation. The violence (in the clinics) would have ended, the Supreme Court decision (that permitted abortions) would have been changed or would have become neutralized (irrelevant), and there would not have been the temptation, need, or necessity (in the minds of a few) to escalate the actions of a few "faithful," misguided or not, depending on your point of view regarding the justification of the use of force and/or violence to slow down or prevent some abortions (which was all that Operation Rescue attempted to accomplish on a given day).

Boy, was I wrong with my plan and projection! Boy, had I overestimated Christians! Boy, had I overestimated the leadership of the clergy in response to needed mercy and justice for the unborn and their willingness to be "discomforted"!

I mistakenly thought those pastors and priests who "thundered from their 'safe' pulpits that 'abortion is murder'!" really believed what they were preaching or were willing to respond appropriately to stop the murdering. I thought when Operation Rescue representatives, locally and nationally, shared with clergy the righteousness/appropriateness/necessity of the "rescue movement," they would, in overwhelming numbers (to the political/civil government system), endorse, join, and lead the rescue movement.

I soon discovered that either the pastors and priests (1) did not believe their own rhetoric; (2) did not really care enough about the babies to make a little sacrifice to save them; (3) had such a false concept of "blind obedience" to the civil government when to do so was clearly sin by refusing to obey God; or (4) were such cowards. I believe all four of the above accounted for the minimal response to what I believe was a "move of God," which the clergy in our country ought to have embraced during a season "when the window of opportunity existed."

I never wanted to believe and it took me a long time to become convinced that the clergy in America does, for the most part, believe that "Caesar is God" and that to disobey Caesar was to "sin against God," even when Caesar endorsed murder and was protecting the murderers and their places of murder! This is clearly to me a false notion about the thirteenth chapter of Romans. One well-known seminary professor at a nationally known Presbyterian seminary here in Jackson, Reformed Theological Seminary, in a discussion with me about civil disobedience stated that, in his opinion, Corrie ten Boom was "sinning" when she and her family were hiding Jews and others marked for extermination during World War II. Can you believe that?

I have since reasoned, *If the clergy in the United States could not see that "disobeying Caesar" in order to "obey God" through peaceful*

129

attempts to rescue little babies from being legally murdered was not a clear case of being called to "obey God rather than man" (Acts 5:29), as Peter advocated and did, then our clergy would "flinch" on any other "issue," even the "issue" of proclaiming the Gospel itself, if told not to. I'm sure few of you agree with this. That's OK. I'm not asking for or expecting unanimity with my opinions. I may be wrong; in fact, I hope so. But what if I am right? Do we think that our government, which protects the right of some to "crush" the skulls of others, is incapable of "crushing" your cleric's propagation of Christianity? Dream on!

I do believe the "rescue"/Operation Rescue/"sit-in"/"solidarity-fidelity with the victim" movement has ended and has failed to the extent that it has ended short of changing hearts and minds as well as civil government's responsibility, through the law, to acknowledge the existence of and prescribe the legal protection of our unborn brothers and sisters. I believe the fault lies principally with the clergy, due to the unwillingness of 99.9 percent of the pastors and priests to do what they are "called" to do, which is to "lead their flocks." The clergy refused to do for the "stranger" what they would all do, I assume, for their children, unhesitatingly, even if such an act of protection were illegal. (Could I be wrong in assuming they would be bold and courageous enough to protect their own?)

In Jackson, between May of 1988 and July of 1993, we had 13 rescues, ranging from seventy-six rescuers (those arrested) to three rescuers. I was arrested in all thirteen rescues. I was sentenced more harshly than anyone else, as expected (as the "leader" and the one arrested more than anyone else), with fines and jail sentences. And only once did I receive a jail sentence after being convicted (only seven days). And I still have not paid all the fines!

All totaled, about three hundred Christians were arrested in Jackson during this five-year interval. Many were arrested four, five, or six times. But the fact is that most Christians in our area, 99.99 percent, have never even as much as gone to an abortion clinic to witness against this atrocity or to sidewalk-counsel pregnant mothers regarding alternatives to abortion. Many who have an opinion about abortion (mostly "I'm against it") have not even lifted a finger in an attempt to save one baby from being murdered.

Many Babies Have Been Rescued by a Few Faithful Christians

A little band of faithful Christian pro-life direct activists have saved many babies. We, as leaders and participants in the Operation Rescue movement, have also forced abortion into the conscience of the community and state. Through our actions, Christians have had to debate when and under what circumstances Christians have a right and an obligation to break "Caesar's law." I believe our acts of "biblical obedience" in Mississippi have been a "key ingredient" in prompting our state legislators to enact the most "fetus-friendly" and "pregnant mother–helpful" laws that are being enforced in the nation today. As I have stated previously, we have three major pro-life laws in our state: (1) the two-parent-parental-consent law (before a minor unemancipated daughter can have an abortion); (2) the informed-consent-with-a-mandatory-twenty-four-hour-waiting-period law; and (3) the abortion-control law. I estimate that these three laws have prevented approximately twenty-five percent of the contemplated abortions in our state. I believe that these three laws are reinforced by the small band of organized faithful (to one another and the babies [and their mothers]), direct activists who witness and sidewalk-counsel at our state's abortion clinics.

I estimate that several thousand, perhaps as many as ten thousand, contemplated abortions have been prevented in our state through the efforts of the dedicated few who have seen to it that these laws have been enacted and who have faithfully been on the sidewalks at the abortion centers over the past fifteen years.

I commiserate in the knowledge that there have been more than two hundred thousand abortions in our state over the past twenty years.

Also, I commiserate that, in my opinion, the Operation Rescue movement is over, passé, washed up, "belly-flopped" (whatever name for failure you want to give it) in Jackson, Mississippi, and throughout the nation. As I have stated, I believe the major reason for this is that the clergy was unwilling to lead and the congregations of those few clerics who participated in rescues were not willing to follow in significant numbers to make a major dent in the abortion industry or to cause needed pro-life legislation.

Why?

Simple! We hate the cross! Not Christ's cross or the crosses of the unborn babies but our own! The burden was too heavy. We, as the Christian body, were not "up" to the job needed, which was to crawl "up" upon our crosses to the "X" mark, the center of the cross, where millions of us ought to have willingly gone on behalf of the babies, our nation, and our "risen" Savior. I believe many of us will go to our "crosses" in one form or another, unwillingly, in the next few years. And it may be that our posterity will stand over our graves and curse us for not being willing to pay a lesser price, when we could have done so, than they will pay one day.

I believe that the abortion debate is all but over in the United States. This is one reason I have reached the conclusion that I have regarding the future of our nation. I believe there will be a few abortion abolitionists willing to make greater sacrifices and to take great risks through the use of force and violence, but I believe it will not appreciably affect the abortion holocaust in this nation. While I believe acts of violence and force are justifiable as a last resort to protect unborn children, I shall not digress into this subject. I believe it will be immaterial and irrelevant in the nation's future abortion policy. I believe Christians will be preoccupied with "rescuing themselves" soon.

I believe there was a "window of opportunity" to end child killing in our nation. I believe that period was between Operation Rescue National's October 1988 campaign in Atlanta, the Siege of Atlanta, through Operation Rescue National's July/August 1991 campaign in Wichita, the Summer of Mercy, to Operation Rescue National's July 1992 campaign in Baton Rouge, the Summer of Purpose. I believe Christianity in the United States missed this great "open window" of opportunity to rescue the children, the nation, and Christianity in this morally (and otherwise) dying culture. I may be wrong. I hope that I am, but I don't think so.

There may be other "windows of opportunity" open in other areas of Christian service and discipleship, i.e., "retaking the social charity" ministry from the civil government, which may give God a reason to spare the United States of America, for now, from His judgment. God is God, not me, and He chooses to "open" and "close" windows, not me, for individuals and for nations, just as He chooses to "open" and "close" women's wombs. Frankly, I do not see any more "open" windows in this nation's future in the long term. I believe our nation is no longer "viable" as a great moral, economic, and military nation and is on "life support" system via the faith and acts of our Christian forefathers.

Remember: God closes windows and gives up on nations just as He does on individuals. Also, He destroys nations and/or allows nations to destroy themselves. I believe He is doing this to our nation due to our nation's wickedness and rebellion before Him as well as for what we have failed to do that is required that is good and for our lack of faith in and repentance to Him.

I Believe Christianity Is in Big Trouble in This Nation and We Are Possibly Facing the Extermination or the Near-Extermination of Christianity in America

Two acquaintances of mine for whom I have a great deal of respect and admiration, Rev. Paul Schenck and his twin brother, Rev. Robert Schenck, wrote a book recently, *The Extermination of Christianity*. They are active in the pro-life movement in the Buffalo, New York, area. The following is recorded in the introduction in their book*:

We are in the middle of the greatest ideological struggle in American history. This dramatic assertion is also a very discomforting one. It seems to me that it would be easier to live some time after it. For instance, I should think that it would have been more comfortable to live in 1850, before the Civil War, or in 1880, after it.

We, who belong to the current generation, have no such luxury. We are living in the midst of a great conflict, indeed, a "combat" of personal and public convictions. It is no secret that this conflict has been brewing for some time—erupting at intervals on the campaign trail, in the legislatures, in the schools, in the courts, and in the streets. These have ranged from tame debate to rancorous antagonism to violent confrontation and even murder.

I am referring to the clash between two competing philosophies or ways of living. One is what has been referred to by Rev. Martin Luther King, Jr., in his "Letter from Birmingham Jail," as the "Judeo-Christian Heritage." This phrase summarizes a world view based on belief in a personal Creator-God who is revealed in Scripture, attested to in the order of creation, referred to by statesmen, scholars, and philosophers, invoked in the great documents like the Declaration of Independence, and revered by the vast majority of American citizens.

This Judeo-Christian heritage hands down to each successive generation common tenets of faith and practice, which include standard definitions of relationships between the sexes, within families, and in society,

---

*Quotes from this book are reprinted by permission of Vital Issues Press.

and certain principles of government. These are held to be applicable and binding on every "tribe and tongue, and people, and nation."

The other competitor is what I have come to call the false consensus. It is an amalgamation of various philosophies and theories, some dating back over 250 years to the Enlightenment, that period when men like Voltaire and Rousseau elevated "Reason" above God. In the early 1960's a group of theologians declared the "death of God," that is the God of the Judeo-Christian tradition. Since that time, the divine throne has been up for grabs—mostly being seized by trendy superstars like Madonna and Michael Jackson.

Some have referred to the false consensus by its parts: secularism, materialism, and humanism, among others. These terms refer to world views that deny the existence of a personal Creator-God; or at least they deny any capacity for any knowledge about His nature and existence, as well as His active role in people's lives.

I have news for those who do not believe in the God of the Judeo-Christian faith; God is not dead! He is not even wounded, which is more than I can say for this nation. I believe this nation/culture/society is wounded fatally. As Paul Schenck said, "**He is a personal Creator-God Who is actively involved in people's lives**." I would add that He is the righteous Judge of individuals, in the here and now (on Earth) and for Eternity, and the righteous Judge of nations only here and now (on Earth).

In the closing paragraph of *The Extermination of Christianity*, Paul and Robert Schenck wrote:

Soon, anyone who identifies himself with the Judeo-Christian way of seeing will wind up as a persona non grata in secular America. While it currently seems unthinkable that religious liberty could be lost altogether in America, a social, political, and cultural environment that is intolerant and hostile to religious faith will in effect nullify the First Amendment and its protection, with the result that religious freedom will have a shallow, hollow ring "from shore to shore."

Much of today's "secularized" Christianity has been a part of the betrayal of the Judeo-Christian heritage, in my opinion. I realize that my accusations against what I call self-identified Christians, who I don't believe are Christians at all, and secularized Christianity are strong, but I believe these accusations are true and necessary to state. If you wanted another "bless us, feel good, let's eat, financial prosperity" book, you have the wrong one. (And there are plenty of those available.) I predict extremely hard times ahead for true Christians, and, in the next chapter, chapter 4, *"Their Destiny Is Their Destruction . . . Their Glory Is Their Shame* (Phil. 3:19)," I will predict some of them.

I will not deny there are some "good signs" that Christianity is awakening in this nation, but I believe these trends are "too little and too late." These "good signs" may well be the seeds of the reconstruction of the nation/culture/society to follow a period of financial depression, rampant violence, and social chaos. I believe for this nation chaos and collapse are near.

During an NARAL, National Abortion Rights Action League, conference, their executive vice-president, James Wagoner, criticized Pat Buchanan's September 1993 speech before Pat Robertson's Christian Coalition "Road to Victory" Conference. Wagoner labeled pro-family activists, such as Buchanan, "religious zealots whose goal is to Christianize America."

Specifically, Wagoner viewed state laws on abortion regulation such as "twenty-four-hour waiting periods," "parental consent," and "abortion reporting" as the "new Jim Crow abortion laws" or "hoops" a woman, even a child, must go through in order to exercise her "right to choose."

Buchanan, God bless him, had said at the Christian Coalition meeting, "We cannot wave the white flag in the cultural war because that war is who we are. Culture is the Ho Chi Minh Trail to power. Our culture is superior because our religion is Christianity."

I pray that we will be willing to "fight" in the matter that God deems necessary for us to fight. I believe we have a "culture war" fight on our hands that will be transformed into a very different kind of "fight" and "war," different, worse than others have predicted. I believe we face a physical fight and a war for the survival of Christianity in the United States, which will transcend the survival of the nation/culture/society as we know it.

Many Christians are saying today what many of the religious people said two thousand years ago on Good Friday: *"We have no other king [God] but Caesar."* Then when asked what to do with Christ, they said, *"Crucify him; crucify him."*

I believe we have reached that "Good Friday" episode for this nation. Many of our "self-identified" Christian friends will turn us in to Caesar for his punishment and then try to wash their guilt off their hands.

I am not, please understand, calling for capitulation. I will stand on my record, one of some shame but much glory.

I ask you to consider what I believe the future holds.

Read the last chapter. If you don't believe it, fine.

If it does not come to pass, fine; you have lost little, reading the ravings of a maniac, perhaps.

But what if I am right?

If I am right, you might want to make some of the preparations that I suggest at the close of the next chapter.

4

"Their Destiny Is Their Destruction . . . Their Glory Is Their Shame" (Phil. 3:19)

On SMEAC, Situation, Mission, Execution, Action, and Critique

"We're on the Road to Being History!"

I do not believe it is an act of pessimism or futility or sin to conclude, "We're on the road to being history!" in the United States of America as a patriot of average intelligence. I am not saying "The sky is falling!" or predicting "the end time" or suggesting that Christianity will soon be banished from the planet or North America. I am not advocating that Christians "walk off the playing field," "give up," or "capitulate." Many of those who disagree with the theme/thesis of this book, "We have gone beyond the point of no return," would say, "Fight on!" and "Never, never, never give up" (as they quote Winston Churchill), have, in fact, (1) never, never, never been more than a little concerned about "the direction" we have (as a nation) been going; (2) never, never, never done any more than watch the war from the grandstands; or (3) never, never, never gotten close to the battlefield.

Yes, I am a little defensive of my belief, "We're history!" when I am called a defeatist. I am many things, some of them negative (that I constantly battle with), but one of them is not a "defeatist." My mom and my wife would say that this is partially due to my being stubborn more than anything else. I would not argue with that. But the fact is that there are only a few of us doing hardly anything at all, or anything noteworthy, to hold back the mounting and rising tide that threatens this constitutional democratic republic, in my opinion.

As you know, I am particularly challenged by God to personally respond in a direct manner to the surgical murder of unborn babies in

137

this land, of which there have been probably more than 40 million since our government endorsed the killing in 1973. This thought and abortions continuance with no relief (for the babies) in the future haunt me, and I struggle with a response. What will I say to my grandchildren and their children when they ask, "Grandpa, what did you do when they were killing babies?"

Shall I answer as Hebrew-language writer Judah Pilch did in 1943 on the response of American Jewry to the Nazi Holocaust to the Jews in Europe? "Shall I tell them that I lived in a generation of weaklings and cowards who were not moved or shocked when they heard of thousands, millions, of their brothers and sisters being led to the slaughter, hour by hour, day by day, week by week, month by month, and year by year?"

In Infantry Officers' Training School one summer at Fort Benning, Georgia, we were taught a class in "strategic withdrawal." It was not a "favorite class" for infantry officers or for the human spirit, especially for Christians, who, naturally, want to "conquer and occupy," to "press on," and to drive "to victory." No one wants to quit or to withdraw. And during combat the enemy, we well understood, usually doesn't accept "time-outs" so its opponent can withdraw peacefully, reorganize, or withdraw in order to reorganize.

The class was not called Giving Up, Lessons in Defeatism, or How to Be a Traitor. We understood and were taught that there are times in combat when our intelligence people, G-2, tell us that we are being overrun and on the verge of extinction. At those times the prudent action is to "perform a 180-degree turn, an 'about-face,' and execute a strategic withdrawal." One could say, "It is time to get the hell out of here!"

Why would an army do that? One answer could be to "draw" the enemy into an ambush. But another reason could be to keep from being destroyed in order to regroup and to contest another day in, perhaps, another place. I ask you to consider under what circumstances you would fight a futile battle. I ask you to consider under what circumstances you would "withdraw." Either might be godly action.

I offer four options that I am convinced Christians in America will face, soon. They are: (1) peaceful secession; (2) abandoning the nation; (3) being driven into exile; and (4) civil war. Why might we have to take one or more of these options? I answer, "To preserve Christianity. To keep it from being exterminated."

I have not come to this conclusion lightly, and I do see dangers, risk taking, sacrificing, and suffering ahead for Christians in the U.S. of A. I believe these circumstances are inevitable regardless of the option/s we have to take. I believe my position is based on "truth" in light of the present-day situation and probable "near-future" situations, as well as "realism" of the growing hostility against Christianity in this nation.

On a Sunday morning in May of 1994, Judge Robert Bork was a guest on *Face the Nation*. The Sunday was the first Sunday after Mrs. Paul Jones had accused Pres. Bill Clinton of the crime of "sexual harassment" in 1991, when he was governor of Arkansas and she was a state employee. The *Face the Nation* media panelists were upset about this charge receiving, in their opinions, too much publicity; tabloid trash, they called it (as they sat there talking about it among themselves). Host Bob Shieffer, disgusted with the "sexual harassment" allegation against the president receiving so much publicity, threw up his hands and said to Judge Bork, who had been sitting there quietly, "Where are we?" To which Judge Bork responded, "We're at the end of Western civilization; that's where we are."

Three Considerations, I Repeat

Referring back to the introduction of this book, I repeat the three considerations that I believe must be accepted before a Christian can seriously contemplate the theme/thesis of this book and acknowledge the few options we face that I listed three paragraphs back. I have (contemplated) and accept (the options) both. They are:

1. One must be convinced that we have, indeed, gone beyond the point of no return.
2. One must conclude that we (Christians) need not, nor does God require, remain for the judgment coming to this land and its inhabitants from a vengeful God.
3. One must believe that we are losing more of "our" people, Christians, especially "our" children, to them and their god/s, the god/s of darkness, than we are winning "them" and "their" children to the God of light.

The same month, May of 1994, in which Judge Bork appeared on *Face the Nation*, *Washington Post* columnist David Broder asked: "If everything is so good, then whey do so many people—including the President—feel so bad?''

I believe that I have the answer. I believe we have ''gone beyond the point of no return'' and many people share this possibility. Pessimists are usually realists. Again, I am not talking about ''the end times'' of the world, nor am I predicting the United States of America or the world is going to be swallowed up by an earthquake or burned alive by fire from Heaven or Hell. What I am referring to is my belief that there will be major and radically different changes in the way we are governed and allow ourselves to be governed. Yes, even in this land governed ''by, for, and of the people.''

Let me refer to the verse in Philippians (3:19) that I have chosen part of as the title of this, the last, chapter of this book: *''Their destiny is their destruction, whose god is their appetite, and whose glory is their shame.''*

Sorry, folks, but I think this describes the nation that you and I love.

More about specific forecasts later in this chapter, but for now let me suggest that the changes will be substantial and, for the most part, much worse and will include the increasing denial of basic freedoms that we have enjoyed and taken for granted. Also, I predict much more crime and much more violent crime, as well as hostility toward Christianity in the near future. I believe that some of the crime and violence will be perpetrated by government police and/or military units in order to keep (1) ''law and order'' and (2) ''peace and tranquility.'' Over the past ten years, especially due to my involvement in ''Operation Rescue,'' I have come to realize that these are more important to government than ''truth'' and ''justice.''

As Christians, I believe only a few of us will ''obey God rather than man.'' Some of us, I predict, will feel the heel of the government boot on our necks as our faces are ground into the dusk and into the pavement while many of our ''self-identified'' brothers and sisters are embarrassed by and deny us as ''fellow Christian travelers.''

A ''Declaration of Sovereignty''

I predict that an unrecognizable culture and society is right around the corner that will be extremely hostile to Christianity if it will even ''tolerate'' Christianity at all. Christians will be tolerated as we are today

140

if we will simply "believe" what we want to, but if Christians try to "practice" our Christianity, we will be denied that opportunity, first by "self-identified" Christians (who are anything but), then by society at large. Such "practices" (that I believe we will be denied), I believe, will include such "works" and acts as "charity" and seeing that "justice" is done for the oppressed and tormented, whose existence the "politically correct" crowd will identify or deny.

The problem, dear hearts, is not nor has it ever been government policies or the "works" and acts of the pagans around us. The pagans and pagan governments are and will continue to act as pagans always have acted and ought to be expected to act. The problem has been with us. When we defy God and rebel against His will and His word, He turns us over to our enemies to rule over us, i.e., *"He gave them into the hand of the nation; and those who hated them ruled over them"* (Ps. 106:41).

Governments and government officials who don't know God or refuse to obey God will do what governments and godless government officials have always done when they are not "ministers of God" (which God calls civil governments of all types to be). They have been, are, and will always been about obtaining (1) control; (2) power; and (3) money. Godless governments and government officials are "trinitarians," too. Their threefold gods are control, power, and money rather than the Trinity, the Father, the Son, and the Holy Spirit.

Sadly, many Christians in government don't understand the fact that their first loyalty is supposed to be to God, the "True Trinity," even as they "serve God" as ministers in civil government.

The Bible is so clear, i.e., Isaiah 3, Deuteronomy 28, Leviticus 26, to name only a few references in Scriptures, that God punishes wickedness in His people. Sure, He punishes those who "know Him not," but "judgment begins in the House of the Lord." Need I recite the words of the Lord Jesus Christ in Luke (12:48): *"To whom much is given much is expected . . ."*

Christianity must decide as it has had to decide throughout the ages whom it will serve. We must decide this as Christians in America today and then affirm our choice to the culture/society/nation. *"As for me and my house, we will serve the Lord"* (Josh. 24:15) ought to be our unified affirmation. We must not only believe this and declare this, but we must prove this by our actions, i.e., through acts of charity and justice. Our actions ought to give a clear witness of our willingness to be living sacrifices to Whom our declaration of sovereignty is to. And it must be for His glory, honor, and purpose or our acts of charity and justice will be but, as Paul said, as "filthy rags."

Christianity must "declare the sovereignty" of the Lord Jesus Christ! We must make it even in another "declaration of independence" from the United States of America, if necessary, and I think it will be. We must, first and foremost, covenant, make a "Declaration of Sovereignty," with the Lord, God. We must declare our dependence upon Him and Him alone.

"The Ink Is Fading and There Is Nothing We Can Do about It."

Cal Thomas wrote in a nationally syndicated newspaper column in the spring of 1994 the following:

> On a recent visit to Philadelphia, I took the tour of Independence Hall. As I stood in the room where the Declaration of Independence was signed, the guide displayed a printed copy of the document and asked how many of us had seen the handwritten original in the National Archives. A few of us raised our hands. The guide then urged the rest of us to see it soon because, he said, "The ink is fading and there is nothing anyone can do about it."
>
> What a metaphor for what ails America! The principles, values, and beliefs that once seemed indelibly written on our hearts, minds, and culture are fading and there seems to be little anyone can do to stop it.*

I don't know that, nor do I have reason to presuppose, Cal Thomas shares my belief: "We have gone beyond the point of no return." Neither Cal Thomas nor any other Christian writers commentators, columnists, radio/television personalities, politicians, or pastors, to my knowledge, have declared what I do: (1) "We have lost our biblical basic for self-government and have lost it irrevocably"; and (2) "Christianity, in America, has made an unholy alliance with Caesar, and we shall pay for it, dearly."

Among those nationally known communicators whom I respect and listen to and whose opinions I read include: Cal Thomas, George Wills, Pat Robertson, Jerry Falwell, D. James Kennedy, Gary DeMar, George Grant, Rush Limbaugh, William Buckley, James Dobson, Chuck Colson,

---

*Copyright, 1994, Los Angeles Times. Reprinted by permission.

David McAlvany, Randy Terry, Marlin Maddoux, and Peter Marshall. I believe all these men profess to be Christians, and I believe them all to be. I would, if I were a waging man and I am not, bet "the farm" that most of our great Christian moral/ethical communicators and leaders have at least entertained doubts as to our nation's continued "viability" much further into the future. I'm sure that each of these men listed above as well as many of our political leaders whom I respect and admire, i.e., Dan Quayle, George Bush, Ronald Reagan, Jack Kemp, Pat Buchanan, Robert Dornan, Alan Keyes, Phil Graham, Bob Dole, Trent Lott, and others of the conservative political leaning, whom I believe all to be Christians, have had their doubts as to what our nation will be like in another twenty or thirty years (or less).

I am sure that these Christian leaders (listed in the last paragraph) believe as I do that a constitutional democratic republic is the best form of government. I believe that these men fear what has happened and is happening in the areas of (1) limitless federal government control and power; (2) deficit spending; (3) erosions of heretofore-established civil and constitutional, individual rights; (4) the devaluation of the intrinsic value of human life; (5) the increasing lack of confidence and respect by the electorate in government and its officials; and (6) the lack of clear definitions of "rights" and "wrongs," "good" and "evil."

I do believe that a constitutional democratic republic government is the best form of civil government, but to be sure, without God, that "best" form of government is nothing more than "mob rule." The "mob rule" can either be (1) by a five to four vote of the "not-the-supreme" U.S. Supreme Court; (2) a 51 to 49 percent vote by the entire electorate on federal election day when we elect the president, 100 percent of the members of the U.S. House of Representatives, and 33 percent of the members in the U.S. Senate; or (3) by the ratification of a constitutional amendment (two-thirds of both houses of Congress and 75 percent of the state legislatures), through which we could nullify any or all of the provisions presently within the U.S. Constitution and its amendments. Understand we could legally "do" whatever injustice has ever been done by any government that exist or ever has existed or will exist. We could, for example, legalize, again, human bondage of black folks, we could legally "round up" and exterminate all Jews living within our nation, or we could legally "march" Catholics, homosexuals, Baptists, or those under the age of two into "gas chambers."

143

There is nothing sacred about a constitutional democratic republic. The pure truth is that a despot/dictatorship/military commander type of civil government is the most efficient form of government. ("Who needs an efficient government?" I state.) However, the fact remains that the despot "could rule more godly" than the shared powers of government by our three branches of government in our constitutional democratic republican form of government. Kings in ancient Israel were both "good" and "evil." The same can be said for any form of civil government.

Perhaps what we need is simply another political party. How does the acronym ACCDRA strike you? We know of the IRA, the Irish Republican Army, in Ireland. The ACCDRA party, or political movement, could stand for the American, Christian, Constitutional, Democratic, Republican Army party.

Am I advocating a "theocracy"? I don't think so in the sense we have been lead to believe, but yes, in the sense that a "theocracy" is a society/cultural/civil government in which God rules over all areas of life. A "theocracy" recognizes the separate spheres of government—(1) family; (2) church; and (3) state—and demands that each follows God's laws.

Some believe that a "theocracy" means "the church" runs the civil government. This is not true; church-run civil government is an "ecclesocracy." While I am writing about the various "——cracies," let me mention two others, "democracies" and "aristocracies." Modern society idolizes the idea of "democracy." Most Americans, I believe, believe that the United States of America is a democracy. To be sure, there are certain democratic elements in our constitutional system of government, not that there have always been (as blacks, obviously, could not vote, women could not vote, non–property owners could not vote, and young people could not vote [still can't today under certain ages]).

The First Amendment of the Constitution states that "the people" have the right "to petition the Government for redress of grievances." The petition of the people, however, is only as good as the character of the people. Knowing the depravity of man, our constitutional framers steered clear of a pure democracy; i.e., only landowners could vote, for example.

James Madison, the framer of the Constitution, wrote that democracies are "spectacles of turbulence and contention." And John Winthrop condemned democracy as "the nearest and worst of all forms of government." I am not against democracies, but I do not believe democracies are any more, or any less, sacred before God than any other form of civil government.

An "aristocracy" is ruled by a small privileged class. Not perfect, not even good, but if the ruling class "loves their neighbors as themselves" and as sacrifically as "Christ loves the Church," I submit, the "ruled class" could be blessed, prosperous, and ruled justly. I would compare the "ruled" to "wives and children" in Christian homes under the headship of Christian husbands and fathers, the ruling class, i.e., the "ruled" by godly husbands/fathers. The "ruled" would live in joy, peace, prosperity, and security just as wives and children would under the authority of Christian husbands and fathers.

Each "———cracy" has strong and weak points, as do civil governments ruled by despots, dictators, military commanders, and kings. The most important characteristic of "good" civil government is that the rulers be "ministers of God" to "do good," which would include "punishing evil" and "rewarding good."

Matthew 4:4 reads: *"It is written, man shall not live on bread alone, but on every word that proceeds out of the mouth of God."* Notice, this passage did not begin with: "Pastors shall not live," or, "Christians shall not live" It said, *"Man shall not live on bread alone, but on every word that proceeds out of the mouth of God."*

The "world," including the citizens of the United States of America (who are not Christians), is not going to take this idea kindly. They (non-Christians) are, in fact, hostile to this truth, always have been and always will be. This is the reason we are in the mess that we are in (nationwide and worldwide). Christianity has not been making this message clear to the "world," including the pagans in our midst.

In fact, most Christians do not understand this eternal principle! The Bible is for all people in all places in all generations and will be for eternity! We have lost this guiding precept in America in the name of "tolerance," "diversity," and "multiculturalism." Tolerance, diversity, and multiculturalism have nothing to do with or everything to do with Matthew 4:4, depending on your view of "religion."

The foundation of Christianity is not the Golden Rule, but our Savior, the Savior of the world, Jesus Christ! And contrary to what most people believe—unfortunately, Christians, too—Jesus did not teach tolerance. He is probably the most intolerant man who ever lived! Compassion and understanding, yes; but tolerance, no! Christ accepted no sin! He gladly forgave all sin. He died for our sin but accepted none.

145

Christ said in John 8:11, *"Go and sin no more."* No one is without sin. Homosexuals and heterosexuals, for example, must all be willing to confess their sins and repent of them to receive salvation in Christ. No one is justified to say, "God, I tried, but you'll just have to be tolerant and accept me as I am." Homosexual thoughts and acts are sin, just as heterosexual thoughts and acts, unless in marriage, are sin.

No amount of giving or good deeds will secure salvation. We are saved "to" good works—not "by" them.

Our present president, Bill Clinton, in my opinion, does not understand, nor do many of our "self-identified" Christian lawmakers, judges, sheriffs, policemen, military personnel, dogcatchers, truant officers, and garbage collectors, that they are "ministers" and "servants" of the Most High God, first, foremost, and always.

If this nation/society/culture does not submit to God in all areas of vocation (private and public as well as "church, state, and family," which are interrelated and interdependent), what William Penn, the first governor of Pennsylvania, said will come to pass: "If men will not be governed by God, then they will be ruled by tyrants."

I shall stick with my book theme/thesis: "We have gone beyond the point of no return." I believe we, this nation, will be ruled by tyrants and more and more of our rights and civil liberties will be denied. More about this in a later section of this chapter.

Isaiah 1:23 has come to pass: *"Your rulers are rebels, and companions of thieves. . . . They do not defend the orphan."* I believe God is allowing this to happen, i.e., Job 9:24: *"The nation is given into the hand of the wicked; He covers the faces of its judges. If it is not He, then who is it?"*

A New "Declaration of Independence" Needed via "the Magna Carta," Being "the Holy Scriptures"

I have read, then reread and reread, the United States' Declaration of Independence and England's Magna Carta, which means "great charter," in preparing for the writing of this chapter.

The Declaration of Independence was written by Thomas Jefferson and on July 4, 1776, adopted by the fifty-six members of the Continental Congress. This historic document declared our freedom from British rule. It stated the reasons for the declaring of independence. It is a fantastic declaration that ought to serve as a "guiding light" for us as we ponder our circumstances and destiny today, as it was for those members of the Continental Congress who had looked at the Magna Carta as they contemplated their circumstances and destiny in the 1770s.

The Magna Carta made a declaration against the throne of England on behalf of those who were subject to the crown. The subjects of the government of England, through their barons, blamed the king of England for many abuses and eloquently expressed their demands for certain unalienable human rights that all subjects of the crown ought to be granted, unconditionally. Through the Magna Carta and later the barons, the subjects of the English crown were to proclaimed specific freedoms and liberties.

The Magna Carta was the document the English barons used to force the king of England, King John, in June of 1215, to grant many new rights to the barons which marked a decisive step forward in the development of a constitutional government in England.

The "carta" in Magna Carta means "charter," and the dictionary defines "charter" as a written grant or specified rights made by a government or ruler to a person or persons. God is the "governor" and "ruler" of the universe and the Earth, the land under our feet. He grants us rights and we are responsible to Him for our use of the rights, liberties, and freedoms that He grants us. This is called stewardship.

Through my reasoning after my reading (and rereading) of the Magna Carta and the Declaration of Independence, I concluded that the Holy Bible is the "great charter" for all nations. When a nation has a "history of repeated injuries and usurpations, all having in direct object the establishment of an absolute Tyranny over these States" (see Bill of Indictment of the Declaration of Independence), "it is time for the people to dissolve the control of the nation over them."

As you read the preamble of the Declaration of Independence, think of the conditions of our nation today:

> When in the course of human events, it becomes necessary for one people to dissolve the political bands which have connected them with another, and to assume among the powers of the earth, the separate and equal station to which the Laws of Nature and of Nature's God entitle them, a decent respect to the opinion of mankind requires that they should declare the causes which impel them to the separation.

Now we offer for you to read, I ought to say reread, as I know that you have read it before (probably long, long ago), the Declaration of Rights of the Declaration of Independence:

We hold these truths to be self-evident, that all men are created equal, that they are endowed by their Creator with certain unalienable Rights, that among these are Life, Liberty, and the pursuit of Happiness.

That to secure these Rights, Governments are instituted among Men, deriving their just powers from the consent of the governed, that whenever any Form of Government becomes destructive of these ends, it is the Right of the People to alter or to abolish it, and to institute new Government, laying its foundation on such principles and organizing its power in such form, as to them shall seem most likely to effect their Safety and Happiness. Prudence, indeed, will dictate that Government long established should not be changed for light and transient courses; and accordingly all experiences hath shewn, that mankind are more disposed to suffer, while evils are sufferable, than to right themselves by abolishing the forms to which they are accustomed. But when a long train of abuses and usurpations, pursuing invariably the same Object evinces a design to reduce them under absolute Despotism, it is their right, it is their duty, to throw off such Government, and to provide new Guards for their future security.

I skip over the Bill of Indictment of the Declaration for the sake of space, even though I encourage you to read it. Now I offer for you to read the Statement of Independence:

In every stage of these Oppressions, We have Petitioned for Redress in the most humble of terms: Our repeated Petitions have been answered only by repeated injury. A Prince, whose character is thus marked by every act which may define a Tyrant, is unfit to be the ruler of a free people.

Nor have We been wanting in attention to our British brethren. We have warned them from time to time of attempts by their legislature to extend an unwarrantable jurisdiction over us. We have reminded them of the circumstances of our emigration and settlement here. We have appealed to their native justice and magnanimity, and we have conjured them by the ties of our common kindred to disavow these usurpations, which, would inevitably interrupt our connections and correspondence. They too have been deaf to the voice of justice and of consanguinity. We must, therefore, acquiesce in the necessity, which denounces our Separation, and hold them, as we hold the rest of mankind, Enemies in War, in Peace, Friends.

We, therefore, the Representatives of the United States of America, in General Congress, Assembled, appealing to the Supreme Judge or the world of the rectitude of our intentions, do, in the Name, and by Authority of the good People of these Colonies, solemnly publish and declare, That these United Colonies are, and of Right ought to be Free and Independent States; that they are Absolved from all Allegiance to the British Crown, and that all political connection between them and the State of Great Britain, is and ought to be totally dissolved, and that as Free and Independent States, they have full Power to levy War, Conclude Peace, contract Alliances, establish Commerce, and to do all other Acts and Things which Independent States may of right do.

And for the support of this Declaration, with a firm reliance on the protection of divine Providence, we mutually pledge to each other our Lives, our Fortunes, and our sacred Honor.

When I read and reread the Declaration of Independence recently, there was one simple fact that kept coming to me: the "founding fathers" of the United States of America, while not perfect or sinless, nor was the nation that they "founded" to be, did acknowledge God. And the simple fact is that this nation no longer does.

Consider these phrases in the Declaration of Independence: "Laws of Nature and of Nature's God"; "Endowed by their Creator with unalienable Rights, that among these are Life, Liberty, and the pursuit of Happiness"; "Appealing to the Supreme Judge of the world"; and "With a firm reliance of the protection of divine Providence, we mutually pledge to each other our Lives, our Fortunes, and our sacred Honor."

I trust that you understand that our lawmakers would never craft legislation with those references to God in them today. And if they did, I trust you understand that the federal courts would rule them unconstitutional in a heartbeat. The Declaration of Independence and the Constitution would never be "constitutional" if written today!

Nations do "come from nations." Ours did. Deuteronomy 4:34 states: *"God takes for Himself a nation from within another nation by trials, by signs and wonders, and by war . . ."*

In the next major section of this chapter, I'll give some personal observations on the "state of the nation" today, and in the next major section of this chapter I will make some predictions as to what the condition of the "state of the nation" may soon be. If I had predicted in the 1960s what would be the moral status of the nation and Christianity in the 1990s, you would have laughed at me. I would have been placed in a "nuthouse." It can get worse and we ought to speculate on what that "worse" may be, and we ought to consider what we'll do in the event those predictions come to pass. Read the possible scenarios from the section titled "On Optimism and Pessimism" later in this chapter.

Civil Government Is Not "Neutral" on Morality; It is Promoting, Openly, Today Increased "Hostility" to Morality and Christian Values

We have reached the point in America that "the State" is openly hostile to Christianity. Contrary to what many "self-identified" Christian civil servants are saying: the state is not neutral on matters of morality but is (1) promoting, in all too many cases, open immorality; (2) funding and advocating immorality, such as endorsing personal "choices"; and (3) protecting immorality by the law, which carries and uses a "stick."

"Civil servants," especially those members of what I call the Imperial Congress (the members of the U.S. House of Representatives and the U.S. Senate), are no longer "civil" or "servants." First, they ceased being "servants"; then they ceased being "civil." This is exemplified through their lifestyles (and salaries, perks, and pensions) and their open "theft" (in many cases) of public property, as well as setting themselves "above the law," over and over again: Dan Rostenkowski, Ted Kennedy, Bob Packwood, and Barney Franks. Usually they are unrepentant and unconvicted (when caught) and settle with government prosecutors with little or no punishment.

"The state," civil government, in America today, does not endorse the "separation of Church and State" but endorses and imposes the "separation of Common Sense and State" as well as the "elevation and deification of the civil government" and the "monsterization" of "the Church," if not the elimination of people of faith in the political process and their effect on the culture.

About the only time our government's "uncivil, unservant" politicians have any use whatsoever for "the Church" is when they can "use" "the Church" in appeals for votes. I am specifically referring to the incumbents running for reelection to the "Imperial Congress" and liberal politicians running for president. While the liberal members of the Democratic Party are the worst (at exploiting the misinterpretation of the "separation between church and state") in the misuse of this phrase, conservative (on economic matters) Republicans, in my opinion, are usually guilty of it, too.

150

It has always fascinated me how the Reverend Jesse Jackson can give a "political speech"—excuse me; a sermon—at a black liberal church, register black liberal congregation members onto the voting rolls, then pass the "collection plate" for a political campaign he is in, and not be criticized by the media or liberals as inappropriately "mixing" "the church" and "the state." The same can be said about President "Brother" Bill Clinton's appeal in a white, liberal, "self-identified" Christian church to promote wickedness through government policies and not be accused by the media or liberals of fostering "an incestuous relation between 'the church' and 'the state.' "

Christianity in this nation is not "imposing" morals on anyone! Christianity doesn't own or control armies or police departments, much less jails, prisons, or concentration camps. Christianity has no control over the judicial system.

Christianity must no longer have an incestuous relationship with "the state" but must distance itself from the "rebel church." As Chuck Colson, the renowned social commentator and former "uncivil, unservant" of Watergate fame in the Nixon White House, said, "The American Church is a 'Church in Exile.' " I submit that it is not now the time for homosexuals to "come out" of the closet but time for the real Church, the "Church in Exile," to "come out" of the closet!

The division between the "rebel, compromising church" and the "Church in exile" must end. How? Christianity must separate itself from the pagan "rebel, compromising church" and call the "rebels" what they are. They are pagans! This is why there is so much confusion between those who truly are and/or want to be Christians and those who are totally pagan as to who true Christians are and what real Christianity is.

This confusion involves, first and foremost, inescapably, the issue of biblical authority, the nature and the mission of Christianity, the scope of Christian discipline, and Christianity's relationship with and responsibility to the civil government.

Regarding a favorite subject of mine, "church discipline," I quote from George Grant's book, *Unnatural Affections*: "A Church which affirms Biblical truth but cannot discipline those who reject them has descended to the level of any other human institution and thus cannot win the world for the Gospel!" (See page 12 of *Unnatural Affections*. Grant quotes from the conservative Episcopal Synod of America.)

This "church discipline" must be level, which means it must apply equally, whether it be to a poor young black in Alabama who has stolen a car for a Saturday-night "joy ride" while claiming to be a Christian or to a rich white former governor of Arkansas who is now president of the most powerful military nation the world has ever known and who endorses the legal extermination of preborn children in his country.

Christians and Christianity (the Church) must realize that we are not one step above the animals, but that we are one step below the angels. We must, in Christian love and charity, for the good of sinners as well as for the integrity of Christianity, call the sinner to accountability for his sin. If the sinner does not repent and change what he believes, says, and/or does (the sin), the sinner must be disciplined, which includes expulsion from Christianity. I realize this is difficult in a nation with a church on every block that practically has its own dogma. I'm not saying it is easy, but I am saying it is biblical.

Otherwise, we will be "turned over to the wicked" as we are being today as clearly prophesied in Job 9:24: *"When a land falls into the hands of the wicked, He blindfolds its judges. If it is not He, then who is it?"* God is allowing Christianity to self-destruct and is allowing its promoters (of the destruction) to be done by those who profess to be "among us."

God and Government: Does It Matter?

Are civil governments to acknowledge God as the Creator and Judge of governments as well as individuals? Of course! And our forefathers understood this simply fact!

In the December 1993 edition of *Biblical Worldview,* editor Gary DeMar wrote in an article titled "God and the Constitution: What Difference Does It Make?" the following:

The first legislative act of Pennsylvania, passed at Chester on the seventh of December in 1682, announced the following to be the goal of a true civil government. The preamble recites, that, "Whereas the glory of Almighty God and the good of Mankind, is the reason and end of government, and therefore, government is a venerable Ordinance of God," therefore, it is the purpose of civil government to "establish such laws as shall best preserve true Christian Civil Liberty, in opposition to all Unchristian, Licentious, and unjust practices, (Whereby God may have His due, and

152

Caesar his due, and the people their due), from tyranny and oppression. . . ."*

DeMar continues as he quotes B. F. Morris, author of *The Christian Life and Character of the Civil Institutions of the United States:*

The frame of government which William Penn (first governor of Pennsylvania) completed in 1682 for the government of Pennsylvania was derived from the Bible. He deduced from various passages "the origination and descent of all human power from God; the divine right of government, and that for two ends,—first, to terrify evil doers; secondly, to cherish those who do well," a clear reference to the Apostle Paul's admonition of civil government in Romans 13. "Civil government," he said, "seems to me to be a part of religion itself,"—a thing sacred in its institutions and ends.

DeMar includes in this article these comments concerning William Penn's farewell address to the Pennsylvania colony:

"You are come to a quiet land, and liberty and authority are in your hands. Rule for Him under Whom the princes of this world will one day esteem it their honor to govern in their place." Penn acknowledged biblical principles of delegated human authority (Romans 13). He expected the colonists to follow his pattern. The future of the colony, Penn believed, depended upon it.

Americans and Christianity in America are in crisis because we have failed to recognize what Penn has said and Gary DeMar has added. Christians, we are in a major crisis as a people in this nation. It is a life-and-death struggle for each of us and our posterity as well as a life-and-death struggle for the continuation of Christianity in this land. We must have the right leadership, accountable to Christianity, and the right vision, "for, without a vision, my people perish," before we can get our energies together and reestablish a safe, productive, caring, and sharing America with strong families and strong neighborhoods.

Hopefully and prayerfully we will be able to look back, whether we are still under a government called the United States of America and on

---

*Gary DeMar, Biblical Worldview, Atlanta, Georgia American Vision; Box 724088; Atlanta, GA 31139

this "hallowed ground" called America or not, on these years and wonder how anyone could have been dumb enough and uncaring enough to have let it get this bad.

I do not object to the beautifully written section of the Declaration of Independence, "The Declaration of Rights," which, as stated earlier, follows the preamble. Remember what it says: "We hold these truths to be self-evident, that all men are created equally, that they are endowed by their creator with certain unalienable rights, that among them are Life, Liberty, and the pursuit of Happiness." But does this portray America today or the direction that America is heading, or does this portray America in a time past and are we moving away from this ideal situation?

I would argue that the sentence in the last paragraph from the preamble of the Declaration would be ruled "unconstitutional" today by the U.S. Supreme Court and most Americans would agree with that ruling.

"How can this be?" I ask. One reason is we don't have villains. And without villains, including no "villains" of Christianity, there will be no heroes!

In an army infantry class three decades ago on the subject of combat patrols, I learned an acronym, SMEAC. It has stuck with me these many years, and I have used it not only to plan and execute military maneuvers, but also in business circumstances and personal life decisions.

SMEAC stands for (S) Situation, (M) Mission, (E) Execution, (A) Action, and (C) Critique. As we continue this chapter and write the conclusion of this book, reflect on these five words.

John Knox, answering Mary Queen of Scots' question regarding the legitimacy of resisting and replacing the government, said, "If their princes exceed their bounds, Madam, it is not doubt that they may be resisted, even by force."

On Security and Prosperity

Impediments To Salvation and Holiness

I believe that "security and prosperity," whether real or perceived, are most often major impediments to "salvation and holiness." Security and prosperity are not moral or immoral assets any more than are other words and phrases that we hear "batted" about such as *freedom, liberty, happiness, lifestyle, good health, a big house, tolerance, diversity, multi-culturalism, ownership* (or *not*) *of a weapon, high* (or *low*) *literacy,* or *high* (or *low*) *IQ.*

All of these "assets," as well as many others, are "value-neutral," in and of themselves, and can be used for "good" or for "evil." They can be used mightily for the Lord by one who has accepted God's plan of salvation and is committed to a holy life and for that life to be used by God for His glory, honor, and purpose.

I remember a recent late-Sunday-morning jog past a huge Baptist church in Jackson not far from our home, Broadmoor Baptist Church. It was almost high noon and the day was clear and the sun, bright; however, there was a security guard pacing about in the parking lot to protect the congregation's assets (their cars and whatever belongings might be in the cars). The guard was there because officials of the church thought they did not have "security" enough (without the guard) and because they had "property" (to protect). This was not wrong, but it was sad. That church was fearful, and probably had reason to be, that their "property" needed security protection, as, I assume, the members of the church would need when they left the relative safety of the sanctuary and "moved" toward their cars. That church has announced they are moving from their longtime location in north central Jackson to a place far, far away from downtown Jackson in a new urban location.

Could it be that if that church were far, far move active and relevant in their neighborhood they would not have felt or had the need for a "paid" security guard or to relocate far, far away (even out of the county)?

Much is made about poverty in America, and some even say we have more than ever before. Some would say this poverty is why we must have security guards at "high noon" to patrol our church parking lots on Sunday. I disagree. I live in Mississippi, by every measure of poverty the poorest state in the fifty. The poorest section in this poorest state is in northwest Mississippi, the Mississippi Delta. Do you know what is the number-one health problem in this poorest region in the poorest state in the nation? It is obesity! I do not make light of the conditions of the people in the Mississippi Delta or in other poverty areas of our nation. But neither "poverty" nor "wealth" (nor "opportunity" or the "lack of opportunity") causes people to act morally or immorally.

And I ask these two questions regarding poverty: (1) "Impoverished compared to whom?" and (2) Who defines "impoverished"? "Sin," and nothing else, causes immorality! Not poverty, not affluence, not oppression, and not tyranny (by others).

Regarding the first question in the last paragraph, I would venture to say that the most desperately poor people in the United States would be considered middle-class or upper-middle-class in many areas of the world, e.g., Calcutta, Rwanda, or Mexico City.

I recall that when I was about ten years old (in 1953), my family did not have a television, air conditioning, or annual vacations. We had one car and Coke to drink but one night per week with supper (a real treat!). I can remember when drinking a Coke was a real joy, a definite rarity. I can remember slowly drinking my weekly Coke (in a bottle) and savoring every drop. I did not feel impoverished and was not enraged by this deprivation. I did not "feel led" to steal Cokes from the rich!

Hardly anyone else lived any better than we McMillans lived in Kosciusko. In fact, I think we were in the upper-middle-income bracket. We certainly lived better than most. We McMillans knew there were those who had two cars and drank Coke with every meal, but we did not envy them or feel sorry for ourselves. I do not remember grieving or whining about our condition in life or contemplate stealing from others to "even things up." And I know my father, a product of the Great Depression, did not believe or expect government to play "Robin Hood" for us by taking from others at the point of a gun (sorry, I mean the point of an arrow) or with the threat of imprisonment (for tax cheaters) in order to furnish "stolen goods" for us.

Sen. Patrick Moynihan, Democrat of New York State (the former People's Republic of Mario Cuomo), "coined" the expression: "We have defined deviance down." I hereby "mint" a new "coin" (term): "We have defined poverty up." "Who are 'we'?" you may ask. "And what do you mean by 'defined poverty up'?"

The "who" is our culture, through our elected civil government lawmakers, and the "what" is the level of income and assets a person and/or a family must have before they are "not" considered impoverished (and eligible for "entitlements").

And why would those within the "Washington Beltway" "define poverty up"? Might it not be those three words you have heard in this book, namely, (1) power; (2) control; and (3) money? Our civil government lawmakers and bureaucrats are modern-day "Robin Hoods."

Government can claim anyone "in poverty" when and if they choose to and as long as we elect them to "rob Peter to pay Paul."

Theoretically, one could be "impoverished" (1) if one does not own his own dwelling place or if one's owned dwelling place is valued less than the nation average, which is $125,000 (in 1994); (2) if one can't afford Cokes for every meal, not to mention at ten, two, and four, (3) if one does not own two (or three of four) automobiles (or televisions); (4) if one can't afford a European month-long vacation annually; (5) if one can't afford the health-care plan or health-care insurance plan of his choice; (6) if one can't afford to abort her first (or each) preborn child; or (7) if one can't afford a $25,000 casket for oneself (or for your pet canary). While not logical, these scenarios are possible.

Many in governments in this democratic republic, I submit, "want" people in poverty just as they want people insecure, whining, and utterly hopeless. And remember why: "power, control, and money!" Why? So they can exercise "power" and "control" over you with your (and others') money! The lawmakers and bureaucrats like "riding those 'white horses,' " the horses of "the good guys" (or so they will tell those to whom they are doling out the "goodies"). They probably stole those "white horses" from the U.S. Horse Farm or from the U. S. Congressional Post Office or from the U. S. Congressional Bank. You don't think they would buy their own horses if they could get you to pay for them, do you?

Members of our "Imperial Congress" and most other government bureaucrats enjoy being "all things to all people." (Translate that to mean "giving away to some what they took from others" and then "giving back to others what they took from some.")

One more example or case of (1) security and (2) prosperity, or the lack of either, that I am familiar with is the existence of 32,000 "outstanding warrants" that are not being and cannot be served (translate that to "imprisoned") by the Jackson Police Department due, primarily, to the fact that our jails are already overfilled. I have more than a passing interest in this fact due to the fact that about half of them (it seems, but the number is probably only about ten) are mine (due to my unwillingness to pay fines for convictions for criminal trespass onto the "hallowed" property of the abortion centers in Jackson). While many of these 32,000 outstanding warrants are for misdemeanor convictions or "failures to appear in court" warrants, a number of them are felony warrants. Sleep well, Jacksonians!

Permit me to regress to the point made four paragraphs ago regarding the average home value in the U. S. (in 1994). In July of 1993 Beverly and I sold the home we had lived in for more than a decade. We did so because our four kids had "left the nest" and were off in colleges or in jobs (living away from home). The home we bought (and now live in) is worth $115,000. (That's what we paid for it). That's $10,000 below the national average! Even though our annual earned income is well over six figures, if substandard housing is "fixed" to include all of those who live in homes less than the national average, ought not Beverly and I expect a "handout" from government even though we "chose" to live where we live and to use much of our income for other purposes, such as, for example, charity? Could not this analogy be used, for example, for many who "choose" not to purchase health-care insurance or air-conditioning?

Fishers of Men and Keepers of the Aquarium

I am convinced there is a relationship between what people think society/government owes them and our perception of "security and prosperity." And there is a great correlation between what we think God owes us and what we owe God, i.e., through our love, concern, and care for others whom He put us here to witness and minister to. We must feed their little (and big) bellies and teach them to fish. We are not only to be "fishers or men" but to be "keepers of the aquarium."

"On (to) the Contrary"

It is reasonable to believe that the blessings of "security and prosperity" ought to bring people to God and His people closer to Him and to holy living as a result of "thanksgiving" to Him for "good and glad-tiding." Unfortunately, in the study of human history, it appears that nothing could be further from the case. "Security and prosperity" have not seemed to draw people to Him and kept those who were "self-identified" Christians living holy lifestyles in the days of the biblical history, the Roman Empire, and the British Empire, and it appears that history is repeating itself in the American experiment in self-government.

A nation that has "known" God, received His enormous blessings, and been the recipient of His holy protection, as well as derived the encouragement from God that comes from being willing to be used mightily by God, ought not to stray away from Him during "times of plenty." Having enjoyed this land and its "milk and honey" should cause Christians in America to remain on the "straight and narrow path," but it is clear we have strayed into a dark, foreboding, dangerous swamp.

Romans 8:28 tells us: *"All things work together for good to them that love God."* That includes security and prosperity, insecurity and poverty, good and bad health, employment and unemployment, rainy and drought days, swampland and terra firma, and all other conceivable conditions and circumstances. Our conditions and circumstances as Christians ought not to have an iota to do with our faithfulness to God, individual salvation and personal holy living, or national righteousness and consensus on and definition of evil and good.

Our conditions and circumstances, what we have and what we do not have, should have nothing to do with our fulfillment of God's desire in our lives and our eternal destinies. Yes, to be sure, God sends good and bad things our way and allows good and bad things to happen to us so that we, as individuals, as Christians, and as a nation comprised of Christians and non-Christians, might "grow" toward Him and in our faith and devotion to Him. I believe God draws people and nations to Him through *"all things."* We choose whether to be moral or immoral in "the best of times" and "in the worst of times." The "good" and the "bad" times are either "blessings" or "cursings"; we make them what they are.

God will bless or curse Christians and Christian or pagan nations according to their obedience to Him in the "here and now" (on Earth). Eternal "rewards" and "punishments" are reserved only for individuals, and there are but two categories on Judgment Day, "the redeemed" and "the condemned."

An example of the plight of the United States in this regard is exemplified by a number of our citizens, Christians and pagans, who are not troubled by the repeated allegations of personal "wrong doings," "alleged sins," made against "Brother" Clinton. So many people see no connection between Clinton's probity and the "common good." As Plato demonstrated from the perspective of reason unaided by Divine Revelations, "Public order depends upon private morality."

President "Brother" Bill's approval ratings are often high because he is the very embodiment of relativism. We live in a relativistic age in this nation today. Most people—sadly again, most Christians, too—do not give any thought to the things of God. Most Christians are not attuned to the workings of the Holy Spirit in their lives.

Most of us (Christians) have been taught to believe that politics will provide us with a secular savior, a person who will solve societal problems while affirming us in moral relativism. President Clinton is able to be more of a "Teflon man" than Ronald Reagan ever was because he is a very good representative of this materialistic, relativistic, and amoral age.

"Where Are We?"

"Where are we?" "How bad is it?" "What is the 'situation' and where are we going?" are reasonable questions.

Do you remember the first major heading of this chapter? Go back and refresh your memory. SMEAC. Remember? It stands for Situation, Mission, Execution, Action, and Critique. This is an old infantry guide to planning the next engagement. The first thing the combat infantry officer must do when he receives an order is assess the "situation." All future plans and goals are predicated on the situation you find yourself in as well as the situation of your enemy.

Our "situation": we are in desperate times, and I believe you would not be reading this book, if you did not share this belief (and fear), too.

National "Code Of Behavior"

Let us explore "where we are now," the "situation," and then in the section of this chapter called "On Pessimism and Optimism" let's predict where we might be in the future. I realize it is going to be difficult to come to a consensus as to the moral condition of our culture today, not to mention a consensus as to what the moral condition will be in the future.

We Americans have a major problem today simply coming to a consensus on a "Code of Behavior." I would like to offer one that ought to be a beginning point, ought to be universal and agreed upon by Christian and pagan alike, and should be a reference point to evaluate our nation's condition or "situation" (or to take the nation's temperature). The "Code of Behavior" is: "Treat your neighbor as you would like to be treated; tell the truth; work hard; be thrifty; be temperate; be self-sufficient; love and support your family; nurture and teach your children these values; and care for the needy.'' If we practiced this code, we would need less government, and the family and Christianity would be in "great shape"'!

This simple code is clear and easy to understand and ought to be adopted and practiced by everyone. Nothing could be further from the case! And we confuse which elements of this code ought to be in the domain of (1) the family; (2) the Church; and (3) the civil government, even among Christians. I understand there are some ''crossover'' responsibilities in this code among these three venerable institutions, and I, too, have a hard time making some of those delineations. I believe the responsibilities are far more discernible than we think they are, and I believe the family, the Church, and the civil government have not tried to define their roles (and ''live'' with them).

I try to draw sharp distinctions between God's role for (1) the family; (2) the Church; and (3) the civil government. I do believe: (A) the family ought to be defined as a husband and wife ''open'' to the gift of children; (B) the Church ought to be Christianity; and (C) the civil government ought to be a constitutional, democratic republic. One thing is for certain: the family, the Church, and the civil government are ''all in this together'' and will either ''live'' together or ''die'' separately. Therefore, this ''Earthly Trinity'' ought to cooperate or to at least ''peacefully coexist.'' Surely it is not God's will that the family, the Church, and the civil government be hostile and obtrusive to one another.

I believe that president and ''founding father'' Thomas Jefferson and Alexis de Tocqueville, a French social observer who visited the United States in 1835, would have at least initialed the ''Code of Behavior'' identified above. I believe in the world of Jefferson and de Tocqueville the values enumerated in this code would not have been abstractions but daily realities and necessities. I believe in their world government's role would be minimal.

If we had been in Philadelphia in 1835, we would have found charities feeding the poor, hospitals caring for the sick, and schools educating children—all without government financial support or intrusion. The Quakers of Pennsylvania didn't wait for a government program, grant, or permission to minister to others but, moved by their faith, did all these things on their own and through their individual and collective initiatives,

161

as did the Catholics in Maryland, the Congregationalists in New England, and the Christians in various denominations in New York.

Thoughtful Americans have always understood the role of their faith in America up until recently. They did not wait for "Mr. Smith" or, worse, "Uncle Sam" to do what needed to be done for others and for themselves and their families (immediate and extended). Our forefathers saw this as their responsibility.

This message of the clear link between "faith" and "responsibility" is not and ought not to be thought of as an exclusively American message. It is a message for all humanity.

None would deny that the moral character of this nation is and has been in decline. Logical questions, therefore, to ask are: "Are we beyond the point of no return?"; and/or "What happens to 'us' and our 'kids' as the decline continues?"

I have one more series of questions: "At what point do we break'?"; "What does 'break' mean?"; and "What do we do before or after the 'break' if a 'break' is inevitable?" The Children's Defense Fund, not one of my favorite organizations and one of the most liberal, antifamily, anti-God, wrong-headed solution-minded organizations on Earth, reported the following facts in a December 1992 report:

A Day in the Lives of American Children

- 17,051 women get pregnant, 2,795 of them teenagers and about one-half unmarried;
- 1,106 teenagers have abortions;
- 372 teenagers miscarry;
- 1,295 teenagers give birth (the majority are unmarried);
- 689 babies are born to women who have had inadequate prenatal care;
- 27 children die from poverty;
- 10 children die from gunshot wounds;
- 6 teenagers commit suicide;
- 135,000 children carry guns to schools;
- 7,742 teenagers are sexually active;
- 623 teenagers get syphilis or gonorrhea;
- 211 children are arrested for drug abuse;
- 4,337 children are arrested for drinking and drunken driving;
- 1,512 teenagers drop out of school;

- 1,849 children are abused or neglected;
- 3,288 children are placed in adult jails; and
- 2,989 children's parents are divorced.

Ten Leading Categories to Gauge the Moral Climate of a Nation

Below are listed ten leading categories from which I believe the moral temperature/climate of a nation can be gauged. The "wellness" or "illness" of a nation can be determined by the temperature and through the changes of the temperature, upward or downward. We can predict whether or not the nation, patient, is improving, holding, declining, or near death. There is a "critical" temperature/climate that can be reached, and at a certain ascertainable degree the patient will be expected to cease to exist (as a living organism).

I believe America is on the critical list and likely to expire soon as other great nations and empires have, e.g., the Roman Empire before the invasion of the barbarians, Israel before the Babylonian invasion and captivity in about 600 B.C., the British Empire, czarist Russia, pre–World War II Germany, and now, conceivably, the United States of America. At a certain elevated fever, a patient's brain is so "cooked" that permanent damage is done. Could that be the "state" of our nation's brain? If so, our moral barometer has been so tainted that a revival of "moral consciousness," the recovery of a "moral impulse," is not possible.

I will grant that this "call" is difficult to make, as it was for the inhabitants of the empires and civilizations listed in the last paragraph. But there was a point of "no return" for those civilizations.

As I have emphasized time and time again, on page after page, the word of God will not be indefinitely mocked. At a point that He determines, His judgment will rain down certainly and perhaps swiftly.

I believe and have emphasized time and time again that the Word of God prescribes the roles of (1) the family; (2) the Church; and (3) the civil government. Never, never are any of these institutions to work against the other institutions. These three institutions are not to contradict one another, and, I submit, the duties and responsibilities are far more identifiable than we think they are in this nation in this generation. These three institutions are to work "hand-in-hand" to support one another for the common good.

For example, the civil government is to provide protection from foreign and domestic foes; this is, clearly, its first duty. But it is appropriate for individuals (especially men), families, and groups of families to "bear arms" in order to protect families, the weak, and the vulnerable when the police or the military are not at hand. Another example: It is the role of Christians and Christianity (through its institutions) through individual initiative and institutional charities, to care for the needy. By our doing so, pagans would emulate us, understanding it is a joy and pleasure to serve others and be drawn "nigh" to the Lord of lords.

Here are my ten leading categories to gauge the moral climate/temperature of a nation:

1. *Propagation of Christianity*
2. *Sacredness and Intrinsic Value of Human Life*
3. *Security: Protection from Foreign and Domestic Enemies*
4. *Health Care, Human Services, and Charity*
5. *Environmental Stewardship*
6. *Rights, Liberties, and Freedoms*
7. *Education: Moral Teaching and General Knowledge*
8. *The Economy: Entrepreneurial Opportunity versus the Social/Welfare State*
9. *Human Sexuality: The Challenge to Affirm Historical Christian Teaching*
10. *Relationships: Memories Are Made of Our Experiences with Others*

Now I shall reflect on each of these ten categories with personal observations on the present condition, temperature, of this nation. Always remember that the family, church, and civil government can have a positive or negative effect on one another and in each of these ten categories. The effect depends upon whether or not each of these three institutions is fulfilling God-ordained roles and is not interfering in the domain/s of the other/s.

I believe that in some areas God would have this "Earthly Trinity" cooperate directly, but in other areas unilaterally. These areas are difficult to ascertain, but I feel we must give this matter much more attention. In no case would God have the family, Christianity, or the civil government work against, or undermine, one another.

Neither the family, Church, nor civil government is more important than the other. God has created everything, including these three vital institutions, and I believe it is essential for the family, Church, and civil government to perform properly in order that other organizations, i.e., vocations, charities, recreation, the economy, the arts and entertainment industry, media, education, medicine, transportation, agriculture, and all other conceivable institutions, to operate properly.

I understand there is a great deal of "overlap" in the ten categories on which I shall now comment. This is inevitable and proper. We are not "islands," nor are any of our institutions, therefore, what we do, say, and think affects others. Anyway, here are my thoughts based on more than five decades of living, forty as a Christian, in these ten categories as to where we are today as a nation/society/culture.

1. Propagation of Christianity

Christianity must continue, and it will, somewhere, for human beings to have access to "eternal truths" and to know "the way, the truth, and the life." Civility of civil government toward Christianity is important in order for Christianity and Christians to be what God would have them be and in order for them to "make disciples of nations" and to carry out the role of Christianity and Christians in the areas of social services, charity, and education, which are (all three) areas that I believe the civil government ought to have little or no importance in or authority over.

The U.S. Constitution says that our government is to "establish justice, insure domestic tranquility, provide for the common defense, promote the general welfare, and secure the blessings of liberty to ourselves and our posterity" in order to "form a more perfect Union."

While there is some room for disagreement in each of these areas as to the role of civil government (local, state, and federal) as it relates to the roles of the family and Christianity (and other private organizations and businesses), I am convinced that our civil government/s has/have far exceeded its/their constitutional authority for the purpose of gaining control, power, and money.

I believe, and I repeat, Christianity and individual Christians are not only called to be "fishers of men" but "keepers of the aquarium." We must be ever mindful that "we" are called to be "salt and light" unto the nations by our God and that "they" (the pagans) are called to be "sugar and darkness" unto the nations by their god/s. And eating a candy bar (sugar) in a closet (darkness) is far more "fun" and "easier" to encourage others to join you in doing than putting salt in wounds and eyes on bright, sunny, and hot days before God and everyone else.

What Christianity and Christians do outside of the church buildings and outside of our homes (where the ''meat meets the street'') is going to impact our nation and its inhabitants as well as other nations and their inhabitants. Over the past three decades in this nation, we have disregarded and failed miserably to be what God would have us be, in my opinion, and we see the consequences of this all around us. We have tried, for example, to be ''nicer than Christ.''

Romans 1:18-23 addresses this. It reads,

> For the wrath of God is revealed from Heaven against all ungodliness and unrighteousness of men, who suppress the truth in unrighteousness, because that which is known about God made it evident to them. For, since the creation of the world, His invisible attributes, His eternal power, and His divine nature, have been clearly seen, being understood through what has been made, so that they are without excuse. For even though they knew God, they did not honor Him as God, or give thanks; but they became futile in their speculations, and their foolish heart was darkened. Professing to be wise, they became fools, and exchanged the glory of the incorruptible God for an image in the form of corruptible man.

While I have considered the fact that this nation might have gone or might be on the brink of having gone ''beyond the point of no return'' at other times, I was convinced of it on Election Night in November of 1992. I had voted (by absentee ballot [for Pres. George Bush and Vice Pres. Dan Quayle]) prior to the election, as I was to be imprisoned prior to Election Day at the Hinds County Penal Farm in Raymond, Mississippi, for a couple of months for refusing to pay a fine of several hundred dollars after having been convicted of yet another ''criminal trespass'' charge at an abortion mill in Jackson. I believe that refusing to try to ''rescue the perishing'' is sin (by omission), and I believe that paying fines to a government that sanctions, endorses, and protects (via fines and imprisonments of those who try to stop the killing) the killing industry might just be sin. (I believe it brings glory to God to refuse to pay the fines and to be as much in solidarity/fidelity with the unborn as one can.)

I was not surprised that election night to realize that the American people, including my precious, wealthy mother (I discovered a couple of years later) had elected a draft-dodging, marijuana-smoking, womanizing

166

adulterer, supporter of abortionist, homosexual perversion, homosexual perversions in the military, and women in the combat arms of our armed services, and habitual liar as president.

Character and honesty did not matter anymore to the electorate. The only thing that mattered to many voters was "The Economy, Stupid," or ought we say, "My personal economy and to hell with anything or anyone else"?

I read that election as the "death nail" to the pro-life movement and for the culture and nation that I had served and loved so intently. I became convinced that a major upheaval in the economy (regardless of the comfort Clinton's economic plan [?] put many in) as well as in the social structure was soon to follow. I came to believe that night as I sat in my cell that protection from criminals and the government was not to be provided for long. I became determined to write this book that night. I wanted to pour my heart out to you as to my belief that the judgment of God is kindled against this nation. Nothing has changed my belief from that fretful, sad night (for me) as I sat weeping in my jail cell, that Tuesday night when I felt like Jeremiah, "the Weeping Prophet."

As I give you a few examples of disasters in the area of "the propagation of Christianity," those of you who are old enough to remember the 1950s and early 1960s please reflect on those days and the situation of our culture then. No, they were not perfect, but they were not anything like today in the area of the "propagation of Christianity."

EXAMPLE: On *Focus on the Family*'s radio program broadcast on June 6, 1994, the fiftieth anniversary of D-day, Dr. James Dobson told of the week-earlier decision of the U. S. Supreme Court that the displaying the Ten Commandments in the Cobb County (Georgia) Courthouse was unconstitutional. How can those nine justices make this ruling with the Ten Commandments on display in the U. S. Supreme Court chamber itself?! And, how long will the statue of Moses holding the Ten Commandments rest atop the Hinds County (Jackson, Mississippi) Courthouse?!

EXAMPLE: The problem is not just that government, particularly the federal courts, is hostile to Christianity and is ignoring and rewriting America's Christian heritage (which is clearly, unmistakenly displayed in many historic documents), but the "faithful" are being "unfaithful"! According to Martin Maddoux, as he stated on the January 31, 1994, edition of his nationally syndicated weekday radio program, *Point of View,* there are 53,000 Christians leaving a Christian church each week to either "drop out" of Christianity or to change "churches." (Some "self-identified" Christian churches ought to be abandoned.)

EXAMPLE: A recent Gallup Poll found that "fewer than 10% of Americans are deeply committed Christians," according to the Christians who were interviewed! (Can you imagine telling God on Judgment Day that you were "not deeply committed to Him"?) The poll revealed that "most Christians in America don't know the basic teachings of Christianity and don't act significantly different from non-Christians in their daily lives."

EXAMPLE: A federal judge in Chicago declared that it is "illegal" for public (read: government) schools to have a vacation day on Good Friday any longer. The June 1994 decision said that such a holiday endorsed Christianity as a government observation.

EXAMPLE: Here in Jackson, Mississippi, Wingfield High School principal Bishop Knox was fired in the fall of 1993 for allowing a student-initiated nonsectarian, nonproselytizing prayer to be read over the public address system.

EXAMPLE: "Express Worship, 22 Minutes," advertised the sign outside the First Lutheran Church in Greenwich, New Jersey. The minister said he was attempting a new way to draw people into "the fold"—limiting the services to twenty-two minutes by omitting sermons and sacraments. Rev. John Kleist told the *(Newark) Star Ledger,* "The idea is to bring people to church who do not have a lot of time or desire to attend church."

EXAMPLE: According to a June 10, 1994, story from the *Chicago Tribune,* the Anti-Defamation League of B'nai B'rith released a report charging that grassroots political tactics employed by the "Christian Right" are significant threats to the constitutional separation of church and state. The report targeted campaigns by "Conservative Christians" to restore school prayer, garner government aid for parochial education, oppose gay-rights initiatives, oppose women's right to choose abortion, and "Christianize" public school curricula as examples of what the report described as "a challenge to American democracy and religious freedom."

Folks, we have come a long, long way, or "gone way, way down," from the days in which John Adams said the following in affirming the Christian spiritual roots of America: "Statesmen may plan and speculate for liberty, but it is religion and morality alone which can establish the principles upon which freedom can securely stand."

2. Sacredness and Intrinsic Value of Human Life

Nearly one-half of Americans believe animals are a "lot like human beings" when it comes to emotions and reasoning ability, according to a *Los Angeles Times* poll published in 1994. Half said they object to wearing fur, while slightly more, 54 percent, said they oppose hunting for sport. Forty-seven percent of those polled said, "Animals are just like humans in all the important ways."

This sort of thinking frightens me. What will "we," Americans, think in thirty years or in ten years regarding the distinction between human life and other animal life? If it is "wrong" to shoot animals for sport, then to use the animals for food or other use, can it be right to "fish" for sport or to "pluck" apples to eat? Perhaps soon it will be "wrong" and unthinkable, maybe soon afterward illegal, to "shoot," "fish," or "pluck" for humans to have something to eat or to defend yourself (as with a charging tiger). What about insects, bugs for example, or what about the "emotional reasoning abilities" of a carrot or a tomato plant?

Next to the propagation of Christianity, studied in the precious section of this chapter, I believe the nation's/culture's/society's view of the sacredness and intrinsic value of human life is Christianity's most important challenge. Yes, the consensus view of the family, Church, and civil government's perspective on the value and sacredness of human life is critical, for without people there will be no families, hence no people, and therefore, no Christianity and no civil governments.

Without people and a regard for their intrinsic value "above and beyond" all other lives, there will be no liberties to enjoy or happiness to pursue. From the eternal perspective, potential Christians must believe they are at least a "cut above" the rat, the leaf, the buzzard, and the petunia. I don't see how a person can believe in God unless he believes in Creationism and believes that human beings are a "special creation" of God, made in "His image," for His purpose. Often I have challenged those "self-identified" Christians who devalue my emphasis on the value and sacredness of preborn human live with a call to evangelism only with this sentence: "How can a person be 'born again' unless he is 'born alive' first?"

Prof. Jerome Lejeune, M.D., of Paris, was asked what sort of legislation would protect innocent human beings and what society should do to prevent technological control over human life. He replied, "There is no pluralism as far as crime is concerned. If society cannot decide what is good, then there is no society left.'' He suggested that legislation protect human life from conception, prohibit the donation of human embryos, prohibit surrogate motherhood, and outlaw genetic engineering except for therapeutic reasons.

The family, Church, and civil government must trilaterally agree and act to protect all innocent human beings from the moments of their conceptions until natural death and then pay due respect to their remains after death. If the family, Church, and civil government do not do this, God promises consequences on Earth for individuals and institutions and eternal damnation for individuals who violate this natural law and eternal law.

I refer to Isaiah 1, verses 10-15 and 20 (printed in the introduction) for rereading. There are two other Scripture readings regarding the subject of ''innocent blood'' and ''blood guiltiness'' that I believe to be appropriate here.

Psalms 106:35–41 reads:

They mingled with the nations, and learned their practices, and served their idols, which became a snare to them. They even sacrificed their sons and their daughters to the demons, and shed innocent blood, the blood of their sons and their daughters, whom they sacrificed to the idols of Canaan; and the land was polluted with the blood. Thus they became unclean in their practices, and played the harlot in their deeds. Therefore, the anger of the Lord was kindled against His people, and He abhorred His inheritance. Then He gave them into the hands of the nation; and those who hated them ruled over them.

II Kings 24:1–4 reads:

In his days Nebuchadnezzar, king of Babylon, came up, and Jehoiakim became his servant for three years; then he turned and rebelled against him. And the Lord sent against him bands of Chaldeans, bands of Arameans, bands of Moabites, and bands of Ammonites. So He sent them against Judah to destroy it, according to the word of the Lord, which He had spoken through His servants, the prophets. Surely at the command of the Lord it came upon Judah, to remove them from His sight because of the sins of Manasseh, according to all that he had done, and also for the innocent blood which he shed, for he filled Jerusalem with innocent blood; and the Lord would not forgive.

170

Former Democratic governor of Pennsylvania John Casey, said this regarding the erosion of the sanctity of life as manifested in abortion and criminal violence as he gave the commencement address at the graduation ceremonies at Christendom College on May 14, 1994; "All of these trends, these disturbing, violent, selfish trends—the problems that we call cultural—come together in the issue of abortion.

"Whatever fine gloss we put on it, here is the ultimate act of unreason, of aggression, of exploitation of the weak by the strong. Abortion is the violent act of a violent society. We have spent a generation constructing a world in which unborn babies are but expendable tissue, a make-believe world of death without tears—and now we wonder why our culture is so violent!" he continued. "We permit the casual destruction of the most meaningful thing on earth at the rate of 1.6 million a year in this nation and then wonder why our lives seem to hold so little meaning."

While abortion has taken "center stage" in the "massacre of the innocent," in this book, I believe we will see the wholesale slaughter of the "useless eaters" on the other end of the life spectrum as we value one's "usefulness" and "quality of life," as Hillary's (and other's) advocacy of a health care/socialistic medicine becomes common.

At a prayer breakfast in Washington, D.C. in the spring of 1994, organized by the Clintons to "woo" evangelical church leaders, a guest soloist from the West Indies spoke briefly with the audience before he sang. His career, he said, was dedicated to his mother, who, when she discovered she was pregnant at age sixteen with him, alone and impoverished, chose to have her baby rather than have him aborted. He said his exceptional talent as a singer was a gift from God that would never have been realized if his mother had chosen to abort him. In reaction to this tribute to God's gift of life, Hillary Clinton, a professed Christian and member of the United Methodist Church, rose and left the room.

As I heard of this episode, I was reminded of Psalms 94:4–6: "They pour forth words, they speak arrogantly; all who do wickedness vaunt themselves. They crush Thy people, O Lord, and afflict Thy heritage. They slay the widow and the stranger, and murder the orphans."

Additionally, we must remember the first three verses of this chapter, Psalms 94:1–3; "O Lord, God of vengeance; God of vengeance, shine forth! Rise up, O Judge of the earth; render recompense to the proud. How long shall the wicked prevail, O Lord, how long shall the wicked exult?"

I don't know how long the wicked shall prevail or exult, but it is less time than it was yesterday. And, who are the wicked? Might "they" include those of us who take little or no risks and make little or no sacrifices while shouting and believing that abortion and euthanasia are murder? Might they include those of us who fund, through our taxes, a government that sanctions, endorses, and protects the "shedding of innocent blood"?

Here are a few examples of the present condition as well as some proof that the sacredness and intrinsic value of human life are eroding steadily and quickly in this nation. As I mentioned earlier, remember the value that our culture placed on innocent and, for that matter, guilty human lives a mere thirty years ago. Also, as you read these examples, ask yourself where we might be in another thirty years or in another ten years (or less).

EXAMPLE: There have been approximately 40 million unborn children aborted surgically (and another approximately 150 to 200 million tiny, unborn children aborted chemically since the medical/chemical industry in the United States "invented" human pesticides over the past fifty years [and used them legally]) since the federal government approved of these killings with very little concern or outrage by Christians and Christianity. Few (as a percent of the population) have taken risks or made sacrifices in efforts to "rescue the perishing," while many "self-identified" Christians have participated in the killing, directly and indirectly, and supported by many Christian denominations. Many "self-identified" Christians at the abortion mills have told me, "God will understand and forgive me," and, "God will have to forgive me," as I offered them alternatives to abortions and challenged the sacrifices of their children. What an imposition on the grace of God; what a frightening presumption of the grace of God; what heresy within the camp of Christendom!, I contend.

EXAMPLE: On Sunday, January 30, 1994, Dr. Jack Kevorkian, "the Doctor of Death," spoke during the worship service of the St. Paul Presbyterian Church in Livonia, Michigan, advocating legal and physician-assisted suicide.

EXAMPLE: A woman, Paula, who has been a "clinic escort" (we call them "clinic deathscorts") at the Jackson, Mississippi, abortion centers for years, told me that when she was living in Berkeley, California (you know the place, out there on the "left" coast, the "land of the fruits and the nuts"), she was on the volunteer staff of the Suicide Hot Line Phone Service. I complimented her for having tried to persuade people not to commit suicide, thinking that she was referring to a suicide prevention service. She quickly responded, ''No, Roy, we were not a suicide 'prevention' service. We took 'no' position on suicide. We were for 'individual choice.' We simply provided a friendly voice and tried to help people considering suicide explore their options and to 'fine-tune' their thoughts relating to suicide.'' At least Paula is consistent!

EXAMPLE: On January 7, 1994, a major U.S. newspaper printed a headline which stated that states were in a bind over abortion funding. The story explained that there was much opposition from state Medicaid directors as a result of an order from the White House to use Medicaid funds, which are a combination of state and federal funds, to pay for abortions for poor mothers who are pregnant as a result of having been raped, even though rape was not defined, or as a result of incest.

Though many states have laws or constitutional amendments that prohibit the use of public funds for Medicaid abortions except when fetuses' mothers' lives are endangered, the directors were to disregard their state laws and constitutions. The White House said that its prerogative supersedes the wishes of the citizens of states. The White House commanded that state and federal monies must mingle with the blood of the innocent human beings whose mothers claimed that they became pregnant as a result of rape or incest. (No proof required nor criminal charges need be made.)

At the rate that we are being required to pay for the executions of poor mothers' children via socialized medicine and federal mandates, I predict it will be as ''hazardous to one's health'' to be in a poor mother's womb as in a rich mother's womb.

EXAMPLE: On Monday, May 2, 1994, a jury in Detroit, Michigan, found Dr. Jack Kevorkian ''not guilty'' of killing his patient (or victim) Thomas Hyde, thirty, even though ''Dr. Death'' acknowledged he had killed Hyde and broke Michigan law. Kevorkian was able to use ''jury nullification,'' which Operation Rescue defendants have tried, almost unanimously unsuccessfully, to use for years, and the jury agreed to his defense. In ''jury nullification'' the jury ''judges'' not only the facts of a case on trial but whether the law that the defendant is charged under is fair or just, according to the ''moral code'' of the jury. (Occasionally juries do this in defiance of judges' instructions.)

EXAMPLE: And how about this for judicial consistence! ''An assault on a pregnant woman that killed her non-viable fetus is murder, California's Supreme Court ruled, giving the state the nation's strictest law on fetal murder. The court made it clear it was not referring to abortion'' an article read in the Wednesday, May 18, 1994, edition of the *(Jackson, Mississippi) Clarion-Ledger* titled ''Ruling tightens Fetal Murder Law.

''In a 6–1 decision Monday, the court said the state could punish fetal murder without regard to the viability of the fetus, the crucial point in U.S. Supreme Court ruling on abortion,'' it concluded.

EXAMPLE: On Tuesday, May 3, 1994, a federal judge in Seattle, Washington, ruled the state's law banning doctor-assisted suicide unconstitutional. The judge, Barbara Rothstein, wrote her ruling borrowing language from the U.S. Supreme Court's 1992 abortion-rights case, *Planned Parenthood versus Casey,* which affirmed *Roe versus Wade.*

Judge Rothstein said, ''Like the abortion decision, the decision of a terminally ill person to end his or her life involves the most intimate and personal choices a person can make in a lifetime and constitutes 'a choice central to personal dignity and autonomy.' ''

I ask, ''Why would Judge Rothstein insert the word *terminal* in defining who can legally be assisted in suicide by a physician? Isn't that discrimination against a 'well' person or a sixteen-year-old who failed a math test and wants to 'check out' now? Why would a twenty-year-old girl not be allowed to be assisted in 'checking out' by a physician if she is jilted by her boyfriend?''

What inconsistence and what blatant hypocrisy! Give them time! They'll come around to the error of their ways and allow ''death on demand,'' physician-assisted execution. And you'll probably be handed the bill by the socialized health ''care'' system! Then why wait for people to ''choose'' death? Society will define who to kill, round them up, and pay the terminators.

EXAMPLE: This is frightening! One infamous sign of public confusion (I hope and pray that what you are about to read is simply confusion; if it is not, it is even worse than I think it is—heaven help us!) is a *New York Times*/CBS poll from 1989 that found that 49 percent of those surveyed said they favored keeping abortion legal, but 48 percent said they believed that abortion is ''tantamount to murder.''

John Donne said, ''No man is an island.'' We are all connected. No one dies or is murdered, even if the murder is sanctified by civil government alone. The decisions we are making today not only affect those yet to be conceived, but impact us all, our moms and our dads, our brothers and our sisters, our husbands and our wives, our sons and our daughters, our neighbors, our friends, our schoolmates, our coworkers, those who know God, those who don't know God, our countrymen, and everyone on Earth or everyone who will ever exist on Earth to one degree or another. What "we" do, individually and collectively, good or bad, pleases God or angers God, now and forever.

I ask you and I ask myself, "What is my life? What is your life? We are but as a leaf upon a tree in a forest of eternity. We are but as mist that appears during a half-exhale on a cold, still winter morning—then vanishes. Isaiah said, *'The grass withers and the flowers fall because the breath of the Lord blows upon them. Surely the people are like grass.'* We do serve at His pleasure!"

No wonder the Bible tells us to *"number our days,"* that we might apply our hearts to wisdom, because this is the kind of wisdom God wants us to apply to our twenty-four-hour slices of time.

Pagans and pagan civil governments would love to tell others that there is nothing to fear beyond the grave, that suffering is something to be avoided at all costs—even if it costs them their lives at the hands of people like Jack Kevorkian, George Tiller, and Warren Hearn. (Tiller and Hearn are well-known late-term abortionists living and killing in Wichita and Boulder, respectively.)

But Christians and Christian nations have something to say. It is the Word of God. Logic, yes. Reason, yes, to be sure. But, first, you and I are called to be fools—"fools for Christ." The Word (and will) and presence of God must always give shape to our views, our thoughts, our convictions, our opinions, our arguments, and our lives. Yes, couch your words in the language of Romans when in Rome; season them with salt; flavor them if you will. But don't forget to present them as the Word of God.

EXAMPLE: Dr. James C. Dobson of Focus on the Family endorsed the peaceful acts of civil disobedience at abortion centers in the middle of the grown of Operation Rescue. I was coordinating Operation Rescue in Mississippi at the time and was so pleased with his position at a time when many Christians and Christian leaders were taking pro and con positions on the morality of peacefully breaking the law in efforts to stop abortions and to call attention to the holocaust.

Dobson drew a logical parallel, in my mind, to the illegal acts in Nazi Germany and its occupied territories to rescue Jews and others in the 1930s and 1940s, as well as the illegal activities that rescued slaves in the United States in pre–Civil War days, and the activities of participants in Operation Rescue.

Dobson said that he believed those who were trying to prevent the slaughter of unborn babies, some of whom were being burned to death by salt poison only days before delivery, would one day be honored for "breaking the law" that sanitized the killing. He stated that he believed that these peaceful acts that transcended the law would be justified one day by history.

Dobson's comments were marvelous and a real encouragement to me and others involved in Operation Rescue at the time. I was praying that Dr. Dobson and other well-known, high-profiled Christian leaders would join us by actually physically intervening to stop the killing. Yes, we appreciated their endorsements, but we needed the "bodies," too.

I believe the "season" for Operation Rescue has passed. I believe we have gone beyond the point of no return in restoring moral sanity regarding the killing of the innocent via abortion. This belief was pivotal in my arriving at my position that this nation has gone beyond the point of no return and that we have lost our biblical base for self-government.

I believe U.S. Supreme Court justice Stephen Breyer's answer during his July 1994 Senate confirmation hearing relating to abortion, which was: "It is settled law," was accurate and I believe it helped seal the fate of this nation before God.

Dr. Dobson's statement was excellent, and he was brave to be willing to publish this controversial endorsement of Operation Rescue. However, I believe his perspective will be but a footnote in history, for winners, not losers, write history (and rewrite history) to suit themselves. I believe the epic struggle (not a "battle" [as some would say] because in real "battles" people literally "fight" for their lives and the lives of others until death and only a handful of Christians have really "waged" any real type of war) for the sacredness and intrinsic value of innocent human life, particularly for those awaiting to be born, is over. And now all other innocent human lives are immediately in danger, especially the lives of the elderly and Christians.

EXAMPLE: These words were spoken by Mother Teresa of Calcutta, India, on February 3, 1994, to an audience of 3,000 people at the annual National Prayer Breakfast in Washington, D.C. Pres. "Brother" Bill Clinton, Vice Pres. "Brother" Al Gore, and their wives, "Sisters" Hillary and "Tipper," were present:

Jesus died on the Cross because that is what it took for Him to do good to us—to save us from our selfishness in sin. He gave up everything to do

176

the Father's will—to show us that we too must be willing to give up everything to do God's will—to love one another as He loves each of us. If we are not willing to give whatever it takes to do good to one another, sin is still in us. That is why we, too, must give to each other until it hurts.

It hurt Jesus to love us. We have been created in His image for greater things, to love and to be loved.

I feel that the greatest destroyer of peace today in the world is abortion, because it is a war against the child, a direct killing of the innocent child, murder by the mother herself. And if we accept that a mother can kill even her own child, how can we tell other people not to kill one another?

By abortion, the mother does not learn to love, but kills even her own child to solve her problems. And, by abortion, the father is told that he does not have to take any responsibility at all for the child he has brought into the world. That father is likely to put other women into the same trouble. So abortion just leads to more abortion. Any country that accepts abortion is not teaching its people to love, but to use any violence to get what they want.

(At this point, most of the audience arose in a prolonged standing ovation. The president quickly reached for his water glass while Mrs. Clinton and the Gores sat and stared without expression at Mother Teresa.)

This child is God's gift to the family. In the "Year of the Family" we must bring the child back to the center of our care and concern. This is the only way that our world can survive because our children are the only hope for the future.

I will tell you something beautiful. We are fighting abortion by adoption—by care of the mother and adoption for the baby. We have sent word to the clinics, to the hospitals, and police stations, "Please don't destroy the child; we will take the child." So we always have someone tell the mothers in trouble, "Come, we will take care of you, we will get a home for your child."

Please don't kill the child. I want the child. Please give me the child. I am willing to accept any child who would be aborted and to give that child to a married couple who will love the child and be loved by the child.

The way to plan the family is natural planning, not contraception. In destroying the power of giving life, through contraception, a husband or wife is doing something to self. This turns the attention to self and so destroys the gift of love to him or her. In loving, the husband and wife must turn their attention to each other as happens in natural family planning, and not to self, as happens in contraception. Once that living love is destroyed by contraception, abortion follows very easily.

I also know that there are great problems in the world—that many spouses do not love each other enough to practice natural family planning. We cannot solve all the problems in the world, but let us never bring in the worst problem of all, and that is to destroy love. And this is what happens when we tell people to practice contraception and abortion.

The poor are very great people. They can teach us so many beautiful things. Once one of them came to thank us for teaching her natural family planning and said, ''You people who have practiced chastity, you are the best people to teach natural family planning because it is nothing more than self-control out of love for each other.'' And what this poor person said is very true. And abortion, which often follows from contraception, brings a people to be spiritually poor, and that is the worst of poverty and the most difficult to overcome.

If we remember that God loves us and that we can love others as He loves us, then America can become a sign of peace for the world. From here, a sign of care for the weakest of the weak—the unborn child—must go out to the world. If you become a burning light of justice and peace in the world, then really you will be true to what the founders of this country stood for. God bless you.

That cannot be improved upon by me regarding the sacredness and intrinsic value of innocent human life.

If we are not a ''burning light of justice and peace in the world,'' as Mother Teresa requests of this nation and as we have been in the past, then we will suffer what God promises to wicked nations in Psalms 107:33–34: *''He turneth rivers into a wilderness and the water-springs into dry ground, a fruitful land into bareness for the wickedness of them that dwell therein.''*

3. Security: Protection from Foreign and Domestic Enemies

I believe I have a fair knowledge of security needs from both potential foreign and domestic enemies. First, I have lived for more than one-half of a century. That ought to count for something. Second, I have been involved in national defense as a member of the U.S. Armed Services, both in the reserves (U.S. Army Reserves and Mississippi Army National Guard) and on active duty in the U.S. Army, as an enlisted soldier and, later, as an officer.

178

Third, having been arrested and jailed/imprisoned sixty times for my pro-life activism, which I believe has resulted from "biblical obedience" rather than "civil disobedience," I have a great deal of experience with law enforcement agencies and the judicial system through its employees (police officers, prosecutors, judges, bailiffs, and jail and prison workers) as well as the "enemies" of "the people" (the civil government/culture/ nation), the other inmates.

Having spent months behind bars (in many cities and states), in penal work details, living environments, and "road gangs," I know and am familiar with the thinking of many of those who are incarcerated. I have ministered to them, witnessed to them, helped those who cannot write correspondence with loved ones and others (including their attorneys, judges, probation officers and workers, family members, and friends), and met many of their family members and friends in person on Visitors' Days.

About 99.9 percent of Americans, including about 98 percent of Christians, do not know how hopeless the lives and the perceived futures are of our citizens who are behind bars. Their families "on the outside" often feel imprisoned too, by their depression, poverty, and fear of the future.

Many Americans feel secure from foreign and domestic enemies. I am not one of them. While I understand the present-day euphoria in the wake of the collapse of the Soviet Union and the knowledge that the United States is unparalleled in military might by any other nation, I know that military preparedness as well as national will to fight and to survive can erode in a short period of time.

The preamble of the Constitution of the United States of America obligates the national (federal) government to "provide for the common defense" and to "insure domestic tranquility." Our governments (federal, state, and local) are required by our founding fathers through their written documents to protect us from "foreign and domestic enemies."

Thomas Jefferson said, "The first and only legitimate function of government is to protect the people." While we could debate how far and from whom (or what), we ought to be protected, we ought to all agree that the protection of our lives and property is, clearly, an essential function of governments. No one will pursue happiness or enjoy liberty if dead.

Protection from Foreign Enemies. The United States is, seemingly, a single national, military (and, to a large degree, economic) world power without equal today. But situations do change and change quickly. Think how quickly the United States responded to the Axis military power advantage between December 7, 1941, and V-J (Victory over Japan) Day in 1945. If there is nothing worth dying for, there is nothing worth living for, and as I look around I do not see many who value anything enough to be willing to die for it (or them) in this nation.

As much as we dominate the world militarily, we are not immune to terrorism in the United States from foreign nations and their agents (or sympathizers [bombers of the World Trade Center]), nor are our citizens and their possessions always safe in other countries (that are friendly to the United States from our enemies and their agents). Think of the times major wars have begun due to aggression against U.S. citizens, their properties, or U.S. property outside our borders.

Also, the possibilities of enemy nations' alliances are real and growing and pose a greater threat to world and U.S. peace as the world "shrinks" via rapid transportation, missile development and delivery systems, communication, and economic interdependence. As our national interests, particularly through economic investment, enlarge abroad (for example in Communist China) the threat to our citizens and their property increases. Our national security is greatly exposed as we depend more on foreign nations and their markets and resources, e.g., the petroleum in Kuwait.

Other risks to our personal and national security could become acute, if and when we cede national sovereignty to regional, hemispheric, or world courts, governments, economic compacts, and military alliances, i.e., the United Nations and it "blue-helmeted peace-keeping" force.

I know that the following hypothetical situation is unthinkable and unlikely, but "what if" the world community of nations recognized that abortion was mass murder, which it is, and the United Nations sent its "blue-helmeted peace-keeping" forces to U.S. shores to close down our abortion mills in order to stop our "killing one another"? While many of us would be pleased to see "the cessation of hostilities" on our shores against our innocent "noncombatants" (the unborn), we would have grave misgivings concerning the loss of national sovereignty to international "peace-keeping" armed forces. You think this is "unthinkable"? Go talk to people in lands that have been occupied by Axis, UN, NATO, SEATO, or other military and political alliances this century. Some of these we agree with. Some of these our armed forces participated in, and others we did not.

As we continue our moral and economic decline, the financial support for our armed services (and domestic law enforcement departments) will most likely shrink. We may very well become vulnerable to foreign enemies and saboteurs. Remember that bullies don't attack a kid whom they think they can't lick. They attack the weaklings.

If our military cannot attract competent personnel, some of those who desire a military career and are the "cream of America's youth" will not join our armed services. This could cause a fast loss of our technological advantage as well as the decline in the "esprit de corps," i.e., sense of pride and honor, within the armed services.

It is imperative that a nation with only 3.5 percent of the world's population be far superior to other nations in military technology, rapid deployment, and a balance between its armed services: army, navy, air force, and marines.

I am also concerned, as a veteran of a combat arms element of the armed services, the infantry, that the admission of women into the combat arms branches will weaken, severely, our ability to wage war. We must remember, as Rush Limbaugh points out accurately, "The purpose of war is to kill people and to break things." The inclusion of women into the combat arms branches of our military, as well as known homosexuals into the military, will deter the ability of our armed services to be prepared to achieve their objectives.

Women are not, by nature, inclined to "kill people and break things," and homosexuals will greatly harm the "esprit de corps." We shall "reap what we sow" as these two trends continue.

EXAMPLE: In a nationally syndicated column in May of 1994, Charley Reese of the *Orlando [Florida] Sentinel* said the following on the subject of women in the military in a column titled "Women, Combat Ships Don't Mix":

> Double standards are common. Men are expected to pick up the slack, and it is instant death to the career of any officer who complains about the deficiencies of female enlistees or their fellow officers. Or for that matter, crosses one. And with the yellow petticoat flying from the Pentagon's mast, no fighting officer can expect help or justice from above.
>
> But what can you expect in the last days of the "Great Decline"? Any nation that makes Roseanne Arnold a famous star and Bill Clinton commander-in-chief is surely dumb enough to put women on warships.*

---

*© 1994 King Features Syndicate Inc. Reprinted with special permission of King Features Syndicate.

Protection from Domestic Enemies. I predict that the greatest danger over the next few years for America will be "from within" and will play a major part in our downfall. To protect its citizens, government will curtail many rights and eliminate others. Security systems, armed guards, armed citizens, bars on windows and doors, curfews, no-picket zones ("Gospel free zones" are a reality in many cities near abortion clinics [for pro-lifers only, that is]), "closed-off neighborhoods," and vigilante justice will continue and expand as Americans "hunker down" in our workplaces, neighborhoods, and homes. We may be rightfully afraid to go into certain areas of our cities and to go anywhere after sundown soon.

Our greatest fear may soon not be Saddam Hussein but the enemies "from within the camp." We may soon be more afraid of the kid next door and the government agent dressed in the BATF uniform or the pinstriped suit that we are of the potential of the barbarians coming over the ramparts at our borders. Also, we are realizing that the government, through the law, is no longer capable of protecting us.

These growing fears, I believe, will cause many to face the fact that peaceful secession, abandoning the nation, being driven into exile, or civil war is inevitable. The "being driven into exile" may be done by the criminal element "among us" rather than by those who are in control (or think they are in control) of our society, i.e., our government officials.

EXAMPLE: In Denver, Colorado, during the 1993 Christian season, so many "on-the-street" Santas (at shopping centers and on the streets ringing bells for charity [as well as for the enjoyment of children and everyone else]) were being "mugged" that the Santas were moved into Denver's police precincts for the "safety sake" of the Santas and the parents/kids (who were being mugged also). Before the Santas were "chased" inside, for their own protection, by lawmen, many parents were probably hoping, "wishing," and praying that they and their children would survive their visits to see Santa.

EXAMPLE: The United States of America leads the nations of the world in the percentage of its population behind bars. There are about 1 million of us in prisons; that's 455 of every 100,000 of us. South Africa is next with 311 per 100,000 of its people. A black man's life expectancy in the United States is less than that of the average person in Bangladesh.

The United States leads the world in per capita crime rates in murder, rape, and other violent crimes. Maybe we *are* the "home of the brave" —brave just to stay here. Perhaps we are stupid to be here or to put up with governments that put up with the criminals. For example, 3.2 million of us walking the streets of America have been convicted of felonies and have been released due to time served, early-release, parole, pardon, or escape. Six of ten of these "prior felons" will be back in jail.

EXAMPLE: An example of the ridiculous way in which the criminals in jail are spending their time is the fact that 53,000 civil rights infringement lawsuits are filed in our courts annually by the inmates against us!

Why do we have so much crime? It's not because of the lack of jobs or poverty or illiteracy or "some are rich" while "others are poor" or any other social or economic condition. It is because of sin! To be sure, social and economic conditions exacerbate problems, but many of the so-called reasons for crime are amoral human conditions and have nothing to do with whether a person lives a moral or immoral life.

Our institutions, including families, Christianity, and civil government as well as educational, political, social and charitable organizations, entertainment, and media are doing a disservice when they claim that there are "rights" without "responsibilities." And "responsibilities" include the fact that we are accountable for our actions, not our parents, pastors, brothers and sisters, gang leaders, teachers, lawmakers, sociologists, presidents, or anyone else. The devil doesn't even make us do it. We do it ourselves.

In my humble opinion, we have tried to eliminate, play down, and soothe the consequences of our sinful actions in this nation over the past thirty years. Phrases such as *I had an episode of brief reactive psychosis. I'm suffering from chronic fatigue syndrome,* and *It wasn't my fault; I'm ailing from posttraumatic stress disorder,* as well as the acceptance by many, have furthered the rise in crime and immorality in this land.

EXAMPLE: In California in 1993 there were twenty-six penitentiaries, with a combined operating budget of $1.5 billion. One hundred and thirteen thousand inmates resided in these facilities. The total cost of maintaining each inmate, annually, is $25,000 (more than the annual costs of many fine colleges and universities to which we send our kids).

Chuck Colson, founder/chairman of Prison Fellowship Ministries, know a bit about the criminal justice system as well as the conditions of the hearts of our prison inmates, as he became a devout Christian as a result of his own prison experience due to his involvement in Watergate. Colson says we will continue to build prisons and put people away in them until one-half of us are behind bars unless we address the root cause of crime and violence in our nation.

Colson wrote an op-ed column for a major U.S. newspaper regarding the subject of our failure to curb the exploding escalation of crime in our nation that was published on April 6, 1994.

Colson said that "morals matter" and immorality was the cause of crime and creating a more moral people was the only solution to the dilemma. He noted that violent crime has risen 50 percent in the past thirty years, 56 percent of which time the Republicans had control of the White House. He criticized the Repubicans for criticizing the Democrats for the surge in crime. Colson stated that politicians are incorrect when they advocate the solution to be only more severe punishments for criminals. He pointed out that over the past twenty years we have quadrupled our prison population but haven't dented the crime crisis. He believes we are not looking at the real cause of escalating crime.

He suggested that it is clearer today than ever before that the root cause of crime is moral decay. And he suggested it will continue to get worse as moral decay increases. He stated that he is frightened by the fact that many lawbreakers today are not motivated by the usual human emotions of hatred, greed, and envy. The fact that many of our young criminals commit violent crimes without remorse places the nation at peril. He said that we are witnessing the most terrifying threat to any society: "crime without conscience."

Relying on more than twenty years of work in prisons around the world as well as his experience in jail, where he got to know a good deal about crime and criminals, Colson stated that he is convinced that America's crime crisis will not be resolved by more cops and more cells and more prisoners. He said that the Bible teaches the same thing that he is preaching and that is that law is written "on our hearts." However, he emphasized that consciences must be trained, just as children must be trained to speak a language. He said that the training of children must begin in the family, where parents must teach their children by example and by required and expected behavior. He quoted Aristotle to make his point. Colson said: "Aristotle wrote, 'We become just by the practice of just actions.' "

Citing divorce and dual careers, Colson stated that parents today spend 40 percent less time with their children than their parents spent with them. And he pointed out the fact that the parents' job of teaching their children acceptable moral standards is made more difficult by the loss of public standards of virtue. He said that modern thinkers have rejected the very idea of objective morality, using as examples Darwin, who, according to Colson, reduced morality to animal instincts; Freud, who, according to Colson, considered moral restraint the source of neurosis; and Marx, who, according to Colson, reduced morality to class self-interest.

Colson believes, according to the op-ed opinion, that under this onslaught commitment to a common morality has crumbled. Modern society, he said, seems determined to scrub the public square clean of even the symbols of our religious heritage, historically the source of moral standards for any culture. He criticized public education, particularly, by claiming that public school teachers are trained to withhold moral judgment in class discussions. He said that when children are raised in this atmosphere, their moral senses will remain unshaped and untutored. Like animals, Colson urged, our children cannot draw moral distinctions.

Colson said that our culture has bred a generation without consciences. He said that until we are willing to deal with the moral crisis head on in our homes, in our schools, and in the public square, we will hear politicians blaming one another, spending more more, building more jails, and locking more people away as the crisis worsens.

He stated that it will become so bad that it will not only be the criminals who are in prison, but we, who remain standing, will be huddled behind our barred doors and windows in our homes.

Amen, Brother Colson. Amen.

4. Health Care, Human Services, and Charity

"We have the power to shape the civilization we want," said Pres. Lyndon Baines Johnson on May 22, 1964, as he spoke at the graduating exercises at the University of Michigan. While the goals of the Great Society were honorable and were centered on improving our society in the areas of rebuilding urban America (feeding, clothing, housing, healing, etc.), combating pollution and other environmental problems, bettering government education, and putting an end to the "cycle of poverty," the results have, by and large, been disastrous.

After three decades of "meddling" in the affairs of others ("the taking from some" for the "perceived benefit of others"), the poverty rate has remained largely the same, while the problems of family breakup, illegitimate births, welfare dependency, an eroding work ethic, and crime all have gotten dramatically worse.

And government did not give us all this "glory" for free; the cost was about $5,000,000,000,000 (did I court the 0's correctly?—yes, twelve, as in trillion), which breaks down to about $50,000 per household. It is interesting to me that this is about what our national debt is today. I wonder how many households could pay their "fair share," fifty grand, if the "bill collector" came today?

In a *World Magazine* article written by Larry Burkett titled "The Not-So-Great Society" published on May 21, 1994, Michael Novak, the 1994 recipient of the Templeton Prize for Progress in Religion, put it this way: "Government has fought a 30-year war to 'improve' our social life—regarding the stability of the family, the condition of the children, the public vulnerability of all of us to violent crime—only to make it worse through the unintentional consequences of government policies."

While civil government has a role to play in health care, human services, and charity, I reject the policies of governments in the United States over the past half-century in this area. Governments can assist private enterprises, charitable organizations, and individuals in identifying problems and the needy and "promoting the general welfare," but I believe it is not within the divine province of civil government to be the primary agent of health care, human services, and charity.

Food, housing, clothing, health care, and education (which are today considered universal "inalienable, constitutional rights" by most civil government employees and the recipients) are, obviously, desired by everyone. But so are transportation such as private automobiles (and auto insurance), air-conditioning, health club memberships, health-care insurance, radios and televisions (and VCRs), indoor saunas, annual European vacations, and life and burial insurance.

But a question to ask is: "Who defines 'universal' government-guaranteed tangible assets (and services) and who is requires to provide these benefits, 'entitlements' for whom?" This is, in a nutshell, the problem! I have stated before: "Morality, like art, begins with the drawing of a line." One could substitute "charity" (or "entitlements") in the place of "morality" and make this statement: "Charity, like art, begins with the drawing of a line."

I try to be a purist, to see things in "blacks" and "whites," to believe there are "rights" and "wrongs," "evils" and "righteousness." I know this is difficult, but it must be considered. I have come to the certain and irrevocable conclusion that civil government ought not to be in the health care, human services, and charity business.

Christ said to "us," his followers (Christians), "Feed my sheep." He said that whenever we failed to care for others in need who could not care for themselves, it was as if we failed to minister to Him.

A Catholic priest here in Jackson whom I love, respect, and enjoy being with said, "Our Christian's perspective ought to be, 'To do unto others as we would have them do unto us," and he believes this "morality mandate" ought to be forced on everyone (Christian and pagan alike) in our nation through the civil government. I disagree with him. I believe this is "legislating morality" wrongly. I believe this is "imposing our morality wrongly on others." I believe this advocacy is tantamount to saying to the citizens of this nation, "Do for others as we would have you do for them, and if you don't agree to this, we will take from you and give a part of what you have to others. If you don't allow us to take from you via confiscatory government taxes, we will put you in jail."

This is not charity! When Robin Hood stole from some to give to others, the victims of Robin Hood's raids were not being charitable; they were being "mugged." And Robin Hood was not being charitable. You can only be charitable when you give what you own to another freely!

It appears logical to me that Christ wants us to "give" freely to others even to the point that it "hurts" so that the recipients of our "sacrificial giving" will know that we truly love them in order to "pave" the way for the story of redemption. Often, in order to "share" with others our knowledge of His saving grace and eternal salvation with Him in Heaven, we must "have the ear" of the "losts." This can be done through "doing for others what we would have them do for us" in the area of physical need and emotional support, whether in the area of charity or seeing that justice is done.

The principles of God's Word guided the decision on which this nation built its foundation. Alexis de Tocqueville, the noted philosopher from Europe in the nineteenth century that I have quoted before, visited America in her infancy to find the secret of her greatness. As he traveled from town to town, he spoke with the people. He examined our young national government, our schools, our centers of private enterprise, but he could not find in them the reason for America's greatness. Not until he visited our churches and witnessed the pulpits of this land ("aflame with righteousness," he said) did he find the secret of our greatness. He returned to France and summarized his findings: "America is great because America is good; and if America ever ceases to be good, then will America cease to be great." How simple! How true! How obvious!

De Tocqueville, a student of governments, located the "soft underbelly," the Achilles' heel, of a democracy and understood that if the people in a democracy cannot control themselves, they will self-destruct, just as many other forms of government can and have. Our "soft underbelly" is the "taking from the public largess" by the citizens through representative government. We have perfected this by even "taking" what is not there and leaving an "I owe you" for our posterity to pay. That "debt" is now $5 trillion.

And now back to de Tocqueville. He worried sixteen decades ago that American democracy might ultimately vest moral authority wholly in the erratic, self-centered, manipulable moods of the populace. "It might be foreseen," he wrote, "that faith in public opinion will become for them a species of religion and the majority its ministering prophet."

That "species of religion," too, should give lovers of liberty anxiety attacks.

I see little evidence that there is a change of heart or mind by the citizens of America in the area of who is responsible for providing health care, human services, and charity to those in need (and to identify those in need). I believe the "die is cast" and that this huge economic welfare state and our social problems will inexorably lead to economic, social, and violent upheaval and chaos.

On this critical matter, I believe we have gone beyond the point of no return. The "house of cards" will soon come tumbling down!

5. Environmental Stewardship

Beware: the "green" menace (evil empire) may replace the "red" menace (evil empire).

Now that "communism is dead" (?), according to many, as a threat to world peace, freedom, and liberty, a case could be made that the "Earth First 'conquerors' " and the "animal rights 'conquistadors' " may take center stage as the next national and international threat to peace, freedom, and liberty as well as loss of common sense.

Christians and Christianity ought to take the leadership, nationally and internationally, in the preservation and stewardship of the environment. After all, God tells us to *"subdue the earth and have dominion over it"* as well as to *"be fruitful and multiply"* (Gen. 1).

188

While governments have a mission in coordinating and encouraging the protection and preservation of the environment and preventing the unwarranted pollution of the land below and the air above, as well as practicing the stewardship on public-owned lands, people and their privately owned institutions must perform the majority of environmental stewardship. And this stewardship includes the caring for and protection of animals, minerals, and vegetables.

Individuals, families (which are made of individuals [no surprise here, right?]), and groups of individuals and families, i.e., businesses, institutions, cooperatives, etc.., who "own" things are at least as likely as civil government to protect, conserve, and expand what is "good" and to eliminate that which is "bad" in the areas of natural resources.

Due to my concentrated efforts in the pro-life movement, especially on the protection and conversation of human fetuses, I have been "branded" by many as a "single-issue" person. I don't deny this, but that is not inconsistent with the protection and conservation as well as the proper use of natural resources (air, minerals, vegetables, and animals).

I am "for" farming. Not just because I admire and like farmers, but because farmers feed human beings. I am "for" medical caregivers. Not just because I admire and like health-care providers but because they care for human beings. I am "for" home builders. Not just because I admire and like home builders and their suppliers, but because they house human beings. I am "for" fishers, hunters, and dairy and beef cattle ranchers. Not just because I admire and like them, but because they feed human beings. And I could go on and on and include every profession, for every legitimate profession serves human beings.

When individuals and their institutions own and make their living "off the land" (and sea and air) through mining, fishing, harvesting, raising, producing, etc., their best interests are served, as are the best interests of those they are engaged in commerce with, through their godly stewardship of natural resources. God entrusts each of us with natural resources, including our bodies, minds, and souls.

While the caring for and conservation of what is "good" is critical, Christians must remember that there is "no future," eternally speaking, for minerals, vegetables, vapors (air [elements]), and animals other than human beings. (I realize the last comment in the last sentence is going to come as a "blow" to some of you when you realize that your pets are not going to be in Heaven with you.) These points are where we and the secularists, atheists, tree huggers, and Earth Firsters part company again. Attention to the "other side of the grave" ("across the Rubicon") is where we must give our first loyalty. The pagans will not give it any validity.

For example, one infamous sign of public confusion is indicated, as I point out again, in a *New York Times*/CBS poll from 1989 which found that 49 percent of those surveyed said they favored "keeping abortion legal," while 48 percent said abortion was "tantamount to murder." I wonder if these 49 percent and 48 percent of the population were to be polled would they call killing a beef cow or cutting an ear of corn off its stalk for human consumption murder? I don't believe I really want to know their answers!

Somewhere deep in the human conscience of all of us is a glimpse of the eternal, the unmistakable humanity of the unborn child. This truth is so fundamental that denying it leads even the best of minds to the most absurd conclusion. Take the late William O. Douglas, a former member of the U.S. Supreme Court. In the 1973 *Roe versus Wade* case, the opinion on which he wrote, which gave us legalized abortion in all fifty states during all nine months of pregnancy. Douglas agreed with the majority that unborn human beings had no right to continued life. Just the year before, in *Sierra Club versus Morton,* Douglas conferred legal rights of continued life to "valleys, alpine meadows, rivers, lakes, estuaries, beaches, ridges, groves of trees, swamplands, and even the air that feels the destructive pressures of modern technology and modern life." And Christians believe I am exaggerating when I say we are in deep, deep trouble.

Most arguments used to defend the killing the unborn babies make sense only if you place the human being as no more than an equal to everything else on Earth, even the air.

I understand from reading an article in a reliable periodical that there has been a loss of 30,000 jobs in the logging industry due to environmental efforts to "save" the spotted owl.

The story went on to say that the Endangered Species Act, which directly caused the loss of these jobs, was a "regulatory straitjacket" for the timber industry. It went on to suggest that loggers, who carry the image of rugged individualist and are the "salt-of-the-earth" husbands and fathers in most cases are out looking for work in distant places while their wives are away from home working to support their families and their children are in day care centers. Many of their families are being split apart, figuratively and physically, which is a change for these men, who are usually men married to females, participants in their children's rearing, and financially responsible for their families' incomes.

Many other families are being affected through the loss of jobs in the ranching, farming, and mining industries because of outrageous environmental regulations at the state and federal levels. Families and their dreams are being shattered by these burdensome regulations as fathers are losing their jobs unjustly.

The spotted owl is only the environmental extremists' weapon of choice of the moment. If the spotted owl is "rescued," they most surely have a forest floor millipede in the wings to trot out onstage next.

In reality, this is a religious fight! Don't forget that.

Environmental stewardship is not incompatible with human existence and progress. But let's remember that the "single issue" is humankind, its protection, advancement, and care for AND its eternal existence.

6. Rights, Liberties, and Freedoms

Ought we to have the "civil rights" to do "civil wrongs"? Do individuals in a "civilized" society have the "liberty" to do that which will inevitably "enslave" themselves and others? Will not unlimited "freedoms," guaranteed and perhaps paid for by the civil government, crush a "civilized" society?

And who defines which rights, including religious rights, liberties, and freedoms (as all perceived "rights, liberties, and freedoms" are ultimately, in the value nature, "religious") are inalienable? And who provides which "rights, liberties, and freedoms" for those who cannot afford them? And ought the consequences of exercised "rights, liberties, and freedoms" be curbed, treated, or eliminated by civil government? Who ought to finance the curbing, treating, and eliminating of the consequences of exercised "rights, liberties, and freedoms"? Are we sure that the curbing, treating, and eliminating of the negative consequences of exercised "rights, liberties, and freedoms" will not exacerbate our societal problems and, possibly, be a leading factor in the collapse of a civilization?

Who is to decide which "rights, liberties, and freedoms" are evil (sin), corrupting to individuals and to society, and counterproductive for individuals and for the whole of the community? Is this (the last question) even a legitimate question to ask? What "rights, liberties, and freedoms" ought to be declared illegal and what punishments are doled out to those who exercise them? Ought we to leave the belief in and exercise of all "rights, liberties, and freedoms" to personal, moral, legal "choice" and allow only personal, moral restraint to control individual or group behavior?

All laws restrict individual or group "rights, liberties, and freedoms" and all laws are a reflection of individuals' (such as kings', potentates,' or military dictators') or a group of individuals' (such as eligible voters in a democracy's, members of a politburo's, or baron's) conceptions of morality. And, I repeat, "Morality, like art, begins with the drawing of a line." We could say, "Law, like art, begins with the drawing of a line." Will there be "drawn lines"; will there be "drawn lines" here or there; or will there be "drawn back" or "erased" lines that had been drawn by past generations? Will we "erase" lines "drawn by God" that He drew for the purpose of the existence of orderly, compassionate, and just civilizations. And will we allow Him to bless those who "keep His commandments" as He promises (*"Righteousness exalts a nation, but sin is a disgrace to any people"* [Prov. 14:34])?

God's sword is two-edged. He promises to "pull down" nations that rebel against Him. *"At one moment I might speak concerning a nation or concerning a kingdom to uproot, to pull down, or to destroy it; if that nation against which I have spoken turns from its evil, I will relent concerning the calamity I plan to bring it. Or at another moment I might speak concerning a nation or concerning a kingdom to build up or to plant it; if it does evil in my sight by not obeying. My voice, then I will think better of the good with which I had promised to bless it"* (Jer. 18:7–10).

Often it is said, "Your rights end where another's nose begins." I dispute that. I say, "All 'rights, liberties, and freedoms' affect everyone else's 'rights, liberties, and freedoms' to a small or large degree."

Listed alphabetically below are a number of "rights, liberties, and freedoms" for you to read and reflect upon. There are comments made after some of the "rights, liberties, and freedoms" after the "rights, liberties, and freedoms" have been defined. All of these "rights, liberties, and freedoms" are "exercised" routinely in this nation and in other nations. Some are legal; some aren't; some are safe; some aren't; some are healthy; some aren't; some are fun; some aren't; some make people feel good; others don't; some are sociably accepted; some aren't; some are expensive; others aren't; but all affect others, specifically, and society, in general.

I have listed these "rights, liberties, and freedoms" alphabetically so that you will, at random, be shocked at the immediate comparisons. For example, "Auto Insurance" sits beside "Ax Murder" and "Sodomy" beside "Speech." Which do you accept as "amoral," "immoral," or "moral"? Which of these do you believe ought to be "legal" or "illegal"? Which of the "legal" (determined as legal by you) rights, liberties, and freedoms do you believe ought to be "provided for" for those unfortunate enough to not be able to engage in due to their financial constraints?

The hypothetical list is: Adultery; Arms Ownership (free for those who can't afford to buy their own, including rival street gangs [?]); Ax Murder; Child Molestation (procuring of children for "would-be"/ "wanta-be" child molesters who don't have a child/children of their own to molest [?]); Cigarette Smoking (free for those who can't afford their own, not to mention are unable to pay the taxes [?]); Cocaine Smoking or Snorting (free for those who are not able to work and buy their own due to their cocaine habits [?]); Clothing (free [?]); Condoms (free and for all ages [?]); Dancing; Dancing Topless; Dancing Totally Nude; Day and Night Care for Moms and Dads during "Moms' Morning Out" and "Moms' and Dads' Nights out" (free [?]); Day Care and Entertainment for Senior Citizens (free [?]); Day Care for Kids (free [?]); Drinking and Driving; Due Process and Fair Trials; Dueling; Food (free [?]); Fornication (procuring of partners for those "would-be"/"wanta-be" fornicators who don't have "partners" [?]); Free Garbage Collection; Free Burial Service; Free Burial Service Insurance; Free Needles for Drug Addicts; Free Print Speech (free printing presses for those who feel they are discriminated against because they can't afford to have enough "free print speech" [?]); Free Verbal Speech (free radio stations and/or programs for those who feel discriminated against because they can't afford to have enough "free verbal speech" [?]); Gambling (free "chips" for poor gamblers [?]); Health Care (free [?]); Health-Care Insurance (free [?]); Housing (free [?]); Husband (or Wife) Abuse (procuring of husbands for women [or wives for husbands] who have not found their own spouses to abuse [?]); Inheritance (what little is left after today's inheritance taxes); Justifiable Homicide (to "defend" oneself or family, a neighbor, or a stranger [sorry, those who feel "justifiable" in defending your unborn neighbor/stranger, as this is not acceptable by 99.999999 percent of society and by 99.99 percent of Christianity]); Lying; Killing and Eating of Black Bears and the Wearing of Black Bear Furs; Killing and Eating of "Unhatched" and "Hatched" Chickens; Killing and Eating of "Unhatched" and "Hatched" Eagles (now legal!); Killing Human (Born) Fetuses (free for those who can't afford to hire the "exterminator"/abortionist [?]); Killing Human Fetuses; Killing of a Panther Who Is Attacking You; Killing of Roaches; Killing of Senior Citizens Who Don't Want To Be Killed; Killing of Senior Citizens Who Want to Be Killed; Killing of Senior Citizens Who We Don't Know Whether They Want to Be Killed or Not; Marijuana Smoking (Free [?]); Murdering and Eating of Ears of Corn; Pornography (free [?]); Rape (procuring of a victim when the "would-be"/"wanta-be" rapist doesn't have an unwilling sexual victim [?]); Religious Freedom; Senior Citizen Abuse and Neglect (by children [?] or by government [?]); Slavery (free, i.e., "government funding as a constitutional right for poor plantation owners" [?]); Theft; Transportation (free [?]); Voting Rights; Wife and/or Girlfriend Abuse and Neglect (procuring of wives and girlfriends for those men who, by no fault of their own, don't have a wife or girlfriend [?]); and on ad nauseam. The list is endless. Make your own. Use your imagination.

It is necessary that the biblical perspective of "promoting the good" and "discouraging the evil" be center stage in the establishing of "rights, liberties, and freedoms" in a nation/society/culture. Many evil acts (example: murder [punished with capital punishment]) that are not for the "common good" ought to be legislated against, and those who defy the law ought to be punished. And good acts (example: donating to charities [favorable tax treatment]) that promote the "common good" ought to be encouraged and rewarded by the civil government.

Christians and Christianity, acting through the civil government, as well as their "good works," ought to support the good and condemn the evil while carrying out missions of mercy and charity for those who need help and are unable to help themselves, whether the recipients became "needy" due to natural acts or as consequences of their acts.

Some acts that are not good for individuals and society ought to be legal, but government ought to never encourage bad behavior by subsidizing the immortal acts. Government ought to never "take away the consequences of sin" of the sinful/hurtful legal acts of its citizens. Christians and Christianity ought to attempt to repair the damage done by sinful acts by individuals, but not to take away the consequences prior to the sinful act. (Otherwise they become part of the sinful act.) Christians and Christianity have a moral responsibility to condemn sinful acts prior to the commission of sinful acts by individuals.

About twenty-five hundred new federal laws and regulations are enacted annually. Tens of thousands more come from our state and local governments annually. Some are good; some aren't; some are needed; some aren't. But each one nibbles away at our "rights, liberties, and freedoms." We are losing many "rights, liberties, and freedoms" via governments' unwarranted and illegal acts, in my opinion. (And I believe it will continue and escalate.) For example, Operation Rescue participants ought to be rewarded (banquets in their honors by Christianity and by civil government), not singled out for special treatment (federal felonies for what ought to be local trespass ordinances) for "doing for others (the unborn) what we would want others to do for us."

In the 1950s, a positive personal attribute was "discriminating taste." Those who practiced appropriate "discrimination" today in many instances are called "hate mongers," or worse. In the 1990s, if one believes that fornication, adultery, and sodomy, for example, are "hurtful" to the individuals who are committing these sins, which, I believe ought to be criminal acts, as well as to the culture at large in many ways, not the least of which is the undermining of our nation's moral vision and the national economy, they are called "bigots" and narrow-minded, hate-filled, right-wing, fundamentalist, extremist, and radical Christians. I stand guilty.

Today, anyone who says, "Whoa, let's wait a minute! Let's hold up the 'throwing money' at the decay in our society and reconsider, based on some of our concepts of Christian, traditional, biblical values, and consider whether we are solving the problems or making them worse. We would like some input. After all, some of the money being used is our tax money. We believe that our values ought to be considered; we believe that Christian, moral principles work," will be bashed and called intolerant and out-of-date and vilified (not to mention called dangerous), then denied a voice in the discourse even though the opposition welcomes our tax monies for their liberal purposes, which have proven an utter disaster.

As Mort Kondracke wrote in *Roll Call* magazine, "Liberals obviously didn't intend for the abandonment of traditional values to lead to an AIDS epidemic, rampant teenage pregnancies, the destruction of the

195

two-parent family, an explosion of child abuse and child poverty, increasing coarseness in popular culture and horrid street violence. But it has.''

But the liberals welcome voices of reason such as Hugh Hefner, founder of the *Playboy* pornography empire, and statements (from Hefner) such as: "Playboy had more to do than any other company with Roe v. Wade. We supplied the money for those early cases and actually wrote the amicus curiae brief for Roe.''

And liberals even sometimes get things right with their perspective of the "legislation of morality.'' Liberal, *Roe versus Wade*'s affirming Thurgood Marshall, the late U.S. Supreme Court justice, made this statement in 1966, when he was solicitor general of the United States: "Laws not only provide concrete benefits, but can even change the hearts of men and women for good or evil. The simple fact is that most people will obey the law and some, at least, will be converted by it.'' Thurgood, tell that to the millions and millions of aborted babies, from wherever you are!

Yes, the "choice'' is ours. We can teach and instruct through the law and moral persuasion, or we can erase any standard of right and wrong. We have freedoms to choose "life or death, blessings or cursings'' as individuals and as nations. We can choose to love life, to help others, and to honor and obey God, or we can choose to hate life, destroy others, and rebel against and disobey God. God has given individuals and nations these choices.

EXAMPLE: In 1992, 1,624,500 Americans were arrested for DWI (Drinking While Intoxicated). The result of this "personal choice'' was the death of 17,699 human beings, many of whom were innocent victims who were at the wrong place at the wrong time. In 1992, many people "chose'' to commit murder. The result of this choice was that 23,760 innocent human beings died. In 1992, approximately 1.5 million pregnant mothers, along with the support of their boyfriends, husbands, parents, grandparents, and others, "chose'' to legally put to death their unborn children.

Soon, it is logical to me, we will hear a hue and cry from the DWIers and the illegal murderers, if they are unfortunate enough to be apprehended, convicted, and sentenced, that they not be punished for their "choices'' either. And they will surely all have extenuating circumstances that they believe ought to mitigate against their culpability.

A phenomenon in Mississippi that many of us regret this decade has been the legalization and rise of a huge casino gambling industry. Gambling casino ships are everywhere, and the state is "reaping'' a "windfall profit," via taxation as well as many new jobs, by "virtue" of this new "growth" industry. But, I believe, Mississippi will "reap what is sown" in years to come, and it will not be a "good harvest" for the state and its people, I predict.

EXAMPLE: Thirty-seven states have legal gambling. Many of the states own the gambling business, and these states actively promote and advertise gambling in order to "make losers" of their citizens. Why? Government's goal is "power," "control," and "money."

Once linked to organized crime and considered immoral by almost everyone, various forms of gambling have edged into the mainstream, quietly accepted by churches and patronized by Christians. Predictions are that by the year 2000 every American will be within a three- or four-hour drive of a casino. Yes, this is another case of government exploiting its subjects by appealing to their dark sides for the "best interest" of the economy (which it is not).

EXAMPLE: The political debate leading up to the passage of the Brady Bill was about "not infringing upon 'sportsmen's rights to hunt.' " There has been little honest debate about a "mere technicality" called the Second Amendment to the Constitution, which says, in part: "A well regulated Militia, being necessary to the security of a free State, the right of the people to keep and bear arms, shall not be infringed."

Do we not understand that not only do criminals desire unarmed victims, but our politicians and government bureaucrats desire unarmed citizens?

Ann Moeller of Clio, Michigan, reiterated this concept when she, as a spoof, created "Blame Someone Else Day" in 1982. Ann declared the first Friday the thirteenth of the year to be "Blame Someone Else Day." Blaming someone else for one's behavior or our misfortune has become not only a "national pastime" but a serious social disease. We need some "Take the Blame Days," I believe.

I recommend that Christians must shoulder our part of the blame and do this, in one way, by considering the thesis of this book, "We have gone beyond the point of no return," and contemplating, if the theme of this book is true, what individual and collectively, short-term and long-term, actions we must take. It may be later than you think.

7. Education: Moral Teaching and General Knowledge

Several years ago, the city of Jackson, Mississippi, "scrapped" government ownership of the garbage collection enterprise/business. We here in Jackson believe that our garbage can be "better served"/handled through private initiative driven by the "profit" motive than by government monopoly. Therefore, we have "turned over" our garbage to private investors/entrepreneurs. If private enterprise does not satisfy its customers, customers can go to another alternative. Not so with clients of government monopolistic services and products. If too many customers discontinue doing business with a private enterprise, the business will cease to stay in business. Not necessarily so with government monopolies.

I maintain that our children are more important than our garbage. If private enterprise can take better care of our garbage than government, I believe private enterprise can better service our children and their educational needs.

Please show me in the U.S. Constitution or in the Bible where it is written, or implied, that civil government/Caesar is obligated to provide a free (it is not free; someone also pays for so-called free government services), government-owned and controlled, educational system for our children (or adults). I believe that government can require parents to see that their children are educated (as well as to not abuse or neglect their children), but I do not believe government is obligated to provide the so-called free education system that most Americans endorse today. It has served us well, but it no longer does.

In the September 1993 edition of *The McAlvany Intelligence Advisor,* Donald S. McAlvany said (reprinted by permission):

John Dewey (the reputed "father of modern education" in America and a leading secular humanist) once said that if the public (government) schools could keep the children occupied from 7 or 7:30 A.M. in the morning, throughout the day, with sports after school, and homework in the evening, that the parents would have less than an hour a day with their children, and that the family's and Christian church's influence over them could be broken in about a generation. Has this happened?

What is the agenda of the government-sponsored school system in America today? Is it to educate our children and prepare them for life or is it to break the influence of the Christian church over them, dumb them down, and prepare them to be obedient, unthinking serfs of the coming socialist America and New World Order? This writer believes it to be the latter three.

Today, our public school system in America is run primarily by secular humanists who share and even promote the agenda of the abortionists, the homosexuals, the radical feminists, the evolutionists, the atheists, the environmentalists, the hedonists, the globalists, the socialists, and more and more the New Age Movement.

If you don't believe what McAlvany has said, visit a government school and study the NEA (National Education Association).

I believe it is past time to "close down" the government school system!

Who would educate our nation's children if we disbanded government schools and sold the schools' assets to the highest bidders at public auctions? Those who believe in private enterprise and those who care about children's education would. How about Christians and Christian institutions as well as anyone else who wants to take a "stab" at it? Christian denominations ought to be eager to expand their education systems from infant day care and colleges and universities to the years in between. Those years are important, too, aren't they?!

Education is ultimately the responsibility of parents. Aren't parents paying enough now (through taxes) for education? If parents had that money, they could "shop" educational institutions just as they shop for "back-to-school" clothes. Parents certainly are able to educate their own children in many areas. These areas could be expanded and they could enroll their children in a variety of educational opportunities if they had the funds they are paying now in taxes.

Christian schools would be (and are [those in existence today]) a great vehicle to teach our moral values, to influence the culture, to win souls to the Lord, and to recruit troops into the Christian army!

We (Christians) ought to dominate the education system in America, if for no other reason than to protect ourselves and our children. We have a vested interest in the culture being "tolerant" of us. If the inhabitants of America knew us and our principles and precepts through our education system, (1) they would see that Christianity works; and (2) there would be less "bashing" of Christians. How many times do you hear the sodomites encourage their own to come out of the closet and be known? They insist the culture endorse their beliefs and behavior and are constantly saying that if we knew them, we would be less "bigoted."

I say that same reasoning (coming out of the closet) could work to our advantage, too. Christians and our reasoned beliefs are about the only ones still "in the closet." We ought to be a part of the great twentieth-century "outing movement," too!

Lincoln said, "What is taught in the schools of America in this generation will be public policy in the next generation." Don't we care what public policy is going to be tomorrow? Don't we want to influence tomorrow's public policy today? What better way than to dominate the educational institutions in this land.

I believe our government schools are unsalvageable. There are times when something can be repaired, and there are times when it cannot be, such as when a hurricane "blows" through a town. Some homes are repaired and others are "bulldozed" over because they can't be repaired. Sometimes the razed homes would have been too expensive to repair, and other times the razed homes would have been unsafe to live in after they are repaired. We have had a hurricane nightmare blow through our government school system, and I believe it is time to "bulldoze" the schools down (auction them off).

And what ought to be the subjects taught in Christian schools? Two groups of three R's should be taught as basic tenents in education. The first group (of Rs), the most important, are (1) religion; (2) rights; and (3) responsibilities, and the second group are (a) readin'; (b) ritin'; and (c) 'rithmatic.

Included in the first group of Three R's ought to be the Bible and the faith of Abraham, Issaic, and Jacob and the life, times, works, and "call" to obedience to God taught by His Son, the Lord Jesus Christ, the Savior and Redeemer of man. Other religions ought to be studied and compared to Christianity, but the eternal truth is that through Christ and Christ alone may man have eternal life. Our belief that "the way, the truth, and the life" is only through Jesus Christ ought to be the centrality of moral teaching in Christian schools. Also, we must teach that God judges everyone and every nation.

In the second group of Three R's, Christian schools may expand to other subjects, i.e., history, civics, sociology, psychology, medicine, journalism, law, typing, chemistry, political science, art, music, biology, and all other studies and vocations; however, the teaching of the Bible must guide education in Christian schools in all other subjects.

Home schooling for Americans is another wonderful alternative educational opportunity. Surely in present-day circumstances, with the disarray in government-controlled secular humanist schools and, unfortunately, some "self-identified" Christian schools, home schooling may be the only choice for some parents.

Civil government ought to allow any organization to enter the education business. The ACLU, People for the American Way, People for the

Ethical Treatment of Animals, the Sierra Club, NOW, nonprofit and for-profit organizations and institutions (such as IBM, Xerox, General Motors, Exxon, General Foods, etc.), secular organizations, and all "religious" groups ought to be allowed to join Christianity in "competing" in the education "marketplace."

Parents ought to be allowed to "choose" which schools to send their kids to. Taxes for education ought to be eliminated, and parents ought to be allowed to shop for their kids' place of education just as they shop for back-to-school notebooks, notebook paper, pencils, glue, and book satchels. Competition would improve education by offering "choice" and eliminate the schools that don't get "votes" (education dollars) from parents.

We are presently spending $250,000,000,000 (that's two hundred and fifty billion dollars) annually for our government-controlled schools, which use government employees to further government policies and beliefs in government-owned buildings. This simply does not add up (not dollars and cents–wise to me [the money spent and the results attained]) and does not have to be!

What are we getting for our money? International education tests show that America's students in our government schools can't spell, can't read, can't write, don't know history, don't know geography but rank high in self-esteem and self-confidence. Isn't that just dandy! The government educational bureaucrats are at least good in the public/student relations effort. They have been using the secular media for years via public service announcements to tell us how great things are (so we'll keep the funds flowing).

Our government school students also know how to put a condom on a banana (even though there is little evidence the little fornicators are practicing "safer sin"; excuse me, "safer sex"), where to buy drugs on the school campus, where to go for an abortion if the condom fails or they forget to use it (we expect these youngsters to carry a condom everywhere they go and to use it properly even though we know they can't remember to get up to go to school, do their homework, or leave gas in the car for their dads the next morning after a hot date the night before), and where to buy a gun on the "black market" so they can go to school armed (135,000 of our students in government schools attend school daily with a handgun; I'm not sure I blame them).

William Bennett, well-known educator and former secretary of education (who recommends the elimination of the federal Department of

Education and did so when he was secretary of education) and former national drug czar, came to Jackson in January of 1994 and spoke to a friendly and enthusiastic audience at our city auditorium. I was there, as was a friend, Dr. Matt Friedeman, a professor at Wesley Biblical Seminary here in Jackson.

Matt is a well-known "personality," as he hosts a one-and-one-half hour week/day radio talk show on popular WJNT during "drive time" (7:30 to 9 A.M.) and writes an "op-ed" column on Wednesday and Fridays in the local newspaper, the *Clarion-Ledger,* the state's largest-circulated newspaper.

In Matt's column of Friday, January 14, 1994, titled "In Response to William Bennett's Speech, Let's Applaud and Then 'Fly,' " Matt wrote, in part, the following (reprinted by permission of Dr. Matt Friedemann and the *Clarion-Ledger*):

Bennett offered a litany of concerns that we ignore at our own peril.

. . . The basic premise—a standard Bennett thought—is that this nation has worked an economic miracle in the last 50 years. Gross domestic product has multiplied, standards of living have soared, and in many ways, the nation has never had it better.

Then why, when polls inquire about the direction of the nation, do 70–75% of the populace say we are headed in the wrong direction? Says Bennett: "It's because we are." And those at the symposium know that he was right. When you hear his data, already documented in previous columns of this writer, it is hard to argue: Since 1960, population has increased 41 percent but in the same period there has been a 560 percent increase in violent crime, a 400 percent increase in illegitimate births, a quadrupling in divorces, a tripling of the percentage of children living in single-parent homes, a 200+ percent increase in the teenage suicide rate, and a drop of 75 points in the average SAT scores of high school students.

In 1940, teachers were asked to identify the top problems in America's schools. Their response: talking out of turn, chewing gum, making noise, running in the hall, cutting in line, dress code infractions, and littering. Same question in 1990 received the answers of drug use, alcohol abuse, pregnancy, suicide, rape, robbery, and assault.

In the industrialized world, we are at or near the top in rates of abortions, divorces, and unwed births and lead the industrialized world in murder, rape, and violent crime. In elementary and secondary education, we are at or near the bottom in achievement scores.

In other words, "substantial social regression."

. . . and so, in response to statistics and stories with which the audience heartily concurred, the crowd stood—I stood—and clapped.

Loud, long.

And I was reminded, again, of the parable from that Danish existentialist, Soren Kiekegaard.

"Suppose it was that geese could talk," begins with the 19th century philosopher in a journal entry entitled "The Tame Geese." In this land the geese had the habit of waddling to church every Sunday. The presiding gander would honk out eloquent sermons about the high goal of their Creator and on such motivational topics as God's generous gift to fowl—wings. With the aid of these feathery propellers, the geese were told, they could "fly away to distant regions, blessed climes, where properly they were at home, for here they were only strangers.

"It was indeed, exciting for the geese to get together at their Sunday 'symposiums' where, in the excitement they would honk, curtsy, bow, and give standing ovations."

"And so it was every Sunday," writes Kiekegaard. "But a strange phenomenon repeated itself weekly, it seems, for after the geese had enjoyed the fellowship of their congregation, heard an outstanding message, and rendered the speaker an ovation or two, they would adjourn," and muses Kierkegaard, "Each would waddle home to his own affairs."

And to the delight of hungry human mouths everywhere they "throve and were well liked, became plump and delicate—and then were eaten—and that was the end of it."

Standing ovations without flight equals "the end of it."

No wonder Kiekegaard was called the "Disturbing Dane."

Our education system, disturbing indeed.

8. The Economy: Entrepreneurial Opportunity versus the Social/ Welfare State

The taxpayers work until late June, almost one-half the year, in Canada to pay their annual taxes, hidden and obvious. In the United States, American taxpayers work until about mid-June to pay their tax liabilities and the number of days we work to pay all levels of government taxes increases each year. In addition to the taxes we pay, governments, particularly the federal government, are supplementing the tax revenues with "borrowed" money in order to have yet more money to spend. And remember: Government is about "power," "control," and "money." How do you gain power and control? Two ways: (1) controlling money, and (2) controlling behavior through criminal and civil law (fines and jail sentences as well as their threats [such as injunctions, which require no law, only a judge's opinion]).

Also, a basic lesson in our capitalistic form of entrepreneurial economy is that whatever the government spends is taken away from taxpayers (that much less taxpayers can spend or invest) in the form of taxes or is borrowed, which reduces the amount of funds available for individuals or businesses/private institutions to borrow or "drives up" the costs (interest rates) of the "loanable" money. The federal government has one more way that it can spend money. It can print money, which has the possible effect of devaluing the value of money and assets.

An example is an area that I am familiar: One of my theories in trying to "close down" abortion centers in my town is to try to persuade pregnant mothers not to kill their unborn babies and to persuade nonpregnant women not to trade with the abortion centers. I realize that abortion centers, just like all other businesses, will close down if they lose a certain amount of business/income, be it 25, 50, or 75 percent, or some other percentage, simply because for-profit (or for nonprofit) businesses must have revenues and clients to remain in business. This is simple logic, simple supply and demand, and simple business reality.

I submit that this same theory applies to a national economies, which consists of individuals' and groups of individuals' (i.e., households', businesses', charities', other institutions', and governments') revenues and expenditures (incomes and outgoes). If the producers, taxpayers, lose or have taken away from them a certain amount of profit (which comes from income ([minus expenses]), which is the incentive for working and investing in the first place, whether the workers/investors (who are taxpayers, too) are individuals, "mom-and-pop" stores, or General Motors, they will either "give up," because the reward (salaries or return on investment) isn't worth the effort, especially if there is another choice (such as a social/welfare state), or be forced to quit by creditors if and when their expenses (including taxes) are greater than their revenues and when they have lost their assets.

This is especially true for those workers/laborers who see fellow citizens, who don't work or pay taxes, having their needs, i.e., food, clothing, housing, health care, transportation, air-conditioning, burial, etc., provided for by others (taxpayers) through government/s via taxes, deficit spending, or "printing money."

And what inalienable rights will the drones (bees) require next from the assets and earnings (via taxes) of the workers (bees)? My *Webster's*

New World Dictionary defines *drone* as a "male, honey bee, which serves only in a reproduction capacity, has no sting, and does not work; an idle person who lives by the work of others; loafer." Do you see similarities here with many welfare recipients? I do not consider the helpless among us to be "human drones," but the term does apply to millions who live off "the honey" produced by the "human worker bees."

What will the "drones" demand next? What else will the government be willing to furnish the "drones" from "the honey" produced by the remaining "workers"? Will so many join the "drones" and will their political influence, through votes and "its' my right" campaigns (or "we'll burn down America if you don't give" threats), be so great to cause the few remaining "workers" to simply quit working or leave the beehive and go to another beehive (or nation)?

A basic tenet of economics is: "The power to tax is the power to destroy." We do not hear this sentence quoted often anymore. Add to that tenet this one: "Whatever is subsidized will grow," and you have a formula for the self-destruction of a capitalist economic system. I am still waiting for a single "tax and spend our way into prosperity" (by government) advocate to answer Rush Limbaugh's question, "Give me one historic example of a nation that has taxed and spent itself into prosperity?" History gives us no example.

God's will, illuminated to us via His Holy Word and inspired by the Holy Spirit, speaks to us in the areas of economics, work, self-reliance, and stewardship. Each of these nouns are, in and of themselves, amoral. We can become self-reliant through evil works or good works; we can be good stewards of the Earth and the "creeping things" or we can be evil stewards; and we can use our economic conditions, i.e., assets or the lack of assets, for good (charity in the one case and, as an example of how the poor can teach the rich, humbleness in the other) or for evil (selfishness in the one case and complaining and/or demanding the redistribution of wealth in the other).

God's role in the economy for the family, Church, and civil government is revealed through the Bible, particularly in the example of the life of Jesus, and guided by the Holy Spirit, I believe. There are some areas in economics that, for me, seem to be "black" and "white" while there are some areas that are "gray." When in Heaven, we'll learn God's perfect will in these matters; however, we must continue to strive for His plan in these difficult matters of the economy.

205

I believe it is the role and duty of civil government to provide a "level playing field" for economic competition and to protect employees from "exploitation" from the employers. I believe civil government ought to provide "incentives" for individuals and groups (businesses, charities, and other organizations) to do "good works" and to reinvest and save. I believe it is the duty of civil government to provide disincentives from some legal activities (such as higher taxes on tobacco products ["sin" taxes] and perfumes ["luxury" taxes] rather than for milk and bread).

God gives us the ability to work as well as a reward for our work. Paul said in 1 Thessalonians 1:2: *"We give thanks to God always for all of you, making mention of you in our prayers; constantly bearing in mind your work of faith and labor of love and steadfastness of hope in our Lord Jesus Christ."*

Hebrews 6:10 says this regarding work and economy: *"For God is not unjust so as to forget your work and the love which you have shown toward His name, in having ministered and in still ministering to the saints."* And in 2 Chronicles the Word of God says: *"You be strong and do not lose courage, for there is reward for your work."*

I believe the direction of our nation into "crippling" private enterprise and initiative is "fixed" and will lead to economic ruin for our nation/culture/society. I do not see a "will" out of this. There is a "way," but I do not believe the politicians will act against the "will" of the citizens, who will say "cut" the government expenses but will also say "but not my benefits"!

Included in a February 7, 1994, syndicated column written by Charley Reese, a columnist for the *Orlando [Florida] Sentinel,* that appeared in the *Jackson, Mississippi, Clarion-Ledger* titled "The 'Crash' Is Definitely Coming!" was this:

If the U.S. government were a private cooperation, it would already be in Chapter 11.

It hasn't taken long for the political rhetoric in Washington to slip away from the painful subject of debt reduction and runaways deficits to the more politically comforting subject of what government can do for us.

Well, to be blunt, government is about to impoverish most of us.

In 1992, 20% of the federal government budget was spent on interest on the debt and another 52% went to entitlement programs such as Medicare and Social Security. Interest payments on the debt—now just over

$4.5 trillion and heading toward $5.0 trillion—cannot be cut. Entitlements are the most politically difficult budget cuts to make because it means taking money away from people who previously were entitled to entitlements.

In 1991, the (federal) government spent more on just three things—national defense, interest on the national debt, and Social Security—that it collected in income taxes.

Do you see where this is heading? Inevitably more taxes and, at some point, ruinous inflation, with the lower and middle classes completely destroyed.

In my opinion, two things are happening right now: The high rollers know the crash is coming and are making all the bread they can while there's still a chance and the politicians are intentionally misleading people about the seriousness of the financial crisis.

You're being deliberately lulled into a false sense of security with an economic disinformation campaign so the high rollers can go on making their killing. When the crash comes, you'll be left holding the bag—and the bag will be empty.*

I close this section with hope for you on the "economic horizon," as seen in Waldo Emerson's poem "Great Men: "

Not gold, but only man can make a people great and strong;
Men, who, for truth and honor's sake, stand fast and suffering long.
Brave men who work while other's sleep, who dare while others fly—
They build a nation's pillars deep and lift them to the sky.

Perhaps the "nation" that Emerson speaks of will be somewhere else or on this land by another name. Prepare for the "coming economic Earthquake."

9. Human Sexuality: The Challenge to Affirm Historical Christian Teaching

A syndicated national column in a major U.S. newspaper dated June 14, 1994, began with the fact that Dennis Dourgalut wanted a traditional wedding, a traditional Catholic wedding. The headline read to the effect that marriage isn't exclusively for heterosexuals anymore. The article went on to say that during a celebratory dinner for their first anniverary of dating Dennis surprised Michael Suddath with a marriage proposal and an engagement ring, asking Michael for a spring wedding.

Dennis persuaded Michael to believe that asking God to bless their union and pledging their love to one another while standing before friends would strengthen their relationship. After receiving Communion, the story went on, they took their vows in a tradional Catholic wedding in Washington, D.C., in 1992 and listened to a twelvth-century prayer, which asked God to preserve their union without jealousy.

The article's last two paragraphs repulsed me and ought to repluse and enrage every Christian as well as cause them to grieve. They stated that Dourgalut and Suddath while studying centuries-old Christian marriage cermonies came across a Boswell, a medieval scholar who wrote a book titled *Same-Sex Union in Premodern Europe*. In this book, Dourgalut and Suddath found services for mixed couples that stressed procreation and multiplication for heterosexuals and "a very beautiful emphasis on love" for homosexuals.

The columnist said that the book was a "bombshell" that would rock assumptions and animosity toward homosexuals. The columnist said that love tugs everyone toward commitment and that all churches and courthouses should welcome all couples, regardless of their sex, preparing to exchange vows. She said that marriage is not just a heterosexual rite any longer.

Consider this: In a recent ABC television editor of *Primetime Live* covering public schools whose health clinics are now surgically inserting Norplant beneath the skin of teenage girls, the practice was debated. The practice is controversial not only because Norplant is a five-year birth control device, but because it is being implanted without the permission or knowledge of the teenager girls' parents. (You do remember parents, don't you?)

One of those interviewed on ABC for the story was a junior high school principal who defended the inserting of Norplant without parental involvement. Her most memorable statement was: "Morality is one thing; reality is another." This is an interesting idea, keeping morality separate from reality. Reality, of course, is everything. Hence morality is restricted to the realm of nothing.

And we have a name for those heterosexuals who use Norplant, take oral contraceptives, and use condoms; in "reality" they will one day be called "parents." Perhaps parents of an unplanned, unwanted, unwelcomed death child killed by abortion but, nevertheless, parents. They will, also, eventually, if they have multiple sex partners, be called "victims of venereal diseases."

We ought to be nothing short of outraged and fighting mad when we read and hear of "real-life incidents" such as the two cases above. Sex between unmarried heterosexuals is wrong/sin, as is all sex between homosexuals. This is the unchanging and historical teaching of Christianity. And I submit that these practices ought to be illegal in all nations in all generations. They are (illegal) in many nations today, but not in the "good old" U.S. of A. In fact, we are tolerating and ignoring these crimes/sins, or, worse, endorsing them through our civil government and, in some cases, sanctifying them in our churches.

Why am I so strongly opposed to the practices mentioned in the last paragraph? Because this standard and practice set forth by God works! Families, Christianity, and civil government must act to instill the fact that virginity, secondary virginity, and abstinence before heterosexual marriage, as well as faithfulness, sexually and otherwise, to one's lifelong partner within marriage, are not only logical but expected. With adherence to this standard come pride, peace of mind, good health, and dominion over one's body.

We are losing the sanctity of human sexuality in Western civilization. With this loss comes (1) men making lewd or suggestive comments to women; (2) the proliferation and acceptance of pornography; (3) women dressing without modesty; (4) disorder between the sexes; (5) widespread and accepted fornication and adultery; (6) masturbation with little thought or comment within families and Christianity (which should condemn it); and (7) homosexuality and sodomy.

Never ought the act of sexual intercourse be practiced without the possibility of the transmission of human life. No exceptions; case closed! Call this opinion prudish, if you like. I call it historically accurate regarding a subject most Christians, including parents and pastors, refuse to consider. Aim at nothing and that's exactly what you'll hit!

While there are many types of love, the only natural love that ought to include sexual intimacy is the "phila" and "eros" love between a man and a woman in a marriage, and God's preferred marriage is between a Christian man and woman committed to one another in body, mind, and spirit, "for richer or poorer, in good or bad health, until death do us part."

"Phila" love, "brotherly love," can exist between many human beings, i.e., brother to brother, sister to sister, brother to sister, father to son, mother to daughter, mother to son, friend to friend, coworker to coworker, employer to employee, etc. But none of these relations allows for sexual intimacy, not in the eyes of nature or in the eyes of God, the Author of Nature, Who is not the author of confusion. The only time that "eros" love, physical love, is allowed is between a man and a woman in marriage, and, I repeat, God's desire is that the marriage be forever and between Christians.

The "false" love between homosexuals, male or female, is sodomy and is repudiated by Scriptures and ought to be repudiated by society, and that ought to include civil government. Unfortunately, this is no longer the case, and I predict we, as a nation, have just begun the downhill slide of a huge and rapid descent into homosexual perversion. Soon there will be no one left in the "hall of 'shame' closet."

EXAMPLE: A homosexual rights lobbying group said in June of 1994 that 71 of 100 U.S. senators pledged not to discriminate against gay employees on their staffs. Why was this even an issue?

EXAMPLE: In May of 1994 a major national news service circulated a news story regarding the explanation to children (and others) about their families who live with a parent and their parent's homosexual partner. The news story begins with the asking of the question as to what a child in preschool day care says when teachers ask the child about his or her family. What a child ought to say to the teacher and his or her peers if asked, "Tell us about your family," and the child's family consists of himself or herself, his or her mommy, and his or her other mommy or daddy, is explored in the article.

In the article, Marla Gold says she knows how to handle the joys and trials of such a situation. Ms. Gold is co-founder of Philadelphia's Family Pride, an advocacy group of gay and lesbian families, and is the mother of a two-year-old boy along with her woman partner. Ms. Gold's goal, according to the news story, is to bring lesbian and gay families into the norm of regular families.

Sadly, we know they exist. That's not the point. The point is that this type of family is a perversion of what a family ought to be! Two women or two men "do not 'make' a family." Two women or two men cannot make a family biologically, if we consider children normal, natural parts of families; and surely not before the eyes of God.

EXAMPLE: An AP story, "Seattle Church 'OKs' Gay Couple as pastors," ran in the June 14, 1994, edition of our Jackson, Mississippi, daily newspaper, the *Clarion-Ledger*. The story said (reprinted by permission of the Associated Press):

> Shortly before 1:30 P.M., Julie Davis slipped into the side office of Seattle's University Congregational Church and placed a call to a private home three blocks away. Anxiously, the Rev. David Shull picked up the receiver, listened to what Davis, head of the pastoral-search committee, had to say, then gasped, "Oh, my God!"
>
> Moments later the news was announced to the church congregation. The shouts and applause that erupted from the sanctuary could be heard outside the church, next to the University of Washington campus.
>
> By an overwhelming 76 percent majority vote, University Congregational Church on Sunday became what is believed to be the first mainline church in the country to "call" a gay couple—Shull, 35, and Rev. Peter Ilgenfritz, 32—to share an associate pastorship.

Can you believe it? The enemy is indeed within the camp, masquerading as some of us. How enraged we ought to be, and how God must grieve.

EXAMPLE: June 2, 1994, *USA Today* carried a story, " 'Allow Homosexuals and Lesbians into Scouts,' says Elders." Former surgeon general Elders was quoted as saying, "Gays and lesbians should be admitted into scout groups and politicians should worry about their own bedrooms."

The article went on to say: "The outspoken Elders defended an interview she gave *The Advocate*, a gay newspaper, in which she urged the Boy Scouts to admit homosexuals. 'I think girls who are lesbians should be allowed to join the Girl Scouts,' she said. 'None of us is good enough, or knows enough, to make decisions about other people's sexual preferences.' "

Our former surgeon general, apparently, knew how the Boy Scouts ought to run the Boy Scouts. She, apparently, did not know how the Girl Scouts were running their organization. She knew so little that she did not even know the Girl Scouts had already capitulated to her desire and welcomed lesbian girls and women (as leaders) into their organization. This surgeon general was an utter disgrace!

EXAMPLE: In late July of 1994, the Census Bureau picked up a new twist to the trend of single parenthood in America: nearly half the children were not the products of divorced parents but were born out of wedlock.

Recently the Census Bureau reported that ten years ago, a child living with one parent was twice as likely to be the product of a broken home as to have been born out of wedlock. Now 37 percent live with a divorced parent, 35 percent with a never-married parent. (And remember there are approximately 1.6 million abortions annually in the United States, 80 percent of which are on single pregnant mothers. There is an incredible amount of sex between single women and men in this country.)

A resident of Eudora, Arkansas, Mr. Haven Bradford Gow is a TV and radio commentator and freelance writer who has published more than 1,000 articles and reviews in 100 magazines and newspapers. A graduate of Boston College, he is the son of the late Mr. and Mrs. Joseph and Elizabeth Gow. He wrote a column titled "Teen Sexuality: A Moral Perspective" he wrote (reprinted by permission):

According to an article in the July of 1993 issue of "McCall's" magazine, "Teenage Sex is a phrase that strikes fear in most parents' hearts. . . . Emotional turmoil, unwanted pregnancies, sexually transmitted diseases—the lists of possible pitfalls is long. And now that the AIDS virus is on the scene, sex is possibly deadly. . . . [T]hese days teens are more sexually active than ever. Today in the United States, half of unmarried girls and 60 percent of unmarried boys, ages 15 to 19, have had sexual intercourse."

The July issue of "McCall's" contained some disturbing as well as thought-provoking comments from sexually active teens. A sixteen-year-old girl in Montclair, New Jersey, said: "I was 14 and had been dating this guy like a week. . . . He had a party, and we had sex in his room while three people who I thought were asleep were lying on the floor." A seventeen-year-old boy in Chapel Hill, North Carolina, had this to say: "My first (sexual experience) was with this girl in the neighborhood who was two years older. When it was over, I just got up and left."

A sixteen-year-old in Springfield, Maine, confided: "Whether you're having sex or not, you're definitely acting like you know about it. People just expect you to be doing it. If you don't, they kind of like wonder what's wrong with you." An eighteen-year-old girl in Houston, Texas, said: "I had decided I wanted to lose it the night of the prom. It's not like anyone made me. I just felt like I was holding this thing back for no great reason. It was a real pain to be a virgin."

"Safe sex" and condom distribution programs in the schools are based on the assumption that teen sex and pregnancies result from "ignorance." But, as the comments from the teens interviewed by "McCall's" magazine make clear, teen sex and pregnancies definitely do not result from "ignorance." Indeed, it would be more accurate to attribute teen sex and pregnancies to such factors as loneliness, lack of self-esteem, peer and societal pressure, and lack of good character.

According to Mrs. Julie Brown, president of the American Life League in Stafford, Virginia, "safe sex" and condom distribution programs in the schools send a terrible moral message to young people. "The message we are sending is that self-control and self-respect are not possible. We cannot tell them to practice abstinence because, we are told, abstinence represents religious belief, even though it represents health and freedom from disease. Why can't we understand that when we tell (young people) to use condoms we are teaching them the basic tenets of the religion of hedonism, that instant pleasure is a basic good. If for that pleasure they happen to acquire a disease that will kill them or leave them sterile for life, no one's telling.

"Why can't we spend more energy improving the learning skills of our children while we renew our dedication to teach 'by our actions' the basic truth that sexual relations belong in marriage where one can find commitment, trust, and happiness?

"Clearly, instead of amoral, secular humanist sex education and condom distribution in the schools; families, churches, schools, social organizations, and the business community must re-emphasize the teaching, learning and practice of virtues like courtesy, kindness, honesty, decency, moral courage, justice, self-respect, and respect for others. When young people develop nobility of mind, spirit, and character, they automatically will know how to conduct themselves in the sexual realm.''

Haven Bradford Gow is an editorial writer and commentator. Julie Brown is a writer, public speaker, educator, and political activist. Thank you both for your beautifully articulated thoughts and opinions.

10. Relationships: Memories Are Made of Our Experiences with Others

Many have written and sung about what memories are made of. Yes, we remember places we have visited and times of solitude. We shall always remember a special sunrise or our first view of the Grand Canyon. However, our greatest and everlasting memories will be of our experiences with others, good or bad times with others.

Often we have been warned to pay attention and give time to relationships. We are told that when we reminisce from our deathbeds, if we are lucky to escape instant deaths by "drive-by shootings," "race wars," instantaneous deaths in auto crashs, or the like, it will be our "relationships" with others that we will reflect upon and that will bless or haunt us in the last days and hours of our lives. We are told that we will not dwell in those last hours of consciousness on business deals, other achievements and awards, or "things," but on "relationships."

God made women as companions for men, and vice versa. He made children to bless and love their parents, and vice versa. He made the short and the tall, the lean and the fat, the black and the white, the strong and the weak, and the optimist and the pessimist to dwell in the "uttermost parts of the earth," to learn from one another, to complement one another, to work with one another, to have fun with one another, to enjoy peace and happiness with one another, and to love one another.

He made us to share with one another what we have, what we know, what we dream, and what we are about with one another (our customs, fears, languages, skills, knowledge, and yearnings). He made us with consciences (He wrote: "The law is written on their hearts"), with a curiosity of who or what made us as well as why, and a wonderment as to whether or not we will have a "hereafter" relationship with the "creator." There is a struggle within each of us, a relationship if you will, that battles between "good" or "evil" centered on whether or not we will be judged for what we have done (as well as what we have failed to do) on our individual judgment day.

Each Christian understands that for "every good and perfect gift" that God intends for us, Satan desires the opposite. Satan created with God's permission, enmity between all human relationships. Satan desires that all of us be at war with one another. In Genesis, Satan put hostility between a woman and her seed (sounds like Satan loves abortion); Satan loves warfare between all humans. This is why relationships that ought to have "pure" love exemplified between parties, e.g., husband and wife, father and son, mother and daughter, and neighbors, are not always "showers" of "natural affections."

No wonder there is so much strife between lesser "natural affectioners," i.e., races, religions, the "haves" and the "have-nots," various economic systems, different types of civil governments, and those who simply do not know or care to know one another.

As Mother Teresa stated so truly, "How can there be peace on Earth when there is war in the womb?"

Obviously, the first place to start in "making 'good' memories" is at home, by seeing that relationships between those whom we know best, ought to love the most, and have mutual dependence with are excellent, honest, and open. This seems logical and easy, but in our "fallen condition" I can't think of anything more difficult. Why? Because we struggle with our "call" to be servants and with putting ourselves "last." This is human nature, and it must be defeated. This is best done and can only be completed by imitating the life of Christ Jesus.

Someone once said (I wish it had been me), "I love mankind. It's just people I can't stand." Amen. Knowing people, having close relationships, does make it difficult to live a Christian life. I think it may well be much easier to be a Christian and live a holy life marooned on an island. It is far easier to love a poor child in India, whom we know only by a photo, than the child next door. It is easier not to be burdened by that child in Calcutta than to care for and love our own children at times . . . the kid in the back bedroom who will not pick up his or her clothes off the floor or stop experimenting with illicit drugs. However, we will not be capable of truly loving the child in Calcutta, witnessed by our prayers and charity, if we are incapable or refuse to love, unconditionally, our own child or wife or husband or mother or brother or sister.

It is indispensable as I see it, to accept and to love the one in the womb, for example, before we can love the one who hates us and is at war with us who lives in Iraq or Iran.

There are some relationships that I believe will test us and add to the crises and chaos that I believe are near for this country. The "landscape" of relationships will dramatically and drastically change soon for the worse and, I believe, will play a significant role in the collapse of our culture/nation/society "from within."

The relationships that I believe will be strained and stretched until many "burst" are: sexual preferences (heterosexuals versus homosexuals); gender (men versus women); age (tax-paying younger workers versus retired senior citizens receiving government funds); economic class conflict (so-called haves versus so-called have-nots); race (whites, blacks, Hispanics, Asians, and others versus one another); geographical residency (urban versus small town, rural, and country); environmental concerns (extreme conservationists versus moderates versus those with no environmental concerns); and religions (Christians versus "self-identified" Christians [who are not Christians] versus secular humanists versus Muslims versus others).

The growing rifts that I believe will be accented in the coming years between the identified groups in the last paragraph will center on economic matters (redistribution of what some have to and for the benefit of others as well as what some may do with what they own) and polarization between "rights" and "wrongs" (with many professing that we can't distinguish between "right" and "wrong" for others [which will, essentially, result in civil government endorsing many "wrongs" that will be disastrous for individuals and the society]).

The "core" issue will be a matter of allegiances and one's worldview. The widening gulf, polarization, will be exacerbated, I predict, as greater division occurs between the "haves" and the "have-nots" (as defined by the growing number of "have-nots" and their government allies) and the moralists, the amoralists, and the immoralists (with many of the "mushy middle" Christians in the camps of the "amoralists" and the immoralists"). I predict as political/ethical discussions become more intensive and the middle class/moral "mushy middle" are squeezed inexorably to one extreme or another (or out of existence), they will have to decide whom they will serve and give allegiance to, God or government.

Much time, paper, and ink could be devoted to each of the relationships that I identified three paragraphs back. I will write just a sentence or two regarding each of them and pray that you'll pick up on the direction I am going:

1. *Sexual Preferences (Heterosexuals versus Homosexuals).* The homosexual movement will continue to grow, I predict, and to force their agenda on society. Homosexuals will only be satisfied when their perverted lifestyle is granted all the privileges and honors afforded presently to married heterosexual couples and when homosexuals are accepted as no different from heterosexuals in all endeavors and vocations of life, such as teachers, scout leaders, military personnel, and others. Homosexuals and their political allies will not be satisfied until all critics of their actions are crushed by "hate crime" speech and opinion and banished to the gulag.

2. *Gender (Men versus Women).* In far too many cases, the fidelity, peace, harmony, and enjoyment of the company between the genders has been replaced by suspicion, jealousy, combativeness, and open hostility, even within marriage. Fifty percent divorce rates, by Christians and pagans alike, and domestic violence testify to the lack of civility between the genders as well as the lack of commitment to marriages and children. The fact that of the approximately 6 million pregnancies annually in the United States, 3 million are not planned testifies to the fact that while men and women are "together," in "that" way, they

are not planning together and often are not even married. The fact there are 1.6 million abortions annually in the country, 80 percent to single mothers, and that more than one-fourth of the babies who survive the womb are born to single mothers gives an eloquent testimonial that men and women are not on the same "wavelength" on one of the most important "relationships" in life, human procreation. Abuse toward genders, physical and mental, in our nation in this generation is a scandal. This must grieve the heart of God enormously.

3. *Age (Taxpaying Younger Workers versus Retired Senior Citizens Receiving Government Funds).* The spreading gulf between the young and the old is becoming painfully obvious. Children who were cared for and protected during their young, vulnerable years are increasingly not feeling responsible for their parents in their old age and are not making plans to care for them or are abandoning them in nursing homes financed by government subsidies or charities. "Absence 'does not seem' to make the heart grow fonder" to children of invalid parents. In too many cases, the mindset that "we have no responsibility" for our parents and "let government take care of my parents" causes capable and financially able children to admit to no responsibility to visit, let alone be responsible for their feeble parents. As America "grays," I feel this unholy trend will increase. Does anyone else visualize "senior citizens" extermination centers beside "abortion" centers?

4. *Economic Class Conflict (So-Called Haves versus So-Called Have Nots).* Democratic civil government politicians have always contended with the conflict between the classes, as we have all other forms of government. Acute to democracies is the temptation by politicians to pit one class against the other. During the past fifty years we have seen this temptation become an "art" by liberals who have preyed on those that they define as the "have-nots" for their own selfish ends. What has been the result? Class envy that I predict will result in open warfare and an erosion of the work ethic among the poor. Also, we now have great contention and mistrust between the economic classes and a worsening of the living condition of all classes.

5. *Race (Whites, Blacks, Hispanics, Asians, and Others versus One Another).* Rather than becoming the positive "melting pot" that we used to be and bragged about, I fear that we are becoming the "meltdown" reactor in the area of race and ethnicity that could explode and incinerate us all. The inability to solve prejudice in our nation and the huge

dependency class in our midst have lead to great polarization, and I predict it will get much worse.

6. *Geographical Residency (Urban versus Small Town, Rural, and Country).* The struggle over environmental matters and government aid between the residents of urban dwellers and those who dwell in small towns, rural areas, and the country are the seeds for disharmony in this nature-rich country. Even though the dwellers of these various areas ought to complement one another and be interdependent on one another, there is potential for great mistrust and envy between these geographical diverse dwellers, particularly in the area of public policy and financial favoritism.

7. *Environmental Concerns (Extreme Conservationists versus Moderates versus Those with No Environmental Concerns).* Hunters, fishermen, farmers, miners, ranchers, loggers, and others whose livelihood comes directly from "Mother Nature" will continue to be pitted against those environmental extremists who do not want "Mother Nature" touched. While those who "live" directly off the land (and the sea, the waters, and the air) have some among their number who are not good stewards of nature, most of them respect nature and will continue to have to defend the "balance" that the moderates believe to be reasonable. However, this is an area for all to be concerned about and an area that can be most volatile and contentious.

8. *Religions (Christianity versus "Self-Identified" Christians [Who Are Not Christians At All but Believe They Are] versus Secular Humanists versus Muslims versus Others).* We are seeing "religious wars" occurring all around the world. Do we believe that as Christianity loses its strong influence on this nation the void will not be filled with other religions, many of whom are committed to destroying all vestiges of Christianity and none of whom desire to be "tolerant" of true Christianity? Major clashes between ethnic, race, and culture religions are upon us. Look for the "balkanization" of religions in this post-Christian land.

EXAMPLE: "Girls, listen up to Texas Gov. Ann Richards's warning about Prince Charming; 'He'll probably leave you with a mortgage and all his offsprings,' " wrote the *Clarion-Ledger* of Jackson, Mississippi, on June 22, 1994. " 'Prince Charming may be driving a Honda and telling you that you have no equal, but that's not going to do much good when you've got kids and a mortgage, and I could add he's got a beer gut and a wandering eye,' the governor said. Richard's prescription: 'Work instead on becoming self-sufficient, so that if you become divorced,' like Richards, 'you won't slip into poverty.' Richards delivered her lecture Monday at Girls' State.'' What a disgrace these negative, gender-divisive comments were!

EXAMPLE: Gov. Kirk Fordice, Republican of Mississippi, in the summer of 1994 took a vacation to Africa and while there went on a ''big-game'' hunt. He received criticism from the usual sources. One criticism came from Randy Bryant of Brandon, who said the following of the governor's hunting trip in a letter to the editor of the *Jackson, Mississippi Clarion-Ledger:* ''The article in the *Clarion-Ledger* on June 26, entitled 'Fordice to hunt big game in Africa' totally turned me against him. Hunting is murder to start with, but for someone to travel thousands of miles and spend thousands of dollars for the sole purpose of murdering innocent animals is beyond sick. The man is quite obviously devoid of compassion for his fellow beings.''

Killing ''innocent'' animals is murder! Fellow beings? If the adjective *innocent* describes some animals, logic must follow that some animals are ''guilty.'' ''Guilty'' of what? Doing what animals do naturally makes some animals ''innocent'' and others ''guilty''? And which acts by animals make them ''innocent'' or ''guilty''? Are mosquitoes ''guilty'' because they ''bite'' us? Are rabbits ''innocent'' because they are cute and get eaten by foxes? Are the foxes ''guilty'' when they catch, murder, and eat rabbits? Are salmon ''innocent'' but sharks ''guilty''? We are in big trouble with this kind of reasoning!

EXAMPLE: ''Minister Plans Male-Only March'' read a headline in a major Mississippi newspaper in July of 1994. The news article went on to explain that Minister Louis Farrakhan gave a speech at the Joe Louis Arena in Detroit in which he called for a million African-American men to march on Washington in October of 1995 to demand reparation from the U.S. government to African-Americans.

Farrakhan, the head of the Nation of Islam, also called for African-Americans nationwide to stop work on the day of the men-only march to call attention to the demand for reparation for the treatment blacks have received since being brought to the United States.

EXAMPLE: In the summer of 1994 Pope John Paul II said that actions that erode the tranditional family, such as government sanctioning of homosexual unions, not only contradict the Roman Catholic Church's position but go against natural law. He said that marriage as the stable union between a man and a woman, open to creating new life, is more than a mere convention of a Christian value.

He stated that heterosexual marriage was an original value of creation and "to lose this truth is not just a problem for believers but a danger for all of humanity." The pope's comments reflected continuing concern over a European Parliament resolution in the spring of 1994 that suggested member nations should provide equal standing to homosexual couples in such matters as adoption, inheritance, housing, and social benefits.

EXAMPLE: "Court Gives Son Back to Lesbian Mother," ran a June 22, 1994, headline in the *Jackson, Mississippi Clarion-Ledger.* The report said (reprinted by permission of the Associated Press):

> A lesbian regained custody of her son Tuesday when a state appeals court ruled that the woman's sex life—though illegal under Virginia law—does not make her an unfit parent.
>
> "A parent's private sexual conduct, even if illegal, does not create a presumption of unfitness," Judge Sam W. Coleman, III wrote in the 3–0 decision by a Virginia Court of Appeals.

Communitarianism

Communitarianism—it's a word, that when mentioned, the most common response is: "A communi-what"? It sounds like a cross between *communism* and some religion. Basically, "communitarians" simply believe that civilizations must align the balance between the rights of individuals and the responsibilities all members of a society have to one another.

To take and not to give is an immoral, self-centered predisposition that ultimately no society can tolerate indefinitely. Will we become intolerant of the sick, self-destructive, and tired relationships we have allowed to develop in this nation that "fly in the face" of God and His "natural law"?

The United States is sick and tired; it is declining and decaying rapidly. The question is: Are we Christians willing to sacrifice and to take back the culture? That's what will make or break the whole thing. It's a question, in my mind, of people taking care of their own fate (God's way) instead of relying on Uncle Sam to take care of them as well as taking care of those who can't take care of themselves (not government) as well as seeing that justice is done via the civil government. I see little evidence that we are "turning the corner" from *"their destiny is there destruction."*

"On Pessimism and Optimism"

G. K. Chesterton said, "The pessimist can be enraged at evil. But only the optimist can be surprised by it." Most Christians in America are optimists regarding the future of our country.

I believe, in general, pessimists are wiser than optimists, but optimists must not be impugned even though they are proven wrong many times. I grant that optimists—in spite of the day of judgment—lead to building and hoping for a better world.

Many or most (no, practically every one) of my friends with whom I have shared my pessimism for the future of this republic believe that I am overly pessimist in my belief that America has gone beyond the point of no return. Few believe what I believe: "We have lost our biblical basic for self-government irrevocably." Hardly anyone believes (or has considered) my perspective that Christianity in America has made an unholy alliance with Caesar (government). That's OK! They might be right; I hope so. But I don't think so. And what if I am right? What if God is (or has) departing (departed) from this land? Ought not this possibility be considered? I think we Christians ignore this possibility at our peril. Ought not we consider contingency plans if we believe this fact to be true?

Now more than at any time during the life of this nation, with the one exception of the period immediately before and during the Civil War, more people believe (1) the survival of this nation is questionable, and (2) we are at a major crossroads. They, most folks, believe the "patient" (the nation) is sick, very sick, but not in an irreversible state. My belief is closer to the conclusion that the "patient" is fatally ill and that death is certain, close, perhaps imminent. There are days when I believe the "patient" is not only "on life support" but is "brain-dead."

I thought this recently when I read that in Wisconsin a "parental consent for abortion" law was under consideration that would allow either parents, judges, or clergy to give consent for a pregnant minor's abortion. Many states have abortion restriction laws that are called parental consent or parental notification laws, which prohibit minors from having abortions without the consent or notification of their parents. The courts (the U.S. Supreme Court ultimately) have required that pregnant minor mothers must be allowed to "bypass" their parents if they can locate a judge who will validate their "need" for an abortion and their "need" to keep parents "in the dark" regarding this surgical procedure. Now comes Wisconsin, a state that is considering allowing a pastor/priest (or a judge) to authorize an abortion while the parents continue to be kept "in the dark."

It is beyond my comprehension to believe there are clerics in this country who will "put their rubber stamp" upon the murder of innocent unborn children! It is my understanding, upon investigation, that clerics have been identified who will readily support the legal extermination of God's most helpless and innocent human beings, made in His image, in Wisconsin.

The Bible does say in numerous passages and in several ways: "And God departed their land." Would God depart America? Anyone who says no is living in a state of false optimism!

Please understand, I am not predicting that the "end time is near" (or that it is not) or that Christianity will not "take hold" and "grow" in fertile ground around the world or return to this land in another generation or exist clandestinely in parts of this land, but I believe the soil in America is polluted and not conducive to Christian life and growth and this will become more true (and more apparent) as time passes. Not only is the "patient" terminally ill, in my opinion, but Christianity is close to being "brain-dead" in this nation that I love so dearly. These are critical times for this nation and Christianity in this land.

Also, I am not saying, "God is dead." I am not saying, "God is sick." God is God and is still alive and well and in charge, but He does "write off nations," and a nation that claims to be a Christian nation and has all the trappings of Christianity, i.e., "one nation, under God" in its Pledge of Allegiance and with "In God We Trust" on its coins, Christian historic statues and memorials on public and private buildings all over the nation, Christian wordings in its historical documents, opening sessions of Congress with prayer, and churches everywhere, but has rejected the "faith of our fathers" to the degree that this nation has through obvious hypocrisy and disobedience to God must anger and sadden the Father of individuals and nations.

And I believe the rage and grief of the Father in Heaven does not end with the civil government in America. A nation with Christian churches on almost every corner at a time when Christianity is so irrelevant to personal piety, so lacking in "works of charity," and so much into apostasy is shaking its collective fists in the face of God Almighty and daring Him to bring judgment and ultimate destruction upon itself.

A formerly well understood Latin phrase in medical schools and medicine, in general, is *primum non nocere*. It means, in English, "first, do no harm." This is the basic reason why abortion, infanticide, and euthanasia are wrong and evil and have been so throughout history in civilized societies. People are forbidden by God (and common justice) from harming themselves, and physicians (and others) are forbidden from killing or injuring their patients.

This principle extends far beyond the medical realm. Families, civil governments, and Christianity are to *primum non nocere,* too. And families, civil governments, and Christianity, as well as all individuals, organizations, and vocations, are to "first, do no harm." With the emphasize on "life" (and "having it more abundantly") in my life, it grieved me in the summer of 1994 to learn that the Catholic bishops in Louisiana, the state in which I was abandoned at birth in February of 1943, called on the state legislature to agree to subsidize (with taxes from Louisianans) the killing of preborn babies in that state who are allegedly (as no proof had to be shown) conceived as a result of rape or incest in order to continue receiving federal tax dollars for social services in Louisiana. (We have defined social services in the United States as the legal murdering of unborn children who happen to have been [again allegedly] conceived in less than ideal circumstances. [Reminds me of the circumstances surrounding the conception of Jesus.]) And who endorses the killing? None other than the Catholic bishops in Louisiana!

The Louisiana legislature, against the will and votes of a few lawmakers led by Rep. Woody Jenkins, "caved in" to federal threats to withhold federal dollars and agreed to *primum nocere* or "first, do harm" to some of its citizens. The people of Louisiana (and the people of every state) should have told President Clinton (and Hillary) and the Department of Health and Human Services that Louisianans would reject federal money rather than use part of it (no matter how small) to kill preborn children.

The United States of America in the fall of 1994 through its considerable influence with the United Nations and its World Population Conference, which was held in Cairo, Egypt, and sponsored by the World Bank (a UN child), quite possibly became the greatest enemy of innocent and vulnerable human life any nation has ever been. I remind you that governments and their agencies, such as the World Bank, are "about" power, control, and money.

Ironically, in the United Nation's "Year of the Family" (1994), this world body, led by the international financial and political strength of the United States, declared war on the family through its "antichild" advocacy of abortion, contraception, and sterilization and its effort to redefine the family through its call to "mainstream homosexuality." Through the United Nations' promotion of abortion, contraception, and sterilization, along with its endorsement of "using sex" with anyone, anywhere, for anything but procreation, the United Nations and the U.S. of A. have adopted an "antichild, antifamily, and anti-God" position unheard of in human history. Rich, white Protestant America has said to the world, "We want more of us and fewer of you." God will not bless a nation with this attitude and purpose!

I believe a major reason that God has allowed this nation to grow and prosper, in every way, through our two-hundred-plus years, even with our flaws, has been the fact that this nation has been a beacon of hope and moral light for people all over the world to see and emulate. American Christianity has exported itself, materials (through charity), and faith "to the ends of the Earth."

When we "cease to be (and do) good," as Alexis de Tocqueville warned, "America will cease to be great." What irony, what a disgrace, for the United States with its failed moral policies in the area of sexuality to be preaching the world, not to mention what will likely become coercing to the nations of the world, to accept and practice what we have done to our families and children, i.e., (1) abortion, contraception, sterilization, infanticide, and euthanasia; (2) easy divorce; (3) undermining of parental authority; (4) disintegration of the family through government social welfare policies rather than "tried and proven" effective private charity; (5) subsidizing immorality in many areas; (6) drowning in sex, profanity, and violence in our entertainment industry; and (7), in too many areas, the calling of "good, evil and evil, good."

As we "export" our failed immorality to other shores, God will not only refuse to tolerate what we do and who we are; He will stop us from working against His Holy will through chastisement, I predict.

Has this nation rebelled against God to the point that we do not believe we are accountable to God as a nation as well as individuals? I have news: Accountability to God for nations and individuals (believers and nonbelievers) is inescapable and inevitable. Accountability to one another, regardless of the relationship (husband/wife, parent/child, neighbor/neighbor, or nation/nation), is healthy and helpful to both parties. But accountability to God must be according to His will and Word, and our mutual accountability to one another must be according to His Word/will/law, too.

Nations and individuals are to follow "biblical values" because they are "traditional values" that are "functional values." Functional because "they work" and traditional because nations and individuals usually repeat "what works." Nations and individuals which and who reject biblical/traditional/function values are hell-bent on self-destruction.

What we are witnessing in this nation in this generation is the clash between law and morality; and when law and morality contradict each other, the Christian citizen has the cruel alternative of either losing his sense of morality or losing his respect and allegiance for and to the law.

I believe we American Christians will face the cruel choice of secession, abandonment, exile, or civil war. I see no other options. More about these alternatives is the section "On Secession, Abandonment, Exile, and/or Civil War."

The Bottom Line, "We're History!"

The bottom line of my conviction is that America (the U.S. of A.) is history! One reason for this belief is that I believe that the great moral, political, legislative, ethical, judicial, and religious debate over abortion is over. As I have stated repeatedly, I believe that a nation calling itself a Christian nation that refuses to acknowledge the existence of its weakest, smallest, most defenseless, and most vulnerable citizens and refuses to protect them, by law, will not be blessed by God, but will be cursed by God.

A nation that espouses in its creed, the Pledge of Allegiance, to be "one nation, under God," yet denies the presence of its tiniest citizens, little unborn babies, and protects their murderers at the rate of 4,500 per day after day, week after week, month after month, year after year, decade after decade is digging for itself a deep pit (grave) in which to be buried.

There are other great moral and national issues and sins this nation has endorsed that will surely add to the judgment of this nation and cause this nation to be added to the "ash heap" of history, but none reach the apex that the legal murder of millions of unborn babies does, in my humble opinion.

Considering the mounting storm clouds that are over our nation, there is much reason for pessimism as to whether we can reverse the immoral "nose dive" this nation is in. Consider these: financial disaster and collapse due to national, family, and individual debt; rampaging crime and violence, as well as appropriate and inappropriate respect and disrespect for law and authority; simple dishonesty and theft in many personal and private relationships (often with no guilt or sense of remorse); accepted deceit and fraud by many of our leaders in business, other institutions, governments, religious institutions, and churches; the AIDS plague; "mainstreaming" of sodomy as an acceptable sexual practice and the acceptance of the cohabitation of unmarried heterosexuals; the "looking for happiness in the wrong places," such as illicit drug use, pornography, or the worship of our bodies via physical fitness, surgery, or makeup fanaticism; the acceptance of pagan religions; suicide; euthanasia; infanticide; the confiscation of firearms and other defensive weapons from innocent people who simply want to be able to protect themselves; the threat to the existence and growth of Christian schools and home schooling through the regulations of these schools and the certification of their instructors (including parents) by government as well as the denial of financial assistance (and incentives) to those who support government schools with their taxes, on the one hand, but receive no financial aid (or benefit) for educating their children in private schools (or home schooling) that are not a financial burden to the government, on the other hand; the drive to global one-world government including multinational or a worldwide armed forces that may one day "impose" world, pagan morality/immorality on other nations; and the persecution of those who claim that "peace and tranquility" and "law and order" ought never to be "deified" above the Author of "truth and justice."

"Future Possible" Scenarios in Each of the (Renamed) "Ten Leading Categories to Gauge the Moral Climate/Temperature of a Nation"

I doubt that many of you have even thought about, much less come to the conclusion that secession, abandonment of the nation, being driven into exile, or civil war are realistic alternatives facing the dwindling Christian population of this nation. You understand that things are "less than perfect" or "less that favorable" probably, but to face secession, abandonment of the nation, being driven into exile, or fighting a civil war as a response to possible future conditions is out of the question for you. I agree that for now it is unrealistic, but what might the future hold?

Furthermore, I doubt many, or any, of you believe that "we have gone beyond the point of no return" or have considered the fact that God does not require us to remain loyal to a nation when loyalty to a nation is treason, disobedience to God. I'm sure few in Nazi Germany pondered their fate and the fate of their fatherland prior to the Second World War, and I'm sure few citizens of the Roman Empire considered, or concluded, that their civilization "had gone beyond the point of no return" when, in fact, it had.

But "What if . . . ? What if this occurred? What if that occurred? What if you were told to do this? What if you were told not to do that? What if you ordered to do this? What if you were ordered not to do that? What if you conclude, to do what you were told to do by the government (that God has ordered you not to do) or to not do what government has told you not to (that God has ordered you to do) caused you to sin against God? What then? Whom do you obey, man or God?"

We do not want to think about "this" and "that" possibilities. I do not enjoy subjecting you, or me, to "this or that" and "these or those" possibilities, but I feel that someone must. We don't like to consider leaving Christian denominations, we don't cherish abandoning political parties, and we abhor separating spouses in a marriage when we object, strenuously, to directions, positions, or circumstances they (denominations, political parties, or families) take or are in. Many times spouses—wives, for example—don't leave their husbands with their children even when there are circumstances and biblical justifications for doing so such as physical abuse or danger such as a natural disaster. For example, a family might be justified to abandon their coast home prior to a hurricane. After the hurricane passes, it may be justified for the husband to return to the home, alone, to assess the damage and stay at the home during repairs while his family stays in a safe environment (away from falling walls or tree limbs or from looters or vandals).

I am not necessarily talking above divorce or separation (in the case of a husband and wife separating for a short or long period of time), even though there are circumstances in which divorce is justifiable (though few). There are, however, times when separation is in order for spouses, such as when counseling and reconciliation are taking place (after, for example, a wife and/or children have been abused). Ought "separation" not to be considered when a nation takes actions (or goes in a direction) contrary to God's law and will? Ought not Christians secede from a nation that has "cast its lot," irrevocably, against God, nature and natural law? I grant that the word *irrevocably* is the key.

I have given this whole matter a lot of thought and prayer, and I am of the opinion that my limits of loyalty and allegiance to this nation are being strained. I am of the opinion that things are not going to improve but are going to get much, much worse.

"Things couldn't get any worse!," some wishful dreamers/optimists say. "Oh, yeah?" I counter. "Of course they could," we both know. I will now give some possible examples in the remainder of this section of this chapter of what could happen in years to come in the U.S. of A. I am going to take you "into the future" and "paint" some possible scenarios from each of the "Ten Leading Categories to Gauge the Moral Climate/Temperature of a Nation." (See "On Security and Prosperity.")

To "fit" future "times," I have renamed these ten categories. They are:

1. *Hostility toward Propagation of Christianity*
2. *Devaluation of the Sacredness and Intrinsic Worth of Human Life*
3. *The Lack of Security from Foreign and Domestic Enemies*
4. *The Erosion of Health Care, Human Service, and Charity*
5. *Environmental Unstewardship*
6. *The Undermining of Rights, Liberties, and Freedoms*
7. *Education: Immoral Instruction and General Knowledge Revisionist Teaching*
8. *The Economy: The Social/Welfare State*
9. *Human Sexuality: Sex Anytime, Anywhere, and with Anyone (or Anything) and without Procreation*
10. *Relationships: "Surely I Will Remember Thy Wonders of Old" (Ps. 77:11)*

1. Hostility toward Propagation of Christianity

Another "time" but not another "place." Could the following pages describe our culture regarding the propagation of Christianity at a time in the future?

One decree "on high" requires that contributions to Christian churches and institutions (including private charities, the few that still exist) not be tax-deductible for individuals, businesses, or other organizations. Another declares that from this point forward churches and their institutions will be taxed just like any other business and that donations must be reported to government auditors. There is much talk (and quiet objection) to these new orders but no disobedience or resistance.

Beginning next year Christians and Christianity are prohibited from "acts of charity" altogether. While Christians, including pastors and the executives of charitable institutions operated by Christianity, claim that this is their right as Americans as well as their duty before their God, not to mention a logical avenue to gain the confidence of those whom they help in order to evangelize to them, government says, "Your evangelizing people is questionably unconstitutional and you (Christianity) are doing so few works of charity, the recipients are becoming confused as to whom to thank, the government or Christianity. This is not good. We can't have that; the government is supreme and 'the people' must acknowledge this!"

"We'll compromise," said a public relations official for the Department of Health and Human Services in Washington, "to the point that we'll 'allow' you to hold seminars for the purpose of telling 'the needy' which government agencies to go to with particular needs, where the agencies are located, and the hours that the government agencies are open. This way you'll be participating in 'acts of charity.' Remember and be consoled in the knowledge that you are accomplishing your goal and responsibility to 'the needy' via your tax dollars to government, which funds our social services, and by your 'steering' the needy to us. You are 'doing unto other' as 'we' would have you do unto 'them.' "

The official closed his prepared text with this: "Rest assured that we'll see that everyone else is charitable through their taxes, or we'll place them in jail cells beside the few pastors and Christian charity organizations executives who defied our 'decrees' and resisted our orders to close down their 'social gospel' works. You Christians can still evangelize and propagate your faith as long as it is legal; we'll take care of 'the needy.' You concern yourselves with your 'hereafter' and the 'hereafter' of others, and we'll take care of people's physical needs." A few Christians remember that these statements were essentially what the communists and Nazi leaders said earlier in this century to the Christians in

Russia and Germany as Christianity became less and less relevant to their cultures. As Christianity became less relevant in Russia in the late 1910s, climaxing in 1933 when Adolf Hitler was named chancellor, the civil governments in Russia and Germany consolidated power, control, and money. The governments of Russia's communism and Germany's Third Reich took control of the social welfare systems from Christianity as they consolidated total control over the people.

Now the U.S. government has said: "We must do more to 'separate church from state'; therefore, you can no longer preach or teach the tenets of your Christian faith on public streets, sidewalks, parks, or anywhere else that is public (government) property. If we allow you (Christians) to speak on government property on matters of faith, a private matter, that would be tantamount to government endorsement of the Christian faith. And we can't have that, can we?"

Some street preachers countered with, "What about free speech? Don't we have the right to proclaim who our God is and to teach His positions on moral matters and matters of justice and charity as much as the secularists?" The federal courts a few years ago plainly said, "No. Your positions are countercultural. Your beliefs have brought division and conflict to our society, and we must maintain law and order and ensure that peace and tranquility reign."

A few fundamentalist Christians have murmured, "Do not truth and justice matter?" Government leaders said, "What is truth? What is justice? We cannot and will not accept your Christian perspectives on matters as important as 'truth and justice' because your opinion is 'tainted' by your religious opinions." Government leaders convinced the "moderate church" leadership to "get the extremist Bible-thumpers" off the streets for the sake of the dignity and reputation of Christianity.

The "lukewarm" Christians have joined the government voice with these seemingly moderate and innocuous measures in order to "protect" the image of Christianity. After all, "those people" protesting the killing of fetuses at the abortion clinics, the newborn at the infanticide clinics, and the elderly at the euthanasia clinics as well as those radicals who participate in the annual March for Jesus walk are getting in the way of the well-planned, dignified, single-day, "in-the-church"-buildings evangelism campaign. And their obnoxious "in-the-streets" witnessing will surely offend many who might otherwise attend our annual Christmas cantatas. These "not so nice,' "easily misunderstood," "in-your-face," and "not coated and tied" radical Christians are offending secularists and will surely cause needless new restraints against Christianity by the government.

And so it goes.

Prohibitions will continue. No Christian message will be allowed on envelopes going through the U.S. Postal System. No Christian bumper stickers will be allowed on autos being driven or parked on public streets or parked in public parking lots. No mention of Christianity will be allowed on any public building, statue, or wall. In fact, all mentions of Christ, Christianity, and/or God will scraped, scratched, sand-blasted, or chiseled off "the public square." Every coin will be "recalled" and either melted down or the slogan "In God We Trust" erased off it.

And those "crosses" must be removed from Christian churches and buildings if they can be seen from public property. No Christian may wear a cross that can be seen in public. The court's thinking on this matter was this: "Just as litter on one's private property is illegal because it is an 'eyesore' to passersby or because it devalues the property values in the area. Christian 'crosses' and other Christian religious symbols are 'offensive eyesores' to some people and we must be tolerant toward them. Either you take them (crosses and symbols) down from your properties now or erect 'a wall of (visual) separation' between your property and the public right-of-way or we will take them down at your expense and put you in jail cells beside the former street preachers and other Christian dissidents."

A decade or so ago Christmas and Easter holidays and other public acknowledged holidays were banned from schools by the U.S. federal court due to the "entanglement" of "church and state." There is a case in the federal court "hopper" now that would ban church bells ringing Christian music. This is a logical continuation of "pollution," i.e., "visual pollution," as it is considered "noise pollution" by some who are offended by the Christian faith. Hardly anyone believes the chiming of church bells will be legal by next year.

Back to "charity," Christian charity. If it is inappropriate to perform "acts of charity" through Christian institutions in the United States and its territories and possessions, such as Haiti (annexed in 1999 without the consent of the Haitians), it stands to reason that the U.S. government would not want to "impose" Christian morality through Christian charity on citizens of other nations even if the charity is authorized by foreign government. These "acts of charity" might be "used" by evangelical Christians to indoctrinate the Christian dogma on vulnerable "needy" people in other lands. The federal government (of the U.S. of A.) is considering a law that would effectively ban acts of charity and evangelism in foreign nations by U.S. citizens and institutions even if foreign government leaders welcome and approve of such activities. One reason the president is considering the ban is that the morality espoused by Christian charity officials runs counter to the morality being exported by the government through its foreign aid department.

While we, as Americans, through our government, pledge ourselves to constitutional, democratic, and representative government reform in other nations (for the good of their citizens, of course), we would consider it an act of "high crimes and misdemeanors," not to mention treason, to export Christian charity and Christianity onto unsuspecting nations and their people.

"What's left for Christians to do in the United States and our Christian citizens residing in other nations in the area of propagating the Christian faith?" a few Christians ask. "You can pray for whatever you desire in your homes and in your 'neutral-looking' and 'neutered-acting' churches," said our president and the heads of the major Christian denominations in America.

2. Devaluation of the Sacredness and Intrinsic Worth of Human Life

Here are some more possibilities to consider at a time when the past is still in the past, only further so; the present is in the more recent past; the near future is now; and the more distant future is still in the future. In other words, this is written as if in the future.

Abortion is not a hot topic anymore. We have settled the "issue," and the debate is, more or less, over. Christians have not only accepted legal abortion as a given legal right but are subjecting their unborn babies to abortion more frequently and through the entire nine months of pregnancy for no or any reason, as are non-Christian women. In fact, the abortion rate for "self-identified" Christians is equal to that of the general population. Pastors no longer address the moral relativism of abortion to the Christian faith for fear of offending their congregations, who, in overwhelming percentages, according to polls, believe abortion is not immoral, even though they understand that abortion kills a living human being.

Christians who still believe that abortion is immoral rely almost exclusively on prayer to save babies and have agreed not to be "disagreeable" on the "matter" of murdered babies any longer, seeing that being "divisive" on this "too long debated 'issue' " brings scorn on Christianity by the general public (for being "judgmental"), accomplishes nothing, and may cause a few Christians women who have had abortions to feel "guilty" for having offered their unborn children as human sacrifices.

Even though child abuse and neglect, not to mention neonatal intensive care costs, were to have been virtually eliminated by abortion through "safe, legal, government-funded, and 'anything but rare,' " national abortion policies, the number of abortions has continued to increase over the more than three decades of legal abortion (despite a much smaller childbearing population). Presently, there are more abortions than live births in the nation and 48 percent of Christian women's pregnancies are terminated by abortion.

Another "lie" has come to be accepted in the United States. Many Christian denominations' pastors/priests/leaders/medical institutions' executives declared in the late 1993s: "We will close down our Christian hospitals and medical centers and clinics before we will allow abortions to take place in them." Also, many Christian physicians and nurses said they would refuse to perform abortions if ordered to by the government or by their superiors. They said they would quit medicine before they would assist in or perform a single abortion. Most Christian medical hospitals and health-care clinics and centers' trustees, executives, and physicians said, "We will not accept government funds in any way, shape, or fashion if accepting the funds means we have to 'shed the innocent blood' of unborn babies." They lied; they all caved in.

When the time came to "put up or shut up," 99.9 percent of the Christian medical hospitals, centers, and clinics as well as Christian medical personnel began to kill the unborn along side their secular peers.

"One who does not take care of his own family is worse than an infidel," the chorus went up by those who said Christians ought to join the killing rather than disadvantage their families via lost jobs or lower incomes. The rhetoric sounded similar to the condemnations of Paul Hill after he was convicted of terminating the life of an abortionist and his armed bodyguard in Pensacola. The day that Hill was executed in Florida, Christians condemned him for abandoning his wife and their three children.

The pro-life physicians who perform many of the abortions executed in hospitals, medical centers, and clinics across the country today are providing well for their families, especially materially, and they aren't doing too badly for themselves as they enjoy nice homes and cars, annual European vacations, seminars in the Caribbean Islands, and weekend, and a few weekday, respites on their yachts in the Long Island Sound, Puget Sound, or the thousands of other yachtsmen's hangouts in the country.

National universal health care mandated "free abortion services" for every woman and required, under penalty of fines and imprisonment by federal law, that health-care facilities and physicians and nurses who perform gynecological care must perform abortions.

These days women are becoming pregnant on purpose in a variety of ways other than the "old-fashioned" traditional way in order to "grow fetuses" for "harvesting" for the humanitarian "cause" of providing "tissue," organs, and "replacement parts" for those who need this type of "treatment." Of course, this "treatment" is paid for via tax funds through universal health care, including the "fee for services" to the women who get pregnant and make "contributions" of their fetuses as well as to the men who offer their "services" via "sperm banks" or volunteer to impregnate women "the old-fashioned way," for the good of the "whole" community, of course (certainly not because of the money or the "good feeling" they receive physically). Humanitarian causes bring out the best in mankind.

It has been well established by logic and practice that "the power to tax is the power to destroy" and "whatever is subsidized will grow." We are seeing this "growth" via "fee for services" in voluntary pregnancies and pregnancy terminations in order to donate (for a fee) fetuses by both women willing to become pregnant and men willing to assist women in become pregnant. Financial incentives or disincentives are being used across the boards in our society today to encourage or discourage certain social and economic behavior. Only a few malcontents complain that government policies place government squarely in the business of affecting ethical/moral/religious policies, which government has used to quiet Christians and Christianity when they were told to stay out of mixing religion and policies ("church and state").

While some recall those bygone days when we debated suicide, first the legality and morality of people killing themselves and, soon afterward, the legality and morality of the medical profession's assistance in killing those desirous of "checking out" early. Few even remember that the

234

debate centered, initially, on those who were terminal (whatever that meant [we are all terminal.]) and one day will be in pain. The logic of "not imposing" a collective will (morality), legally on those who were not terminally ill and/or not in pain who wanted to die and be assisted in dying was certain to give way.

A few others remember the debate shifted to whether or not there ought to be any criteria at all regarding who ought to be allowed to commit suicide and assisted in dying, i.e., age, including parental consent and/or notification, emotional stability, economic situation, educational attainment, mental condition, or IQ. At first, the law required a three-physician panel to agree that suicide (and assistance in dying) was warranted, but that soon gave way when three or more "physicians" were banding together to create euthanasia centers, which became known as "discontinuation clinics." Many of these "D.C." centers are presently geographically restricted to medical business areas that are set aside for the killing and harvesting of "tissue," organs and "body parts" from those who have recently died or been killed in abortion clinics or infanticide clinics.

Did I forget to chronicle the "infanticide movement"? Please excuse and pardon me. How clumsy of me! The devaluation of human life has been so swift and the killing so pervasive that it is easy to overlook some of the tragedy. Some of us "old-timers" remember something called the domino effect, which was a major reason for the U.S. military involvement in Southeast Asia, in general, and Vietnam, in particular. Many Americans were concerned that the "cancer" of communism might spread and eventually engulf the whole world. Some of us thought it was noble to do more than pray for the Vietnamese people who were being overrun by superior and outside military forces. Many Americans supported and many of us interfered physically with military power in order to try to help the Republic of Vietnam maintain its national integrity and destiny. Americans who supported the U.S. military involvement in the Vietnam War believed we were acting to stop the spread of communism to other nations in Southeast Asia and, possibly, to other nations throughout the world.

Using that same logic, "the domino effect," in this nation as well to try to stop the legal killing of the first group of innocents under attack at the time, the innocent unborn, many tried to protect these victims, illegally and peacefully, through sit-ins at the doors of the abortion centers. We thought the peaceful attempts to protect the unborn would not only save babies but stem the tide of the "death ethic" (the "domino effect") that was beginning to dominate our culture. We failed to change the hearts and minds of our countrymen and women and abortion continued to not only take untold casualties of our unborns, but perpetuate the legal killing of other citizens. First, the unborn, then the newborn, and then the old born. We are at a point where everyone is "fair game" for the meat market. I recall telling an Operation Rescue rally in 1993, "When fetuses are nothing more than 'raw meat,' then we all will be nothing more than 'raw meat.' "

The debate over "when life (or meaningful life) begins" was renewed when infanticide was being discussed in earnest at the beginning of the twenty-first century. The debate really was not of much concern to honest people, because they acknowledged the newborn was a human being, just as everyone finally acknowledged in the abortion debate back in the latter decade of the twentieth century that the fetus was a human being from the moment of conception. The question in the debate about legal infanticide became (as it had in the abortion debate), "Who decides?" "Who," according to the pro-choice enthusiasts, "should decide whether to allow a newborn to continue to live or to die (or to be killed) ought to be the parent/s." They convinced the general public that it was immoral for some (the "antichoicers") to "legislate their morality on others" (in this case, parents who wanted to "let die" or "kill" their newborn child/ren).

The infanticide enthusiasts "waxed eloquent" that it was not a matter in which government ought to get involved. "Infanticide is a moral matter and civil government must not impose its morals on parents of newborns," they argued. "Besides," they stated correctly, "infanticide would 'cut' health-care costs for the society as a whole." Some suggested we could cut, or even eliminate, all health-care costs (including health-care workers, hospitals, pharmaceutical companies, not to mention health insurance companies) if, through government policy, we encouraged suicide and the killing of those who are ill. Some extremists in the "killing to solve social, moral, medical, ethical, and economic problems" even suggested the required killing of everyone who was "sick, feeling bad, or having a bad day." Some "death ethicists" suggested a government grant be awarded to those (for their dependents, heirs, or charities) who were willing to be killed. Clearly, many spouses and children of the "sick" and "in pain" elderly, as the "death with dignity" and "death to solve problems of those with sick relatives" movement grew, believed it to be compassionate to kill those for whom we were responsible.

Out of this mindset came a new "growth industry," the killing of the newborn, "infanticide," as well as a collateral industry, the use of body parts for "recycling."

This mentality, morality, ushered in the national decision that a newborn "life" was not to be protected from its parents' decision to kill at the "beginning" of the born end of life until that life "could walk." Many would never be able to walk, or walk "meaningfully" due to physical complications, i.e., "the hand they were dealt." Some advocated that it would not only be good for society to kill these "potential toddlers" for the good of the "whole" but would be the charitable, compassionate thing to do for the kids. So we permitted infanticide clinics to be set up beside the abortion clinics and euthanasia clinics. These districts are called terminator alleys.

Nevada and New Jersey have lost their tax advantage over other surrounding states now that gambling barriers have collapsed in all states. Nevada, which has a long history of being on the "cutting edge" as a tourist mecca, has been innovative in tourist recreation and entertainment. One of those entertainments has been simulated dueling in the streets of Carson City and other historically significant towns and cities. The Nevada legislature has approved "dueling" and the federal courts have approved the measure as a "privacy right" and a "state's right."

A headline announcing the federal judicial approval of "dueling to the death" read: "Legalized Dueling to Fatten Public Coffers." The story read: "To bolster a sagging economy, due to lost revenues and taxes caused by out-of-state gambling competition, Nevada has legalized dueling. Private companies are preparing to invest in 'dueling matches' similar to those held in Tombstone in 1881 when Wyatt Earp, his two brothers, and 'Doc' Holiday dueled it out at high noon with a rival gang at the O.K. Corral."

The proponents of "legal dueling" say, "If the duelers are willing, government ought to stay out of it. It ought to be a legal choice. Besides, people are 'dueling it out' in the streets across America every day and innocent people are accidentally being killed and wounded.

"We recommend making dueling 'safe and legal' (for the general public, that is)," they reason. "Plus, we could offer cash prizes to the 'contestants' as we make 'games' of dueling, say $100,000 to winners (survivors) and $50,000 to losers (the dead, with the proceeds going to their dependents, estates, heirs, and/or charities). We could charge for admission to the 'games' as well as profit from gambling (betting on winners), paying prizes from these two sources of revenue.

"Of course," they contend, "all of this would have to be government-regulated, which means we would have an employment increase not only in the private sector but also in the government section. And this industry would provide additional tax resources for local, state, and federal governments. All winners and no losers, unless you call the 'contestants' shot dead 'losers.' But they (those shot dead) really would not be losers, in one respect, because they would 'choose' to compete (or not) and can 'exit' their way, with drama, reminiscent of Paul Anka's song 'I Did It My Way.' "

"We recommend," advocates of legalized dueling suggest, "standing the duelers back-to-back on the fifty-yard lines in our football stadiums (when the stadiums are not in use [another advantage, additional use of public facilities]), have the duelers pace off twenty steps, turn, and open fire on one another with handguns (this will please the advocates of the confiscation of handguns [the guns used in dueling will be "off the streets" and out-of-the-homes of law-abiding citizens]), and continue shooting until one contestant is dead as a door knob. The surviving dueler would be the winner! Presto, instant wealth and notoriety! We would protect the 'sports fans' in the stands much like we protect sports fans at hockey arenas from errant flying hockey pucks by erecting portable, bulletproof, see-through walls."

The arguments of the advocates of legal dueling seemed reasonable and were compelling to the U.S. Supreme Court when they approved the venture in 1999. For once the high court used historical evidence in making their decision, as they pointed out that dueling was legal when the U.S. Constitution was enacted.

The gaming industry was thrilled! Local and state governments (Nevada first, New Jersey second, now other states are joining in "the games") envision the influx of new gaming tax revenues. The medical community was skeptical at first, but after it was pointed out that legal dueling would "expand the resources of donor tissue, organs, and body parts," they endorsed "the games." And the population control people and the environmental enthusiasts see the advantage of this growth industry, the elimination of (evil) people, particularly if the new tax revenues are earmarked for environmental conservation efforts and if they are assured that no errant bullets would strike a spotted owl or a snail darter.

Licenses to marry and certification to bear children are new government regulations. While state legislatures wrestle with legalized dueling and allowing the gaming industry to encourage and promote it or leave ownership of the "matches" to local government, another controversial issue has surfaced. There is a new federal regulation requiring registration and approval (by the regional health-care alliances) prior to marriages for heterosexual couples and certification and approval for heterosexual couples prior to conceiving and bearing children after they have become legally married.

Homosexual couples are exempt from the requirement (government approval to marry) due to the fact that they can't reproduce (by themselves, that is). Also, homosexuals are encouraged to marry, sort of an "affirmative action" resulting from years of discrimination. Homosexual couples simply give notice of their marriages to government; they do not need government approval to unite. Another type of "affirmative action" to assist homosexual couples is that homosexual couples need not obtain permission to have children, as do heterosexual couples. A number of available methods of child conceiving, bearing, and adopting are scientifically possible and sociably accepted today.

These two regulations requiring prior approval by the regional health-care alliances, (1) marriage, and (2) conceiving and bearing of children by heterosexual couples, have two purposes: to keep up with who is living where and with whom and to control population, not that population growth is a concern now that the U.S. population growth is not "growth" at all anymore. The population has been declining for more than two decades and is far below replacement level. The population of the United States was increasing in the last few decades of the twentieth century and the first decade of the twenty-first century due to legal and illegal immigration, but now few immigrants are desiring to reside in the U.S. due to the bad economic opportunity and the loss of rights, liberties, and freedoms here.

Single women who become pregnant are, in almost all circumstances, required to have abortions. Married heterosexual couples are forced to have abortions if they do not ask for and receive permission to conceive first.

Criteria the regional health-care alliances use to deny or grant permission for heterosexual couples to marry and, subsequently, to have live births include but are not limited to these considerations: health of the fetus, mother, and father; number of living children; predicted IQ of the fetus; assets, liabilities, and income of the couple; sex of the fetus (in an effort to "balance the sexes," for in some regions there is an imbalance of male children [too many] due to smaller numbers of children in families [families with one child prefer male children] and "selected" abortions of female fetuses by the "choice" of many parents [desiring to conceive a male child later]); professions of parents; and faith/religion or lack of faith/religion of parents. (Some say the last reason [faith/religion of parents] is being used to eliminate Christians by denying Christians the right to marriage or to bear children once marriage is approved.)

One often-heard complaint, not made public, is that the members of the regional health-care alliance board are anonymous.

"Living wills" (called death wishes by some) "no wills," and "no say" are topics of interest today regarding what to do with or to sick old folks. Understandably, there has been continuing debate and conflict over the withholding and withdrawing of treatment (which includes feeding and oxygen tubes for those who can't swallow and/or need oxygen rather than room air). It is more reasonable these days to accept the allowing of sick folks when they enter the "autumns" of their lives to voluntarily prescribe what is to be done "for" or "to" them when they are unconscious through "living wills" due to the acceptance of "privacy rights" over one's own body (such as in abortion rights) many years ago.

By the turn of the century, there was little conflict over allowing people to die or to be killed by euthanasia who had explained ahead of time via a legal document that this is what they preferred to be done to them when they became unconscious.

A real problem arose when no guidelines were left by unconscious persons regarding what was to be done "to" or "for" them. Without instructions, the preferred "treatment" would be unclear. Ought health-care workers to treat, feed and clothe, resuscitate, or kill their patient? While it appeared logical that the next of kin or friends ought to "speak for" the unconscious, a few objected to this because of the possibility that the next of kin or friends might be influenced by a financial motive or the motive of not wanting to continue to be responsible for the patient. These motives might influence the kinfolk or friend to order the medical team to kill the patient. Some suggested that physicians and attorneys would be better suited to make the judgment as to health care for a critically ill person who was unconscious due to the fact that the physicians and attorneys would be "removed from personal involvement" and would not have a financial incentive. But many of the physicians making

240

the call practiced "medicide," a new specialty in medicine (a specialty in killing patients), and some attorneys, desirous of estate business, had a financial vested interest that is improved with dead patients and clients. These attorneys are called "hearse packers," a take-off from the phrase *ambulance chasers.*

As it "takes a village" to raise a child, it has generally become accepted to allow "the village" to determine whether or not to kill a member of "the village," to continue treatment, or to do nothing. These decisions began to be made by "committees." The "committee" usually is represented by heirs, friends, medical people, legal people, and financial consultants and always a member of the regional health care alliance. The "committee" considers the health of the person and the health of "the village" in deciding when or if to kill the relative/patient/client/taxpayer/health-care user or to treat, feed and clothe, resuscitate, and house the person who is unconscious and has failed to indicate in writing or with verbal instructions what to do "for" or "to" him. "Living wills" may be required in the near future.

A brewing confrontation today is this: What do we do with those who are conscious that "the village" has decided ought to volunteer to be killed and who are not willing to be killed? There is considerable anguish these days as to what to do with those who are conscious and seemingly logical and reasonable who have not "opted" to be killed even after "the committee" has recommended death as the best medical option for "them" and "the village." Social workers, physicians, attorneys, family members, friends, and, you guessed it, representatives of the regional health-care alliances are giving excellent instructions in the art of personal persuasion by auxiliary "encounter groups" to the "sick and stubborn" who have not yet signed "living wills" or agreed to "move out" now.

About the only group immune from being killed are those living in our prisons who have been convicted of first-degree murder. Our culture is sensitive to these people and will not even allow these prisoners to choose to be executed and their bodies sold to medical institutions for "tissue," organs, and "spare parts." Funny, some think of this denial as unconstitutional, but they are few and far between. Most say that these convicted murders are really special; they are the "victims" of our society. And they must be protected, even from their own folly and bad choices.

We are in another "brave new world" now, indeed. Many are "brave" in their advice and declarations as to who should live and who should die or be killed. We do have a few "cowards" left; they are, however, confined to the group "targeted" for extinction: the Christians. Many citizens of this nation believe this hatred group with much persuasion and "prayer" will soon become more brave and willing to enter "the great beyond" or abandon the nation.

3. The Lack of Security from Foreign and Domestic Enemies

When open-minded, reflective citizens, Christians and non-Christians, look back into recent history from their perspective in the future, they will be able to identify times when domestic violent lawbreaking escalated totally out of control. We ought to be able to understand by then that there have been, are, and shall always be "causes" and "effects" of crime, and this is true regarding the senseless and random, out-of-control violence that is gripping this land.

Crime has become a trademark, a legacy, of this generation. To be sure, the moral meltdown of our culture, particularly the breakdown of the family unit as well as the lack of the fear of God by Christians (and non-Christians), is the root cause of the criminal violence across our land, but civil government has contributed to this shameful condition, too. The lack of punishing criminals and the decriminalization of many crimes, along with the absence of successful rehabilitation programs in jails and prisons, have played a part in the escalation of crime in this land. The deemphasis on citizen's protection of themselves via the confiscation of weapons of protection and an unwillingness of citizens to be their first line of protection against criminals have given criminals more boldness as they understand that most of their potential victims are unwilling or unable to protect themselves, their families, and their property. Last, our civil government has become the "criminal element" in many areas as it confuses "good and evil." Our civil government, our citizens (in a government "of, by, and for the people"), must take heed from Amos 5:15: "Hate the evil and love the good and establish judgment in the gate." Might the following be scenarios with us tomorrow?

The Criminal Control Act of 1994 was a broad plan to curb crime by spending $30 billion that the federal government did not have and "spraying" the funds into social programs, law enforcement, judicial

242

reform, and new penal institutions. And more crimes were designated "federal crimes."

It was "too little and too late." Midnight basketball games in urban gyms, sponsored and paid for by federal dollars, was a great idea for the kids who could evade their local police, who were enforcing local 10:00 P.M. curfews. The public saw this as silly, wasteful, and the grasping at "the last straws," and the criminals saw this as hilarious.

Another direction of government that fostered great hope for continued success and protection for criminals and "wanta-be" criminals was the disarming of the citizens by government. This occurred first through the banning of certain types of weapons, then the registration of all weapons, and then, finally, the confiscation of all weapons. None believed the banning of weapons would occur swiftly. Most thought the U.S. Supreme Court would honor the constitutional provision of "the right to bear arms," which is clearly defined in the Second Amendment of the U.S. Constitution. But in the hysteria to "buy back," "pick up," "confiscate," and "melt down" as many weapons as possible, the Supreme Court nullified the Second Amendment by fiat, just as it had done in previous years to other enumerated rights, liberties, and freedoms that had been taken for granted for generations.

The criminals were armed, are armed, and will stay armed, and they knew (and know and will continue to know) what the disarming of Americans would do for them. They knew it would make for "safe, illegal, and 'anything but rare' " sacking, raping, and plundering of America. There is now no doubt that criminals prefer unarmed victims. And with the approximate forty-five minute average response time by law enforcement personnel to 911 emergency calls, criminals can "linger" around the crime scene to catch their breath, "tidy" up a bit (including the elimination of evidence that might incriminate them), and sack, rape, and plunder again, then leave.

About the only two points left that are now being debated in public about domestic crime are (1) what to do with the citizens who refuse to "turn in" their illegal weapons (and are frequently used while trying to protect themselves when victimized); and (2) ought we now move to disarm our law enforcement officers in the hope that criminals will not use weapons while on their crime sprees? There are pros and cons on each side of these two propositions.

Some say that we ought not to be too severe on those few citizens who have been unwilling to relinquish their firearms. The government efforts to confiscate firearms from those who had registered their weapons, according to government mandates to do so several years ago, cleared our society of practically all weapons from most of the law-abiding citizens. (So government thought, until they realized that many people did not register their weapons when ordered to do so.) As you can imagine, government officials are having a major problem locating the weapons of both the criminals and the noncriminals who did not register their weapons when ordered to do so. (I guess that makes these noncriminals criminals, too.) Government fears "all" armed citizens.

The second phase of the weapons control efforts in the 1990s and the 2000s became known as "the firearms regulation and registration acts." In the early 1990s, the first phrase, the banning of specific rapid-fire weapons, was followed quickly by the second phase, which, as has been mentioned, was the registration of some, then other, and finally, all firearms.

The third phase was the unashamed banning of all firearms by the federal government, which was implemented, initially, by confiscation of the firearms from those who had registered their firearms when told to do so. Of course, government officials and politicians had told gun owners, even promised them, that registration of guns would not lead to confiscation. The government lied. Hunters and sportsmen, who used firearms for target practice, were told they would continue to be able to own and use their firearms for those purposes. Hunting for sport and/or food with firearms is now moot, as the ownership of any firearm is illegal.

Recently in a small west Texas town there was a bit of flack when a housewife (and mother of two preschool children) whose husband was out of town on a business trip was jailed for having an illegal handgun in her home. She was given the maximum sentence, five years, for the violation, which was "the illegal ownership/possession of a firearm." She used the handgun in a "threatening matter" against an intruder in her home in the middle of the night and was given the maximum sentence for this offense, "threatening the life of another with an illegal weapon," which was seven years. She is now serving a twelve-year sentence for the two federal felony convictions.

The deputy sheriff discovered her illegal possession of the handgun when he answered the call to the sheriff's office she made when she realized an intruder was in her home. When the deputy sheriff arrived, forty-two minutes after the 911 emergency call, the housewife/mother told the deputy of being awakened by a noise downstairs, discovering an

244

intruder in her home, calling for help, confronting the intruder/burglar in the upstairs hallway, and ordering him to leave after telling him she had a gun and knew how to use it. She told the deputy sheriff that the intruder was armed with a handgun. The deputy read the lady her Miranda rights, arrested her, and took her to the county jail for illegal possession of a firearm and threatening a person with it.

The intruder/thief was apprehended one month later when he attempted to pawn the housewife/mother/family's television and a few other items in Lubbock. He confessed to breaking and entering the family's home as well as committing grand larceny but denied the woman's allegation that he was armed with a handgun when he was scared out of her home. He acknowledged that she had threatened him with a handgun and testified to that fact at her trial. He pleaded guilty to the two crimes and "threw himself at the mercy of the court." He was given a lecture by the judge and a two-year suspended sentence with one-year probation.

Meanwhile, the lady pleaded "not guilty" to the two federal felony crimes that she had been charged with, believing a jury of her peers in west Texas would find her "not guilty" or at least be "deadlocked" through her planned attempt to use "jury nullification" on the two violations with which she had been charged. She was mistaken; she was convicted and is serving twelve years in prison at an undisclosed federal penitentiary in Arizona.

Unfortunately, this case is typical of "justice" in America today.

The National Police Chiefs' Association is standing united behind the proposed federal legislative initiative that will ban firearms from police officers in the United States. Their belief is that if the criminal element is convinced that both citizens and law enforcement officers are unarmed, there is less likelihood that criminals will commit crimes armed. The NPCA spokesman said, "We have tried everything else. Should we not try this now?" He calls the proposition a truce (with the criminals) effort and asks that Congress pass the proposal.

Policemen on the "beat" have strongly disagreed with their superiors. They say, "This proposal is not a 'truce' but a 'surrender'!" Offering a different perspective on this initiative is the National Police Officers' Association. The NPOA is comprised of the "footsoldiers" who are not willing to face possibly armed criminals unarmed in another "social" experiment. Their recent strongly worded news release said: "If the police chiefs are willing to experiment with law enforcement officers' lives for a short 'test trial' period, we are willing to agree to this if the chiefs are willing to change roles with us for the 'trial period'."

While the police chiefs and their subordinates debate this through their national organizations, the general public will add their "two cents" on talk radio programs and through letters to the editors of newspapers and magazines. And politicians will craft legislation that will try to reach a compromise, a happy balance, that will satisfy neither side fully.

One lawmaker calls her alternative proposal the "Peace in Our Time" bill. This New York congresswoman's bill is really weird. Among other things, she suggest that police officers be armed on Mondays, Wednesdays, and Fridays and be unarmed on Tuesdays, Thursdays, and Saturdays during a one-year test period. She suggested that the results of the test period be studied after the experiment. Oh, yes, when asked about Sundays, she advocates that police officers be given the day off in an effort to promote "family values/time together" for police officers and their families (as the divorce rate for police officers is 82 percent) as well as to cut law enforcement costs. Only from New York state, "the Former People's Republic of Mario Cuomo," could this be suggested seriously? Right?!?!

There is understood and natural frustration among Americans over our inability to curb crime, particularly violent crime. Neighborhoods are receiving local government permission to "seal off" their subdivisions at night with iron gates and other roadblocks. Even moderate-income neighborhoods have hired private security guard companies to patrol their neighborhoods twenty-four a day. "Neighborhood Watch" programs are common, not the exception, in every city and town in the nation. Alarm systems and emergency exits are being installed and cut into rooms, especially bedrooms, as homes are being built and remodeled. New homes and apartments are being designed with security alarms and sensors and bars over windows and doors as well as emergency exists from almost every room.

The criminal justice system has tried about everything, to no avail. "Truth in sentencing," "no sentencing," "halfway houses," " 'three strikes, you're out' sentencing," "life without parole sentencing," and " 'just promise us you'll not do it again' sentencing" have all been tried unsuccessfully. Social programs, appointing and electing of chiefs of policies, judges, and parole officers, more jails, no jails, "no frills" cells, "all the frills" cells, rehabilitation of inmates and former inmates, "kinder and gentler" treatment of inmates, and so on and on, have been tried.

Some, in exasperation, are now even proposing that we legalize all crime! It would certainly "cut government costs" and "reduce the crime rate." We could eliminate law enforcement, judicial, and penal costs and a few other costs. And no one would be made to "feel guilty" for having done something wrong, immoral, evil, or antisocial. Self-esteem among our "thugs" would rival the self-esteem enjoyed by our "students" in government schools.

The U.S. armed services are really staying busy these days, now that our nation has been officially named the "police force of the world" by the United Nations. Along with supporting and financing "peace" on every continent via the U.S. armed forces, the home forces of the armed services are "seeing" a great deal of action in most all of our urban areas.

And we now have elements of the Mobile Strike Force, comprised of elite airborne, light infantry, and military police troops, in all fifty states. These "special forces" units are specialists in civil unrest and political stabilization and may be deplored by the president, the commander-in-chief, at any time and anywhere in the country regardless of the wishes of the governors or mayors. We learned, bitterly, in the Detroit riots of 1998 and the Atlanta riots of 1999 that local police departments, state patrols, and state national guard units were incapable, at times, of quelling urban civil disturbances. The federal government reasoned that if state and local governments were going to ask and expect the federal government to rebuild cities (with federal relief funds) after they have been destroyed by natural or man-made disasters, the federal government ought to be allowed to "step in" and "stomp out" rioting with federal armed forces.

In the opinion of most Americans, regarding both the national and international scenes, there is no longer the will, finances, or patriotism to continue to resist the aggression of our federal government (and the world government [the United Nations]). During the mild confrontations with government and minor acts of civil disobedience and small amount of destruction (by today's comparison) of the 1960s (for the civil rights of African-Americans), the 1970s (protests against U.S. participation in the Vietnam War), the late 1980s and early 1990s (by the antiabortion movement), and the late 1990s (for the civil rights of the homosexuals), Americans were resolute in not allowing the frustration and lawlessness to "break" the restraints of government or the will of the people to live in a land of uncompromised rights, liberties, and freedoms. The general consensus now is that a totalitarian government must emerge from the rubble one day soon to establish order.

"Who are these 'blue-helmeted' soldiers that are billeted in every major urban area of our country and where did they come from?" some still ask. Most know precisely who they are, where they came from, and who their commanders are.

On the international front, Americans ought to be sleeping well, as we are now being protected by the United Nation's "blue-helmeted" troops. They are intermingled with U.S. troops on all military installations at home and abroad. There are many advantages to this situation, which has evolved gradually over the past twenty years.

From "hot spots" around the world brought about by civil war, ethnic cleansing, border clashes, and outright warfare between nations to the crushing of governments due to the fact that citizens from certain other nations were defecting to those nations by boats, airplanes, and foot, the "blue-helmeted" U.S. troops are "keeping the peace" around the world after they have destroyed resistance by the former governments, which were declared illegitimate by the UN General Assembly. Some nations have approved of their citizens' becoming cocitizens of more than one nation. The democratically elected president of Mexico approved of cocitizenship for Mexicans with the United States in the mid-1990s, paving the way for multinational citizenships.

Even the UN governing body, the UN military high command and brain trust, and, especially, the ground troops trying to keep the peace while dodging the local inhabitants' gunshots aimed at them and at "countrymen" when civil war exists have not always been pleased with the new forms of governments or the new leadership imposed on them by UN military commanders. Some believe that the "peace-keeping" forces were, first, "invasion forces."

Some Americans are wondering what might eventually happen if we elect or appoint political leaders in this country who are not endorsed by the UN political or military leaders or if we intensify our "ethnic cleansing" of the few Christians left between the Atlantic and the Pacific Oceans and between the Canadian and Mexican borders. Now that we do not have the independent economic or military strengths that we had when America was a totally independent sovereign nation, some have speculated as to what would happen if the United Nations threatens to invade our shores if the United States does not "toe" the world body "party line" someday.

What might be our national resolve if we don't change governments or leaders (or the type of government or economic system) when or if the UN high command orders us to? If "blue-helmeted" UN forces invade our nation in an attempt to bring down our political leaders will there be any resistance? Most folks don't see that there would be anything left worth fighting or dying for.

How true, how shameful; how sad.

4. The Erosion of Health Care, Human Services, and Charity

Where might we be in providing health care, human services, and charity to the inhabitants of this nation in two or three (or less) decades? Will we have a balance between government and private providers in these three critical areas or will our drift toward a social/welfare state have eliminated private competition and private charity? Might the rights, liberties, and freedoms as well as the responsibilities of individual Christians and Christian health care, human service, and charity institutions collapse due to the lack of support or be banned by the government? Might the landscape of America in these areas be radically changed soon as portrayed by the following pages?

Things are not going well in the areas of health care and human services in the nation now that religious charity has been outlawed by the federal courts and due to the fact that so many mentally competent and able-bodied people are refusing to work and are being sustained by government grants, entitlements, and aid.

In the late 1990s—1999, I think it was—the U.S. Supreme Court, in the now-famous *United States versus Catholic Charities* case, ruled religious charity unconstitutional. Even though Catholic Charities and the few other Christian charitable institutions that were still in business had agreed not to proselytize those whom they served several years before the decision, the Court ruled that allowing Christian organizations to receive tax-deductible contributions and to be tax-exempt was a "veiled" way of circumventing the "wall of separation between church and state."

In this particular case, Catholic Charities had not been accused of attempting to "propagate" their Christian faith (Catholic Charities had long ago refrained from doing that as per government requirements, as

Catholic Charities had been taking enormous funds from various government agencies to carry out their aid [as much as two-thirds of their operating funds came from government sources as far back as 1995]); however, the Supreme Court justices decided in a 9–0 decision that the provision of material goods and medical care to the needy "is construed as an attempt to promote the 'one-God' concept of Christianity and to 'witness' through 'good deeds'," a phrase from the Christian Bible.

In the oral arguments, the U.S. solicitor general, who argued the case for the federal government, pointed out that a few of the Catholic Charities' facilities had failed to remove or conceal, as they had agreed, crucifixes, crosses, painting of "the Madonna," and other Christian emblems. While it was "settled law" that these institutions could not display "their religions" or "voice their religion," the Court agreed with the solicitor general when she maintained that, from a practical point of view, this could not be done. She said, "Even the name, Catholic Charities, conveys a religious preference."

The National Conference of Catholic Bishops countered that Catholic Charities had instructed their facilities to "wipe clear" any visual images and to be "void by voice" of any relationship with the God of the Catholic Church. The bishops admitted that some of its volunteers and employees disregarded these instructions. There was an affidavit in the presentation submitted by the solicitor general signed by a Catholic priest who acknowledged that he tried to always offer charity to the needy with the statement: "Christ told me that whatever I do unto the least of these, I do unto Him." The attorney for the National Conference of Catholic Bishops stated that this priest has been removed and is being disciplined for not obeying their regulations.

Many government employees who work in local, state, and federal social service agencies have been encouraging lawmakers for more than two decades to eliminate tax preferences, such as tax-deductible contributions and tax-exempt status, for religious institutions that perform charitable work. These financially conservative government employees succeeded in eliminating tax-deductible contributions for churches in the early 2000s and have been the driving force calling for the banning of religious and other charitable institutions altogether.

These "progressives," as they call themselves, represent both the Democratic and Republican parties and are elected and are civil service government employees. They have ushered in a new age of social services in which there is no more confusion as to who is the benefactor of charity. It is now, clearly, only the government/s.

One major reason for the lack of desired and projected "contributions" by individuals and corporations into government-owned and- controlled charities when those "contributions/donations" were added to earmarked tax revenues by government/s was the belief, by taxpayers, that our society was confusing "rights and entitlements" (by the recipients), on the one hand, and "blackmail and extortion" (by the providers), on the other hand. Many taxpayers objected to their taxes being used to "sustain an unacceptable lifestyle" by many of the recipients while the beneficiaries refused to work as volunteers for the community improvement.

Another reason taxpayers were not making government-requested "voluntary contributions" to government charities, above and beyond their tax liabilities, was that the few people still working had so little left after taxes and from dwindling profits that they could not afford to make donations.

Federal inheritance tax is now 90 percent across-the-board (regardless of a donor's estate or the donee's wealth); federal income tax is as high as 80 percent for those with an annual income of $150,000 ($50,000 in 1995 dollars) or higher; and the average taxpayer works until late October each year to pay his tax "contributions" to the many government taxing units he is subjected to.

As one reflects on the growing crisis in health-care delivery and the providing of basic human service needs of the poor through all levels of governments' social services agencies, it is clear that through the 1970s, 1980s, and 1990s many of the nation's so-called working poor gave up on low-income jobs when they saw that those who were not employed who were receiving government grants, entitlements, and aid were living substantially as well as they were. Many of these low-income wage earners were being denied government assistance, subsidies, and social services because they were making "too much money" and were receiving no health care and no support in other "vital needs" areas as well as living in housing worse or no better than those whom they knew who did not work at all, had no intention of working, and were laughing at them for working.

Being laughed at by friends and relatives who were "sucking at the governments' teats" was the last straw for many of these low-income wage earners who had self-respect and were trying to do what they thought was right. Now they are unemployed, by choice, and have time to lie around and create illegitimate and legitimate children, who will be soon be on government assistance, too. They have "idle hands" (the "Devil's workshop") and many of them are increasingly becoming addicted to illicit drugs and are having to steal (or to sell their government benefits for cash) in order to buy their drugs. The "needy" who are addicted to illicit drugs complain that their drugs are too expensive and blame that on the fact that the illicit drugs are illegal. They call for decriminalization of illicit drugs and government funding for their "recreational drugs." Many can be seen at the midnight basketball games operated and financed across the nation by our federal government through its Crime Prevention Program.

Now that health care, housing, food, clothing, transportation, haircuts, recreation, education, out-of-state annual vacations, and other "rights and entitlements" are being provided by a benevolent society through its centralized federal government, there is a heavy financial burden on those very few who still have jobs and are willing to work, as well as those who have assets and are stilling willing to risk them in this almost collapsed capitalist/mixed government-owner and -operated economic system.

Government has instituted many programs to ensure that some taxpayers and business asset owners do not evade their responsibility to be "responsible" citizens. Multinational corporations are almost nonexistent in this country now. By government policy, assets, jobs, incomes, and investments must be maintained in the United States by its citizens. Foreign investments in land, businesses, art, gold, silver, or anything else that can be "nailed down" must be maintained in the United States. Few foreign investors are investing in assets or businesses in the United States because the profits are so low, taxes are so high, and the government's restrictions are enormous.

The "semi capitalist" economic system, as it has been renamed, has two phrases that now apply, *nationalized* and *nationally controlled.*

Our citizens who still own assets and are still willing to work have been migrating to other nations in droves. But that is being strongly discouraged these days through tax and confiscation policies as well as new "migration" regulations. Many recall, humorously, when we debated what ought to be the U.S. "immigration" policies when so many people, particularly those from Vietnam, Cambodia, Haiti, Cuba, and

Mexico, were coming to our nation illegally and clandestinely for political and economic reasons.

Today, many formerly patriotic, hard-working, and productive Americans are leaving for those same reasons.

The Health and Human Services Department is now playing "we'll take away" and "we'll keep" your kids with parents of some American children. Years ago some people, who were called alarmists and who "sprang" from what was dubbed the religious right predicted that the federal government would take away from parents children who were being "abused," according to a liberal interpretation of the word *abuse.*

Christians and the general public agreed that government ought to "take away" from parents children who were clearly being physically abused and neglected. The "religious right" agreed in those cases, but "abuse" did not stop with that which was "abuse and neglect." The "religious right" predicted, rightfully so, that government would usurp parental rights in areas such as discipline and religious training.

The "religious right" was right (again)! Corporal punishment was banned in the early 2000s, and "inappropriate religious indoctrination" was banned a few years later. As usual, bureaucrats expanded the definition of "indoctrinations" to include almost anything that placed a religion, particularly the Christian faith, against the state.

Institutions called redirectional institutions, have been established for the children that have not only been taken away from their parents by the federal government but "kept away" from parents, permanently, it appears. The "redirectional institutions" are, essentially, "reprogramming centers." Some call these institutions orphanages. This is a misnomer because these children "do" have loving and caring parents whose first priority is their children (after God). These parents are able to support their children, miss them badly, love their children very much, and are searching for them. Many of these parents would flee America with their kids if they could find them but will not leave without them.

These parents will continue to search for their kids, and they are among the potential revolutionists feared by government leaders. As these parents look for their kids in various cities and states, they are binding together with many "underground elements" of the "religious right," whose faith was banned two years ago.

Another policy of Health and Human Services that has recently been adopted and is sort of strange was the change in the federal income tax law regarding the tax credit for dependent children. The new policy clearly discourages parents from having children. The HHS's pressure on the federal income tax law brought about a surcharge per child. It began a few years ago at a modest $2,500 per child. It is now up to $7,500, and there is talk on Capitol Hill of increasing it to the round figure of $10,000. After you compute your annual taxable income, you multiple the number of dependent children you have times $7,500 and add the amount to your taxable income. Remember the days when the government gave parents a tax break for children through tax deductions for children? This is another U.S. government policy that defies Scriptures. To our government children are not "a gift from God" but a curse from Hell.

Few remember when the nuclear family (comprised of husband and wife with children, if children were in nature's plan [God's plan]) was the cornerstone of the nation, of civilization. Strangely, civil servants, who are, presently, neither "civil" nor "servants," don't seem to understand that without families and children, there will be no taxpayers or other people to boss around.

5. Environmental Unstewardship

"The earth is the Lord's, and all it contains, the world, and they that dwell therein. For He hath founded it upon the seas, and established it upon the floods. . . . " *reads Psalms 24:1–2 . Everyone in this nation and almost everyone on the planet Earth understands that we need the Earth and the Earth doesn't need anyone or anything. The Earth just "is." It is not a being. The Lord desires that we not desecrate the Earth but that we guard, tame, and possess it for His purposes.*

He made man "in His image and likeness," not the volcanoes, elm trees, rivers, or deserts; therefore, it is man who is not one step above the spotted owl or the snail darter, but one step below the angels. Man does not exist for the benefit and pleasure of the Earth and its "creeping and crawling things," but the Earth exists for man. Likewise, man exists to glorify, honor, worship, praise, and serve God and to use the Earth for the purposes of God in our lives while we are temporarily occupying the Earth. And our bodies will one day become a part again of the Earth. We are not, I repeat, we are not "on" Earth to worship the Earth, for the Earth will not and cannot "save us" from Hell or "accept us" into Heaven. We must work toward understanding that balance and exercise a respect for the Earth, but we dare not compromise our use of the Earth for His will and purpose.

God says, in Psalms 82:8, that He will "judge the earth." *He will judge us, individually and collectively, for our moral attitudes as well as our theological knowledge of the whole of His creation. I fear our nation is placing the Earth and the "creeping and crawling things" above the Heavens and humans! Could this movement, "Earth first worship (which is sacrilegious)," lead to the following situations?*

Hunting was outlawed; then came along the outlawing of fishing. After all, both are "cruel and unusual" punishments to our feathered, skinned, and scaled fellow beings. A newly created subdivision of the HHS, Health and Beings Services, was established in the early 2010s to protect other "beings" from human beings, who have been abusing and neglecting other "beings" for centuries, we are told. Homeless shelters for animals who had been domesticated and, later, abandoned have been established. The thinking on this one was that these animals, once domesticated, could not survive in the wilderness if "turned out" and left to their own devices.

The animal rights enthusiasts, joining other "politically correct" activists, denounced the use of the words *wild* and *wilderness* last year due to the perception of animals as "wild." The proper terms, they said, for "wild" and "wilderness" are *uninhibited* and *uninhibited areas.* Many of these government-owned areas, formerly known as "wilderness areas," are situated beside the orphanages that house the homeless children who have been taken away from their parents as well as abandoned by their parents and/or guardians. The children living in these government redirectional institutes are about as uncivilized as the uninhibited beings residing in the government "uninhibited zones."

Zoos are pretty much relics of the past. It became too politically incorrect to incarcerate animals against their wills if we are going to liberate humans from normal and natural moral restraints. And as we slowly and surely decriminalized crime and opened the doors of our jails and prisons, it was necessary to emancipate the jailed and imprisoned animals in our zoos.

As the "free the animals" (from zoos) movement grew, there was picketing and civil disobedience at many zoos. Many of the demonstrations and protests became violent, reminding some of us of the days at the abortion centers when there was picketing and protesting, some of which led to the use of force and violence in efforts to try to protect unborn human beings. The animal rights enthusiasts learned from other

255

protest groups and forced their agenda into the media and national conscience. They achieved their objective, making relics of zoos, whereas the abortion protestors failed.

As a passing note, in an effort to compromise with the growing "close the zoos" movement, zookeepers offered a "come-and-go" "open-door" policy for the zoo animals. Too many of the animals, especially the flesh-eating animals, refused to come back to their cages at night. It is suspected that the carnivorous animals did not come back due to the recent policy that changed their diets from meat to vegetative. The policy change was instituted because it was decided that those being feed to the carnivorous animals were being treated "cruel and inhumane."

With the decade old ban on hunting and fishing, which now includes the banning of eating meats, including poultry and fish, there are signs that the "vegetarian only" legal diet has improved the health of many of our citizens. But there are a lot of long faces from those who remember the good old days of the "Quarter Pounder" and the "Big Mac." Our citizens may be healthier, but many are suspected of defying the "vegetarian only" diet imposed by the U.S. Food and Drug Administration. (Those persons would be the ones who are still overweight and smiling.)

Of concern to the Population Control Council of the United States, a division of the United Nations' Population Control Administration, is the frightening possibility that life spans of human beings in the United States may be lengthened due to the "vegetation only" diet. They fear that Americans' living longer could have disastrous effects on the planet, especially if other nations and societies join the "no meat" movement. Their major concern is that those in the "ending stage" of their lives, who are nonproductive, often called useless eaters, might injure the Earth by drinking too much of its water, eating too many of its plants, breathing too much of its air, and walking too much on its soil.

The "plant rights" people are angering the leadership of the "animal rights" people because they are stealing away "some of their thunder" and plagiarizing their slogans and speeches from the 1980s and 1990s. Privately, "animal rights" leaders are frightened at the number of their members who are defecting from their cause (believing that "animal rights" are secure) and joining the fledgling, but growing, "plant rights" movement. Off camera, the "animal rights" leaders see the logic of extending certain unalienable rights to plants. After all, plants can "bleed" (sap) when cut, are being "raised" and "harvested" for various human purposes, e.g., to make houses, tires, paper, ornaments, medicine, and clothes, as well as to be eaten.

Many "plant rights" activists, like "animal rights" activists, feel as if plants are being degraded and exploited by "profit-minded only" capitalists. Some suspect the new "rights" movement is trying to "horn" or "muscle" in on the old "rights" movements' financial support for their own political agenda.

Many U.S. citizens are disregarding laws that they do not accept and obeying those they do accept. Law enforcement officers and the courts are doing about the same thing as they close their eyes to laws being violated that they believe to be absurd and that citizens, en masse, are refusing to obey. The law enforcement personnel and judicial system employees understand there are enough jails to house the minor lawbreakers and there is no way to force payment of fines on those who refuse to willingly pay their fines. Many are becoming convinced that the government is almost impotent to do anything about crime, disrespect for the law, and immorality in our culture.

Growing hostility is likened to a burning fuse between the "animal" and the "plant" rights groups as well as between those who are selectively obeying the laws with which they agree with and disobeying the laws with which they disagree. Government is almost irrelevant and will probably be a nonfactor if these two groups or any other "cause" groups conflict. Could open armed, hateful rebellion break out between these opposite forces or other forces that are in conflict? Government law enforcement officials fear that it could and don't cherish the possibility of being caught between any two strong factions.

Many people believe that when, not if, but, I repeat, when, these clashes occur a totalitarian government will emerge to restore order. Few believe that life for anyone will be better than the days of the mid-1940s through the mid-1970s. The thirty-year period following the era of 1945-1975 has been dubbed "the Golden Age" of America. Many of us believe it was the age of the "decline of the nation" and the period of "the choking of American Christianity." A conference held in March of 2004 had as its theme "The Implications of Life Under Totalitarian Government."

6. The Undermining of Rights, Liberties, and Freedoms

There is no question that because of two things: (1) the increasing rate and violent nature of crime in the United States; and (2) the increasing burden of taxes, which are shared only by the producers (taxpayers,

257

those citizens who are paying the taxes and who are losing economic freedom), all law-abiding, taxpaying citizens are losing rights, liberties, and freedoms.

I believe, as stated in the last paragraph of the last section, we will eventually evolve into a totalitarian state in order to have order restored. Not only is the U.S. Constitution being ignored by the courts and time-honored and successful, functional traditional values being abandoned by the citizens, but "rights, liberties, and freedoms" that we have held dear for so many generations are being systematically repealed by the federal and state lawmakers. Biblical history teaches us that nations, Christian and non-Christian, go through the following five cycles: (1) peace and tranquility, law and order, respect for others and their property, economic and developmental progress, and blessings to (2) rebellion, violence, disrespect for others and their property, rejection of authority, economic decline, and cursings to (3) tyranny, repression, depression (economically, physically, mentally, and spiritually), and totalitarianism to (4) repentance and renewal to (5) confrontation (usually war) and deliverance and then back to 1. The cycle is proven in human and biblical history over and over again without fail just as surely as business cycles record "up" and "downs."

I believe we are in the final stages of number 2 and I believe the characteristics of number 3 are coming down soon on our "collective ears." Are not the following possibilities in the offering in the areas of "rights, liberties, and freedoms"?

Not only do we consider our "rights, liberties, and freedoms" to be far different now than we did back in the 1980s, but speaking from a practical standpoint, many of our "rights, liberties, and freedoms" that we took for granted and enjoyed have been and are being taken away via federal judicial interpretations of the Constitution and legislation enacted by our federal and state legislatures, which have been and are being approved by court review.

Most citizens applaud these changes, obviously for the desired purpose of bring about greater protection of our "bodies and properties" through accent on "law and order" and "peace and tranquillity." "Truth and justice," along with "rights, liberties, and freedoms," are being compromised or ignored and sacrificed in an effort to prevent our culture/society from plummeting into the pit of earthly hell. We are making these tremendous personal sacrifices in these three areas out of necessity and for what we believe to be "the good of the whole." We do so at our peril.

Here are a few examples. Media reports, including letters to the editors, editorials, personal columns, and management positions on matters of public policy (by radio and television stations, primarily), not to mention all news reports, must be "approved" by Regional Media Alliances now. So much so-called disinformation has been "forced" on readers, listeners, and viewers by the media, according to government officials, that government control became necessary in order to ensure "accurate, unbiased, and centrist" news and opinion by the media, which are still mostly owned and operated by the private sector.

In the past, privately owned and operated independent (of government censorship) media, especially those owned and operated by Christian organizations, were considered the best sources for accurate information and news as well as logic and fair news analysis and opinion. It was believed that the unfettered reporting of news and opinion (before the fact) by privately owned and operated news media, while not perfect, was the best method of presenting news and opinion to the general public. (By *unfettered* we mean "not controlled or censored by government" and *before the fact* we mean the media is "fair game" for libel and slander "after the fact" in civil court when and if libelous and slanderous statements are reported.) At that time, consumer choice was the arbiter of success or failure in the reporting and dissemination of news and opinion by the media.

Accurate and balanced news reports along with fair news analysis and opinion combined with two other ingredients, a literate (educated) and unselfish (altruistic) population, are necessary for a democratic government to exist. As has been stated before, I believe, "Without God the best form of civil government, a constitutional representative democracy, is nothing more than mob rule." The mix of (1) truth; (2) the ability of the citizens to comprehend the truth; and (3) the willingness of the people to act unselfishly with the truth is essential to justice, law and order, and peace and tranquillity. These are godly principles that ought to guide and guard a society.

Contrary to these principles, the U.S. government acted in the early part of this century, the twenty-first, to suppress and control the media because the media was "a stumbling block" in the government's move toward totalitarism. First, it was the Christian media and programming that were deemed "harmful and hostile" to government policies and

259

"slanted and biased" against public (read: government) actions, which were called "against the public interests" by the U.S. Supreme Court in the *United States versus Focus on the Family* case rendered on January 22, 2003, the thirtieth anniversary of the *Roe versus Wade* decision (which received little publicity; interestingly, Focus on the Family was a longtime dissenter against that U.S. Supreme court opinion).

This decision "shut down" the Christian voice via their Christian magazines and newspapers, radio and television stations and network, and denominational periodicals if they "ventured into matters of public policy morality." Incidentally and ironically, the ACLU, People for the American Way, People for the Ethical Treatment of Animals, and Americans United for Separation of Church and State were "friends of the court" through their amicus curiae briefs on behalf of the U.S. government in the *United States versus Focus on the Family.* All four of these organizations have since been closed down by the Justice Department.

Some secularist media executives understood that what was happening to Christian media could happen to them. But their voices and numbers were too little and too late. All media now must gain "approval" of what they are going to say or publish from the Regional Media Alliances.

Many of the secularist media executives and owners who gave encouragement to the Christian media privately during the public debate over the *United States versus Focus on the Family* decision contradicted that support publicly by calling for censorship of religious media via the so-called separation of church and state plank of the Constitution (which does not exist). Their belief and opinion that public policy and morality, always formed by one's religious perspective, can be separated eventually led to the restriction of their independence, too.

Interestingly, and sadly, many Christian-magazine editors and owners/managers of Christian radio and television stations and networks were glad to see Focus on the Family lose their federal court case because they did not like the "black eye" Focus on the Family and other Christian media, such as *The 700 Club* and *Point of View,* were giving the Christians in the industry and Christianity through their involvement in "nonspiritual" matters, such as public and private morality and national and individual accountability before God.

Most of these Christian critics (of other Christian media) in the Christian media would rather "switch than fight." They would rather print and broadcast noncontroversial things such as Christian gospel music and discussion of "morally neutral" matters. (Their problem is that there are none.) While they were singing "We'll Fly Away," their media independence and livelihood were "flying out" the window, for they, too, have now been closed down by the Regional Media Alliances due to censorship, financial restraints, and other government regulations and taxation. They wrongly believed that they would receive less "flack" from the FCC, Federal Communications Commission, when "those troublemaking" Christian media outlets were taken off the air and out of print. While a few of the critics of the growing government control of media via censorship, particularly Christian media, complained, their voices were "drowned out" by Christian media types and pastors/priests who shouted, "Live and let live!" They did not understand that the Devil and his minions don't play that way. They have no intention of "playing fair."

Another area where we have lost huge amounts of rights, liberties, and freedoms has been the area of the practice of our religion and propagation of our Christian faith to our children as well as to others. (See the first section of this chapter.) Governors and presidents, state and federal lawmakers, and state and federal judges have continuously taken away Christian rights, liberties, and freedoms because, they claim, Christians and Christianity were "interfering with public policy." We believe in addition to this they realized that if they could take away basic rights, liberties, and freedoms of Christians, it would be easier to take rights, liberties, and freedoms away from everyone else.

Public officials have been persuasive in convincing the general public that religious people, especially Christians, had nothing positive to contribute to society and were only critical of the lifestyles of others and determined to "legislate morality" of others.

Unfortunately, there is truth to this criticism, because the few pastors and other Christian leaders who were speaking about public policy in their churches and to the community in other ways were not offering many or any positive or easy solutions to the dilemmas the culture was in. It is true that the recommendations offered by Christians would usually "cripple" individuals' free choices to live their lives as they wanted to regardless of personal or collective consequences.

The word *charity* had been taken from the new *Webster's Dictionary* and replaced with *government entitlements*. A few old-timers still whisper about the days when their churches and individual Christians were the agents of charity and Christians had, and deserved, a place at "the table of public opinion." They, the old-timers, said it was deserved and people, including pagans and government officials, listened to the opinions and recommendations of Christians and their organizations. They described those days as the "days before the 'spiritual/moral meltdown' " of our culture.

The decade-old ban on private ownership of any type of firearm has not deterred much crime or violence. Most say the restrictions on travel outside one's home or neighborhood after 7:00 P.M. unless on government business or government-approved trips did more to restore "law and order" than the weapons ban, even though the curfew eventually helped the criminal elements know for sure where and when their next victims could be located.

Speaking of weapon bans, there is a bill in the U.S. House of Representatives, H.B. 9, known as the "No, You Can't!" bill, which would ban the manufacture/sale/ownership of knives longer than nine inches. The killings of Nicole Simpson and Ronald Goldman with a knife led to this legislation. Few believe this bill will pass in this year's legislative session, but with the increased use of knives in the commission of violent crimes, who knows what will happen next year?

Major successes have occurred over the past four years in expanding the number of minority groups added to "hate crimes" as well as increases in the severity of fines and prison sentences for those who commit "hate crimes." Triple and quadruple fines are the norm, and maximums for civil damages have been eliminated for "hate crimes."

To well-established victimized minorities such as feminists, African-Americans, homosexuals, and Jews have been added Mexican-Americans, Canadian-Americans, environmentalists, naturalists, animal rights advocates, welfare recipients, health-care enthusiasts, and one-world governmentalists.

There is a move afoot that would reverse some of the excesses of "hate crime" legislation. The sponsors of this legislation in Oregon claim there is one unprotected/unidentified minority group left, the male WASP (White, Anglo-Saxon Protestant) and this group must be brought under "hate crime" legislation. One proponent of this bill has proposed that crimes against male WASPs ought to be reduced by one-half. In other words, if a crime is committed against a male WASP, say an assault with a deadly weapon, and the usual prison sentence is five years, the sentence for a person who can prove he attacked a male WASP with a deadly weapon because he "hates" male WASPs would be reduced to two and one-half years.

A small plaque was discovered on a wall in a government indoctrination center, formerly called government schools, noting "Ten Character Traits Worth Developing." The traits were: Be honest; demonstrate integrity; keep promises; be loyal; be responsible; pursue excellence; be kind and caring; treat all people with respect; be fair; and be a good citizen.

A federal court jury in Colorado ruled the plaque unconstitutional because these traits were called "moral values–biased," rather than "moral values–neutral," called for by the Federal Civil Rights Act of 2001. The jury reasoned, in light of the C.R. Act of 2001, that "these traits might be interpreted as endorsing or suggesting that children live up to moral values that might be embarrassing or humiliating (or hard to attain) for them." Therefore, the ten traits were ordered removed or rewritten to be "morally neutral."

After the case was sent back to a lower federal judge for revision, the judge renamed the new plaque "Ten Neutral Traits of Non-discrimination." The ten traits now are: "Be honest or dishonest; demonstrate and define right and wrong as you wish and as it suits your circumstance; don't make promises; be loyal or disloyal; be responsible or irresponsible; pursue mediocrity for the common good or common bad; be selfish if it makes you happy and makes you feel good; treat yourself to everything that makes you feel good and happy; be free; and be what you want to be."

Written on the side of a stone mountain in Utah was "Freedom is found in acknowledging, obeying, and serving moral law." Not only was this sentence chiseled off the mountain, but, before this was done, fingerprints were taken. The author of this profound truth is being hunted down not only for defacing public property, but also for "insensitivity to the citizens of the United States," as defined in the Civil Rights Act of 2001.

7. Education: Immoral Instruction and General Knowledge Revisionist Teaching

No instruction on matters of ethics is amoral. Teaching by those in authority, whether the instructor is a parent, a king, a schoolteacher, or a president, is either "moral" or "immoral." Teachers, by word or example, ought not to leave "right" and "wrong," "good" and "evil," up to the conclusion of the impressionable student, particularly when the student is a young person, to decide. Morally correct instruction is "holy teaching." If a teacher attempts to teach moral neutrality, the teacher is not a teacher but a facilitator of information or the presenter of a situation/s, which leads to "situational ethics" instruction.

God did not, does not, and will not leave the people of God without His teachings. He made us and as our loving Creator, Teacher, and Instructor as well as the Creator of our environment and all truth, He (1) left us a book of instructions, the Bible; (2) gave us an example, a perfect Teacher, His son, the Lord Jesus Christ; and (3) provided a guiding light, the Holy Spirit.

All truth is knowable, whether it is mathematics, earth science, or moral human behavior toward others and "things." And our search for truth in order that we might act in accordance with His perfect will matters to Him. He cares that we "know" truth and the we "act" morally, and because He cares, we ought to "care," too. Don't let others convince you that amoral conduct ought to be taught by parents, Sunday school teachers, public and private school teachers, senators, public health nurses, mayors, baseball stars, military rulers, presidents, or anyone else by word and/or deed. Amorality, or moral vacuums, will be replaced or filled with morality or immorality, and if the teachers exclude teaching moral necessity, immorality will reign. It is nonsense to believe or to try to teach that amorality is good conduct for family members, people of faith (or no faith), or citizens of a nation.

We are living at a time when our public school teachers, in particular, and other teachers, in general (and sadly, many Christian parents and Christian school teachers) are "teaching" (by what they say and do) that conduct can be amoral and that "all truth" is unknowable. What might this lead to in the area of education? Could the following come to pass?

Some complain about the elimination of "choice" in education, but most have a clear reasoning as to why government outlawed/banned all education other than government education. And most folks are resigned to the reality that there will be "no more" parochial education. And most folks are resigned to the reality that there will be "no more" parochial education, including religious education, particularly Christian schools. Some hold out hope for a return to legal home schooling. "In their prayers and dreams!" I say.

After government, spearheaded and inspired by our federal government's Department of Education, which now finances 90 percent of the nation's education, and the National Education Association, overcame the clash with the religious community regarding "moral values education" in their schools to students who resented, along with many of their parents, sad to say, religious schools' "brand" of moral values, the next step is enforcing conformity for religious outcome-based education was relatively simple. After all, the federal government desired a specific outcome in knowledge and conduct for every kid and was controlling the purse strings.

Eventually parents of Christian denominations that sponsored schools, usually on church property and often in church buildings, capitulated to the national education goal (and accepted the federal government's financial assistance through "choice" vouchers, tax deductions, student loans, and/or other financial incentives). And Christian educators and church leaders who owned and operated the schools "bowed under" when pressure, including the withholdings of favorable tax treatment for the sponsoring churches of many Christian schools, to close down their schools, and, probably, the churches was exerted.

Many students led "the progressive moment," as it was called, in educational reform (reminds us of the inmates running the insane asylum), sometimes to the dismay of their parents and at other times, sadly, with the encouragement of their parents. These students wanted to be able to decide for themselves what was "right" and what was "wrong" for themselves, believing that what is "right" or "wrong" for one may not be "right" or "wrong" for another.

The situation regarding federal government regulation of parochial education had become so discouraging a few years ago that almost everyone gave a "sigh" of relief when all schools other than government-owned, federally regulated schools were prohibited. It was, at that time, almost the "only game in town," because so many parochial schools had closed due to government regulation and interference.

A still sticky point has been the home schooling movement for government. Government educational professionals consider parents who are refusing to enroll their children into government schools to be the "last remaining countercultural" pocket of resistance to total government control of the education of the nation's children.

While federal regulations require that parents be licensed before having children and that parents license and enroll their children into government schools at age three, many parents are refusing to do the latter and a few are refusing to do the former. These last holdouts to what is clearly the turning over of children's minds and bodies to the state object to both of these government requirements on two points: (1) children are not the property of government or even the property of their parents but the property of God; and (2) they, furthermore, object to what children are being taught in government schools in the areas of "values clarification," sex education, revised history (U.S. and world), natural science, including evolution, and environmental conservation.

It is suspected by federal authorities within the Department of Education that some parents are not reporting the births of children to the National Population Department, much less getting approval for conceiving these children. Most of all these lawbreakers are, understandably, not registering or enrolling their children into the federal education system when they are three years old as required by the Department of Education.

By not obeying the law in these three areas, these parents are circumventing federal population control and education policies altogether. The president has called for a closer working relationship between the National Population Department and the Department of Education in order to apprehend these criminals. God help the parents who are violating these laws if they are caught!

A crackdown on these violations has resulted in about ten thousand parents being arrested, convicted, and imprisoned. With the government control of media and the federal judicial bureaucracy, which has all but taken over all law enforcement, the judiciary, and incarceration from state and local control, little is known about the condition or whereabouts of these parents or their children. About the only thing known for sure about the parents of children who were conceived, birthed, and not registered or enrolled in the government schools when they turned three is that these parents have no control over their children now and do not even know where their kids are.

All areas of education in our colleges and universities are now centralized through the Bureau of Higher Learning, a major branch of the federal government's National Education Department. Many parents who were sending their children to private colleges and universities are presently making the tremendous sacrifice of sending their college-age kids to schools in other nations. There is legislation in the U.S. Senate that would ban this. America's colleges and universities are calling for various forms of protection. The most extreme suggestion is the banning of America's kids attending colleges and universities out of the nation. Other

266

measures included "out-of-country tuition" fees for those kids attending colleges and universities in other nations.

This is a sad turnabout when one considers that our colleges and universities, just like our hospitals, were once the envy of the world and many foreign students attended them only a few years ago. These schools are now too expensive and are not worth the costs when compared to the costs and quality of higher education in other countries, especially those in the Middle and Far East.

One more point about the costs of education today in the United States: While the government schools for those students three through twenty are open to everyone regardless of their qualifications, there is a tuition cost for all students. The costs are based on a sliding scale based on their parents' ability to pay. This compulsory tuition is a clear disincentive to parenthood.

One thing is clear in the area of education today in this country. It is that the professional federal educators and bureaucrats have "learned" that they can "shape" the minds of the nation's youths via the centralization of education. Affixing public policy in the minds of the people can best, and peacefully, be done through the educational/indoctrinational system, for what is taught in one generation will be public policy in the next.

When we became a pagan nation, Christianity became endangered. At that point we tried to educate pagans, and when you education pagans, you worsen your condition.

8. The Economy: The Social/Welfare State

Social and economic reform during the Great Depression began the long road that America has taken toward a social/welfare economic state. People were hungry, homeless, and jobless. Few jobs were available from the private sector when the depression began in 1929. Franklin Delano Roosevelt and the federal government "stimulated" the economy through the government becoming the employer of many and by making loans to individuals, private businesses, and institutions. We shall not criticize what was done during the years of the depression and its recovery as well as the World War II era in this vital area. Most historians and economists agree, I believe, that during the Great Depression and World War II crises desperate measures were necessary, including the government becoming the employer of last resort and deficit spending, in order

267

to save our free-enterprise economic system as well as democracy, liberty, and freedom here and around the world.

However, soon after these two crises had been solved and resolved, "greed," not "need," fueled the path that has led us on our social/welfare economic state journey that this nation has been on for the past forty years. Make no mistake about it: the economy can get worse, much, much worse. It will if we evolve deeper into a ruinous, social/welfare economic state marked with huge national deficits. Might the following scenarios be in our future economic condition?

Economists universally agree that the United States is clearly in a "post mixed economy."

The country began with an almost "laissez-faire" economy, meaning that there was little or no interference by the government/s in competition between the producers and the owners of good and services and their employees and consumers. That meant that the control and use of the means, materials, and monies utilized in the production of goods and services were privately owned and prices, products, and wages were regulated only by the "give and take," the competition, if you will, between employers, employees, and consumers, with little or no government interference. Profits for the entrepreneurs were their goal, and it was predicated on the "supply and demand," costs of "the means" of production as well as the ability to sell products and services.

The economy moved imperceptibly to a mixed economy as government regulated disputes and frictions between employers and employees and buyers and sellers and began to take over enterprises that either had performed poorly (in the opinion of government) by private enterprise or had not been provided.

Today we are in a near "pure-socialist" economic system of producing goods and services. Today government, according to government leaders, operates for the "pleasure" of its citizens and thereby provides everything "essential" for everyone. Many of us say that this is a lie. We claim that government does not serve, but the workers serve, and the workers serve where, when, and for how much and how long those in charge of government require. How did we get here? Gradually.

Essentially, we got "here" because this is what the citizens, the majority, believed they wanted. First, "the people" wanted and then demanded a "bureaucratic Santa Claus" to provide for them the goods and services they wanted at the prices they were willing to pay. If government had to "invent" money to pay for the goods and services out of thin air (by printing money) or had to borrow money (deficit spending) to provide, "so shall it be done," said the citizens.

Why did the citizens not simply buy the goods and services for themselves from one another? Over a period of time, the citizens redefined what goods and services were "essential" and agreed that whoever could not afford them would have them provided for at a lesser cost initially and at no cost later. Some could not afford items such as homes, food, clothing, and health care or did not want to pay the price dictated by supply and demand. At that time, "the people" demanded that the prices be reduced for "essentials" for those who were willing to purchase goods and services at a lower price and provided free for those who could not afford these "essential" goods and services.

What was desired soon became what was demanded, as "essentials," from a smaller and smaller group of willing workers by a larger and larger group of nonworking consumers/voters. Such items and services as autos and health-care insurance, entertainment, haircuts, child-behavior counseling, lawn mower services, summer vacations, and other goods and services became the "necessities of life."

Elected officials (who were not dumb) saw "the route to reelection" tied to providing these "necessities of life" demanded by more and more people, "voters." At first, the governments' economists, whose jobs depended upon satisfying the elected leaders, found the solution in (1) managing elements of the economy through the establishment of minimum prices for products and services produced by the private sector; and (2), providing goods and services by government desired by the citizens (again, "voters") that were not being marketed by the private enterprise economic sector.

Then "a funny thing happened on the way to the forum" (the place where goods and services were to be purchased). That "funny thing" was that investors/owners/managers of privately owned enterprises were no longer making a "profit." (Remember that word? It was once not only fashionable but good to do and to repeat, even essential to the survival of all privately owned and operated businesses. That was before *profit* became a dirty word synonymous with the word *sin*.) After a few years of "no profits," the businesses either went broke or chose to go out of business before they went broke. The chain reaction continued with employees losing jobs and the government losing tax revenues that had come to it as a result of the taxation of business profits.

The "I went bust," and the "I've had it; I'm quitting," comments by former businessmen and their workers were followed by their presence at the government social services agencies demanding entitlements that they had been providing for others via their paid taxes. These two new groups of people and their dependents joined the millions who were already in lines at the "entitlements" offices. Was it ever crowded there then! People were there and there by the many, many millions.

"The people" demanded goods and services from their elected and hired government "servants." The "servants" knew that if they did not provide "the 'new' people" and "the 'old' people" with what they wanted, they would not be "servants" the day after the next election. And the "hired servants" (as opposed to "elected servants") knew that if they did not "make it happen" through the availability of "entitlements" (via the bureaucracy that they [the "hired servants"] ran), they, too, would be "entitlement shopping" the day after "the day after" the next election (as they would be fired by the newly elected "elected servants"). That would be the best-case scenario for the "servants," both "elected and hired," if they did not provide the "entitlements for 'the people.' " At worse, they would be hung from the nearest tree (probably located in a nearby government-owned and -operated neighborhood park).

The "servants" realized at that desperate time that the only way to meet the demand for goods and services for the people would be for the government to own the means of production, hire the workers, procure the raw materials, and "market" the goods and services.

This is how we got to where we are today, in a nutshell.

Some look back and understand that in order for Uncle Sam to "feed, clothe, house, and heal" the people, Uncle Sam would have to tax (steal, take) what government needed from those who owned what was needed and invest in assets from which government could produce goods and services. Many clearly see, in retrospect, that in order to have prevented the social/welfare economic system of government, government should have gotten out of the social services business, called the Social Gospel by Christianity for many years, in the late 1990s. One reason the government did not was because Christianity was not clamoring for the opportunity to retake their responsible position as provider of social services for the needy, whom they should have defined by biblical terms.

By the time a few people saw (1) the problem; (2) what lay ahead if things were not changed drastically; and (3) the solution, Christians and Christianity had totally collapsed due to the moral and spiritual "meltdown" that had occurred within the individual hearts of the overwhelming, majority of Christians, the lack of vision by Christian leaders, and the persecution of Christians and Christianity by non-Christians and government officials. By that time the government had seized the seat, or throne, of charity and did not want to release it. When government realized that the costs of "entitlements" were changing the face of government as they desired it, government officials did not know how to "release it" and get out from under the enormous debt and continuing deficit spending. How do you let go of the tail of an angry tiger? The government, for many years, saw only power, control, and money as its sphere of influence grew through its self-destructive "entitlements" programs.

Some understand now that within both the Democratic and Republican parties were socialists, even though many did not know or acknowledge it, who not only wanted government to feed, clothe, house, and heal the "needy" as they defined "needs" of the "needy," but "to deliver us from" disasters, educate us, and instill government/s' values into us and our children. Those "values" began with the acknowledgment that "we are servants of the 'most high' god," the state.

In other words, "the people" wanted a social/welfare "messiah" to be our "provider," "deliverer," and "savior." Christians began to worship the state and sing to it, "From Whom All Blessings Flow," and this was idolatry.

When the nation lost its soul, exchanging it for "Materialism," it lost its heart to take care of itself as well as others and it became a pagan nation. And when you make a pagan or a pagan nation rich, you worsen his or its condition. Instead of getting drunk only once a week on weekends, he or it can then afford to drink steadily.

9. Human Sexuality: Sex Anytime, Anywhere, with Anyone (or Anything) and without Procreation

This section's heading seems unthinkable and is bizarre, but if you consider what sexual acts have boiled down in this country over the past few decades, it may not be too far from truth. The majority of sexual intercourse in America today is either between homosexuals or heterosexuals, married or unmarried, who have "closed out" procreation as a possibility or a desire.

This is depravity and this is what has occurred in our culture over the past thirty to forty years. And it has not gone without notice in the heavens. Our artificially manipulating and circumventing the normal functions of healthy human organs—in this case, our sexual organs—I believe, will have natural and supernatural consequences on individuals and our society.

"Frightening" is what may lie ahead in this important area, human sexuality and human relationships. Few seem to care and even fewer seem to speculate what may lie ahead: Read of what our folly may usher in.

"Five Lesbians Establish a 'Family' in Seattle," "Seven Homosexuals 'Call' Their Marriage a Family in Boston," and "Preacher Marries Man and Donkey in 'Union' in Peoria" ran headlines in major newspapers in the late 1990s. From the "left" coast and the "right" coast as well as from points in between (Peoria), "the family" and accepted sexual behavior are being redefined by government, and, most sadly, Christianity is offering little protest. Not only is Christianity not calling these (and other) sexual activities depraved, but much of Christianity is endorsing them!

Among those who were choosing various sexual lifestyles "choices" were married heterosexual couples (in the late 1990s and early twenty-first century) who were choosing to artificially prevent procreation (or naturally prevent conception without sound natural or spiritual reasons). They sought respect for their chosen "choice" of not having children. These couples gave enormous credibility to those other "unions" that did not choose or could not choose to have children, and it mattered not if these relationships were platonic and/or sexual.

Those who wanted to establish a redefinition of "the family" had taken to the streets along with other new "civil/human rights" groups. They were teaching and "preaching" a new and harsher wave of objecting to "intolerance" as they sacked government buildings, looted shopping districts, ransacked and fire-bombed churches and parachurch organizations that opposed their agendas, and killed individuals who, they claimed, "preached hate-filled bigotry, intolerance, and a 'oneness' of morality."

272

The new breed of civil/human sexual rights activists shouted, "One size does not fit all!" as they denounced and mocked the defining of the family in the "narrowness" of a man and a woman, committed for a lifetime, who willingly unite in marriage and accept children as gifts from God, if nature blesses them with children.

A Christian businessman was burned to death in his clothing store the day after the *Los Angeles Times* featured these comments spoken by him in a newspaper story in which the headline read: " 'Redefinition' (or Any 'Definition') of the Family" ":

> The very word "platonic," which some call their relationships with their partners, especially with animals, means "impractical."
>
> Many of these new "families" are anything but "practical," the businessman said, "seeing as they do not allow for and many times it is impossible for offsprings to enter their 'families.' Children have always been the major reason for the existence of families and it ought to continue."

The article went on to say:

> A spokesperson for Humankind ("mankind" is out these days as it is not "politically correct") and Everything Else, an organization dedicated to the removal of "stumbling blocks" between persons and "other living things" that people love through the unitive process called marriage, says that it is a civil/human right to merge anyone with another or any other thing. The spokesperson for Humankind and Everything Else pointed out that so many "human being" marriages between heterosexuals exclude plans for human reproduction (via sterilization, contraception, and abortion) that the lack of reproduction capabilities ought not to handicap marriages of any sort or person with another living person or thing.
>
> Humankind and Everything Else backed up their reasoning with statistics such as the fact that the average heterosexual couple in the United States has but .45 children. Their spokesperson said, "There are today more fetuses aborted than born alive, 50% of heterosexual couples enter marriage with one or both partners sterile, and all Christian denominations recognize contraception, sterilization, and abortion as morally acceptable options (even for their members) for all humans who are capable of reproduction in a pluralism society."

I recall in 2007 the shooting of a Los Angeles Roman Catholic cardinal, one of the last dissenting voices in the Catholic Church in

America to the movement of the culture to what he called the abyss, soon after he spoke on the status of the family in an October "Respect Life" homily. In his homily, he said, "Our society is rent by division over the most basic principles of morality. As a result, the family, in particular, has been battered. Even before *Roe versus Wade* and the onslaught of legalized abortion, popes and bishops predicted that the abortion license and the acceptance of sex divorced from commitment and procreation would have devastating effects on marriage and the family."

In the shirt pocket of a homosexual female arrested for the fatal shooting of the cardinal was the column written by the cardinal, which closed with this sentence: "Those predictions have proven true beyond most people's wildest expectations." A jury exonerated the young woman for the murder of the cardinal due to the fact that she had been "verbally abused" by several priests and ministers who had denounced homosexual acts as abhorrent and sinful as well as destructive to the family and, consequently, the cultural, for violation of the California "Hate Crime Act" of 1999.

In the trial of these three priests and two ministers who had written a letter to the editor of the *Los Angeles Times* after the "Hate Crime Act" was passed, the closing argument to the jury by the prosecutor made it clear that no abuse, including verbal abuse (including homilies and sermons that call homosexual acts sin, harmful to those who engage in them, and destructive to society), will be tolerated. The prosecutor, who is now attorney general of California, said "Our society cries out for an end to the violence and hatred that tear us apart. This can only happen through the discovery of respect, through the practice of tolerance, and through the affirmation of dignity to all human beings."

Quietly and only among those who know the ones they are speaking to, people shared their opinions regarding the insanity of the "hate crime" prosecutions, including "verbal abuse" crimes. "Ministers are in jail because they gave their theological opinion that homosexual practice is harmful to those engaged in what these few pastors, who are willing to give a theological opinion, believe to be sin?," some question. "An apology to a lesbian who assassinated a Catholic cardinal, not to mention an acquittal of the charge of murder by a jury, because the cardinal committed a 'verbal abuse' hate crime when he published a homily in a diocese periodical for Catholics?" some ask. This ought to be the case only in a horrible dream or in some weird sort of speculative fiction.

A few believe that the court would probably order the cardinal to apologize to the lesbian who shot him dead if it could. The governor or California has apologized on behalf of the people of his state to this lesbian woman who "was driven" into killing the cardinal (so the governor said as he pleaded with her not to be "hard" on herself for what she did to the Cardinal). A sidebar to this case: A million-dollar civil award judgment was given to the lesbian woman by a jury against the Catholic diocese for what the deceased cardinal had said against her and other homosexuals. The killing of the cardinal was declared "justifiable homicide" by the jury, as noted in the last paragraph.

"Tolerance" for those who seek to "redefine" the family is not the only goal of the various civil/human rights groups that are advocating sexual and platonic relationships be recognized by society. They intend to and are affecting public policy through the law.

These groups are being most successful in state and federal courts as well as in the U.S. Congress and in state legislatures in persuading government to elevate marriages between homosexuals and humans and "other living things" to the same level once held only by heterosexuals. There is not perfect unity between these various new civil/human rights groups regarding their agendas. For example, they disagree as to whether or not there ought to be "reparation" for past discriminations against homosexuals. Act-Up has filed suit in the First District of the U.S. Federal Court seeking a $250,000 judgment for every homosexual in the nation for past discrimination. The money would be paid by the U.S. government to every avowed homosexual.

Act-Up believes that this legislation would act as an incentive for timid homosexuals to "come out of the closet," but other homosexual rights groups believe nonhomosexuals may claim to be homosexuals just for the money. Act-Up says; "We have a solution for that possibility. We'll make them prove it!" The quarreling between the various homosexual groups has been amusing to many. To others, sad.

The North American Man/Boy Love Association, NAMB, is seeing (in a state court) in Oregon a mandatory annual state holiday, the first weekend in April, to celebrate "Gay Pride Weekend." The theme will be the success of the long struggle for equal rights under the law for their cause. They believe that their civil rights struggle, like the civil rights struggles for blacks and for women, ought to be given official recognition (such as the national holiday memorializing Dr. Martin Luther King).

Their proposal is that the first weekend in April each year be set aside in Portland for a state-sponsored (read: government-financed) three-day picnic/"outing" and educational campaign for all homosexuals and their friends, with a requirement that all young men between the ages of six and seventeen must attend (and camp out with Act-Up volunteers both nights in tents). NAMBA would be in charge of the two-night, three-day event, naturally.

The North American Woman/Girl Association, NAWGA, initially filed a countersuit against the NAMBA suit, but has since withdrawn it and is reconsidering their legal opinions in light of their goal to "further the 'interfacing' of their members with girls between the ages of six and seventeen also." If NAMBA is successful, they may follow "suit" with a "suit" of their own.

Moving onto the center stage in the "redefining" of the family has been a growing new organization, Human and Other Animals' Civil Rights, HOACR. On the heels of the epic struggle to gain rights for *Homo sapiens*, HOACR seeks to bring whom and what they call fellow travelers into "our mutual journey through life" in the areas of life, liberty, and the pursuit of happiness.

HOACR wants to franchise "the disenfranchised" and reminds *Homo sapiens* that other animals and vegetables have been left out "in the cold" too long. HOACR constantly reminds *Homo sapiens* skeptics of the early efforts of their various civil/human rights group and the resistance they faced when they were simply asking for a "place at the table." HOACR leaders are optimistic but are realistic as they lay out their long-range and short-range goals.

The minerals proclaim, one environmentalist enthusiastically believes, *Hurry up! We are out here "in the cold" and we want to "come in," too!*

10. *Relationships:* "Surely I Will Remember Thy Wonders Of Old" *(Ps. 77:11)*

Memories, remembrances, are so important. "Those who forget the past are destined to repeat it." Scripture tells us (in Ps. 77:10–11): "I say, this is my infirmity; but I will remember the years of the right hand of the most High. I will remember the works of the Lord; surely I will remember Thy wonders of old. I will meditate also on all Thy works and talk of Thy doings."

276

"Memories are made of these," sang Perry Como in the 1950s (in one of his hits by that name). As Christians, our first memories ought to be made of the things "that He hath done" *and* "Thy wonders of old." *And our meditations ought to be* "of Thy works," *and our talk ought to be of the* "things He hath done" *in our lives, the lives of those whom we have helped make memories for, and of* "Thy works" *in our midst.*

Proverbs tells us: "Without a vision, my people perish." *We are to look ahead, yes; but we are to look backward, too, as a warning and for guidance into our future. Our* "Song of the night" *(Ps. 77:6) is both sweet and bitter. And it must be remembered and learned from for good, not evil. The text of Psalms 77:6 is:* "I call to remembrance my song in the night; I commune with mine own heart; and my spirit made diligent search."

It is essential that God's people remember that God blesses those who are within His will and curses (including bringing curses upon and allowing others to curse them) those who are not. We have seen in the mere centuries of our nation His blessings and His cursings. "His remembrance shall perish from the earth, and he shall have no name in the street" *(Job 18:18) is followed by this verse:* "He shall be driven from light into darkness and chased out of the world."

Would God do that to the United States of America and its Christian citizens?

Of course He would! And this land, this nation, is questionably Christian today. I am troubled by two major occurrences today within Christianity in this nation: (1) the questioning of the authority and "believability" *of Scripture, and (2) the forsaking of the concept of holiness, living* "holy lives" *(the necessity of living righteously.) Might a writer one day write the following about our nation and about Christianity in this nation in our posterity?*

There is much hopelessness among our people today. Few see much chance of a more peaceful and tranquil society around the corner. Hardly anyone can remember the days when simple folks, average families, stayed together, loved and cared for one another (not to mention enjoyed one another's company), and went to church together on Sundays and Wednesday nights. Those were the days when churches were "everywhere" and, while not perfect institutions with imperfect members, were relevant to the communities and their pastors were honored leaders of the culture.

Those were the days when most Christians believed the Scriptures were "the Word of God." People believed and obeyed the Scriptures and God and believed both were instructive and necessary in their lives and relative to their relationships with others, not to mention relative to their relationships with Him. Almost all Christians believed that there was but one Sovereign Lord of our lives as well as everyone else's lives (whether the nonbeliever believed it or not).

Current and modern memories do matter today. But the nature of relationships, partially influenced by recent memories, has changed drastically when compared to relationships of past generations. The relationships that appear to matter today, it seems, are only those that result in personal fulfillment, as opposed to the time-honored and encouraged mutually fulfilling relationships of the past. It could be said that the most important relationship today is that bond between the individual and the state, our benefactor. Civil servants who provide almost everything for us tell us they protect us (some say we only need protection from them) and provide for us, and that seems to be the key to our individual and collective well-being today. Government is shaping our memories.

There is much dissatisfaction, gloom, and grief concerning the state of our culture and the state of the "state." The small Christian community believes this is, in large part, due to the lack of a concrete personal relationship with Jesus Christ among the "many" who claim to be Christian but have "forsaken any semblance of Christian beliefs and duties."

For example, many Christians doubt if there is a life after death or if they are accountable to their God for what they do (that Scripture tells them not to do) and for what they fail to do (that Scripture tells them to do) or if they believe Jesus is who He says He is (in Scripture).

Many Christians believe that all they "have" to do (to get to Heaven) is acknowledge that God is their Creator and that they are to acknowledge and to honor and praise Him for that singular act. There is little joy or happiness in the mortal lives of "self-identified" Christians. "Ought not the mortal Christian life concentrate on immortality?" I ask. "How can there be joy in the present if there is not hope in the future (life)?"

*   *   *

I am convinced that God is departed from this land due to the rebellion, disobedience, and apostasy among the Christians and Christianity.

I am convinced that our federal government is an illegitimate and illegal government due to its "crimes against humanity" (abortion and infanticide by approval of "partial birth abortions.") And I am convinced that most of our organized and denominational Christian church leaders are apostate and without moral authority for refusing to call the government illegal and illegitmate. There is a remnant left, but it is shrinking and may face extinction here. I believe the time has come for the few true Christians left to answer the call of God and to take drastic, sacrificial risks and immediate actions, including the consideration of the theme/thesis of this book.

There is a paralysis among the few Christians left due to fear of rejection or persecution by their friends and relatives, not to mention the culture at large, if they profess their strongly held beliefs and fears, much less "live for eternity rather than for today."

When one considers that the Bible says (in Matt. 7:16): *"You will know them by their fruit,"* one wonders how many Christians would be convinced today for "being a Christian" based on the evidence.

The paralysis has escalated from "timidity" to "fear to act."

Fear has the power to make cowards of us all. But it need not. Christianity calls us to "acts of heroism," and heroism is doing what is necessary in the face of fear with eyes set on eternity.

It is as if the feet of most Christians are made of clay and are embedded in rock or steel. Christians must recall what was written in Job 13:11–12 regarding fear and unwillingness to act when the Lord leads: *"Shall not His excellence make you afraid? And His dread fall upon you? Your remembrances are like unto ashes, your bodies to bodies of clay."*

On Secession, Abandonment, Exile, and/or Civil War?

What if on a Monday in 200?, we heard over the news broadcasts that the stock market had "crashed" and that evening stockbrokers and stock owners were "diving" out of skyscrapers to their deaths?

What if by Tuesday noon the president had "closed" all banks and other financial institutions under his recent authority to declare "martial law" due to a "run" on the money supply and transfer of funds to foreign savings accounts that had begun earlier that day?

What if by Thursday evening all the gasoline stations and grocery stores in the nation were "out" of gasoline and food because of a panic "run" on them? What if by the weekend all the stores were closed due to marauding bands and gangs of thugs looting, raping, plundering, and murdering at will for goods or simply because there was no one there to stop them? By Saturday, no commerce, no jobs, nothing but "you're on your own!"

What if all of America's urban areas looked like South Central Los Angeles, "the City of Angels," did during the hours and days that followed the "not guilty" verdict of Rodney King's police assailants in the early 1990s? What if policemen, national guardsmen, and federal troops as well as their commanders refused orders to try to quell the rioting because they were scared to leave their precincts, armories, bases, "forts," and other installations? What if our law enforcement personnel refused to protect us because to do so would mean they must abandon their families and homes? Would you blame them?

If this dreadful scenario occurs, and I believe the possibility exists, I suggest we, "you," will be, if you are a typical family, about one gas tank away from being immobile except by foot or bike. You will be about two weeks away from starvation. You will be about three or four weeks away from having no electricity, gas, or water at your home, as the employees of the utility companies will be home protecting and trying to provide for their families, too. Those employees will not be venturing onto the unprotected streets and highways to go to work at the utility companies any more than the law enforcement personnel or firemen will.

Under this scenario there would be no mass media communications, no education system, no churches, no businesses, and "no order." What would you do? Have you ever considered what you would do if such a situation existed? How prepared are you to protect and provide for your family and property without outside help?

What if it happened next Monday?

What you, "we," would do depends on what you have done in preparation for "such a time as this." (Remember what Mordecia in the book of Esther said to Queen Esther after he had fasted, rent his clothes, and put on sackcloth and ashes? As Esther prepared to see her husband, the king, Ahasuerus, by putting on her "queen" clothing and committing to ask him to "spare" the lives of her people, the Jews, Mordecia encouraged her with this statement from Esther 4:14: *"Who knows whether you have attained royalty for such a time as this?"*)

Recommended preparation that I suggest are: (1) be of the mindset that this possibility exists; (2) be prepared to defend yourself and your family physically through the possession of arms and ammunition and the "know-how" and will to use them; (3) store sufficient amounts of water and food for you and your family to survive for at least six months; (4) have a site (a cabin with land suitable for the growing of vegetables) that you own or have access to that you can migrate to (I suggest it be fifty miles, at least, from an urban area); (5) develop the knowledge and obtain the supplies necessary to grow food for survival at the site mentioned in 4; (6) learn and be prepared to act on a skill that you could use for "barter" if the monetary system collapses (and it surely will); and (7) be prepared to help create a community and civilization out of the "rubble" that would exist if the scenario suggested here does occur.

If this projection does not occur and you prepare for it, you have lost very little and you will have been drawn closer to nature, self-sufficiency, your family, and God, I believe. You would have the comfort of Boy Scouts, who are to "Be Prepared."

I believe that the collapse of our government, including the financial underpinnings, is going to happen. If this occurs, there is going to be little that you, anyone, can do individually or collectively in the short run other than simply survive. Martin Luther King gave this insight, which I believe to be a good note for preparation for whatever is to come for each Christian and for Christianity, when he said, "The ultimate measure of a man is not where he stands in moments of comfort and convenience, but where he stands in times of challenge and controversy."

And the order that would be "God-honoring" by a newly constituted civil order, civil government, if such a collapse occurs, that I have suggested is possible would be that order that affirms this sentence spoken by Pres. Thomas Jefferson as he was leaving office on March 31, 1809; "The care of human life and happiness, not their destruction, is the first and only legitimate objective of good government."

Our Golden Age As the Sun Sets on America

I believe we have gone beyond the point of no return as a nation. I believe that a constitutional, democratic republican form of government is the best form of government; but, I believe, without God, this "best" form of civil government is nothing more than "mob rule." That is what our government has become. I believe that God is and will continue to "depart" and "turn His back" on the United States of America due to

281

our rejection of Him as "sovereign over nations" and our disobedience to "His Holy Word." I believe that calling ourselves a Christian nation but refusing to, as a nation, live "the Christian life" is idolatrous. I believe the judgment of God hangs, kindled, over our heads!

What does the future hold for Christians and Christianity in America? I believe we face many most difficult choices.

How long will we remain patriotic to a government with our allegiance, taxes, obedience, and prayers when our culture/government is "mocking, denying, and cursing" God as well as forcing Christians to participate in great national sin via "do not do what God requires" and via "do what God forbids"? There are, clearly, two individual and collective types of sin, "commission" and "omission."

I repeat. Sin is not only doing what God tells us not to do; it is also refusing, failing, to do what God has told us to do, i.e., *"Defend the poor and the fatherless. . . ."* (Ps. 82:3); and this, in my opinion, includes the unborn.

While the United States, just like all nations, has never been a perfect nation, it has always, until recently, acknowledged the God of Abraham, Isaac, and Jacob as the Lord of lords, the King of kings, the Judge of judges, and the ultimate Judge of individuals and nations. Until recently our culture/society/government has believe this and has understood that Jesus Christ was and is (and always shall be) the Son of God Almighty. Our nation, including our civil government, has clearly now rejected these beliefs and is a post-Christian nation.

Can this be changed; can our direction be reversed? This is the 64 dollar question. I don't believe it can be in the context of peaceful political reform. I don't think it can through repentance, renewal, and restoration by the Christian community due to the facts that (1) we, Christianity, do not recognize the authority of Scriptures; and (2) we do not fear God as we do not recognize the call of God in our collective lives to "be holy, as I am holy." I may be wrong; I hope so. But what if I am right?

In the days of William Shakespeare, when oratory flourished, John Donne was, in my opinion, the greatest preacher in England. Donne is principally remembered as a great scholar and a famous poet who wrote fairly erotic love poems. While, like many of us, Donne grew up in a Christian family, he rejected his and his parents' faith during university days and devoted himself to writing poetry and advancing in the government as a diplomat. He later fell out of favor with powerful men and decided to join the Anglican clergy in spite of his unbelief.

282

When his wife died, however, Donne experienced a drastic conversion and became an eloquent speaker for a personal faith and trust in Christ. His religious poetry still can move both the heart and the intellect, giving us expressions like "death be not proud," "no man is an island," and, "never send to know for whom the bells toll; it tolls for thee." These three short sentences, I believe, speak to our nation; death, an island, and toll.

We American Christians, the few that are truly Christian, in my opinion, are yoked, unequally, with our pagan nation and "self-identified" Christians who are no more Christian than the tree outside my window. I believe this will become increasingly more obvious as time passes. If we are not able to extricate ourselves, we will suffer the consequences of this burden along with the pagans with whom we are harnessed. As I have stated elsewhere in this book, "they," the pagans, are influencing us and our children more than we are influencing them and their children.

Is the United States of America facing Donne's acknowledgment of death: "Death be not proud"? Donne understood that we are inexorably linked to others: "No man is an island." Are the "bells tolling" for America as Donne predicted for "thee" in his time?: "It tolls for thee."

God anoints us, in a literal and figurative way, by giving us "gifts," skills, talents, desires, insights, and, yes, even heavy burdens that others don't have. These lead us, through obedience and the use of our "measure," to fulfillment by achieving our special assignment/s and purpose/s.

Samuel said in I Samuel 10:1, *"Is it not because the Lord hath anointed thee to be captain over his inheritance?"*

God calls and expects us to see our "inheritance" for our good and for the purpose that He alone has ordained. As Christians, our common elements are love, compassion, faith, discipline, premarital chastity, sexual loyalty in marriage among heterosexuals (only), commitment to children, hard work, protection and the acknowledgment of the intrinsic value of innocent human life, and, finally, growing old gracefully. These are what we are about, what families are about, and what our culture/society/nation/government is all about fostering.

This is not the reality that exist today in the United States. It is full of nostalgia and warmth, but today these beliefs are highly offensive to many and controversial in most circles in our culture. Some would say, "These elements do not depict the real world; they sound like *Ozzie and Harriet* to me." Critics of Christian morality (sadly, many of the critics are professing Christians) chant, "The traditional family never really existed—and if it did, there's nothing left of it today."

The *Ozzie and Harriet* and *Leave It to Beaver,* Wally, Ward and June Cleaver families have never been a majority of American households. But while they may have been unrealistic, they were idealistic. They challenged us to purity!

And the questions I raise that haunt me are these: "What will the future hold? Will I remain loyal no matter what the culture/society/nation/government endorses, does, or forces me to submit to? Will my children, grandchildren, and great-grandchildren adore us for what we did and stood for or will they curse our graves for our bad actions or lack of good actions?"

Renunciation of U.S. Citizenship?

When there was still time, would it have been morally correct for a Christian citizen to have renounced his citizenship in the democratically elected Adolf Hitler administration, the Third Reich in Nazi Germany? Would not that single public act by one person have been a positive and moral thing to have done if that person was convinced of "what was to come"? Perhaps that single public act by one person would have ignited others, perhaps by hundreds, perhaps by thousands, perhaps by millions, to join in the renouncing of citizenship and allegiance. Perhaps the Holocaust, Germany military aggression into other nations, and World War II could have been averted if German Christians had not consented to "do evil" or to "cooperative with evil."

What if one, then a few, then hundreds, thousands, and millions in pre–World War II Germany had considered, then concluded that their nation "had gone beyond the point of no return" when Hitler first ceased the reign of power and refused to "be a part" of what was to come?

Would not a statement such as: "I am held captive to my conscious and I can do nothing else. I can't be a part of my nation any longer. May God have mercy on me if I am wrong. May God have mercy on my homeland if I am right; and if it is His will that His judgment brings destruction to my homeland, may others in our nations tremble in the knowledge that God's judgment does not sleep forever." Would this personal declaration not have been a righteous and courageous act to a nation and to the world by an individual Christian or by a group of Christians in Nazi Germany in the late 1930s?

Of course, predicting then the "coming of the Third Reich" and its horrible acts against humanity would have had to be the key to determining whether the statement (in the last paragraph) would have been a statement of courage or a declaration of treason. Knowing "the signs of the times" reveals, and always has, the thin line between either righteous rebellion or suing for independence or treason. God, help us to see "the signs" that allow us to predict the future and to know if and when it is God's will that we choose secession, abandoning the nation, being willing to be faithful to God and to "do" the acts that would cause "us" to be driven into exile, and/or civil war.

Our founding fathers debated this possibility and concluded that the "War of Independence" was the "way to go." I am sure there was much "wrestling of conscience" among those who considered it and those who would not consider it, especially those with a Christian conscience, before the fifty-six men in 1776 signed the Declaration of Independence, which read, in part: "When in the Course of human events, it becomes necessary for one people to dissolve the political bands which have connected them with another, and to assume among the powers of the earth, the separate and equal station in which the Laws of Nature's God entitles them, a decent respect for the opinions of mankind requires that they should declare the causes which impel them to separate."

They went on, as you know, in the Statement of Independence, to declare: "And for the support of this Declaration, with a firm reliance on the protection of divine Providence, we mutually pledge to each other our Lives, our Fortunes, and our sacred Honor."

While others were surely thinking it, one person (in the pre–War of Independence days) had to have been the first to say to another or others, in "so many words," what I have suggested you and others may soon conclude regarding our "bands" to this nation, which are presented in the first two paragraphs of this section, "Renunciation of U.S. Citizenship?" or the opinion that it is "sin before God to profess allegiance to and be loyal to this government through our pledge, our finances, our obedience, and our prayers."

To denounce the government of the United States of America as a "tyrant" that can no longer be "given allegiance" and to renounce one's citizenship in "the government" would cause what reaction by our government? By your former fellow citizens? Are you ready for this? Would you ever be ready for it?

Not dissimilar to an "illegal alien," one would probably be denied "free government charity," i.e., California's 1994 Proposition 187. One might expect to be stoned and branded by "loyalists," with no protection from law enforcement personnel. One could expect to be imprisoned for certain "disobedience" if one refused to cooperate to degrees in specific matters, e.g., refused to pay taxes. One might even be deported, but to where (assuming you did not have citizenship in another country)?

Short of advocating the "violent overthrow of government," I don't know exactly what government officials would do if a person, others, hundred, thousands, or millions, "resigned" as citizens as a matter of moral "consciousness." We understand that we are to "first, do no harm." What if a Christian concluded that to participate as a citizen in the United States is to "do harm" and quietly (or loudly, as Martin Luther did when he nailed his Ninety-five Theses on the door of the church in Wittenberg on October 31, 1517) nailed his resignation, perhaps along with his reasons, to the door of the federal office building in any of our nation's large cities?

Might this be enough (before God)? Perhaps. Perhaps not.

One might choose a "better place" to live, another nation, an uninhabited island. One might apply for citizenship in another nation, receive citizenship in another nation, and move to that new nation and then 're-sign" his American citizenship by mail. "A better place" in another nation is beyond the scope of this book. There may be better, more godly, nations to live in now or in the future. These possibilities are beyond the scope of this book, too.

I believe it is unfair, however, to assume that the resigning of one's citizenship in the United States without an advocacy for violent overthrow of the government (which I am not calling for) may lead to a person abandoning the nation or being driven into exile by the civil government.

While we are seceding from the United States peacefully, abandoning the nation for another nation (or for an uninhabited island), being driven into exile by the civil government as a result of illegal activity one believes he must do in order to obey God, or establishing a new nation as a result of a civil war if peaceful secession is resisted by the civil government, "the New Jerusalem" will not be invented. But it may be that a new, better, improved, and "more perfect" nation might be constituted.

My question for you is this: What would the United States government's action/s and policy/ies have to be before you would "bolt from the fold?'' What, if anything, could the United States of America embrace, endorse, commit, sanction, allow, perpetrate, force, attack, and/or reject before you would refuse to give your loyalty, allegiance, taxes, obedience, and prayers to it? I think these are fair questions as we continue, deeper, into a post-Christian nation. Ponder these principles.

With a full understanding that sin is both ''the commission of what God tells us, nations, too, not to do'' and ''the omission of doing what God requires that we, nations, too, do,'' I ask, ''What, if any, are the boundaries in your character and Christian life to which you would not, could not, comply?'' Is it enough to be ''against present'' policies and to try to change them? On what public policy matter might you cooperate with via commission or omission while holding a Christian perspective that the matter is sinful and unjust and inhumane to others?

I believe it is fair for Christians in this nation to consider these questions now. Christians not only ought to consider these questions but ought to go before the Lord in serious prayer regarding our relationship with our government and to search the Scriptures for answers. We ought to communicate with one another on these questions.

Read what God said to us in Hosea 8:4: *"They have set up kings, but not by Me; they have appointed princes, but I did not know it. With their silver and gold they have made idols for themselves."* So much for those who interpret Romans 13 as saying that God ''approves'' of all civil governments and desires or even expects us to regard all civil governments as ''of God'' and not to oppose any government.

As we pray regarding these grave issues, we must remember that prayer is not to get our will done in Heaven or here on Earth, but to see that God's will is done on Earth.

A Possible Scenario:
A Thanksgiving in the Confederate States of North America

On Thanksgiving Day in 20?? during the noon meal, heads were bowed in thanksgiving prayer in the dining rooms of homes all across the Confederate States of North America. This predominately Christian nation recognizes that nations are allowed to be established and exist through His grace and that His will is that all nations recognize Him and be His ministers for good. The new nation, the Confederate States, acknowledges the existence of the God of Abraham, Isaac, and Jacob and has pledged to God, in its Constitution, that it will not deny Him, but will serve Him and encourage individuals and families to know and serve Him within the boundaries of the new nation and throughout the world.

The president of the Confederate States of North America asked the citizens of the country two days ago to thank God for delivering them out of the chaos in the United States of America that began two decades ago when the United States of America collapsed.

Most of the citizens of the Confederates States are old enough to remember that "fateful Monday" in 200? when the news "flashed" that the stock market had collapsed. That day will go down in history in North America as the "Day of Infamy II," with the "Day of Infamy I" being December 7, 1941, the day that the U.S. Naval base at Pearl Harbor was attacked by the Japanese Imperial Navy.

As the citizens of the United States are aware of its "roots" in England and other Western European countries, the citizens of the new republic, the Confederate States of North America, are aware and appreciate the fact that its "roots" were grounded in the United States of America.

Similar to the founding fathers of the United States, the founding fathers of the Confederate States of North America clearly took bold action when they drafted the Articles of Confederation, the Declaration of Independence (from the United States), and the Constitution of their new nation. They believed and recorded that they believed that God had decreed the collapse of the United States of America in order that a new nation, the Confederate States of North America, could rise from the debris and ruins of the United States as "one nation, under God." They were confident that the United States had brought on its demise and destruction as well as its near irrelevance in matters of national moral courage on "the stage of nations" of the Earth because it had rejected God and committed crimes against humanity on its own soil as well as on the soil of other nations.

The founding fathers of the Confederate States of North America believed that the United States of America's government's failure to recognize God as sovereign over nations and to recognize that their nation owed their very creation and continued existence to Him brought about God's judgment on their land. The United States, the founders of the new nation believed, precipitated its own destruction at the hands of an angry God.

288

In 1963, through its God-rejecting U.S. Supreme Court, the United States denied the existence of God in the U.S. government schools via the banning of prayers to Him as well as the reading, studying, and referring to His Holy Word as the foundation of morality. In the mid-1990s, the U.S. Congress, the federal and state courts, the state legislatures, and the America people debated whether or not to allow prayer and the recognition of God back into its government schools. The consensus was to reject the acknowledgment of the God of Abraham, Isaac, and Jacob as well as Jesus Christ as the Son of God as the God of the nation. This decision meant that the children of the nation who attend government schools were not to be taught Whom they, as individuals, were accountable to nor Whom the nation was accountable to. All children, regardless of where they attended school, were being raised in a nation that rejected God.

Christian leaders, pastors/priests, and layman condoned this "separation of the United States of America from God" by calling it separation of church and state. What they did was separate "truth and God" from "common sense and reality." The Christian leaders, pastors, priests, and laymen, for the most part, said, "This is our job and our job alone." A few Christians said, "Beware when the nation, through its civil government, does not acknowledge God as the God of the nation." This minority voice believed that there would be a continual "meltdown" morally as a result of not teaching our children in all three areas of discipline and education: (1) the body; (2) the mind; and (3) the spirit.

As we mentioned above, vivid in the memory in most citizens' minds of the Confederate States of North America is that first week that followed the stock market collapse of 200? Within the first week after the "crash," there was rioting from Seattle to Miami and from San Diego to Bangor.

Not only were those whom government had "taken care of" generation after generation through its social charity agencies looting and pillaging, but a host of others were taking what they needed and wanted, realizing that government had failed to "provide" for them, as it had for others, and government was unable to "protect" property and people. The rapists and murderers were having "a field day" taking "whatever" and "whomever" they wanted, as well as "taking out" whom they pleased.

The financial system failed first, then the government collapsed, and then there was no "law and order," no "peace and tranquillity" (the two things that government and, sadly, most citizens "worshiped" along with education and materialism).

Jobs, goods and services, utilities, communication systems, fire and police protection, the military, and common decency fell to the wayside. As we reflect back to those turbulent months and years, we understand, in hindsight, that when the standard of God is removed from the public conscience, from the public square, there is no definition of "common decency."

During those heart-rending days there was much despair and much reason for grief! It was a "low water mark" the day the president was assassinated, not to mention two weeks later when a mob invaded the Supreme Court chamber and killed all nine members of the Court. That was the day the entire Washington, D.C., police force left the streets of the "then capital city" to protect their families and property. (A provincial government headed by the joint chiefs of staff of the Armed Services was set up in Virginia, across the Potomac, at the Pentagon when the federal civilian government dissipated. The chairman of the joint chiefs of staff declared martial law with the consent of the other members of the joint chiefs of staff.)

The United States of America had arrived at the point identified in the last verse of Judges (21:25): *"In those days there was no king in Israel; every man did that which was right in his own eyes."*

Many were killed and many starved in those first months after the collapse of the United States of America. Many left the country; many wished they could. There was a "reverse 'boat lift' " to Haiti, Cuba, and Mexico, not necessarily because the American refuges believed things would be better in Haiti, Cuba, Mexico, or Canada economically, but because they believed they would be safer in those nations due to strong police forces who had already declared martial law in their countries, crushed resistance, and prevented complete mayhem by abrogating rights, liberties, and freedoms early enough that things could not get "out of hand."

The "Seeds" for Confederate States "Planted" at a Time for Secession? Convention in Jackson, Mississippi

A number of self-described Christian free-thinkers and visionaries, who were dubbed "hatemongers," traitors, and much worse by the media and others, met in Jackson, Mississippi, July 3–5, 199?, at Colonial Heights-Parkway Baptist Church to investigate theologically, this question: "Under what conditions, if any, would Christians have an obligation before God to consider (1) peaceful secession; (2) abandoning a nation; (3) being willing to challenge the culture, including the civil government, even to the point of peaceful, massive disobedience to the point they would be driven into exile; and/or (4) civil war?"

The convention planners and organizers began planning the three-day conference in the fall of the year prior to the convention and began disseminating convention details (dates, times, place, speakers, speakers' subjects, and motel/hotel accommodations) by the first of the year of the conference. They expected and hoped for a crowd of approximately five hundred delegates.

Due to the massive amount of preconvention publicity, most of it negative, by the secular and Christian media, more than four thousand Christians attended the convention. Three months prior to the convention another, larger Baptist church was selected to be the host facility for the conference.

The "Time for Secession?" convention was titled *"We Must Obey God, Rather than Man"* (Acts 5:29). No consideration of the advocacy of "violent overthrow" of the U.S. government was on the agenda or allowed to be discussed for two reasons: (1) the convention planners were not sure if this was an acceptable biblical option (some thought this was never a biblical option, much less something that could be considered at that time by Christian citizens of the United States), and (2) the convention planners realized that this would clearly be an illegal act under the U.S. Constitution as previously interpreted by the U.S. Supreme Court.

The question of the "violent overthrow" of government would probably "trigger" the U.S. government to not allow the convention to be held due to its potential "treason" decision (even if the issue was discussed theoretically) and would dissuade people from attending the convention to discuss the other possibilities. Convention planners agreed that this discussion would go beyond "free speech" as permitted by the federal government. Some planners did believe that this issue might come up in cloakrooms/bathrooms/standing in the parking lot conversations. This was inevitable but would not be sanctioned or encouraged by convention leaders, speakers, and organizers.

Not only did the convention planners never dream that 3,000 delegates would preregister for the convention and 4,000 attend; there were other surprises, some only to be discovered months, or years, later. Four governors, representing Alabama, Louisiana, Mississippi, and South Carolina, attended the convention. The governor of Mississippi spoke at the Opening Session, giving a "Welcome to Mississippi" greeting. In addition to welcoming the delegates to "the land of the magnolias and the mighty, muddy Mississippi [River]," he complimented the delegates for their courage and insight in attending the convention. He acknowledged that the "questions to be raised here are 'heavy' and 'troubling,' but the times we live in are 'disturbing.' "

Unknown to the Mississippi governor (and convention officials) when he gave the Keynote Address at the last banquet of the convention was the fact that representatives of five other governors were attending the convention. The governor of Mississippi and the conference officials also did not know that there were eighteen undercover agents of the federal government's Department of Justice in attendance, too.

The governor's speech (at the final meeting of the conference) was titled *"Have No Fellowship with the Unfruitful Works of Darkness"* (Eph. 5:11).

The southern governor questioned, as a professed, devout Christian, his very own salvation considering that he, as governor, had ordered (1) the arrest of Christians, including two of his own grandchildren, as they sat, peacefully, at the doors of Jackson abortion clinics and gave testimony that abortion was murder (a belief that he shared); (2) the enforcement of a federal injunction that denied children in public/government-owned schools the right to acknowledge their profession of Christianity during "open discussion" periods of exchange between students conducted by students, praying to the God of Abraham, Isaac, and Jacob, or professing their belief that Jesus Christ is the Son of God to other students during recess or other "free" times; (3) the enforcement of a federal court order that required those who commit crimes against homosexuals to be punished twofold, through fines and/or jail sentences, while those who commit crimes against Christians have their punishments reduced by one-half; and (4) the national guard to "search" homes that were "allegedly" violating weapon-ban laws. His executive order compelled the national guard personnel to confiscate any weapons found and to arrest the home owners/occupants.

Regarding the last case, the governor said that some of his relatives had been arrested for firearms possession violations and that a colonel in the Mississippi National Guard refused to allow troops under his command to arrest his grandmother, who lived alone out in the country near the rural community of Carrollton, which is Carroll County in northwest Mississippi. The colonel was court-martialed.

The Mississippi governor recounted two other incidents that troubled him greatly. The first was the reduction of a life sentence to ten years, with parole allowed after five years, for a man who was convicted of killing a woman. The evidence that this was a "hate" crime against a Christian, which allows for less than the usual sentence, was very suspect in that the "proof" that the man knew she was a Christian was not at all clear. The second was the story of a family of five, mother and father and three small kids, ages one, three, and five, who were robbed, the mother raped, her throat cut, and her body mutilated, and the father and kids killed with gunshots into their heads. The "gang" leader of the thugs that committed this atrocity was arrested and convicted. When he was arrested for his part in these heinous crimes, there was a newspaper article in his shirt pocket with the names and addresses of people who had recently been prosecuted for weapons ban violations. Once convicted, these citizens had their weapons confiscated by state law enforcement personnel. The family that had been murdered was on the list of people convicted of weapons possession, and their name and address had been marked in yellow. The governor said he felt personally responsible for the deaths of these people.

A close friend of the governor told him that he knew this family well and that they were wonderful, God-fearing Christians. This friend of the governor said that he was filled with grief at the loss of his good friend and his family and that he and others who had attended the mass funeral and burial of the family were filled with rage at the murderers and the government for confiscating the husband/father's firearms.

Among the topics/titles of presentations presented at the convention were: "Federal Edicts without Federal Funds"; "State Protection of Abortion, Infanticide, and Euthanasia Centers"; "Elimination of Religion from Government Schools and from the Public Property"; "Alabama Marker at the Mississippi/Alabama State Border: "We Dare Defend Our Rights' "", and "Tyranny of Government."

A former president of Gunowners of America gave the last seminar mentioned in the last paragraph. He began with this quotation from Thomas Jefferson: "When governments fear the people, this is liberty. When people fear the government, this is tyranny." He chronologically noted the moves by the federal government to ban firearms to Americans and the elimination of his association as a legal organization by the federal government.

Delegates to this convention had about as many new questions to surface as they heard questions explored and/or answered. There was no doubt that "blind loyalty and obedience" to government was dispelled and unless major changes in this direction in many areas occurred and occurred soon the alternatives of peaceful secession through the petitioning of states, abandoning the nation by individuals, families, and groups of families, and being driven into exile would be cruel options that Christians would have to take.

Even though "violent overthrow" of government was banned from discussion formally at the convention, the topic of "civil war" and "open, violent rebellion" by individuals, families, states, and regions in cases where the federal government would not "leave people and states" alone was talked about informally. Yes, *"wars and rumors of war"* (Matt. 24:6) was discussed in theoretical circumstances.

The last act of the delegates to the conference was that annual conferences be held. The fact that Jackson, Mississippi, is the capital of the Confederate States of North America is due in no small part to the fact that the first "a time for secession?" convention was held in Jackson in July of 199? and that the governor of Mississippi took such a positive, direct involvement in the first convention. Mississippians were the catalyst for that first conference.

"Without 'Hope' in the Future, There Is No 'Joy' in the Present"

Many of those in attendance at the convention considering what conditions must exist for Christians to warrant (1) the belief that a nation has gone beyond the point of no return in the eyes of God through biblical study, Christian and human history, common sense, and prayer, and (2) a "break with a government" that they are and have been subjects of when conditions of 1 exist.

While the first convention was discouraging in many, or most cases, there was the sense of encouragement in that it was realized and pointed out by speaker after speaker that God is in control of the affairs of men and of nations, including the demise of some nations and the creation of new nations.

The fact that convention speakers of the first and subsequent conventions outlined conditions that would require us to "separate ourselves from the civil government" and that secession, abandonment of the nation, being driven into exile, and civil war are all possibilities, there was solace taken from the fact that the delegates had taken these questions "head on" and would continue to meet, at least once a year, to exchange points of view regarding the theme/thesis of the first convention and to monitor changes in current events. Also, an executive committee was elected and would meet quarterly.

One woman from North Carolina who attended the third convention said, "While I am fearful of what lies ahead, it has been good for us to discuss some of the realistic dreadful possibilities. This gives me 'hope,' for without 'hope' in the future there is no 'joy' in the present."

A Christian Nation Arises From the "Rubble" of Disaster

During the seven years between the first convention of those who met in Jackson, Mississippi, in July of 199? and the collapse of the United States of America in 200?, there were seven conventions for those Christians who were trying to decide what to do, if anything, regarding their allegiance to the nation and their allegiance to God. They studied the present circumstances, tried to predict the short-term and long-term futures, and cried out to God for Him to make it clear to them what they were to do (and what they were not to do).

They questioned their loyalty to the United States via their allegiance, finances (paying taxes), obedience, and prayer. The movement received a great deal of national publicity before, during, and after each annual convention, and much continued to be written and said, mostly negative, in the secular and Christian media regarding their "questions," "answers," and "inescapable conclusions." It became more clear that a national "trainwreck" lay dead ahead!

During the third annual convention of the movement, the delegates named themselves "The Secessionists." They defended their meetings as protected by the First Amendment's right of "free speech," "assembly," and "religious freedom."

When an illegal investigation of "The Secessionists?" was confessed by the head of the Federal Bureau of Investigation, the executive director of "The Secessionists?" listed before a packed news conference in Washington, D.C., the four critical elements that government must abridge before "a people" have the right to ask to be allowed to secede. They were: (1) a moral consensus; (2) personal liberties; (3) unlimited and unrestrained government; and (4) denial of self-government. The executive director said, "I question whether these four bedrock principles exist today in the United States of America, and I am convinced that this nation is clearly not a nation 'under God' any longer. I believe we have rejected the God of Abraham, Isaac, and Jacob.

"We will soon 'reap what we have sown'; and this will include the 'fruit' of the rejection and denial of God in this land," he continued. "Jesus Christ warned His disciples in Matthew 6:24, *'You cannot serve God and mammon.'* In this verse Christ further warned, *'You will love one and hate the other, you will hold to one and despise the other.'* We, in America, love the secular state 'god' and despise God.

"Our government is taking away our liberties and may soon carry out what Mao Tse-Tung (of Communist China history) said: 'I will rule at the point of a gun.' I am reminded," he continued, "at this time Thomas Jefferson said, 'Indeed, I tremble for my country when I reflect that God is just and His justice cannot sleep forever. The God who gave us life gave us liberty. Can the liberty of a nation be secure when we have removed a conviction that these liberties are the gifts of God?' As Jefferson was fearful of the judgment of God for the national sin of slavery that the nation was conceived in, we in America today love the secular state 'god' and all that it is giving us and despise God."

In July of 200?, almost on the seventh anniversary of the first convention of "The Secessionists?", the financial collapse of the United States occurred (which has been already described). The twenty months that followed that "Bloody Monday" and week were marked by terror and havoc. Millions were killed; millions were to starve; the world was plunged into economic, then chaotic, ruin. Bands of roving marauding gangs raped, looted, and murdered and committed arson. Ethnic hordes attacked other ethnic groups. People took from others and nations invaded nations.

The strong and the prepared survived, not that "chance," or, better said, "the hand of God" did not protect many.

Those who had joined "The Secessionists?" stayed in contact with one another, via shortwave radio and survived at a high rate. They came to help one another. They moved into the homes, cabins, and caves of one another. As order (at the point of a gun), communications, transportation, law, and authority were being restored, leaders of "The Secessionists" met and outlined a plan to consecrate a new nation.

The Secessionists! Convention

As an unelected president, who gained his power as a result of being the chairman of the joint chiefs of staff of the U.S. Armed Services, consolidated military control, proclaimed himself "in charge," and established "law and order" through martial law, members of the executive committee of "The Secessionists?" met in Birmingham, Alabama, in April of 200?, some two years after the collapse of the U.S. federal government.

They concluded that the new "president" of what "he" called the United States of America could and would not restore the nation to the biblical, Christian basis upon which it had been founded. The committee was convinced that they did not want to be a part of what was arising from the former United States of America.

The third day of the meetings of the executive committee, the committee voted, unanimously, to draw up a Declaration of Independence and a Constitution for a new nation, which they named the Confederate States of North America. Both of these documents were drafted similarly to the United States of America's Declaration of Independence and Constitution.

On the fourth day of sessions of the executive committee's conference, they changed their name from "The Secessionists?" to "The Secessionists!"

The "die had been cast"! The delegates, representing twelve former states of the United States, agreed to return to their state executive committees with drafts of the new Declaration of Independence and the new Constitution of the proposed new nation, the Confederate State of North America, as well as a petition for peaceful secession, and to "sell" their local leadership on ratifying the petition, Petition for Peaceful Secession from the United States of America and the two other documents.

The date they set to reconvene and to hopefully officially establish a new constitutional, democratic republic was July 4, 200? That was accomplished, and on that date. After that, citizens from other states were invited and encouraged to become residents and citizens of the new republic. The twelve states that initially comprised the new republic were the eleven states that had seceded from the United States in 1861 to form the Confederate States of America (Alabama, Arkansas, Florida [the northern half], Georgia, Louisiana, Mississippi, North Carolina, South Carolina, Tennessee, Texas and Virginia) and Oklahoma.

297

While the news of the effort of these states to secede from the United States spread across the country, the executive committee tried to prevent a number of things from happening. First, many inquiries came from citizens of other states who wanted to explore the possibility of their states or regions of states joining the new republic. Second, the president/military dictator of the United States and others who were trying to revive the United States were threatening to take military action against "breakaway" states that were promoting secessionist movements.

The executive committee of "The Secessionists!" nevertheless was committed to the new nation and believed that if they acted swiftly, before those in command of the United States splintered military could reestablish "law and order" through "power and control," the new nation could be conceived, born, and weaned from the "fatherland/motherland."

A major decision came within six months when the executive committee recommended to the secessionists convention and the secessionists convention delegates from the twelve states concurred that immigrants to the new nation would be welcomed and given land to settle and develop and those who wanted to remain loyal to the United States, who were called Loyalists, would be reimbursed for their land and property, which they could not take with them as they migrated to U.S. territory.

The Convention of Secession ratified the Declaration of Independence from the United States of America and the Constitution of the Confederate States of North America. The Declaration of Independence made it abundantly clear that the new nation was "created by" and would be a "minister of" God. The Constitution declared that the nation would abide by biblical principles, and as it would be "given the light by the Holy Spirit." The Declaration of Independence declared that the nation would urge its citizens to follow "the example of Jesus Christ, who is God Incarnate, the man from Galilee."

While no citizens would be required to adhere to Christianity, the government would encourage its citizens to become Christian and acknowledge the nation as a Christian nation. Christian denominations would be supported, but not financially, by the government, and other religions would be supported, but not financially, by the government, and other religions would be allowed to exist and would not be oppressed by the government or allowed to be persecuted by Christianity or any other religion. The framers of these documents acknowledged that the nation was dependent on Christianity making "disciples" of citizens of the country.

The Constitution set limits on the role and "works" of the civil government and emphasized a statement that Thomas Jefferson had made: "The care of human life and happiness, and not their destruction, is the first and only legitimate object of good government."

Only one of the twelve states proposed and accepted for membership in the new confederation of states and did not join the union as a contiguous state. That state was Florida. The top half of Florida seceded from the United States and joined the Confederate States, while the south half seceded from the United States and vowed to "go it alone."

While there were a few pockets of loyalty to the United States in the Confederate States' territory, none was so steadfastly loyal to the United States as to commit their young men to fight (and die) in a war with the Confederate States to reunite their states to the United States. Consequently, there was next to no violence in the twelve seceding states with the U.S. government and its military forces or with Loyalists within the seceding states.

The people of North America were tired, tired of violence and starvation, tired of governments not working, tired of elected people and civil servants acting as elitists and being out of touch with the needs and desires of the common people, and tired of arguing and fighting. Those "tired" and "worn-out" worked for the good of the seceding Confederate States of North America.

The "self-proclaimed" president and military dictator of the United States and his military command staff were having enough problems ending the open violence and rebellion within the borders of the thirty-six remaining states (Alaska and Hawaii had seceded and had formed new nations) to be concerned with the withdrawal of the twelve Confederate States. They knew they were helpless to stop the secession, and they knew the leaders of the new nation knew it. By a mutual defense pact, the twelve state legislatures comprising the new nation agreed that "an attack against one was an attack of all," no matter who the aggressor/s was/were.

Many Christians and non-Christians from the thirty-eight other states to the north, east, and west of the new nation moved to the South and hoped they were migrating to "the Promised Land" of deliverance, opportunity, and protection "on Earth," at least for a "spell." While not perfect, those early days of the new republic were promising, exciting, spirited, and unifying. One man from Oregon said, "As I got out of my camper with my family, I felt as Noah must have felt when he opened the door of the Ark."

"Only a Life Lived for Others Is a Life Worth Living"

Initially, the governor of Mississippi was one of the leaders of "The Secessionists?" movement. He spoke at the inaugural convention held in Jackson in July of 199? Nine years later he was elected the president of the Confederate States of North America during the first meeting of the new nation's first Electoral College. The sons of governors of Louisiana and South Carolina who had attended the first convention of the movement were the governors of their states and led their delegations to the Electoral College as they had to the political party convention of the Christian Democratic Republican Party several months before.

When the governor of Mississippi was sworn in as the first president of the Confederate States of North America, he prayed for divine guidance for himself, his small group of advisers and cabinet members, and the members of the two legislative branches of the confederation's government, the House of Proportional Representatives and the Confederate Senate.

He prayed (1) for peace of mind during hard times ahead for everyone in the new nation; (2) that everyone would understand that "less" is not always "worse," but that "as we grow less, He becomes more"; (3) that the citizens of the nation would acknowledge that God "governs in the affairs of nations as well as in the affairs of men"; (4) that "we must build our nation, our 'house,' on the authority of God rather than on 'sand' " and (5) that we would remember that "obedience to God goes for nations as well as for individuals."

He closed his inaugural address on the steps of the Old Capitol Building in downtown Jackson, where Gen. Andrew Jackson, who had served the United States as its seventh president (1829–37), had spoken to Mississippians on January 18, 1840. (Jackson spoke to Mississippians from the same spot in the Old Capitol of Mississippi that the new president of the Confederate States of North America was inaugurated and gave his inaugural address. It was the same spot that the governor of Mississippi had read the Ordinance of Secession from the United States, which had been ratified on January 8, 1861, making Mississippi the second state to join the Confederate States of America. [South Carolina had seceded on December 20, 1860.] Jefferson Davis of Mississippi five weeks later became president of the Confederacy.)

"General Jackson," the new president said, "was a son of the South who understood the yearning of man to be free, to love peace, and to serve others." The new president noted that General Jackson had stood his ground when necessary and was a man of principle. "People realized what Old Hickory was made of more than a century and one-half ago as he spoke to them from this place," he added. "May it be that our effort will result in success, in peace, and for the liberation of mankind, not its enslavement to others or to an evil nation."

The newly inaugurated president of the Confederate States of North America closed his remarks by quoting these words from the great Jewish scientist Albert Einstein: "Only a life lived for others is a life worth living." The governor said that he hoped and prayed that the citizens of this republic would remember the words of Einstein and promised that he would "live for others and for 'King Jesus.' "

Blackmail, Restitution, or Foreign Aid

One of the first orders of business for the new nation was to negotiate with the nation from which it had seceded, the United States of America.

There was a unanimous resolution affirmed as the first order of business of the Confederate States' Congress that pledged the new nation to "make every effort to reach a peaceful secession from the United States of America." The diplomatic staff had been in contact with the U.S. State Department prior to the secession. In fact, several of them as well as several members of the Confederate States' Congress had high positions in the U.S. government while sporting bumper stickers on their automobiles that read: "Peaceful Secession: 'Who Needs the Federal Government?' " The slogan reflected the sentiments of the citizens of the new nation regarding what many perceived as the U.S. government's intrusion into the affairs of state governments and into areas were the civil government ought not to venture, principally into the social charity business.

Due to the horrible financial plight of the U.S. federal government as well as many state governments and other governmental entities, the elected officials of the Confederate States explored the possibility of making a payment or a series of payments of gold to the United States. The move was suggested for the purposes of (1) showing good faith and sympathy to the nation from which they were seceding for its enormous debt, and (2) helping an aging and ailing friend, "a parent," in great financial need.

However, the questions arose: "Would this financial assistance be considered a reparation? Would it matter? Would it be considered blackmail? Would it matter? Would it be foreign aid? Would it matter? Would it be a charitable thing that God would have one nation do for another nation in such horrible financial distress, for an offspring nation to do for its 'fatherland/motherland'?"

The Congress of the Confederate States of North America passed and the president signed a bill that would be offered to the United States. The law, called the Foreign Aid to United States Act of 200? Pact, would obligate the new nation's Congress to consider making an annual donation each year to the United States for twenty-five years. The "grant," if any, would have to be approved by the Congress annually and would be based on the ability of the nation to pay it.

The fact that the amount, if any, would not be predetermined or guaranteed satisfied those who did not want anyone to think the monies (gold) given to the United States to be the "purchase of peace" or a "retribution for peace." It would, in fact, be considered foreign aid with "no strings attached," and as in the case of all foreign aid, the aid could be accepted or rejected by the donee nation.

The Peaceful "Break" with the United States of America

A delegation of the diplomatic corps from the Confederate States of North America was sent to the new capital city of the United States of America: Charleston, West Virginia. (During the most violent and turbulent times of the collapse of the United States, the capital was removed from Washington, D.C., which was almost completely burned down, to Arlington, Virginia [housed in the Pentagon], and finally, to Charleston.)

The diplomats were calmly received by the president, who was also the chairman of the joint chiefs of staff of the U.S. armed services, the joint chiefs of staff, the secretary of defense, the secretary of state, and the secretary of insurrections and insurgence, a new cabinet-level position.

302

The fact that the United States was in clear disarray was no surprise to the delegates and was not hidden from the delegates or the officials of the United States. The secretary of state of the Confederate States of North America asked for and was granted a dissolution between the twelve states that had been among the united states of the United States of America. The secretary said that the decision of what "we must do" was clear, and the secretary confessed his love for his native land and "wished it well."

There was a sense of bewilderment among the representatives of the United States and a sense of relief and sadness among the representatives of the Confederate States. It was quiet clear that the United States was not capable of reversing what the Confederate States had concluded they must do and were doing.

During the several hours of completely candid conversation between the two diplomatic staffs, the secretary of state of the Confederate States said with sadness and no condemnation of the president of the United States and his cohorts that he, too, was sorry about the dissolution of much of the United States of America and for the problems of their country and that he, personally, felt partly to blame for what had happened.

"As a Christian," the secretary of state of the Confederate States said, "in a nation that was becoming more and more non-Christian, I now believe that we Christians ought to have more boldly proclaimed the truth that nations cannot serve two masters any more than individuals can. We must not serve two masters; if we serve one, we must deny the other.

"Isaiah," he emphasized, "tried to tell us that nations must accept God as their ruler. *Isaiah* in the Hebrew language stands for 'salvation of the Lord.' Isaiah tried to tell of the coming of the Messiah to whom nations and individuals must bow their knee to. Isaiah, in his Emmanuel prophecy that foretold the birth of a Messiah, Isaiah 7:14, told the head of the civil government, King Ahaz, that he had nothing to fear if he accepted the coming of Christ as the one '*on whose shoulder governments would rest.*'

"Isaiah 9:6 says: '*For unto us a child is born, unto us a son is given; and the government shall be upon His shoulder, and His name shall be called Wonderful, Counsellor, Mighty God. The Everlasting Father, the Prince of Peace,*' " the secretary said. "We Christians are and have been irresponsible for not acknowledging his truth. This is the reason the United States is being 'split apart'! This is the reason that God is not protecting, guarding, and guiding this nation and its people, including its leaders.

"Civil governments are to protect those in the margins, those who are in the beginning of life, 'the dawn of life,' and those who are in the ending of life, 'the dust of life,' as well as those in the shadows of life, 'the weak, the poor, the oppressed and persecuted.' But civil governments are not to be the agents of charity; that is the duty of Christians and Christianity. We rejected these biblical truths, and we have been and are paying the price for our error, our rebellion to God.

"Isaiah saw, almost twenty-eight hundred years ago, that the political troubles in Judah were religious troubles, that our government leadership problems would be religious problems. He warned the people of Israel then, and he warns us today, that people should trust in God, not in political schemes or systems. Isaiah told us that if we did, we would be saved.

"We have been too obsessed with 'not infringing' on the religious rights of others, of pagans," he lamented. "What we did not realize that those who do not believe in God, in the Trinity of the Father, the Son, and the Holy Spirit, were wrong, that they were worshiping false gods. We did not understand that they would have far more religious freedoms, be better protected, and be more prosperous in a land that 'trusted in God.' God desires nations recognize the authority and sovereignty of God. He desires that nations and individuals further the knowledge of God 'even unto the ends of the Earth.' "

* * *

The foretold scenario may be the way by which God establishes a new nation on the Earth from what may be the ruins of another nation (in this scenario, this nation). It would be nice to have the possible transition occur, if a "split" does occur, peacefully and agreeably as I have fictionally written.

Perhaps the United States will fade away, dissolve, or disintegrate without much fanfare or notice. Perhaps it will happen soon. Perhaps it will not; perhaps the United States will "heal thyself." Perhaps it will continue for decades or for centuries. I hope so. One thing is for sure: the United States and every other nation and institution will perish, as everyone and everything on Earth one day will "return to dust." Perhaps there will be a civil government dissolution or civil war here in the United States; perhaps soon, perhaps not.

Perhaps, like Jonah at Nineveh, these warnings and predictions will not happen because God may "repent" of His planned wraft as Jonah 3:10 says: *"And God saw their works, that they turned from their evil way; and God repented of the evil, that he said that he would do unto them; and he did it not."* Perhaps God will bring "vengeance" and destruction on this land and its people, saved and unsaved, for national and individual sin, not in a few years, but in many years to come. We can rest assured that this nation, just like each of us (in our human flesh) will, one day "return to dust."

Contemplate the same region (the twelve states) of the United States that seceded in the fictional scenario being willing and able to secede and the United States being willing and able to fight to "preserve" the Union (as it did in the bloody Civil War of 1861–65). Would not that be sad!

Perhaps none of this will happen; perhaps the theme/thesis of his book is totally wrong. But what if something similar to what I have portrayed does come to pass? Are you, would you be in the future, ready to act, to secede, or to abandon the nation? Would you be willing to obey God even if that obedience means that you would be driven into exile or to fight a civil war for King Jesus?!

Perhaps: "Abandoning the Nation" or "Being Driven into Exile"

I attended a medical meeting with my physician wife in Bermuda recently. I like the "lifestyle" medical doctors live during their meetings at swanky hotels in beautiful places. I like the way I live when I'm attending medical doctors' meetings when I'm there as the spouse of a physician!

Bermuda! What a lovely place! It consists of more than three hundred islands, twenty of which are inhabited. In addition to its beautiful beaches and coral reefs, its rolling hills and year-round perfect weather make it a paradise in which to vacation. I'm sure it would be a suitable place to live. It covers about twenty-one square miles. It is about twenty-two miles long and no more than one-half mile at its widest point.

Knowing that I would be writing this section in this book one day, I could not help but speculate what it would be like for me to live in Bermuda, when I was there, or other places I've been (out of this country [or in a wilderness area in the United States]) since I became convinced of four eventual outcomes, "choices," in my life ahead for Christians in America: (1) peaceful secession; (2) abandoning the nation; (3) being driven into exile (or into the wilderness); and (4) civil war. I've recalled other nations that I have visited in other regions during my life, too.

Yes, I have thought about one day living in Bermuda or some other nation or on a uninhabited island. Why?

I state again that I believe it is not out of the range of possibilities that Christians in large (or small) numbers will believe that God would have us abandon the United States or that God would allow us to be driven into exile.

What could be the circumstances? Two things come to mind immediately. First, Christians may one day confront the fact that it would be "sin" to stay in the United States and/or to retain citizenship in this nation (which could lead to the government forcing Christians to leave the country). This is beyond the scope of this book, as is the possibility of being fugitives within the borders of the country who are being hunted for exile or imprisonment. How would you feel if you were on the "run" and went into a post office in a city you were passing through and saw your "mug shot" on a WANTED poster? What if the poster read: "Wanted: Dead or Alive"? Perhaps God will have us flee into exile from this nation. It certainly has happened before to "God's people."

The second possible scenario is quite interesting and extremely speculative. I just don't see any possibility of Christianity rising up, peacefully or violently, to confront the government, which, for example, has endorsed and sanctioned violence against unborn human beings and even protects the killers not only with the "weight of the law" but, in Jackson and many other cities, with federal marshals living alongside abortionists twenty-four hours a day, seven days a week, 365 days a year.

At one Jackson abortion mill, there is a federal injunction against me and other Christians, pro-life Christians, that is, that prohibits us from being on the sidewalk (public property) in front of and alongside an abortion mill. Pro-abortion "Christians" are welcome on the public sidewalks alongside this one abortion mill to affirm pregnant mothers' "choices" to kill their unborn children and, perhaps, to hand them money to help pay for the execution fee. Meanwhile, pro-life Christians must stay at least twenty-five feet from the clinic property. Yes, we are banned from being on the public sidewalks alongside this one abortion mill. Sidewalk counseling is negated at this one mill for those who would like to try to persuade pregnant mothers that terminating the lives of their unborn offsprings ought not to be done, as well as offering Christian alternatives to abortion. Praying on this public sidewalk is forbidden if you are pro-lifer but not for a pro-deather.

Things could change, I will admit. I realize that ten or fifteen years ago I never would have dreamed that I would be arrested sixty times by my government for doing something that seems so obvious and reasonable; peacefully interfering to prevent the killing of an innocent human being child. Understand that it is illegal, by man's law, in the United States today to try to prevent the execution of an unborn child. What I have been arrested and imprisoned for so many times, peacefully intervening, and for many months seems to me to be a reasonable thing to do.

After all, unborn humans are people, too, and they deserve and ought to be protected from being torn limb from limb just like newborn children are (for now). Perhaps God is raising up a legion of "peaceful" and/or "violent" soldiers to "do His will" and in confrontation with the powers of Earth that have "called good, evil" (rescuing babies from the hands of murderers) and have "called evil, good" (the slaughter of the innocent and the staining of this land with the blood of the innocent).

Make no mistake—the blood of these tens of millions of innocents who have been unjustly put to death cries out to Heaven for vengeance.

I can tell you that there are a number of states that I do not go into and another group of states that I drive and walk "gently" through due to "outstanding warrants" for my arrest. Perhaps one day there will be hundreds, thousands, millions of us in the same boat—rather, "on the same land."

Is it not possible that to pledge allegiance, pay taxes, be loyal, and obey the laws that tell us to "sin" either by omission or by commission may one day cause us, before God, to feel and be culpable as good citizens who remained loyal to the fuhrer of the Third Reich in Nazi Germany and were told by Adolf Hitler, "Conquest is not only a right, but a duty"? Did not Christians have a "right," a "duty" before God, to refuse to carry out the horrible orders of the dictator of Germany?

We must be aware that this could happen again and could happen here!

Yes, I agree, it would be nice for our government/nation/culture/laws/civil leaders/some so-called Christian leaders to change direction and return to God! But what if it does not happen? What if God has willed it not to happen?

Perhaps, and I pray that it be so, there will be "the will" and the vision by large numbers of Christians to regain the land via repentance and godly action that will touch the heart of God and cause Him to hear our prayers and heal our land. Frankly, I believe the chances are few, even slim, and getting slimmer each day.

Perhaps there will be enough Christians willing to secede peacefully if we are "called" to secede. Perhaps of those there will not be enough of them, us, if necessary, to fight in a civil war. What if our will is too weak, our talents and resources too small, or our determination too fleeting? We deserve no better.

Some Christians may be required to leave the nation via abandoning the land or being willing to be driven into exile. Other Christians may be required to be destroyed with the nation, may be imprisoned and/or executed by the civil government authorities, or may cooperate with a godless government against the will of God.

There are many times of late when I am ashamed of my nation. And it is getting worse and worse. Some call me cynical; I call myself a realist. There are days when current events cause me to "doubt" my patriotism. There are many days when I am more convinced than others that "we have, indeed, gone beyond the point of no return" and that we must plan contingency plans to withdraw from this land sooner than I believe necessary.

Some days I believe we, those who feel the same way that I do, could all live in a telephone booth.

****

I close with a quote from visionary Catholic, Conchita Gonzales of Garabandal, Spain: "The warning, like the chastisement, is a fearful thing; it is a fearful thing for the good, as well as for the wicked. It will draw the good closer to God and warn the wicked that the end of time is coming."